SHAKESPEARE'S CRITICS

Shakespeare's Critics

From Jonson to Auden: A Medley of Judgments

Edited by
A. M. Eastman
and
G. B. Harrison

Ann Arbor The University of Michigan Press

Third printing 1969

Library of Congress Catalog Card No. 64-10651
Published in the United States of America by
The University of Michigan Press and simultaneously
in Don Mills, Canada, by Longmans Canada Limited
Manufactured in the United States of America

Book design by Quentin Fiore

Acknowledgments

We gratefully acknowledge the permissions to reprint materials granted by the following publishers and individuals.

Barnes and Noble, Inc., New York, New York:
E. M. W. Tillyard, *Shakespeare's Last Plays.*
John Vyvyan, *The Shakespearean Ethic.*

Basil Blackwell, Publisher, and the Shakespeare Head Press:
Robert Bridges, "On the Influence of the Audience" from *The Works of William Shakespeare*, Volume 10.

The Bodley Head Ltd., London, England:
J. B. Priestley, *The English Comic Characters.*

The British Academy, London, England:
Kenneth Muir, "Shakespeare and the Tragic Pattern" from *Proceedings of the British Academy,* Volume XLIV.
R. W. Chambers, "The Jacobean Shakespeare and 'Measure for Measure' " from *Proceedings of the British Academy,* Volume XXIII.

University of California Press, Berkeley, California:
Willard Farnham, *Shakespeare's Tragic Frontier.*

Cambridge University Press, New York, New York:
Cambridge History of English Literature, Volume 5.
Harley Granville-Barker and G. B. Harrison, eds., *Companion to Shakespeare Studies.*
Harley Granville-Barker, *The Study of Drama.*
Arthur Quiller-Couch, *Shakespeare's Workmanship.*
Enid Welsford, *The Court Masque.*
John Dover Wilson, *The Essential Shakespeare.*
———, *What Happens in Hamlet.*
H. B. Charlton, *Shakespearian Tragedy.*
Caroline Spurgeon, *Shakespeare's Imagery and What It Tells Us.*

Jonathan Cape Ltd., London, England:
John Middleton Murry, *Shakespeare.*

Chatto and Windus Ltd., London, England:

John Lawlor, *The Tragic Sense in Shakespeare.*

E. M. W. Tillyard, *Shakespeare's History Plays.*

———, *Shakespeare's Last Plays.*

William Empson, *The Structure of Complex Words.*

Patrick Cruttwell, *The Shakespearean Moment.*

M. C. Bradbrook, *Shakespeare and Elizabethan Poetry.*

The University of Chicago Press, Chicago, Illinois:

From *The Meaning of Shakespeare* by Harold C. Goddard. Copyright 1951 by the University of Chicago.

The Clarendon Press, Oxford, England:

Robert Bridges, *The Testament of Beauty.*

Bertrand Evans, *Shakespeare's Comedies.*

George Gordon, *Shakespearian Comedy and Other Studies.*

S. C. Sen Gupta, *Shakespearian Comedy.*

Arthur Sewell, *Character and Society in Shakespeare.*

Nevill Coghill, Merton College, Oxford, England, and John Murray Publishers, Ltd.:

Nevill Coghill, "The Basis of Shakespearean Comedy," from *Essays and Studies* 1950.

Columbia University Press, New York, New York:

Patrick Cruttwell, *The Shakespearean Moment* (1955). Pp. 94–97, 100–104.

English Institute: *English Stage Comedy* (1955). Pp. 56, 58–61, 72–73.

English Institute: *Essays* 1948 (1949). Pp. 67–70, 72–73.

Bernard Spivack, *Shakespeare and the Allegory of Evil* (1958). Pp. 43–49, 429, 446.

Brents Stirling, *Unity in Shakespearian Tragedy* (1956). Pp. 199–202.

Constable and Company Ltd., London, England:

Logan Pearsall Smith, *On Reading Shakespeare.*

Doubleday and Company, Inc., New York, New York:

From *Archy and Mehitabel* by Don Marquis. Copyright 1927 by Doubleday and Company, Inc.

E. P. Dutton and Company, Inc., New York, New York:

Eric Partridge, *Shakespeare's Bawdy* (Dutton Paperback Series).

Faber and Faber Ltd., London, England:

W. H. Auden, *The Dyer's Hand.*

Louis MacNeice, "Autolycus," from *Collected Poems.*

J. F. Danby, *Shakespeare's Doctrine of Nature.*

Francis Fergusson, Princeton, New Jersey:

Francis Fergusson, "Measure for Measure," from *The Human Image in Dramatic Literature* (Doubleday Anchor Book).

Mrs. Doris Franklin, Canton, Ohio:
E. E. Stoll, *Poets and Playwrights.*
———, *Hamlet: An Historical and Comparative Study.*

Trustees of the Helen and Harley Granville-Barker estates, ℅ Field Roscoe and Company, London, England:
Harley Granville-Barker, *Prefaces to Shakespeare.*

Ginn and Company, Boston, Massachusetts:
G. L. Kittredge, Introduction to *Hamlet.*

Harcourt, Brace and World, Inc., New York, New York:
Cleanth Brooks, *The Well Wrought Urn.*
From *On Reading Shakespeare* by Logan Pearsall Smith. Copyright 1933 by Harcourt, Brace and World, Inc., renewed 1961 by John Russell.
John Lawlor, *The Tragic Sense in Shakespeare.*
From *The Art and Life of William Shakespeare* by Hazelton Spencer. Copyright 1940 by Harcourt, Brace and World, Inc.

Harper and Row, Inc., New York, New York:
Alfred Harbage, *As They Liked It.*

George G. Harrap and Company Ltd., London, England:
L. L. Schücking, *Character Problems in Shakespeare's Plays* (1922).

Harvard University Press, Cambridge, Massachusetts:
From Hyder Edward Rollins, editor, *The Letters of John Keats.*
From Geoffrey Bush, *Shakespeare and The Natural Condition.* Cambridge, Mass., Harvard University Press, Copyright 1958, 1956, by The President and Fellows of Harvard College.

W. Heffer and Sons Ltd., Cambridge, England:
L. C. Knights, *How Many Children Had Lady Macbeth?*

Heinemann Educational Books Ltd., London, England:
John Masefield, *William Shakespeare.*

Hollis and Carter, Ltd., London, England:
Derek Traversi, *Shakespeare: The Last Phase.*

Holt, Rinehart and Winston, Inc., New York 17, New York:
From *Shakespeare* by Mark Van Doren. Copyright 1939 by Mark Van Doren.

Hope Leresche and Steele, London, England:
John Vyvyan, *The Shakespearean Ethic.*

Houghton Mifflin Company, Boston, Massachusetts:
Havelock Ellis, *Impressions and Comments.*

Henry E. Huntington Library, San Marino, California:
Lily Bess Campbell, *Shakespeare's "Histories": Mirrors of Elizabethan Policy.*

Hutchinson and Company Ltd., London, England:
From *The Story of My Life* by Ellen Terry (1908) by permission of The Hutchinson Publishing Group.
Indiana University Press, Bloomington, Indiana:
B. Ifor Evans, *The Language of Shakespeare's Plays.*
Katherine Jones, London, England:
Ernest Jones, *Hamlet and Oedipus.*
Alfred A. Knopf, Inc., New York, New York:
John Crowe Ransom, *Poems and Essays.* Copyright 1947 by Alfred A. Knopf, Inc., Vintage edition.
J. Middleton Murry, editor, *The Journal of Katherine Mansfield.* Published 1927 by Alfred A. Knopf, Inc.
Longmans, Green and Company Ltd., London, England:
J. I. M. Stewart, *Character and Motive in Shakespeare.*
The Macmillan Company, New York, New York:
From *Last Poems and Plays* by W. B. Yeats. Copyright 1940 by George Yeats.
From *Shakespeare's History Plays* by E. M. W. Tillyard. Copyright 1946 by The Macmillan Company.
From *Shakespeare and the Nature of Man* by Theodore Spencer. Copyright 1942, 1949 by The Macmillan Company.
E. A. Robinson, "Ben Jonson Entertains a Man from Stratford" from *The Man Against the Sky* by E. A. Robinson. Copyright 1916 by The Macmillan Company, renewed 1944 by Ruth Nivison.
From *Ideas of Good and Evil* by W. B. Yeats.
From *The Wheel of Fire* by G. Wilson Knight.
From *William Shakespeare* by John Masefield. First published in the U.S.A. in 1954.
Macmillan and Company Ltd., London, England:
John Palmer, *Political Characters of Shakespeare.*
Sir Walter Raleigh, *Shakespeare.*
A. C. Bradley, *Shakespearean Tragedy.*
W. B. Yeats, "Lapis Lazuli," from *Collected Poems of W. B. Yeats.*
W. B. Yeats, *Ideas of Good and Evil.*
St. Martin's Press, Inc., New York, New York:
Sir Walter Raleigh, *Shakespeare.*
A. C. Bradley, *Shakespearean Tragedy.*
Methuen and Company Ltd., London, England:
G. Wilson Knight, *The Wheel of Fire.*
Wyndham Lewis, *The Lion and the Fox.*
B. Ifor Evans, *The Language of Shakespeare's Plays.*
New Directions, Publishers, New York, New York:
From *The Structure of Complex Words* by William Empson. All rights reserved.

W. W. Norton and Company, Inc., New York, New York:

From *Hamlet and Oedipus* by Ernest Jones. Copyright 1949 by Ernest Jones.

From *Shakespeare's World of Images* by Donald A. Stauffer. Copyright 1949 by W. W. Norton and Company, Inc.

Oxford University Press, Inc., New York, New York:

M. C. Bradbrook, *Shakespeare and Elizabethan Poetry* (1952).

Louis MacNeice, "Autolycus" from *Collected Poems* (1963).

Partisan Review, New York, New York, and Mr. George Barker:

George Barker, "William Shakespeare and the Horse with Wings" (Series 4, July–August 1953).

Penguin Books, Inc., Baltimore, Maryland:

Maynard Mack, editor, *Antony and Cleopatra* in the *Pelican Shakespeare.*

Penguin Books Ltd., Harmondsworth, and L. G. Salingar, Cambridge, England:

L. C. Salingar, "The Elizabethan Literary Renaissance" from *Pelican Guide to English Literature,* edited by Boris Ford (1955).

Laurence Pollinger Ltd.:

John Crowe Ransom, *Poems and Essays.*

Laurence Pollinger Ltd. and the Estate of the late Mrs. Frieda Lawrence, London, England, William Heinemann Ltd., and the Viking Press Inc.:

D. H. Lawrence, "When I Read Shakespeare" from *The Complete Poems of D. H. Lawrence.*

D. H. Lawrence, "Introduction to These Paintings" from *Phoenix.*

Princeton University Press, Princeton, New Jersey:

From *Prefaces to Shakespeare* by Harley Granville-Barker. Copyright 1946 by Princeton University Press.

From *Dramatic Providence in Macbeth* by G. R. Elliott. Copyright 1958 by Princeton University Press.

From *Shakespeare's Festive Comedy* by C. L. Barber. Copyright 1959 by Princeton University Press.

From *The Sense of Shakespeare's Sonnets* by Edward Hubler. Copyright 1952 by Princeton University Press.

Random House, Inc., New York, New York:

W. H. Auden, *The Dyer's Hand.* © Copyright 1958, 1960, 1962 by W. H. Auden.

Routledge and Kegan Paul Ltd., London, England:

Eric Partridge, *Shakespeare's Bawdy.*

The *Sewanee Review*, Sewanee, Tennessee, and Francis Fergusson:

Francis Fergusson, "The Comedy of Errors and Much Ado About Nothing" (Vol. LXII, No. 1, Winter 1954).

Sidgwick and Jackson Ltd., London, England:
E. K. Chambers, *Shakespeare: A Survey.*

Public Trustee and The Society of Authors, London, England:
Ellen Terry and Bernard Shaw: A Correspondence.
Extracts from *The Saturday Review* written by George Bernard Shaw.
George Bernard Shaw, "Tolstoi: Tragedian or Comedian?"

The Society of Authors as Literary Representative of the Estate of the late Katherine Mansfield:
J. Middleton Murry, editor, *Journal of Katherine Mansfield.*

The Society of Authors as Literary Representative of the Estate of the late Havelock Ellis:
Havelock Ellis, *Impressions and Comments.*

University of Toronto Press, Toronto, Canada:
Harold S. Wilson, *On the Design of Shakespearian Tragedy.*
G. G. Sedgewick, *Of Irony.*

Roy Walker:
Roy Walker, *The Time Is Free.*

University of Washington Press, Seattle, Washington:
Robert B. Heilman, *This Great Stage.*

J. Dover Wilson:
J. Dover Wilson, *What Happens in Hamlet.*

The World Publishing Company, New York, New York:
Margaret Webster, *Shakespeare Without Tears.* Copyright 1955 by The World Publishing Company.

The *Yale Review,* New Haven, Connecticut:
Maynard Mack, "The World of Hamlet." Copyright Yale University Press.

Yale University Press, New Haven, Connecticut:
Tucker Brooke, *Essays on Shakespeare.*
Merrell R. Davis and William H. Gilman, editors, *The Letters of Herman Melville.*

Mrs. W. B. Yeats:
W. B. Yeats, "Lapis Lazuli" from *Collected Poems of W. B. Yeats.*
W. B. Yeats, *Ideas of Good and Evil. Essays and Introductions.*

For convenience, volume and page references have been supplied to the following editions:

Coleridge's Shakespeare Criticism, ed. T. M. Raysor, Cambridge, Mass., 1931. Everyman's Library.
Essays of John Dryden, ed. W. P. Ker, Oxford, 1926.
The Collected Works of Bernard Shaw. Ayot St. Lawrence Edition. New York, 1930–32.

Introduction

Shakespeare, said Ben Jonson, is for all time. No, said Shaw, he is for an afternoon. The disagreement may stand as metaphor for the range and diversity of opinion with which the centuries have regarded Shakespeare and which this volume attempts to exhibit. In the following pages are more than 350 pieces of Shakespearean criticism from 120 English-speaking authors. The earliest is Shakespeare's ill-tempered contemporary, Robert Greene, who condemned Shakespeare as "an vpstart Crow," a plagiarist of bombast, who was "in his owne conceit the onely Shake-scene in a countrey." The latest critics are a score or more of the still-living who find in Shakespeare something uniquely his own and who recognize him not as "the onely Shake-scene," but surely as the best. In between there is a dialogue of many voices and many views.

Shakespeare is like a God, says Melville: "If another Messiah ever comes twill be in Shakesper's person." Pope sees Shakespeare as a plain businessman writing "for gain, not glory." Shakespeare scarce blotted a line, brag his fellow players; "Would he had blotted a thousand," groans Jonson. "Was there ever such stuff as a great part of Shakespeare?" cries George III; and as if in reply Coleridge writes: "If we do not understand him, it is our own fault or the fault of copyists and typographers."

There is disagreement whether we can discover the man in the plays. "No man can walk abroad save on his own shadow," says Raleigh; "No dramatist can create live characters save by bequeathing the best of himself to the children of his art." Emerson asserts that "though our external history is so meager, yet, with Shakespeare for biographer . . . we have really the information which is material." Wordsworth says of the sonnet that "with this key Shakespeare unlocked his heart"—to which Browning replies, "Did Shakespeare? If so, the less Shakespeare he!" And Henry James declares that "The man himself, in the Plays, we directly touch . . . positively nowhere."

Have Shakespeare's plays unity? That of action, says Dr. Johnson; "to the unities of time and place he has shewn no regard."

Coleridge discovers both a unity of feeling and a union of high and low, gay and sad. Lowell perceives the Shakespearean plot as "an interior organism." But Rymer and Dryden and Pope find no unity in Shakespeare's tragicomedy, and Santayana devastatingly asserts that "Shakespeare's genius shines in the texture of his poems rather than in their structure, in imagery and happy strokes rather than in integrating ideas."

Is Shakespeare's natural bent for comedy or tragedy? The critics disagree. Is his wit false or true, on the surface merely or in the universal comic depths? Again they disagree. Is he moral? No, says Rymer; by accident says Dr. Johnson; yes, says Emerson. Shakespeare is obscene, repines Bowdler, and brings out his *Family Shakspeare* so that a father may "read one of Shakspeare's plays to his family circle . . . without incurring the danger of falling unawares among words and expressions which are of such a nature as to raise a blush on the cheek of modesty, or render it necessary for the reader to pause, and examine the sequel, before he proceeds further in the entertainment of the evening." Anticipating such misapprehension Coleridge has already said that although there are in Shakespeare a few gross speeches, "it is doubtful . . . if they would produce any ill effect on an unsullied mind." (Take that, Mr. Bowdler!) But Logan Pearsall Smith sides with Bowdler. Not only does he find in Shakespeare bawdy jokes of the usual playhouse variety, but "recondite improprieties which must have been far above the vulgar apprehension," as well as "the indelicacies with which he spiced the sugared sonnets written for his private friends."

The debates touch on everything, for a great author has no privacy unless it be that of his bath. To some Shakespeare is serious, to some frivolous; to some pagan, to some Christian. He is Protestant, says one school; Catholic, another; he is either, neither—unknowable—asserts a third. The disputes carry over to his characters, not just to the Hamlets and Iagos, Shylocks and Cleopatras, but to them all. Are they knowable? How? In what respects? To some the characters are people; to others, *personae;* to yet others, attitudes gesturing at meanings. To Pope "every single character . . . is as much an Individual, as those in Life itself." Johnson replies: "In the writings of other poets a character is too often an individual; in those of Shakespeare it is commonly a species." To Coleridge characters are individual *and* species. To Edgar Allan Poe they are mere phantoms, their complexities but the reflections of "the conflicting energies and indolences of the poet." Vyvyan finds that they baffle psychological analysis for another reason: "They are human beings and allegorical figures at the same time." Poet laureate Bridges discovers a different explanation for their ambiguity. To arouse interest, he says, Shakespeare "will risk, or even sacrifice, the logical and consistent"; he shrouds motives and mixes them to engage our attention, but so subtly that we do not perceive it.

We stress the ubiquity of disagreement about Shakespeare—and it obtains in the discussion of every play, every character, every scene—because it is tribute to the vitality of his art. It is the dominant principle of order in this volume. We could have put the book together chronologically, of course, and that would have made clear certain points about the history of Shakespearean criticism which the present order masks. Chronological arrangement would have shown that though Shakespeare's plays held the stage and acquired an ever-enlarging reading public, they ran for two centuries counter to the canons of contemporary criticism. Jonson, Dryden, Pope, Johnson, and hundreds of lesser critics promulgated the doctrines of instruction, decorum, restraint, regulation, the unities; yet Shakespeare flourished. The great neoclassical critics found cause to praise Shakespeare as highly, perhaps, as ever mortal has been praised; but they regarded him as human, hence frail, and as the victim of the popular taste of his times, and so in a level-headed way they censured him. It is not until the end of the eighteenth century that Shakespeare comes into what might be called his own. Then he is regarded in a new way, with veneration, awe, reverence, adoration. His mysteries are now approached as religious mysteries. Now come the joyous enthusiasms of Morgann, the elaborate profundities of Coleridge, and out of these the deepening explorations of Shakespeare's characters that culminate in Bradley's *Shakespearean Tragedy*. Bradley marks the end of an era, but our own century has fruitfully pursued new inquiries. Granville-Barker and Stoll have led us into Shakespeare's dramaturgy; Spurgeon opened the way into his imagery; Tillyard and Lily Bess Campbell have pioneered investigations of the plays against their Elizabethan and Jacobean background.

We have sacrificed the historical order to highlight controversy because controversy points to and defines the enduring questions about Shakespeare and his work. Our arrangement has attempted to serve other ends. By placing Whiter's observations about Shakespeare's imagery beside Miss Spurgeon's, we have invited recognition that the critical road down which she traveled so successfully had been entered, and at almost exactly the same place, over a century before. By placing Poe's observations about Shakespeare's characters as *personae* beside those of critics of half a century later, we again invite recognition that "modern" awarenesses are, often, recoveries of older views. At other places, other principles have governed the order of selections. When we come to individual plays, our goal has been to link the selections in the order that a good conversation might take, so that one set of remarks modifies or grows out of another, or clearly starts out on a new line of inquiry. For illustration, the reader may look at the selections dealing with *Troilus and Cressida.*

Dryden speaks first in splendidly casual condescension about the rubbish he has removed from the play in creating his own version thereof. Swinburne follows, observing that "the hysterics of the eponymous hero and the harlotries of the eponymous heroine remove both alike beyond the outer pale of all rational and manly sympathy." Like Dryden, Swinburne clearly finds something distasteful in the play, but he discovers evidence as well of Shakespeare's genius, especially in the bitter portrait of Cressida. Tucker Brooke replies, however, that there is no bitterness in this portrait: Shakespeare "shows us the pathos of a daintiness reaching vainly after nobility, a wistful sincerity which knows it lacks strength to be the thing it should be." Coleridge then invites our attention to another character, Thersites—"the admirable portrait of intellectual power deserted by all grace, all moral principle, all not momentary purpose." Now Harold Wilson tries to look beyond individual characters to the vision of the play as a whole. He finds it a naturalistic vision of reversed human values. "There is," he asserts, "nowhere any implication of a power that transcends the human measure . . . This is the world of men, and it is a disordered world." But Brooke closes out the dialogue with another view, an allegorical reading of the play that sees Cavalier and Puritan instead of Trojan and Greek, a reading that makes of the play's history a prophecy of the divisions and disasters that in the decades to come were to trouble England.

Our selections are not complete essays—there are already enough collections of these; nor are they mere snippets culled from the *New Variorum* or its recent imitations. We have started afresh and wandered wide, seeking passages that are high in quality and justly representative of their authors. Readers familiar with Shakespearean criticism will inevitably complain that we have included critics whom they would have omitted and overlooked others who have a greater claim. In defense we would observe that some critics, especially of the past thirty years, are so detailed and analytical that a short or representative passage could not be selected. Other critics, whom our older readers will remember as so fresh and sparkling twenty years ago, today on rereading have become weary, stale, flat, and unprofitable. Criticism, it seems, is almost as short lived as the daffodils. In one instance we have been denied permission to reprint from a critic's work, and so our readers will miss Mr. Eliot's elaboration of his remark that Othello in his suicide speech is "cheering himself up." The reader will miss certain other things we have deliberately excluded. The only criticism included here is that written in English —for reasons of space. There is little on historical scholarship, on Elizabethan rhetoric, or on politics or sociology as these bear on Shakespeare. Nor have we had space to include remarks on the sonnets and other poems. There is none of the weary old controversy about who wrote the plays. It is said that the *Iliad* was written not by Homer but by another blind poet with the same name. Perhaps similar reasoning will account for the plays we call Shakespeare's. At any rate, the plays are here before us, and their interpretations. These are what matter. Finally, there is none of the criticism implicit in textual annotation, in stage directions, in descriptions of the performances of great actors and actresses; space is our reason. We have, in fact, omitted virtually all modern editorial comment except for a remark or two by Professor Kittredge.

If we fail to give the reader these things, however, we hope we tease and delight him with others he had not anticipated—Lowell's fine observations on the world of *Hamlet,* for example, or Rymer's grumpy condemnation of *Othello,* or Geoffrey Bush's probing into the meaning of revenge in Shakespeare's plays, or the series of high praises from the pen of G. B. Shaw. (The reader should be warned, by the way, that this book contains far more about the individual plays than appears under the titles of the separate works. There are fine things about *Hamlet* and *Coriolanus* and *Richard II* and the other plays in the section on General Criticism, which he will find by using the Index.) Like the tailor's pattern book, our specimens give but glimpses of the larger whole to which we hope he may be attracted.

Contents

I. General Criticism

Shakespeare has surface beneath surface, to an immeasurable depth, adapted to the plummet-line of every reader; his works present many phases of truth, each with scope large enough to fill a contemplative mind. Whatever you seek in him you will surely discover, provided you seek truth. There is no exhausting the various interpretation of his symbols; and a thousand years hence a world of new readers will possess a whole library of new books, as we ourselves do, in these volumes old already.

—Nathaniel Hawthorne. *Our Old Home.* 1863.

If all that has been written upon Shakespeare by Englishmen were burned, in the want of candles, merely to enable us to read one half of what our dramatist produced, we should be great gainers.

—Samuel Taylor Coleridge. *The Lectures of 1811–12.* IX. Raysor II, 165.

Attitudes

Bardolatrous

[1] *Maurice Morgann*

Shakespeare . . . differs essentially from all other writers: Him we may profess rather to feel than to understand; and it is safer to say, on many occasions, that we are possessed by him, than that we possess him. And no wonder;—He scatters the seeds of things, the principles of character and action, with so cunning a hand yet with so careless an air, and, master of our feelings, submits himself so little to our judgment, that every thing seems superior. We discern not his course, we see no connection of cause and effect, we are rapt in ignorant admiration, and claim no kindred with his abilities. All the incidents, all the parts, look like chance, whilst we feel and are sensible that the whole is design. His Characters not only act and speak in strict conformity to nature, but in strict relation to us; just so much is shewn as is requisite, just so much is impressed; he commands every passage to our heads and to our hearts, and moulds us as he pleases, and that with so much ease, that he never betrays his own exertions. We see these Characters act from the mingled motives of passion, reason, interest, habit and complection, in all their proportions, when they are supposed to know it not themselves; and we are made to acknowledge that their actions and sentiments are, from those motives, the necessary result. He at once blends and distinguishes every thing;—every thing is complicated, every thing is plain. . . . A sceptre or a straw are in his hands of equal efficacy; he needs no selection; he converts every thing into excellence; nothing is too great, nothing is too base. Is a character efficient like *Richard,* it is every thing we can wish: Is it otherwise, like *Hamlet,* it is productive of equal admiration: Action produces one mode of excellence and inaction another: The Chronicle, the Novel, or the Ballad; the king, or the beggar, the hero, the madman, the sot or the fool; it is all one;—nothing is worse, nothing is better: The same genius pervades and is equally admirable in all. Or, is a character to be shewn in progressive change, and the events of years comprized within the hour;—with what a Magic hand does he prepare and scatter his spells! The Understanding must, in the first place, be subdued; and lo! how the rooted prejudices of the child spring up to confound the man! The Weird sisters rise, and order is extinguished. The laws of nature give way, and leave nothing in our minds but wildness and horror. No pause is allowed us for reflection: Horrid sentiment, furious guilt and compunction, air-drawn daggers, murders, ghosts, and inchantment, shake and *possess us wholly.* In the mean time the *process* is completed. *Macbeth* changes under our eye, *the milk of human kindness is converted to gall; he has supped full of horrors,* and his *May of life is fallen into the sear, the yellow leaf;* whilst we, the fools of amazement, are insensible to the shifting of place and the lapse of time, and till the curtain drops, never once wake to the truth of things, or recognize the laws of existence.

An Essay on the Dramatic Character of Sir John Falstaff. (1774) 1777.

[2] *Samuel Taylor Coleridge*

Shakespeare knew the human mind, and its most minute and intimate workings, and he never introduces a word, or a thought, in vain or out of place: if we do not understand him, it is our own fault or the fault of copyists and typographers; but study, and the possession of some small stock of the knowledge by which he worked, will enable us often to detect and explain his meaning. He never wrote at random, or hit upon points of character and conduct by chance; and the smallest fragment of his mind not unfrequently gives a clue to a most perfect, regular, and consistent whole.

The Lectures of 1811–12. Raysor II, 145.

[3] *Thomas Carlyle*

Whoever looks intelligently at this Shakspeare may recognize that he too was a *Prophet,* in his way; of an insight analogous to the Prophetic, though he took it up in another strain. Nature seemed to this man also divine; *un*speakable, deep as Tophet, high as Heaven: 'We are such stuff as Dreams are made of!' That scroll in Westminster

Abbey, which few read with understanding, is of the depth of any Seer. But the man sang; did not preach, except musically. We called Dante the melodious Priest of Middle-Age Catholicism. May we not call Shakspeare the still more melodious Priest of a *true* Catholicism, the 'Universal Church' of the Future and of all times? No narrow superstition, harsh asceticism, intolerance, fanatical fierceness or perversion: a Revelation, so far as it goes, that such a thousandfold hidden beauty and divineness dwells in all Nature; which let all men worship as they can! We may say without offence, that there rises a kind of universal Psalm out of this Shakspeare too; not unfit to make itself heard among the still more sacred Psalms. Not in disharmony with these, if we understood them, but in harmony!—I cannot call this Shakspeare a 'Sceptic,' as some do; his indifference to the creeds and theological quarrels of his time misleading them. No: neither unpatriotic, though he says little about his Patriotism; nor sceptic, though he says little about his Faith. Such 'indifference' was the fruit of his greatness withal: his whole heart was in his own grand sphere of worship (we may call it such); these other controversies, vitally important to other men, were not vital to him.

"The Hero as Poet." 12 May 1840. *On Heroes Hero-Worship and the Heroic in History.* 1841.

[4] *Ralph Waldo Emerson*

What point of morals, of manners, of economy, of philosophy, of religion, of taste, of the conduct of life, has he not settled? What mystery has he not signified his knowledge of? What office, or function, or district of man's work, has he not remembered? What king has he not taught state, as Talma taught Napoleon? What maiden has not found him finer than her delicacy? What lover has he not outloved? What sage has he not outseen? What gentleman has he not instructed in the rudeness of his behavior? . . . He wrote the airs for all our modern music; he wrote the text of modern life; the text of manners: he drew the man of England and Europe; the father of the man in America; he drew the man, and described the day, and what is done in it: he read the hearts of men and women, their probity, and their second thought and wiles; the wiles of innocence, and the transitions by which virtues and vices slide into their contraries: he could divide the mother's part from the father's part in the face of the child, or draw the fine demarcations of freedom and of fate: he knew the laws of repression which make the police of nature: and all the sweets and all the terrors of human lot lay in his mind as truly but as softly as the landscape lies on the eye. And the importance of this wisdom of life sinks the form, as of Drama or Epic, out of notice. 'T is like making a question concerning the paper on which a king's message is written.

Shakspeare is as much out of the category of eminent authors, as he is out of the crowd. He is inconceivably wise; the others, conceivably. A good reader can, in a sort, nestle into Plato's brain and think from thence; but not into Shakspeare's. We are still out of doors. For executive faculty, for creation, Shakspeare is unique. No man can imagine it better. He was the farthest reach of subtlety compatible with an individual self,—the subtilest of authors, and only just within the possibility of authorship. With this wisdom of life is the equal endowment of imaginative and of lyric power. He clothed the creatures of his legend with form and sentiments as if they were people who had lived under his roof; and few real men have left such distinct characters as these fictions. And they spoke in language as sweet as it was fit. Yet his talents never seduced him into an ostentation, nor did he harp on one string. An omnipresent humanity co-ordinates all his faculties. Give a man of talents a story to tell, and his partiality will presently appear. He has certain observations, opinions, topics, which have some accidental prominence, and which he disposes all to exhibit. He crams this part and starves that other part, consulting not the fitness of the thing, but his fitness and strength. But Shakspeare has no peculiarity, no importunate topic; but all is duly given; no veins, no curiosities; no cow-painter, no bird-fancier, no mannerist is he: he has no discoverable egotism: the great he tells greatly; the small subordinately. He is wise without emphasis or assertion; he is strong, as nature is strong, who lifts the land into mountain slopes without effort and by the same rule as she floats a bubble in the air, and likes as well to do the one as the other. This makes that equality of power in farce, tragedy, narrative, and love-songs; a merit so incessant that each reader is incredulous of the perception of other readers.

This power of expression, or of transferring the inmost truth of things into music and verse, makes him the type of the poet and has added a new problem to metaphysics. This is that which throws him into natural history, as a main production of the globe, and as announcing new eras and ameliorations. Things were mirrored in his poetry without loss or blur: he could paint the fine with precision, the great with compass, the tragic and the comic indifferently and without any distortion or favor. He carried his powerful execution into minute details, to a hair point; finishes an eyelash or a dimple as firmly as he draws a mountain; and yet these, like nature's, will bear the scrutiny of the solar microscope.

"Shakspeare; or, the Poet." (A lecture delivered in Boston, 1846.) *Representative Men.* 1850.

[5] *Herman Melville*

Dolt & ass that I am I have lived more than 29 years, & until a few days ago, never made close acquaintance with the divine William. Ah, he's full of sermons-on-the-mount, and gentle, aye, almost as Jesus. I take such men to be inspired. I fancy that this moment Shakspeare in heaven ranks with Gabriel Raphael and Michael. And if another Messiah ever comes twill be in Shakesper's person.

Letter to Evert A. Duyckinck, 24 February 1849. *The Letters of Herman Melville.* Ed. Merrel R. Davis and William H. Gilman. 1960.

[6] *Harold C. Goddard*

Shakespeare is like life. There are almost as many ways of taking him as there are ways of living. From the child lost in one of his stories as retold by Charles and Mary Lamb, to the old man turning to his works for fortitude and vision, every age finds in them what it needs. Every new lover of them finds himself, as every generation, from the poet's to our own, has found itself. One by one all the philosophies have been discovered in Shakespeare's works, and he has been charged—both as virtue and weakness—with having no philosophy. The lawyer believes he must have been a lawyer, the musician a musician, the Catholic a Catholic, the Protestant a Protestant. Never was there a more protean genius. Whether his dramas should be taken as plays or as literature has been disputed. But surely they should be taken as both. Acted, or seen on the stage, they disclose things hidden to the reader. Read, they reveal what no actor or theater can convey. And how many ways of reading them there are! Not merely that each fresh voice makes them unique. The lover, the student, the teacher, the scholar, the director, the actor—every one of them finds something that the others miss, until we begin to wonder how many Shakespeares there were. I do not refer to the man Shakespeare, though he too is variously held to have been everything from a shrewd businessman to a dreamer and mystic—or even a myth in the sense that someone else wrote his works under his name. I refer to the Shakespeare we find in the plays. There at least is the playwright, the dramatist, the psychologist, the thinker, the humorist, the prophet, and the poet—to name no others.

The Meaning of Shakespeare. 1951. Chap. I.

Judicious

[7] *Ben Jonson*

I remember the Players have often mentioned it as an honour to *Shakespeare,* that in his writing, (whatsoever he penn'd) hee never blotted out line. My answer hath beene, Would he had blotted a thousand. Which they thought a malevolent speech. I had not told posterity this, but for their ignorance, who choose that circumstance to commend their friend by, wherein he most faulted. And to justifie mine owne candor, (for I lov'd the man, and doe honour his memory (on this side Idolatry) as much as any.) Hee was (indeed) honest, and of an open, and free nature: had an excellent *Phantsie;* brave notions, and gentle expressions: wherein hee flow'd with that facility, that sometime it was necessary he should be stop'd: *Sufflaminandus erat;* as *Augustus* said of *Haterius.* His wit was in his owne power; would the rule of it had beene so too. Many times hee fell into those things, could not escape laughter: As when hee said in the person of *Caesar,* one speaking to him; *Caesar, thou dost me wrong.* Hee replyed: *Caesar did never wrong, but with just cause:* and such like; which were ridiculous. But hee redeemed his vices, with his vertues. There was ever more in him to be praysed, then to be pardoned.

Timber. 1640.

[8] *John Dryden*

Shakespeare, who many times has written better than any poet, in any language, is yet so far from writing wit always, or expressing that wit according to the dignity of the subject, that he writes, in many places, below the dullest writer of ours, or any precedent age. Never did any author precipitate himself from such height of thought to so low expressions, as he often does. He is the very Janus of poets; he wears almost everywhere two faces; and you have scarce begun to admire the one, ere you despise the other.

The Conquest of Granada by the Spaniards with *Defence of the Epilogue, or an Essay on the Dramatique Poetry of the Last Age.* 1672. Ker I, 172.

[9] *Alexander Pope*

. . . of all *English* Poets *Shakespear* must be confessed to be the fairest and fullest subject for Criticism, and to afford the most numerous, as well as most conspicuous instances, both of Beauties and Faults of all sorts.

★ ★ ★

To judge . . . of *Shakespear* by *Aristotle's* rules, is like trying a man by the Laws of one Country, who acted under those of another. He writ to the *People;* and writ at first without patronage from the better sort, and therefore without aims of pleasing them: without assistance or advice from the Learned, as without the advantage of education or acquaintance among them: without that knowledge of the best models, the Ancients, to inspire him with an emulation of them; in a word, without any views of Reputation, and of what Poets are pleas'd to call Immortality . . .

★ ★ ★

I will conclude by saying of *Shakespear,* that with all his faults, and with all the irregularity of his *Drama,* one may look upon his works, in comparison of those that are more finish'd and regular, as upon an ancient majestick piece of *Gothick* Architecture, compar'd with a neat Modern building: The latter is more elegant and glaring, but the former is more strong and more solemn. It must be allow'd, that in one of these there are materials enough to make many of the other. It has much the greater variety, and much the nobler apartments; tho' we are often conducted to them by dark, odd, and uncouth passages. Nor does the Whole fail to strike us with greater reverence, tho' many of the Parts are childish, ill-plac'd, and unequal to its grandeur.

Preface. *The Works of Shakespear.* 1725.

[10] *Samuel Johnson*

Shakespeare with his excellencies has likewise faults, and faults sufficient to obscure and overwhelm any other merit. I shall shew them in the proportion in which they appear to me, without envious malignity or superstitious veneration. No question can be more innocently discussed than a dead poet's pretensions to renown; and little regard is due to that bigotry which sets candour higher than truth.

Preface. *The Plays of William Shakespeare.* 1765.

[11] *Matthew Arnold*

. . . the imitators of Shakespeare, fixing their attention on his wonderful gift of expression, have directed their imitation to this, neglecting his other excellences. These excellences, the fundamental excellences of poetical art, Shakespeare no doubt possessed them—possessed many of them in a splendid degree; but it may perhaps be doubted whether even he himself did not sometimes give scope to his faculty of expression to the prejudice of a higher poetical duty. For we must never forget that Shakespeare is the great poet he is from his skill in discerning and firmly conceiving an excellent action, from his power of intensely feeling a situation, of intimately associating himself with a character; not from his gift of expression, which rather even leads him astray, degenerating sometimes into a fondness for curiosity of expression, into an irritability of fancy, which seems to make it impossible for him to say a thing plainly, even when the press of the action demands the very directest language, or its level character the very simplest. Mr. Hallam . . . has had the courage . . . to remark, how extremely and faultily difficult Shakespeare's language often is. It is so: you may find main scenes in some of his greatest tragedies, King Lear, for instance, where the language is so artificial, so curiously tortured, and so difficult, that every speech has to be read two or three times before its meaning can be comprehended. This over-curiousness of expression is indeed but the excessive employment of a wonderful gift—of the power of saying a thing in a happier way than any other man; nevertheless, it is carried so far that one understands what M. Guizot meant, when he said that Shakespeare appears in his language to have tried all styles except that of simplicity. He has not the severe and scrupulous self-restraint of the ancients, partly no doubt, because he had a far less cultivated and exacting audience: he has indeed a far wider range than they had, a far richer fertility of thought; in this respect he rises above them: in his strong conception of his subject, in the genuine way in which he is penetrated with it, he resembles them, and is unlike the moderns: but in the accurate limitation of it, the conscientious rejection of superfluities, the simple and rigorous development of it from the first line of his work to the last, he falls below them, and comes nearer to the moderns. In his chief works, besides what he has of his own, he has the elementary soundness of the ancients; he has their important action and their large and broad manner: but he has not their purity of method. He is therefore a less safe model; for what he has of his own is personal, and inseparable from his own rich nature; it may be imitated and exaggerated, it cannot be learned or applied as an art; he is above all suggestive; more valuable, therefore, to young writers as men than as artists. But clearness of arrangement, rigour of development, simplicity of style—these may to a certain extent be learned: and these may, I am convinced, be learned best from the ancients, who although infinitely less suggestive than Shakespeare, are thus, to the artist, more instructive.

Preface. *Poems by Matthew Arnold.* A New Edition. 1853.

Iconoclastic

[12] *Robert Greene*

. . . there is an vpstart Crow, beautified with our feathers, that with his *Tygers hart wrapt in a Players hyde,* supposes he is as well able to bombast out a blanke verse as the best of you: and beeing an absolute *Iohannes fac totum,* is in his owne conceit the onely Shake-scene in a countrey.

Greenes Groats-worth of Wit. 1592.

[13] *Ben Jonson*

Though neede make many *Poets,* and some such
As art, and nature haue not betterd much;
Yet ours, for want, hath not so lou'd the stage,
As he dare serue th'ill customes of the age:

Or purchase your delight at such a rate,
As, for it, he himselfe must iustly hate.
To make a child, now swadled, to proceede
Man, and then shoote vp, in one beard, and weede,
Past threescore yeeres: or, with three rustie swords,
And helpe of some few foot-and-halfe-foote words,
Fight ouer *Yorke,* and *Lancasters* long iarres:
And in the tyring-house bring wounds, to scarres.
He rather prayes, you will be pleas'd to see
One such, to day, as other playes should be.
Where neither *Chorus* wafts you ore the seas;
Nor creaking throne comes downe, the boyes to please;
Nor nimble squibbe is seene, to make afear'd
The gentlewomen; nor roul'd bullet heard
To say, it thunders; nor tempestuous drumme
Rumbles, to tell you when the storme doth come;
But deedes, and language, such as men doe vse:
And persons, such as *Comædie* would chuse,
When she would shew an Image of the times,
And sport with humane follies, not with crimes.

Prologue. *Everyman in His Humour.* 1601.

[14] *Thomas Rymer*

From all the Tragedies acted on our English Stage, *Othello* is said to bear the Bell away. The *Subject* is more of a piece, and there is indeed something like, there is, as it were, some phantom of a *Fable.* The *Fable* is always accounted the *Soul* of Tragedy. And it is the *Fable* which is properly the *Poets* part. Because the other three parts of Tragedy, to wit the *Characters* are taken from the Moral Philosopher; the *thoughts* or sence, from them that teach *Rhetorick:* And the last part, which is the *expression,* we learn from the Grammarians.

This Fable is drawn from a Novel, compos'd in Italian by *Giraldi Cinthio,* who also was a Writer of Tragedies. And to that use employ'd such of his Tales, as he judged proper for the Stage. But with this of the *Moor,* he meddl'd no farther.

Shakespear alters it from the Original in several particulars, but always, unfortunately, for the worse. He bestows a name on his *Moor;* and styles him the Moor of *Venice:* a Note of pre-eminence, which neither History nor Heraldry can allow him. *Cinthio,* who knew him best, and whose creature he was, calls him simply a *Moor.* We say the Piper of *Strasburgh;* the Jew of *Florence;* And, if you please, the Pindar of *Wakefield:* all upon Record, and memorable in their Places. But we see no such Cause for the *Moors* preferment to that dignity. And it is an affront to all Chroniclers, and Antiquaries, to top upon 'um a *Moor,* with that mark of renown, who yet had never faln within the Sphere of their Cognisance.

Then is the Moors *Wife,* from a simple Citizen, in *Cinthio,* dress'd up with her Top knots, and rais'd to be *Desdemona,* a Senators Daughter. All this is very strange; And therefore pleases such as reflect not on the improbability. This match might well be without the Parents Consent. Old *Horace* long ago forbad the Banes.

Sed non ut placidis Coeant immitia, non ut
Serpentes avibus geminentur, tigribus agni.

[But not that the savage should join with the gentle,
nor serpents with birds, nor lambs with tigers.
Horace. *Art of Poetry.* Lines 12–13.]

★ ★ ★

What ever rubs or difficulty may stick on the Bark, the Moral, sure, of this Fable is very instructive.

I. First, This may be a caution to all Maidens of Quality how, without their Parents consent, they run away with Blackamoors.

Di non si accompagnare con huomo, cui la natura & il cielo, & il modo della vita, disgiunge da noi. Cinthio. [Not to go with a man whom nature & heaven & manner of life separate from us.]

Secondly, This may be a warning to all good Wives, that they look well to their Linnen.

Thirdly. This may be a lesson to Husbands, that before their Jealousie be Tragical, the proofs may be Mathematical.

A Short View of Tragedy. 1693. Chapter VII (mis-numbered V).

[15] *George III*

"Was there ever," cried he [George III], "such stuff as great part of Shakespeare? only one must not say so! But what think you?—What?—Is there not sad stuff? What?—what?"

"Yes, indeed, I think so, sir, though mixed with such excellences, that—"

"Oh!" cried he, laughing good-humouredly, "I know it is not to be said! but it's true. Only it's Shakespeare, and nobody dare abuse him."

1785. *Diary and Letters of Madame D'Arblay.* Ed. Barrett and Dobson. (1904). II, 344.

[16] *G. B. Shaw*

Shakespear is for an afternoon, but not for all time.

"The Immortal William." *The Saturday Review.* 2 May 1896. XXIV, 166.

[17] *G. B. Shaw*

[Our theatre's] greatest catch, Shakespear, wrote for the theatre because, with extraordinary artistic powers, he understood nothing and believed nothing. Thirty-six big plays in five blank verse acts, and (as Mr. Ruskin, I think, once pointed out) not a single hero! Only one man in them all who believes in life, enjoys life, thinks life worth living, and has a sincere, unrhetorical tear dropped over his deathbed; and that man—Falstaff! What a crew they are—these Saturday to Monday athletic stockbroker Orlandos, these villains, fools, clowns, drunkards, cowards, intriguers, fighters, lovers, patriots, hypochondriacs who mistake themselves (and are mistaken by the author) for philosophers, princes without any sense of public duty, futile pessimists who imagine they are confronting a barren and unmeaning world when they are only contemplating their own worthlessness, self-seekers of all kinds, keenly observed and masterfully drawn from the romantic-commercial point of view. Once or twice we scent among them an anticipation of the crudest side of Ibsen's polemics on the Woman Question, as in All's Well that Ends Well, where the man cuts as meanly selfish a figure beside his enlightened lady doctor wife as Helmer beside Nora; or in Cymbeline, where Posthumus, having, as he believes, killed his wife for inconstancy, speculates for a moment on what his life would have been worth if the same standard of continence had been applied to himself. And certainly no modern study of the voluptuous temperament, and the spurious heroism and heroinism which its ecstasies produce, can add much to Antony and Cleopatra, unless it were some sense of the spuriousness on the author's part. But search for statesmanship, or even citizenship, or any sense of the commonwealth, material or spiritual, and you will not find the making of a decent vestryman or curate in the whole horde. As to faith, hope, courage, conviction, or any of the true heroic qualities, you find nothing but death made sensational, despair made stage-sublime, sex made romantic, and barrenness covered up by sentimentality and the mechanical lilt of blank verse.

All that you miss in Shakespear you find in Bunyan, to whom the true heroic came quite obviously and naturally. The world was to him a more terrible place than it was to Shakespear; but he saw through it a path at the end of which a man might look not only forward to the Celestial City, but back on his life and say:—"Tho' with great difficulty I am got hither, yet now I do not repent me of all the trouble I have been at to arrive where I am. My sword I give to him that shall succeed me in my pilgrimage, and my courage and skill to him that can get them." The heart vibrates like a bell to such an utterance as this: to turn from it to "Out, out, brief candle," and "The rest is silence," and "We are such stuff as dreams are made of; and our little life is rounded by a sleep" is to turn from life, strength, resolution, morning air and eternal youth, to the terrors of a drunken nightmare.

"Better than Shakespear." *The Saturday Review.* 2 January 1897. XXV, 1–3.

Box Office

[18] *Alexander Pope*

Shakespear, (whom you and ev'ry Play-house bill
Style the divine, the matchless, what you will)
For gain, not glory, wing'd his roving flight,
And grew Immortal in his own despight.

The First Epistle of the Second Book of Horace, Imitated. 1737. Lines 69–72.

[19] *Don Marquis*

pete the parrot and shakespeare

i got acquainted with
a parrot named pete recently
who is an interesting bird

pete says he used
to belong to the fellow
that ran the mermaid tavern
in london then i said
you must have known
shakespeare know him said pete
poor mutt i knew him well
he called me pete and i called him
bill but why do you say poor mutt
well said pete bill was a
disappointed man and was always
boring his friends about what
he might have been and done
if he only had a fair break
two or three pints of sack
and sherris and the tears
would trickle down into his
beard and his beard would get
soppy and wilt his collar
i remember one night when
bill and ben jonson and
frankie beaumont
were sopping it up
here i am ben says bill
nothing but a lousy playwright
and with anything like luck
in the breaks i might have been
a fairly decent sonnet writer
i might have been a poet
if i had kept away from the theatre

yes says ben i ve often
thought of that bill
but one consolation is
you are making pretty good money
out of the theatre

money money says bill what the hell
is money what i want is to be
a poet not a business man
these damned cheap shows

i turn out to keep the
theatre running break my heart
slap stick comedies and
blood and thunder tragedies
and melodrama say i wonder
if that boy heard you order
another bottle frankie
the only compensation is that i get
a chance now and then
to stick in a little poetry
when nobody is looking
but hells bells that isn t
what i want to do
i want to write sonnets and
songs and spenserian stanzas
and i might have done it too
if i hadn t got
into this frightful show game
business business business
grind grind grind
what a life for a man
that might have been a poet

well says frankie beaumont
why don t you cut it bill
i can t says bill
i need the money i ve got
a family to support down in
the country well says frankie
anyhow you write pretty good
plays bill any mutt can write
plays for this london public
says bill if he puts enough
murder in them what they want
is kings talking like kings
never had sense enough to talk
and stabbings and stranglings
and fat men making love
and clowns basting each
other with clubs and cheap puns
and off color allusions to all

the smut of the day oh i know
what the low brows want
and i give it to them

well says ben jonson
don t blubber into the drink
brace up like a man
and quit the rotten business
i can t i can t says bill
i ve been at it too long i ve got to
the place now where i can t
write anything else
but this cheap stuff
i m ashamed to look an honest
young sonneteer in the face
i live a hell of a life i do
the manager hands me some mouldy old
manuscript and says
bill here s a plot for you
this is the third of the month
by the tenth i want a good
script out of this that we
can start rehearsals on
not too big a cast
and not too much of your
damned poetry either
you know your old
familiar line of hokum
they eat up that falstaff stuff
of yours ring him in again
and give them a good ghost
or two and remember we gotta
have something dick burbage can get
his teeth into and be sure
and stick in a speech
somewhere the queen will take
for a personal compliment and if
you get in a line or two somewhere
about the honest english yeoman
it s always good stuff
and it s a pretty good stunt

bill to have the heavy villain
a moor or a dago or a jew
or something like that and say
i want another
comic welshman in this
but i don t need to tell
you bill you know this game
just some of your ordinary
hokum and maybe you could
kill a little kid or two a prince
or something they like
a little pathos along with
the dirt now you better see burbage
tonight and see what he wants
in that part oh says bill
to think i am
debasing my talents with junk
like that oh god what i wanted
was to be a poet
and write sonnet serials
like a gentleman should

well says i pete
bill s plays are highly
esteemed to this day
is that so says pete
poor mutt little he would
care what poor bill wanted
was to be a poet

archy

archy and mehitabel. 1927.

Approaches

"Interpretive" or Submissive

[20] *Samuel Johnson*

Let him, that is yet unacquainted with the powers of *Shakespeare,* and who desires to feel the highest pleasure that the drama can give, read every play from the first scene to the last, with utter negligence of all his commentators. When his fancy is once on the wing, let it not stoop at correction or explanation. When his attention is strongly engaged, let it disdain alike to turn aside to the name of *Theobald* and of *Pope.* Let him read on through brightness and obscurity, through integrity and corruption; let him preserve his comprehension of the dialogue and his interest in the fable. And when the pleasures of novelty have ceased, let him attempt exactness; and read the commentators.

Preface. *The Plays of William Shakespeare.* 1765.

[21] *George Saintsbury*

But it is quite certain that anyone who, with fair education and competent wits, gives his days and nights to the reading of the actual plays will be a far better judge than anyone who allows himself to be distracted by comment and controversy. The important thing is to get the Shakespearean atmosphere, to feel the breath of the Shakespearean spirit. And it is doubtful whether it is not much safer to get this first, and at first hand, than to run the risk of not getting it while investigating the exact meaning of every allusion and the possible date of every item. The more thoroughly and impartially this spirit is observed and extracted, the more will it be found to consist in the subjection of all things to what may be called the romantic process of presenting them in an atmosphere of poetical suggestion rather than as sharply defined and logically stated. But this romantic process is itself characterised and pervaded by a philosophical depth and width of conception of life which is not usually associated with romance. And it is enlivened and made actual by the dramatic form which, whether by separable or inseparable accident, the writer has adopted. Thus, Shakespeare—as no one had done before him, and as people have done since far more often in imitation of him than independently—unites the powers and advantages of three great forms: the romance (in verse or prose), pure poetry and the drama. The first gives him variety, elasticity, freedom from constraint and limit. The second enables him to transport. The third at once preserves his presentations from the excessive vagueness and vastness which non-dramatic romance invites, and helps him to communicate actuality and vividness.

"Shakespeare: Life and Plays." *The Cambridge History of English Literature*. 1910. V. Chap. VIII.

[22] *G. Wilson Knight*

Criticism is a judgement of vision; interpretation a reconstruction of vision. In practice, it is probable that neither can exist, or at least has yet on any comprehensive scale existed, quite divorced from the other. The greater part of poetic commentary pursues a middle course between criticism and interpretation. But sometimes work is created of so resplendent a quality, so massive a solidity of imagination, that adverse criticism beats against it idly as the wind that flings its ineffectual force against a mountain-rock. Any profitable commentary on such work must necessarily tend towards a pure interpretation.

★ ★ ★

. . . our imaginative focus is generally right enough. In reading, watching, or acting Shakespeare for pure enjoyment we accept everything. But when we think 'critically' we see faults which are not implicit in the play nor our enjoyment of it, but merely figments of our own minds. We should not, in fact, think critically at all: we should interpret our original imaginative experience into the slower consciousness of logic and intellect, preserving something of that child-like faith which we possess, or should possess, in the theatre. It is exactly this translation from one order of consciousness to another that interpretation claims to perform. Uncritically, and passively, it receives the whole of the poet's vision; it then proceeds to re-express this experience in its own terms.

The Wheel of Fire. 1930. Chap. I.

Biographical

a. *The question: Can the man Shakespeare be known?*

[23] *Donald A. Stauffer*

Now let us consider for a moment the form of the drama itself. Its material, says Aristotle, is men in action. This is also the material of morals. The first three of its six component elements, still according to Aristotle, and philosophically the most important, are plot, character (or *ethos*), and what may be called "reasoning," or the intellectual statement of a position or a belief. Most Shakespearean agnostics content themselves with considering this third element—as if a play were composed of independent opinions expressed by opposed characters, with the dramatist showing his peculiar professional powers by remaining aloof. But Aristotle seems to give precedence over *dianoia* or reasoning to the second of his elements, *ethos* or character. Surely it is an inhumane, almost fantastic, conception of the drama to suppose that the dramatist does not take sides in the portrayal of character. Is a play to be no more than a Madame Tussaud's waxworks of unrelated figures speaking their little pieces? Does the dramatist lead his reader-spectator through a menagerie saying in simple description, "This is a giraffe, a lion, a zebra"? Let us hope rather that he composes a great picture made up of individual character studies, comparable, say, to Raphael's *School of Athens* or Rembrandt's *Night Watch.* Moral ideas will shine in the characters themselves as revealed in their talk, action, and impact upon others. And not even the apotheosized Shakespeare can be so inhuman or superhuman as to leave his likings out of these portraits. It is not so simple as to say that he approves of virtue and is against sin. There is more individuality in this elusive playmaker. Why are the cards stacked so cruelly against well-meaning Polonius and the inoffensively compliant Osric? Why are the citizens in his crowds such dolts and weathercocks? Why the sympathetic weighting of the character of the Duke in *Measure for Measure,* who to the average reader seems weak, vacillating, and a refugee from responsibility? Do the unusual presentations of usual virtues and vices in almost all of his plays tell us nothing of Shakespeare's own beliefs?

Postscript. *Shakespeare's World of Images.* 1949.

[24] *Thomas Carlyle*

But I will say, of Shakspeare's works generally, that we have no full impress of him there; even as full as we have of many men. His works are so many windows, through which we see a glimpse of the world that was in him. All his works seem, comparatively speaking, cursory, imperfect, written under cramping circumstances; giving only here and there a note of the full utterance of the man. Passages there are that come upon you like splendour out of Heaven; bursts of radiance, illuminating the very heart of the thing: you say, 'That is *true,* spoken once and forever; wheresoever and whensoever there is an open human soul, that will be recognized as true!' Such bursts, however, make us feel that the surrounding matter is not radiant; that it is, in part, temporary, conventional. Alas, Shakspeare had to write for the Globe Playhouse: his great soul had to crush itself, as it could, into that and no other mould. It was with him, then, as it is with us all. No man works save under conditions. The sculptor cannot set his own free Thought before us; but his Thought as he could translate it into the stone that was given, with the tools that were given. *Disjecta membra* are all that we find of any Poet, or of any man.

"The Hero as Poet." 12 May 1840. *On Heroes Hero-Worship and the Heroic in History.* 1841.

[25] *Ralph Waldo Emerson*

. . . though our external history is so meagre, yet, with Shakspeare for biographer, instead of Aubrey and Rowe, we have really the information which is material; that which describes character and fortune, that which, if we were about to meet the man and deal with him, would most import us to know. We have his recorded convictions on those questions which knock for answer at every heart,— on life and death, on love, on wealth and poverty, on the prizes of life and the ways whereby we come at them; on the characters of men, and the influences, occult and open, which affect their fortunes; and on those mysterious and demoniacal powers which defy our science and which yet interweave their malice and their gift in our brightest hours. Who ever read the volume of the Sonnets without finding that the poet had there revealed, under masks that are no masks to the intelligent, the lore of friendship and of love; the confusion of sentiments in the most susceptible, and, at the same time, the most intellectual of men? What trait of his private mind has he hidden in his dramas? One can discern, in his ample pictures of the gentleman and the king, what forms and humanities pleased him; his delight in troops of friends, in large hospitality, in cheerful giving. Let Timon, let Warwick, let Antonio the merchant answer for his great heart. So far from Shakspeare's being the least known, he is the one person, in all modern history, known to us.

"Shakspeare; or, the Poet." (A lecture delivered in Boston, 1846.) *Representative Men.* 1850.

[26] *Walter Raleigh*

It would be pleasant, no doubt, to unbend the mind in Shakespeare's company; to exchange the white-heat of the smithy for the lazy ease of the village-green; to see him put off his magic garment, and fall back into the dear inanities of ordinary idle conversation. This pleasure is denied to us. But to know him as the greatest of artisans, when he collects his might and stands dilated, his imagination aflame, the thick-coming thoughts and fancies shaping themselves, under the stress of the central will, into a thing of life—this is to know him better, not worse. The rapid, alert reading of one of the great plays brings us nearer to the heart of Shakespeare than all the faithful and laudable business of the antiquary and the commentator.

★ ★ ★

No man can walk abroad save on his own shadow. No dramatist can create live characters save by bequeathing the best of himself to the children of his art, scattering among them a largess of his own qualities, giving, it may be, to one his wit, to another his philosophic doubt, to another his love of action, to another the simplicity and constancy that he finds deep in his own nature. There is no thrill of feeling communicated from the printed page but has first been alive in the mind of the author; there was nothing alive in his mind that was not intensely and sincerely felt. Plays like those of Shakespeare cannot be written in cold blood; they call forth the man's whole energies, and take toll of the last farthing of his wealth of sympathy and experience. In the plays we may learn what are the questions that interest Shakespeare most profoundly and recur to his mind with most insistence; we may note how he handles his story, what he rejects, and what he alters, changing its purport and fashion; how many points he is content to leave dark; what matters he chooses to decorate with the highest resources of his romantic art, and what he gives over to be the sport of triumphant ridicule; how in every type of character he emphasises what most appeals to his instinct and imagination, so that we see the meaning of character more plainly than it is to be seen in life. We share in the emotions that are aroused in him by certain situations and events; we are made to respond to the strange imaginative appeal of certain others; we know, more clearly than if we had heard it uttered, the verdict that he passes on certain characters and certain kinds of conduct. He has made us acquainted with all that he sees and all that he feels, he has spread out before us the scroll that contains his interpretation of the world;—how dare we complain that he has hidden himself from our knowledge?

Shakespeare. 1907. Chap. I.

[27] *William Wordsworth*

Scorn not the Sonnet; Critic, you have frowned,
Mindless of its just honours; with this key
Shakspeare unlocked his heart

"Scorn Not the Sonnet." (1827). Lines 1–3.

[28] *Robert Browning*

"'*With this same key*
Shakespeare unlocked his heart,' once more!"
Did Shakespeare? If so, the less Shakespeare he!

"House." *Pacchiarotto, and How He Worked in Distemper: with Other Poems*. 1876. Lines 38–40.

[29] *Henry James*

The man himself, in the Plays, we directly touch, to my consciousness, positively nowhere: we are dealing too perpetually with the artist, the monster and magician of a thousand masks, not one of which we feel him drop long enough to gratify with the breath of the interval that strained attention in us which would be yet, so quickened, ready to become deeper still. Here at last the artist is, comparatively speaking, so generalised, so consummate and typical, so frankly amused with himself, that is with his art, with his power, with his theme, that it is as if he came to meet us more than his usual half-way, and as if, thereby, in meeting *him,* and touching him, we were nearer to meeting and touching the man. The man everywhere, in Shakespeare's work, is so effectually locked up and imprisoned in the artist that we but hover at the base of thick walls for a sense of him; while, in addition, the artist is so steeped in the abysmal objectivity of his characters and situations that the great billows of the medium itself play with him, to our vision, very much as, over a ship's side, in certain waters, we catch, through transparent tides, the flash of strange sea-creatures. What we are present at in this fashion is a series of incalculable plunges—the series of those that have taken effect, I mean, after the great primary plunge, made once for all, of the man into the artist: the successive plunges of the artist himself into Romeo and into Juliet, into Shylock, Hamlet, Macbeth, Coriolanus, Cleopatra, Antony, Lear, Othello, Falstaff, Hotspur; immersions during which, though he always ultimately finds his feet, the very violence of the movements involved troubles and distracts our sight. In The Tempest, by the supreme felicity I speak of, is no violence; he sinks as deep as we like, but what he sinks into, beyond all else, is the lucid stillness of his style.

Introduction. *The Tempest.* The University Press Shakespeare, Renaissance Edition. 1907. XVI.

b. Shakespeare in the plays

[30] *Walter Whiter*

The Association of Ideas is a fruitful and popular theme in the writings of metaphysicians; and they have supplied us with innumerable examples, which prove at once the extent and the activity of its influence. They have taught us that our modes of reasoning, our habits of life, and even the motions of our body, are affected by its energy; and that it operates on the faculties by a kind of fascinating controul, which we sometimes cannot discover, and which generally we are unable to counteract. The consideration, however, of this doctrine (curious and extensive as it may appear) has commonly been confined to the admirers of metaphysical researches; nor has the theory, I believe, ever been systematically discussed as a point of taste, or as a subject of criticism. We have seen the question totally exhausted, as it refers to the general powers of the understanding, and the habitual exercise of the reasoning faculty; but we may justly be astonished that the effects of this principle should never have been investigated, as it operates on the *writer in the ardor of invention,* by imposing on his mind some remote and peculiar vein of language, or of imagery. If, in the ordinary exertions of the understanding, the force of such an association has been found so powerful and extensive, it may surely be concluded, that its influence would predominate with absolute authority over the vigorous workings of a wild and fertile imagination. In the pages of the poet, therefore, may we expect to be supplied with the most curious and abundant materials for the discussion of this principle; and in none can we hope to find such frequent and singular examples of its effect, as may probably be discovered by the diligent reader in the writings of Shakspeare.

"An Attempt to Explain and Illustrate Various Passages of *Shakspeare,* on a New Principle of Criticism, Derived from Mr. Locke's Doctrine of The Association of Ideas." *A Specimen of a Commentary on Shakspeare.* 1794.

[31] *Caroline F. E. Spurgeon*

I believe it to be profoundly true that the real revelation of the writer's personality, temperament and quality of mind is to be found in his works, whether he be dramatist or novelist, describing other people's thoughts or putting down his own directly.

In the case of a poet, I suggest it is chiefly through his images that he, to some extent unconsciously, 'gives himself away'. He may be, and in Shakespeare's case is, almost entirely objective in his dramatic characters and their views and opinions, yet, like the man who under stress of emotion will show no sign of it in eye or face, but will reveal it in some muscular tension, the poet unwittingly lays bare his own innermost likes and dislikes, observations and interests, associations of thought, attitudes of mind and beliefs, in and through the images, the verbal pictures he draws to illuminate something quite different in the speech and thought of his characters.

The imagery he instinctively uses is thus a revelation, largely unconscious, given at a moment of heightened feeling, of the furniture of his mind, the channels of his thought, the qualities of things, the objects and incidents he observes and remembers, and perhaps most significant of all, those which he does not observe or remember.

My experience is that this works out more reliably in drama than in pure poetry, because in a poem the writer is more definitely and consciously seeking the images; whereas in the drama, and especially drama written red-hot as was the Elizabethan, images tumble out of the mouths of the characters in the heat of the writer's feeling or passion, as they naturally surge up into his mind.

The greater and richer the work the more valuable and suggestive become the images, so that in the case of Shakespeare I believe one can scarcely overrate the possibilities of what may be discovered through a systematic examination of them. It was my conviction of this which led me to assemble and classify all his images, so as to have in orderly and easily accessible form the material upon which to base my deductions and conclusions.

Shakespeare's Imagery and What It Tells Us. 1935. Chap. I.

[32] *Walter Whiter*

Pelleted is again used with another term derived from the same source [the kitchen] in *Antony and Cleopatra.*

By the *discandying* of this *pelleted* storm.

(Act III. S. ii. p. 538.)

Discandying is the dissolving what is *candied.* So in this same play,

Their wishes do *discandy**, melt their *sweets.*

(Act IV. S. x. p. 557.)

Antony. Fortune and Antony part here; even here
Do we shake hands. All come to this?—The hearts,
That *spaniel'd me at heels,* to whom I gave
Their wishes, do *discandy;* melt their sweets
On blossoming Caesar.

(*Antony and Cleopatra,* Act IV. S. x. p. 557.)

No let the *candy*'d tongue *lick* absurd pomp;

*The whole of this passage and the succeeding quotations are well worthy of the reader's attention. [What follows is from Whiter's note.]

And crook the pregnant hinges of the knee,
Where thrift may follow *fawning*.

(*Hamlet*, Act III. S. ii. p. 302.)

Will these moist trees,
That have outlived the eagle, *page* thy *heels*
And skip when thou point'st out? Will the cold brook,
Candied with ice, caudle thy morning taste,
To cure thy o'er night's surfeit?

(*Timon of Athens*, Act IV. S. iii. p. 101.)

Why what a *candy* deal of courtesy,
This *fawning greyhound* then did proffer me!

(*Henry IV*. Part I. Act. I. S. iii. p. 144.)

These passages are very singular. The curious reader will observe that the *fawning obsequiousness* of an animal, or an attendant, is connected with the word *candy*. The cause of this strange association I am unable to discover; though the reader must know but little of the human mind—of Shakspeare—or even of the ordinary doctrine of *chances*, if he imagines that these matters were in *four* passages connected by *accident*.—When the reader shall be convinced respecting the truth of this observation; his curiosity will be much gratified by the following lines from the *Tempest;* in which he will perceive that the same association still occupied the mind of the Poet, though a single *word* only is apparent, which relates to one portion of the preceding metaphor.

Seb. But, for your conscience—
Ant. Ay, Sir; where lies that? if it were a *kybe*,
'Twould put me to my slipper; but I feel not
This deity in my bosom: twenty consciences,
That stand 'twixt me and Milan, *candy'd* be they,
And *melt*, ere they molest.

(Act II, S. i. p. 45.)

Surely the reader cannot doubt but that the introduction of the word *kybe* is to be referred to the former expressions, "page thy *heels*,"—"spaniel'd me at *heels*," though it is applied to a very different metaphor.

"An Attempt to Explain and Illustrate Various Passages of *Shakspeare* on a New Principle of Criticism, Derived from Mr. Locke's Doctrine of The Association of Ideas." *A Specimen of a Commentary on Shakspeare*. 1794.

[33] *Caroline F. E. Spurgeon*

By far the clearest and most striking example that I have met with of this tendency to group repeatedly a certain chain of ideas round some particular emotional or mental stimulus, is another group of ideas centring round an animal. This is so marked in its repetition that it has been noted by others—I mean the dog, licking, candy, melting group, called up inevitably by the thought of false friends or flatterers.

It is quite certain that one of the things which rouses Shakespeare's bitterest and deepest indignation is feigned love and affection assumed for a selfish end. He who values so intensely—above all else in human life—devoted and disinterested love, turns almost sick when he watches flatterers and sycophants bowing and cringing to the rich and powerful purely in order to get something out of them for themselves. It is as certain as anything can be, short of direct proof, that he had been hurt, directly or indirectly, in this particular way. No one who read his words carefully can doubt that he had either watched someone, whose friendship he prized, being deceived by fawning flatterers, or that he himself had suffered from a false friend or friends, who, for their own ends, had drawn out his love while remaining 'themselves as stone'.

★ ★ ★

The explanation of this curious and repeated sequence of ideas is, I think, very simple. It was the habit in Elizabethan times to have dogs, which were chiefly of the spaniel and greyhound type, at table, licking the hands of the guests, fawning and begging for sweetmeats with which they were fed, and of which, if they were like dogs today, they ate too many, dropping them in a semi-melting condition all over the place. Shakespeare, who was unusually fastidious, hated the habit, as he disliked all dirt and messiness, especially connected with food.

So there come to be linked in his mind two things he intensely dislikes, one in the physical everyday world, the other in the world of the mind and emotions: the fawning cupboard love of dogs, their greed and gluttony, with its sticky and disagreeable consequences, and the other fawning of insincere friends, bowing and flattering for what they hope to get, and turning their backs when they think no more is coming to them.

Shakespeare's Imagery and What It Tells Us. 1935. Chap. X.

[34] *Sidney Lanier*

And this dream-relation of youth toward the Real brings us immediately to our point; for it is precisely such a relation which the *Midsummer Night's Dream* expresses in the most ravishing terms of fancy. Death, and the cross of love, and the downward suctions of trade and politics, and the solemn stillness of current criticisms in all ages, and the compromise of creed, and the co-existence of God and misery, and the insufficiency of provision whereby some must die that the rest may live, and a thousand like matters: to these things the youth's senses, made purposely unapprehensive in part, are in a state which is described with scientific accuracy when it is called the state of a dream; and this is the state revealed in the *Midsummer Night's Dream.* Here we have the cross of love—two mad for one, Oberon quarrelling with his wife; but no thought of heartbreak. Here Bottom and his fellow patches show us Shakspere conscious of the fashionable degradations of his art; but there is no mourning over it, as in the later sonnet, "Tired of all these, for restful death I cry," and several others. Here we have the stupid ass-worship of contemporary criticism in all times—Titania, or current applause, doting upon the absurd monster; but it is matter for smiles, only, not indignation. *Certainly, Wrong is abroad, that is clear; but meantime one is young; and this is a dream:* such appears to be the fair moral outcome of this play.

★ ★ ★

Hamlet, as compared with *A Midsummer Night's Dream,* is as much as to say, *ten years later.* Here the ills and wrongs which youth admits in a theoretical sense not at all interfering with one's gayety, have come upon our poet in the shape of actual matters: as they do come, one way or another, to every man soon after his manhood. Immediately in his path young Shakspere finds a grave; it is so real that a voice appears to come out of it, saying, *either explain me or fill me.* Here also, sitting on either side the ugly hole, are the two figures of Sin and Punishment; and a multitude of less definite shapes flit terribly about. No debonair waving away of these now into the vague recesses of youthful unconcern. Once for all, death and crime and revenge and insanity and corruption *are,* and I have personal relations to them. For the first time he realizes the Real.

Every man of forty, many a man of thirty, knows this phase.

If we call that of youth the Dream Period, we may designate this as the Real Period. It comes after one has seen the frightful shifts of his fellow-tradesmen, or fellow-politicians, or, alas, fellow-artists; or after one has deadened to some love, of wife, child, or mother, found unworthy, and therefore loved by grace and not by attractive necessity; or after one has by turns begged, threatened, and wept in the face of death, at the parting of one's best-loved, and found oneself scorned with the scorn of death's imperturbable Nothing; or from one of a thousand other directions. Turn which way one will, there is the Devil grinning. The most familiar references show us the universality of this phase; it crops out from all Bibles, histories, biographies; the eating of the fruit which brought the knowledge of good and evil; the giving over of Job into Satan's hands, the Temptation in the wilderness, the sequestration of Moses, the hideous groans of Mohammed, the cry for the actual truth at the Renascence, the rise of Science: these all occur in each life, and represent from various standpoints the condition of Shakspere's mind which expressed itself in the play of *Hamlet*. Again postponing for a moment the parallel questions of actual date and artistic advance: let us pursue the matter of moral growth to the third play of our series, *The Tempest*.

Here the world is resolved. Man—who in the *Midsummer Night's Dream* was the victim of Puck, or tricksy Chance, and the slave of Nature; who, in *Hamlet* has advanced only so far from this *status* that he is *inquiring* into Nature, puzzling over death, analyzing revenge, and struggling with fate;—is, in *The Tempest*, ruler of Ariel (Puck's apotheosis), and lord of the storm, (which here brings good instead of the evil of Titania's freshets). In the Dream Period man is the sport of fate; in the *Hamlet* period man is still beneath fate, but the thing has gone beyond sport, for man inquires and suffers and struggles; in the *Tempest Period* man is master of the universe. And—what is here essential—this masterhood of Nature is accompanied by a supreme moral goodness to fellow-man. *The Tempest* is motived upon an enormous Forgiveness. The whole plot is, in three words, a *storm* and a *fairy*, used as *servants* by a *man* (Prospero), for a beneficent purpose which embraces in its scope even the man's *cruelest enemy*.

Out of the Real, or Inquiring, or Scientific (these terms become convertible from the point of view herein urged) Period of *Hamlet*, our poet emerges into what we may fairly call, by a nomenclature based on logical extension of the thought started with, the Ideal Period of *The Tempest.*

"Chaucer and Shakspere." (1880). *Music and Poetry.* 1898.

[35] *Edward Dowden*

First Period.—Returning now from our more detailed classification, let us glance once more at the four periods into which we divided Shakspere's career of authorship. The first, which I named *In the workshop,* was the period during which Shakspere was learning his trade as a dramatic craftsman. Starting at the age of twenty-four or twenty-six, he made rapid progress, and cannot but have been aware of this. The works of Shakspere's youth—experiments in various directions—are all marked by the presence of vivacity, cleverness, delight in beauty, and a quick enjoyment of existence. If an industrious apprentice, he was also a gay and courageous one.

Second Period.—As yet, however, he wrote with small experience of human life; the early plays are slight or fanciful, rather than real and massive. But now Shakspere's imagination began to lay hold of real life; he came to understand the world and the men in it; his plays begin to deal in an original and powerful way with the matter of history. "The compression of the large and rough matter of history into dramatic form demanded vigorous exercise of the plastic energy of the imagination; and the circumstance that he was dealing with reality and positive facts of the world, must have served to make clear to Shakspere that there was sterner stuff of poetry, material more precious—even for purposes of art—in actual life, than could be found in the conceits, and prettinesses, and affectations which at times led him astray in his earlier writings." During this period Shakspere's work grows strong and robust. It was the time when he was making rapid advance in worldly prosperity, and accumulating the fortune on which he meant to retire as a country gentleman. I name the second period therefore *In the world.*

Third Period.—Before it closed Shakspere had known sorrow: his son was dead; his father died probably soon after Shakspere had written his *Twelfth Night;* his friend of the *Sonnets* had done him wrong. Whatever the cause may have been, the fact seems certain that the poet now ceased to care for tales of mirth and love, for the stir and movement of history, for the pomp of war; he needed to sound, with his imagination, the depths of the human heart; to inquire into the darkest and saddest parts of human life; to study the great mystery of evil. The belief in human virtue, indeed, never deserts him: in *Lear* there is a Cordelia; in *Macbeth* a Banquo; even Troilus will be the better, not the worse, for his disenchantment with Cressida; and it is because Timon would fain love that he is driven to hate. Still, during this period, Shakspere's genius left the bright surface of the world, and was at work in the very heart and centre of things. I have named it *Out of the depths.*

Fourth Period.—The tragic gloom and suffering were not, however, to last for ever. The dark cloud lightens and rolls away, and the sky appears purer and tenderer than ever. The impression left upon the reader by Shakspere's last plays is that, whatever his trials and sorrows and errors may have been, he had come forth from them wise, large-hearted, calm-souled. He seems to have learned the secret of life, and while taking his share in it, to be yet disengaged from it; he looks down upon life, its joys, its griefs, its errors, with a grave tenderness, which is almost pity. The spirit of these last plays is that of serenity which results from fortitude, and the recognition of human frailty; all of them express a deep sense of the need of repentance and the duty of forgiveness. And they all show a delight in youth and the loveliness of youthful joy, such as one feels who looks on these things without possessing or any longer desiring to possess them. Shakspere in this period is most like his own Prospero. In these "Romances," and in the "Fragments," a supernatural element is present; man does not strive with circumstance and with his own passions in darkness; the gods preside over our human lives and fortunes, they communicate with us by vision, by oracles, through the elemental powers of nature. Shakspere's faith seems to have been that there is something without and around our human lives, of which we know little, yet which we know to be beneficent and divine. And it will be felt that the name which I have given to this last period—Shakspere having ascended out of the turmoil and trouble of action, out of the darkness and tragic mystery, the places haunted by terror and crime, and by love contending with these, to a pure and serene elevation—it will be felt that the name, *On the heights,* is neither inappropriate nor fanciful.

Shakspere. Literature Primer. 1877. Chap. V.

[36] *J. I. M. Stewart*

The artist does not get the essence of his characters from camera-work, as Mr. Draper would suppose; nor yet from a filing-cabinet of traditional literary types, which is the belief Professor Stoll constantly expresses with what softening word he can. He gets his characters from an interplay of these with something inside. And it is because he has a particular sort of inside, or psychic constitution, that he is obliged to get them. Falstaff and his peers are the product of an imagination working urgently from within. The sum of the characters is a sort of sum—nay, gives something like the portrait—of Shakespeare: a truth which Walter Bagehot realises in his essay, *Shakespeare—the Man.* ("If anybody could have any doubt about the liveliness of Shakespeare, let him consider the character of Falstaff.") But we do not quite express the matter by saying (what is obvious enough) that Shakespeare had immense perceptive and apperceptive power; that he could recognise in himself all the elements variously combined in the motley humanity about him, and so draw, with an original authority, the characters of many men and many women. To this we must add that there is typically in the artist an instability; a reluctance of elements, in themselves abnormally numerous, available and potent, to combine hierarchically in the formation of one permanent character; a corresponding impulse to build up now one and now another impermanent configuration of traits. "Now Master up, now Miss"—said Pope, projecting an extreme of this constitution upon his enemy. And here too is what Keats recognised as the chameleon nature of the poet.

The inquiries of James and others into the phenomena of conversion, and of later investigators in the field of multiple and split personality (did Falstaff indeed have a Dr. Jekyll who drove the common tenement of clay hoarse with halloing and singing of anthems?) have shown how, in abnormal individuals not artistically endowed, either a co-presence or a succession of perfectly "real" personalities can be a psychological fact. And a man writes plays or novels, I conceive, partly at least because he is beset by unexpressed selves; by the subliminal falling now into one coherent pattern and now into another of the varied elements of his total man—elements many of which will never, except in his writing, find play in consciousness. It is this that gives the characters their "independence as well as relation"; their haunting suggestion of reality and of a larger, latent being unexhausted in the action immediately before us; their ability to beckon beyond the narrow limits of their hour. And here, too, we see how characters "come alive"—how Falstaff came alive. It was not that Shakespeare took a traditional figure and clothed it with the spurious animation of a dazzling dress. It was that he took that figure and infused into it as much—and only as much—of the Falstaff-being in himself as the exigencies of his design would admit. Of what more there was unused the bouquet, it may be, floats across the stage in those "secret impressions" which Morgann felt. And sherris and ambrosia mingle there.

"The Birth and Death of Falstaff." *Character and Motive in Shakespeare.* 1949.

[37] *John Middleton Murry*

At this moment [of writing *King John* and *Richard II*], when Shakespeare was striving to deepen and enrich the drama of English history, and determined to

> let the world no longer be a stage
> To feed contention in a lingering act,

there is a sudden cessation of the casual metaphors of the theatre with which *Richard III* is replete, and there appears, in each of the two new histories, a theatrical metaphor of a quite different kind. It is indeed by contrast to the new metaphors that the peculiar quality of those in *Richard III* is apparent. The stage-metaphors of *Richard III* are metaphors of an abstract stage; the audience is not included in them; and the performance to which they have reference is one which in no sense at all depends upon the spectators: it might be played to an empty room. The play is, so to speak, an intellectual form, not a human event.

The new metaphors are quite different. In them it is the audience which matters. 'By heaven!' cries the Bastard,

> By heaven, these scroils of Angiers flout you, kings,
> And stand securely on their battlements,
> As in a theatre, whence they gape and point
> At your industrious scenes and acts of death.
>
> (II. i. 373–5)

That picture of the theatre is not drawn in the mind's eye: it is the concrete Elizabethan playhouse, the den of 'the blunt monster with uncounted heads', who solidly refuses to be kindled by the industry of the actors, or the labours of the playwright. To-day the theatre is refined; the thread which connects it with the Elizabethan playhouse is almost too tenuous to be a connection at all, and so the force of such an image is lost upon us. It is rather the memory of some pathetic troupe of tumblers in a continental market-place that we must invoke in order to feel the brutal indifference which is implied in Shakespeare's image here—an indifference which can become a torture to a sensitive third-party.

It is this same brutal indifference which is the theme of the still more striking image of the theatre in *Richard II*.

> As in a theatre, the eyes of men,
> After a well-graced actor leaves the stage,
> Are idly bent on him that enters next,
> Thinking his prattle to be tedious;
> Even so, or with much more contempt, men's eyes
> Did scowl on gentle Richard; no man cried 'God save him!'
> No joyful tongue gave him his welcome home:
> But dust was thrown upon his sacred head,
> Which with such gentle sorrow he shook off,
> His face still combating with tears and smiles,
> The badges of his grief and patience,
> That had not God, for some strong purpose, steel'd
> The hearts of men, they must perforce have melted
> And barbarism itself have pitied him.
>
> (V. ii. 23–36)

Better not let the imagination dwell too long on the implication of this image. One does not need to be unduly tenderminded even today to suffer acutely when some poor *artiste*—a Miss Moss of Katherine Mansfield's *Pictures*—'gets the bird' from a ruthless audience in a music-hall. He would be a bold man who believed that he was in any human respect more sensitive than Shakespeare. And Shakespeare was the actor, not the detached third party.

It is more comforting to reflect that the use of these metaphors at this moment is double-edged. If they record, as I believe they do, something of Shakespeare's reaction to the brutal indifference against which he had to struggle in his double effort, to make a living and to humanize the drama of his day, they record also a resilient capacity to take advantage of that indifference. We may be sorry for the man who had had to endure what is hinted at in these two metaphors;

but we must admire the smiling recovery of the man who could risk the words on the Elizabethan stage. If the scroils had flouted him, he was flouting them.

This resilience reaches a height of easy familiarity in the Induction to *Henry IV*, Part II. It is the moment in the sequence of the historical plays when we might expect such a change of attitude. With Falstaff and Hotspur, Shakespeare had found a way of his own, if not to their hearts, to some fundamental human stuff in his audience. He could make them laugh with a kind of language which lifts clowning on to a pinnacle of the imagination; he could make their ears ring with the noise of a rhetoric which sounds like the very challenge of youth and bravery. There is nothing in grain in *King John*, which does not come to a magnificent harvest in *Henry IV*. If there is a strain of lyricism and philosophy in *Richard II* which does not enter into the subsequent pattern of a Shakespeare history, it seems to be for want of room rather than from any doubt of his power to carry it over. That may be illusion. Perhaps Shakespeare had been forced to sacrifice something, after all.

But if he was, it did not weigh on him. If he had come to terms with his audience, the terms seem to have been pretty completely his own terms. He had found a vein which interested him and interested his audience, too. Falstaff may have been nothing distinguishably different from 'fat meat' to them; but they knew at least that it was a kind of fat meat that no one else could provide: they knew, too, that when it came to tearing a passion to tatters, it was somehow more satisfying to have it done in the 'natural' speech of a passionate man like Harry Percy of the North. Shakespeare was no longer afraid of his audience, or resentful of it. It is what it is, and by it he must live. He has found a way that pleases it and himself. So his impertinence takes a different tone; it is so direct as to be disarming; and it declares itself in the very first words of the play which followed his triumph.

Enter Rumour, *painted full of tongues.*

RUM: Open your ears; for which of you will stop
The vent of hearing when loud Rumour speaks?
. . . Rumour is a pipe
Blown by surmises, jealousies, conjectures
And of so easy and so plain a stop
That the blunt monster with uncounted heads,
The still-discordant wavering multitude,

Can play upon it. But what need I thus
My well-known body to anatomize
Among my household?

(II Hen. IV. Ind. 15–22)

The impertinence is colossal; or it would be, if it were merely impertinent. It happened to be truth as well.

Shakespeare. 1936. Chap. V.

[38] *J. Dover Wilson*

Another personal clue, also with a close parallel in the literature of to-day, is the strain of sex-nausea which runs through almost everything he wrote after 1600. "Sweet Desire" has turned sour! It has become ferocious also; Venus and the boar have changed roles; and Shakespeare was to have no security until the beast is fast chained to the rock beneath Prospero's cell. Whatever the cause, whether it had something to do, as many think, with the dark-eyed mistress of the Sonnets, though that episode must have been long past in 1601, or simply to the general morbidity of the age, certain it is the change is there. And that it was not a mere trick found useful to a practising dramatist is, I think, proved by its presence in the ravings of Lear, where there is no dramatic reason for it at all. Further, it is difficult to avoid associating it with personal jealousy of some kind. Jealousy is the mainspring of no less than four plays: *Troilus and Cressida, Othello, Winter's Tale,* and *Cymbeline,* while there are traces of it in *Antony and Cleopatra,* and one may suspect that it furnished material for the scene between Hamlet and his mother. That "couch for luxury and damned incest", which, unseen, is ever present to the mind both of Hamlet and of the audience, is, I think, symbolic. Far more than the murder, it is this which transforms the Prince's imagination into something "as foul as Vulcan's stithy". The imagination of Othello is as foul and more explicit. Even Lear, as I have just said, broods "over the nasty sty" and begs "an ounce of civet to sweeten his imagination", while to Posthumus and Leontes is given utterance scarcely less outspoken than Othello's. Above all in *Timon of Athens,* which breathes a hatred of mankind that rivals Swift's, nearly a whole act is devoted to the unsavoury topic. Collect these passages together, face them as they should be faced, and the conclusion is inescapable that the defiled imagination of which Shakespeare writes so often, and depicts in metaphor so nakedly material, must be his own.

The Essential Shakespeare. 1932. Chap. VI.

[39] *Ernest Jones*

It is surely plain that an emotional experience to which Shakespeare responded by writing "Hamlet" must correspond in its nature with the underlying themes of the tragedy. Now it is true that the two facts just mentioned, deaths of a father and of an obvious father-substitute, accord in part with this criterion, but we entirely miss in them any allusion to the almost physical disgust at sex that is so prominent in "Hamlet." Such a misogyny is hardly possible except from a sense of bitter disappointment at the hands of the opposite sex. This may be wholly constitutional, dating from early childhood experiences, a state of affairs that can be excluded when one thinks of the happy young Shakespeare writing his love comedies, or only partly so and then reinforced by a tremendous experience of the same sort in adult life. What we would expect, therefore, is some overwhelming passion that ended in a betrayal in such circumstances that murderous impulses towards the faithless couple were stirred but could not be admitted to consciousness.

Now, as is well known, Shakespeare himself in his Sonnets gives an unmistakable description of just such an experience, and from its intensity more critics than not have regarded it as a personal one.

Hamlet and Oedipus. 1949. Chap. VI.

[40] *Eric Partridge*

If ever there were a man filled with the joy and sap of life, it was Shakespeare; and if ever there were a man compact of spiritual needs and loveliest and noblest aspirations, it was Shakespeare. He could muse and meditate with the most meditative, also could he talk and do things with the best conversationalist and the most energetic man of action. Thinker, yet not remote from the stressful hurly-burly; dreamer, yet practical businessman; deliberate sater of that desirous, sex-hungry body, yet merciless contemner of his own yielding; condemning too his dark mistress, yet continuing to love the woman she might have been—and, for his happiness, should have been; never finding the ideal love, yet forever seeking it, for he knew that such love is, this side heaven, man's most abiding joy and content and safety; expressing the physical aspect of love in its most intimate details, either with frank joyousness and animal spirits or with a self-reviling brutality and as if moved by an irresistible need to cleanse, not merely his bosom but his entire system, of this most perilous stuff, yet with his eyes upon a starry portal that might allow him, spirit-weary, mind-lorn, body-aching, to enter a house of tranquillity: complete and enduring union with such a woman as could joyously, unquestioningly, bring him the peace and the bliss of perfect understanding, unreservèd sympathy, and an unflawed compatibility. He never found that woman, that home, that peace.

Introductory. *Shakespeare's Bawdy*. 1948.

[41] *Eric Partridge*

In my study of Shakespeare's sexuality and bawdiness, I have come to feel that, from his plays and poems, there emerges something basic, significant, supremely important and most illuminatingly revelatory.

Although he never even hinted this, Shakespeare seems to have held, and to have consistently acted upon, the opinion; nay, the belief; that:—

To write is, in fact, to create; and to make love is potentially to create:

to write provides a means of releasing one's intellectual and spiritual energy, whereas to copulate is a means of releasing one's physical energy:

the desire to write is at least as urgent and powerful, intellectually and spiritually, as the desire to make love (especially, to copulate) is on the physical plane:

composition is superior to love-making as a means of satisfying the need for self-expression (or 'the creative urge'); almost equal to it as an anodyne to that loneliness with which all of us, but especially the literary and artistic and musical creators, are beset, and as a comfort and a solace:

moreover, to write of sex and love serves both to satisfy—and perhaps to justify—the intellectual and spiritual need to create and homoeopathically to assuage one's physical desires by that modified form of sublimation which consists in a not ignoble substitution.

Valedictory. *Shakespeare's Bawdy*. 1948.

Historical

[42] *Lily B. Campbell*

Perhaps it will help explain my point of view in regard to Shakespeare's plays if I venture to state my own credo. I do not believe that a poet exists in a vacuum, or even that he exists solely in the minds and hearts of his interpreters. I do not believe that he can write great poetry without conviction and without passion. I do not believe that his reflection of his period is casual and fragmentary and accidental. Rather, it seems to me the poet must be reckoned a man among men, a man who can be understood only against the background of his own time. His ideas and his experiences are conditioned by the time and the place in which he lives. He is inevitably a man of feeling. If, however, he is not merely a poet but a great poet, the particulars of his experience are linked in meaning to the universal of which they are a representative part. If he is a great poet, his feeling becomes an intense passion. It is not that he does not write out of his experience that sets him as a man apart; it is rather that he penetrates through experience to the meaning of experience. For this reason he has generally been reckoned a seer and a prophet. It is not lack of feeling but a passion for universal truth that takes his hatred and his love out of the realm of the petty and into the realm of the significant. In this sense, and in this sense only, is he impersonal. Further, the greatest poets have always in their work been philosophers; that is to say they have developed, as they matured, consistent patterns of thought. They have seen life as a whole, not in fragments.

I hope no one will misunderstand me as saying that a poet expounds a philosophy in set words or invents a system of the universe. The poet is as much conditioned by the material he works in as by his experience. If he is a dramatist, he has to do first and fundamentally with plot. The characters may, indeed, express his philosophy or their own, but the plot is bound to express the author's philosophy; it is bound to relate particular characters and their particular actions to universal law. Macbeth may say that "Life is a tale told by an idiot," but the play of *Macbeth* is not a tale of a world run by an idiot. It is a tale of a world of clearly defined moral law, in which Macbeth and his particular actions meet with the indestructible and the universal. Poets today have another philosophy, and their plots reveal their uncertainties. But Shakespeare's plots were clear and sure because he had a definite, fundamental conception of universal law.

It is to a study of Shakespeare's historical plays from this point of view that this book is directed. The first problem involved is the definition of a history play, for that definition must lead to the background of thought and purpose which affords the basis for interpreting individual plays.

Shakespeare's "Histories" Mirrors of Elizabethan Policy. 1947. Chap. I.

[43] *L. C. Salingar*

The world of the play [*Hamlet*] is a corrupted world of Renaissance civility; and Hamlet, the stage figure, is as much a humanist who has turned to satire as an avenging son frustrated by melancholia. His friendship with Horatio shows his leaning towards the stoicism of the day; and the mood and topic of his formal speeches are those of contemporary satirists (of Marston, for example), from the invective against woman's frailty in his first soliloquy to his baiting of Osric's humour at the end. His disgust with the world is more savage, but no more effective, than Jaques'; and when his meeting with the Ghost betrays his terrible inadequacy, he too can only determine to 'put an antic disposition on'. In his dealings with the court he becomes very largely the Fool of popular tradition, with his snatches of ballad and proverb, his dark riddling wisdom, his mockery and irresponsibility, his sudden violent mischief. But while Folly in the comedies shows civility and practical reason inverted, in *Hamlet* they are agonizingly broken into fragments. The supreme 'antic' is Death itself (IV.iii, V.i), the skull of Yorick the jester in the graveyard scene. One by one, in the tradition of the Dance of Death, Hamlet reduces the murderer, the politician, the courtier, the land-purchasing lawyer, the court lady, even Alexander himself, to the same ignoble ending as the clown:

> . . . Now get you to my lady's chamber, and tell her, let her paint an inch thick, to this favour she must come; make her laugh at that.

This is the final biting mockery of traditional satire against the disguises of civility.

"The Elizabethan Literary Renaissance." *The Age of Shakespeare, A Guide to English Literature*. Ed. Boris Ford. 1956. Vol. II.

[44] *D. H. Lawrence*

It is an old fear, which seemed to dig in to the English soul at the time of the Renaissance. Nothing could be more lovely and fearless than Chaucer. But already Shakespeare is morbid with fear, fear of consequences. That is the strange phenomenon of the English Renaissance: this mystic terror of the consequences, the consequences of action. Italy, too, had her reaction, at the end of the sixteenth century, and showed a similar fear. But not so profound, so overmastering. Aretino was anything but timorous: he was bold as any Renaissance novelist, and went one better.

What appeared to take full grip on the northern consciousness at the end of the sixteenth century was a terror, almost a horror of sexual life. The Elizabethans, grand as we think them, started it. The real "mortal coil" in Hamlet is all sexual; the young man's horror of his mother's incest, sex carrying with it a wild and nameless terror which, it seems to me, it had never carried before. Oedipus and Hamlet are very different in this respect. In Oedipus there is no recoil in horror from sex itself: Greek drama never shows us that. The horror, when it is present in Greek tragedy, is against *destiny*, man caught in the toils of destiny. But with the Renaissance itself, particularly in England, the horror is sexual. Orestes is dogged by destiny and driven mad by the Eumenides. But Hamlet is overpowered by horrible revulsion from his physical connexion with his mother, which makes him recoil in similar revulsion from Ophelia, and almost from his father, even as a ghost. He is horrified at the merest suggestion of physical connexion, as if it were an unspeakable taint.

"Introduction to These Paintings." *The Paintings of D. H. Lawrence.* 1929.

[45] *E. M. W. Tillyard*

At a time when so much has been said about the principle of order and of the hierarchies in English literature of the Renaissance tradition, it is not likely that anyone will question my conclusion that Shakespeare's Histories with their constant pictures of disorder cannot be understood without assuming a larger principle of order in the background. I hope I have proved by illustration how steadily aware Shakespeare was of that principle throughout his History Plays from the very beginning, and that by this awareness he allies himself to the more philosophical writers of his day.

★ ★ ★

The question of the epic and how far Shakespeare took into account the contemporary ideas of the epic brings with it the general interpretation of the whole series of Shakespeare's Histories. At one time I followed a common opinion in looking on them less as self-sufficient dramas than as experiments in a solemn mode leading him to his true goal of tragedy. Men thought of Shakespeare caught up in his youth by the new and exciting self-realisation of England, in a way deceived into thinking the political theme his true theme, lured on to picturing, as his climax, the perfect king, Henry V. Then, at the culminating moment he realises that the man of action is not his real hero, that his imagined hero has let him down; and, schooled by this experience, he turns to the type of man who fundamentally attracts him, the man whose interests are private not public, whose sphere of thought is the universe and not the body politic. And, let down by his political hero, Shakespeare finds his true outlet in Brutus, Hamlet, and the other great tragic heroes.

I now think this scheme is wrong as a whole, though it contains elements of truth. First, Shakespeare turned the Chronicle Play into an independent and authentic type of drama, and no mere ancillary to the form of tragedy. He did this largely because he grasped the potentialities of the old Morality form, never allowing the personalities of his kings to trespass on the fundamental Morality subject of Respublica. In the total sequence of his plays dealing with the subject matter of Hall he expressed successfully a universally held and still comprehensible scheme of history: a scheme fundamentally religious, by which events evolve under a law of justice and under the ruling of God's Providence, and of which Elizabeth's England was the acknowledged outcome. The scheme, which, in its general outline, consisted of the distortion of nature's course by a crime and its restoration through a long series of disasters and suffering and struggles, may indeed be like Shakespeare's scheme of tragedy; but it is genuinely political and has its own right of existence apart from tragedy. But in addition to this concatenated scheme, Shakespeare in *Richard II* and *1* and *2 Henry IV* gave us his version, which I have called epic, of what life was like in the Middle Ages as he conceived them and in his own day. This version was entirely successful and presents not even a parallel to the form of tragedy. It is one of Shakespeare's vast achievements and it stands unchallengeable: something entirely itself without a jot of suspicion that it ought to be, or ought to lead up to, something else; and achievement sufficient to put Shakespeare among the world's major poets. Nevertheless *Henry IV* led to *Henry V,* a play whose hero was no longer Respublica but Rex, and, once there was a change of hero, the form created by Shakespeare collapsed and the problem of tragedy thrust itself forward. Prince Hal had had nothing to do with tragedy and did not let his creator down; Henry V admitted the problems of tragedy and let his creator down very badly indeed. Thus it is that in a very minor and exceptional way, and at the very end of its exploitation, the History Play served as a transition to authentic tragedy. In *Macbeth* Shakespeare settled the adjustment of the political man of action to the other parts of the tragic world.

"Conclusions." *Shakespeare's History Plays.* 1946.

[46] *C. L. Barber*

Shakespeare was the opposite of primitivistic, for in his culture what we search out and call primitive was in the blood and bone as a matter of course; the problem was to deal with it, to master it. The Renaissance, moreover, was a moment when educated men were modifying a ceremonial conception of human life to create a historical conception. The ceremonial view, which assumed that names and meanings are fixed and final, expressed experience as pageant and ritual—pageant where the right names could march in proper order, or ritual where names could be changed in the right, the proper way. The historical view expresses life as drama. People in drama are not identical with their names, for they gain and lose their names, their status and meaning—and not by settled ritual: the gaining and losing of names, of meaning, is beyond the control of any set ritual sequence. Shakespeare's plays are full of pageantry and of action patterned in a ritualistic way. But the pageants are regularly interrupted; the rituals are abortive or perverted; or if they succeed, they succeed against odds or in an unexpected fashion. The people in the plays try to organize their lives by pageant and ritual, but the plays are dramatic precisely because the effort fails. This failure drama presents as history and personality; in the largest perspective, as destiny.

Shakespeare's Festive Comedy, A Study of Dramatic Form and Its Relation to Social Custom. 1959. Chap. 8.

[47] *Wyndham Lewis*

. . . the *master-subject* of Shakespeare's plays has been reached, and, I think, its essential nature exhibited. . . . This was, of course, immediately and historically, the reflection of the struggle between chivalry, "celtism," christian mysticism, on the one hand, and the "scientific spirit" of the renaissance mind and of the modern world on the other. It was the struggle that gave such force and point to the work of Cervantes and Rabelais. And Shakespeare was more positivist than Cervantes, and less so I think than Rabelais: his was a mean position, but into this mean he gathered the excesses of his time as well. That is why with all his measure he had so much force.

The fact that this is also with Shakespeare, as with Cervantes and Rabelais, the master-*motif* of his work has not been given the salience it deserves. So far the *alto-fronto* type, originating or at least finding its rough archetype in *The Malcontent,* has received beyond doubt the most advertisement. The Hamlet-problem is the most obviously conspicuous one in all the mass of his plays. But there is, running through all of them and turned a hundred ways, another fundamental preoccupation of the mind, which is a universal problem but also a problem especially of his time—and now of ours. And Machiavelli (abused or ignored, in the nature of things, by every true machiavellian) is still the best textbook for much to-day being accomplished in the political field.

This preoccupation as manifested in Shakespeare could be styled the battle of the lion and the fox: the contest or the tragedy arising from the meeting of the *Simpleton* and the *Machiavel,* the Fool and the Knave. Othello is the most obvious instance of this preoccupation and nothing else; but it springs up everywhere in Shakespeare's plays. Coriolanus, and Hotspur, Ajax, Hector, in varying degrees, are other instances of simpletons with whom, I think, contrary to what is generally believed, Shakespeare had little sympathy. Coriolanus is certainly not the hero, or the object of admiration, for Shakespeare, that he is generally supposed to be, any more than is the unintelligent and morbid chivalry of Percy. There is no love lost between these figures and their intelligent creator, as there is between Don Quixote and his. And it is at this point we once more will find how difficult it is to reconcile all the troubled elements, sometimes confronted on the same stage, in these creations. The sort of contradiction to which I refer is this, for example: that Hotspur and Coriolanus are as good physical heroes as Othello, but they do not apparently recommend themselves to Shakespeare: and therefrom their physical heroism itself seems to become disgusting or ridiculous. The quality in Antony and Othello that is capital for their dazzled creator, in the other two seems taken for granted, and now and then appears almost an offence. The cause for this seems to be in the fact that the latter heroes have not the necessary magnetism to transform their exploits into poetry, and to destroy in these the *real.* There is the stench of battle, and its "shop," about both of them; mechanical, sanguinary, perspiring events are their inferior element, and they neither of them have Cleopatras or Desdemonas.

Coriolanus, a figure that occupies a great deal of space, is at no point allowed anything that could be described as charm. He is in a state of stupid tutelage, and remains a "boy" to the end. The Coriolanus of Shakespeare seems to have the qualities and defects of the english public-school boy, the really successful type of which has for its rationale a military or administrative objective, for which he is prepared by a castration of the imagination. Essentially also his training permits of no development: throughout life he remains the schoolboy he has been taught to be for ever, so that at sixty the same jolly, healthy face shall be there as at the beginning. No amount of physical courage can compensate for the defects of dullness and meanness inherent in such a system. And Coriolanus, who is crabbed, sullen and pompous, has none even of the features that redeem that.

If you were brought to accept that view of Shakespeare's feeling about these two characters, only Coriolanus and Hotspur, for instance, it would involve a radical modification also of the generally accepted estimate of Shakespeare's political tendencies. In short, the wedge successfully introduced at those points would bring to the ground the house of cards of theologico-political shakespearian criticism that has been built during a century (the first transcendental stones of which were laid by Coleridge and Gervinus), and which is being gnawed at to-day by most contemporary critics. But it is always an open question on *which side* the edifice will fall; and my own inclination would be to see it fall to a side favourable to Shakespeare.

The Lion and the Fox The Rôle of the Hero in the Plays of Shakespeare. 1927. Part VI, Chap. I.

Aesthetic

[48] *Oscar Wilde*

Art begins with abstract decoration, with purely imaginative and pleasurable work dealing with what is unreal and non-existent. This is the first stage. Then Life becomes fascinated with this new wonder, and asks to be admitted into the charmed circle. Art takes life as part of her rough material, recreates it, and refashions it in fresh forms, is absolutely indifferent to fact, invents, imagines, dreams, and keeps between herself and reality the impenetrable barrier of beautiful style, of decorative or ideal treatment. The third stage is when Life gets the upper hand, and drives Art out into the wilderness. This is the true decadence, and it is from this that we are now suffering.

Take the case of the English drama. At first in the hands of the monks Dramatic Art was abstract, decorative and mythological. Then she enlisted Life in her service, and using some of life's external forms, she created an entirely new race of beings, whose sorrows were more terrible than any sorrow man has ever felt, whose joys were keener than lovers' joys, who had the rage of the Titans and the calm of the gods, who had monstrous and marvellous sins, monstrous and marvellous virtues. To them she gave a language different from that of actual use, a language full of resonant music and sweet rhythm, made stately by solemn cadence, or made delicate by fanciful rhyme, jewelled with wonderful words, and enriched with lofty diction. She clothed her children in strange raiment and gave them masks, and at her bidding the antique world rose from its marble tomb. A new Caesar stalked through the streets of risen Rome, and with purple sail and flute-led oars another Cleopatra passed up the river to Antioch. Old myth and legend and dream took shape and substance. History was entirely re-written, and there was hardly one of the dramatists who did not recognise that the object of Art is not simple truth but complex beauty. In this they were perfectly right. Art itself is really a form of exaggeration; and selection, which is the very spirit of art, is nothing more than an intensified mode of over-emphasis.

But Life soon shattered the perfection of the form. Even in Shakespeare we can see the beginning of the end. It shows itself by the gradual breaking up of the blank-verse in the later plays, by the predominance given to prose, and by the over-importance assigned to characterisation. The passages in Shakespeare—and they are many—where the language is uncouth, vulgar, exaggerated, fantastic, obscene even, are entirely due to Life calling for an echo of her own voice, and rejecting the intervention of beautiful style, through which alone should Life be suffered to find expression. Shakespeare is not by any means a flawless artist. He is too fond of going directly to life, and borrowing life's natural utterance. He forgets that when Art surrenders her imaginative medium she surrenders everything.

Goethe says somewhere:—In der Beschränkung zeigt sich erst der Meister. It is in working within limits that the master reveals himself, and the limitation, the very condition of any art is style. However, we need not linger any longer over Shakespeare's realism. *The Tempest* is the most perfect of palinodes. All that we desired to point out was that the magnificent work of the Elizabethan and Jacobean artists contained within itself the seeds of its own dissolution, and that, if it drew some of its strength from using life as rough material, it drew all its weakness from using life as an artistic method. As the inevitable result of this substitution of an imitative for a creative medium, this surrender of an imaginative form, we have the modern English melodrama. The characters in these plays talk on the stage exactly as they would talk off it; they have neither aspirations nor aspirates; they are taken directly from life and reproduce its vulgarity down to the smallest detail; they present the gait, manner, costume and accent of real people; they would pass unnoticed in a third-class railway carriage. And yet how wearisome the plays are! They do not succeed in producing even that impression of reality at which they aim, and which is their only reason for existing. As a method, realism is a complete failure.

"The Decay of Lying." *Intentions*. 1891.

[49] *Edgar Allan Poe*

In all commentating upon Shakspeare, there has been a radical error, never yet mentioned. It is the error of attempting to expound his characters—to account for their actions—to reconcile his inconsistencies—not as if they were the coinage of a human brain, but as if they had been actual existences upon earth. We talk of Hamlet the man, instead of Hamlet the *dramatis persona*—of Hamlet that God, in place of Hamlet that Shakspeare created. If Hamlet had really lived, and if the tragedy were an accurate record of his deeds, from this record (with some trouble) we might, it is true, reconcile his inconsistencies and settle to our satisfaction his true character. But the task becomes the purest absurdity when we deal only with a phantom. It is not (then) the inconsistencies of the acting man which we have as a subject of discussion—(although we proceed as if it were, and thus *inevitably* err,) but the whims and vacillations—the conflicting energies and indolences of the poet. It seems to us little less than a miracle, that this obvious point should have been overlooked.

Review of *The Characters of Shakspeare,* by William Hazlitt. *Broadway Journal.* Aug. 16, 1845.

[50] *Arthur Sewell*

Is Falstaff a coward? One might answer that the facts say that he is, but our impression of him, our attitude to him, says that he is not. Falstaff ran away, pretended to be dead; and to do these things was to put the safety of his skin above his human dignity, and this might be thought to be a sort of 'cowardice'. But not when we are dealing with Falstaff, for Falstaff was very doubtful about 'honour', and if we do not believe in 'honour' the word 'cowardice' has no meaning. Falstaff is not to be judged, as a real person might be judged, in terms of the ordinary moral categories. His running away, his pretending to be dead, his speech on 'honour' are all part of his attitude to his world, and it is this that calls from us the ambiguous, even face-saving, judgement of laughter. We do not ask, Was Falstaff a coward? just because we are ourselves infected with Falstaff's notion that perhaps, after all, the question is not so important as we thought it was.

Falstaff is a character, not a real person. What wholeness and consistency he has comes not from within but from the address of his personality *vis-à-vis* his world as it transforms itself into speech and behaviour. The world is his stooge and, so magnanimously does he present himself, he is his own stooge. He subdues and transforms the matter of the moment—even his own monstrous belly—to the purposes of his superlatively comic vision. Such a representation of personality is to be found in a work of art, and its consistency is not psychological but aesthetic. It is the notable distinction of Falstaff's being that he has been conceived quite independently of psychological motivation. His delights, like ours, are aesthetic, even though they have their play in the uncertain world of our moral scruples.

Character and Society in Shakespeare. 1951. Chap. I.

[51] *Elmer Edgar Stoll*

But Shakespeare was not a political or moral theorist. He was not a theorist at all, not even, in any abstract or analytic sense of the word, a thinker. He was an artist, which is something widely different. His morals and his politics, his science and his history, were those of his time or one still earlier; but his art was for the ages. He was not a philosopher, a seer, an oracle, as some worshippers have taken him to be; he was not, of course, a prophet living in spirit in the nineteenth century while working in the sixteenth; but he was a man and dramatist as others were—Sophocles, Molière, Lope de Vega—and as such he was not very different from a great painter, sculptor, or musician. Like theirs, his work was to reveal not truth but beauty, to imitate and ennoble life, not analyze or expound it. Plot and situation, dialogue and character, style and meter,—these are the elements of his art in which he wrought as he strove to produce the illusion of life upon the stage. These are the things that we should attend to as we, in turn, strive to discover how far he succeeded in producing the illusion of life upon the stage.

Poets and Playwrights. 1930. Chap. II.

[52] *Harley Granville-Barker*

Our would-be Shakespeare of to-day, with a Hamlet for his subject, has only to note that the wretched fellow was suffering from an Oedipus-complex and the mystery is solved. Why does no one take Shakespeare's *Hamlet* (as Shakespeare possibly took Kyd's) and re-write it on these lines? Let Claudius, whose mind and conscience even as we have them are most supple, allow Hamlet to return to Wittenberg (it is never made clear why he did not), where some psycho-analyst must surely await him. He can return in the next act freed from the doubts and hesitations which so intolerably prolong the present play. Whether he will not also have been freed from belief in the Ghost and the need to revenge his father, that is for our would-be Shakespeare to decide. But the theme will at least have been lifted to a more enlightened plane; and we shall be spared those useless reflections upon duty and honour, death and immortality, matters upon which even the New Psychology has nothing very new to say.

Freudianism can be a great help to the critic too. I have recently been told that Othello was a "Narcissist", because, while

Desdemona loved him for the dangers he had passed, he loved her because she pitied them. There is likewise skulking about some queerly obscene explanation of the relations between Lear and Cordelia. Would "dirty nonsense" be too strong a term for such talk? I do not use the "dirty" abusively, but to connote the more material side of our nature, which was formed, as we know, out of the dust of the earth. For the grain of truth in the matter, forced to such inappropriate and pretentious growth, lies not at all in the plays themselves, but in the primitive—and therefore powerful, and admittedly most interesting—stuff out of which they are moulded. But the virtue of Shakespeare's work is that he took this stuff, the crude story, or the murky legend of blood feud and lust, and transmuted it into spiritual tragedy. That has been plain enough ever since his sources were known; and it is in these, therefore, and even behind them again, not in the plays, that the Freudian critic should seek his quarry.

The Study of Drama. (A lecture given at Cambridge on 2 August 1934.) 1934.

[53] *Richard G. Moulton*

Amongst ordinary readers of Shakespeare, Character-Interest, which is largely independent of performance, has swallowed up all other interests; and most of the effects which depend upon the connection and relative force of incidents, and on the compression of the details into a given space, have been completely lost. Shakespeare is popularly regarded as supreme in the painting of human nature, but careless in the construction of Plot: and, worst of all, Plot itself, which it has been the mission of the English Drama to elevate into the position of the most intellectual of all elements in literary effect, has become degraded in conception to the level of a mere juggler's mystery. It must then be laid down distinctly at the outset of the present enquiry that the Drama is to be considered throughout relatively to its acting. . . . The interpretation of a character must include what an actor can put into it; in dealing with effects regard must be had to surroundings which a reader might easily overlook, but which would be present to the eye of a spectator; and no conception of the movement of a drama will be adequate which has not appreciated the rapid sequence of incidents that crowds the crisis of a life-time or a national revolution into two or three hours of actual time. The relation of Drama to its acting will be exactly similar to that of Music to its performance, the two being perfectly separable in their exposition, but never disunited in idea.

Shakespeare As a Dramatic Artist. 1885. Chap. XVI.

[54] *Bertrand Evans*

This book attempts an approach to the comedies through one of Shakespeare's notable dramaturgical characteristics—his uses of awareness and control.

★ ★ ★

To my own mind, what most emerges from the present study is a view of Shakespeare as the shrewdest of dramatic engineers. True, shrewdness in the management of awarenesses is not all there is to dramatic shrewdness, nor is dramatic shrewdness all there is to Shakespeare. But I offer this study as one more item in the enormous and swiftly growing body of evidence that Shakespeare as dramatist (like Shakespeare as poet) was about as remote from that warbler of 'native woodnotes wild' of Milton's as it is possible to get. I, for one, have never believed in that warbler, and this study of but one facet of Shakespeare's dramaturgy has made me even surer that his deliberateness was anything but that of Fancy's child. Several of his habits as dramatist are set in relief when the plays are examined from the point of view of the uses of awareness: his habit of making assurance doubly sure that we *cannot* miss an effect that he has been at pains to prepare—and he is *always* at pains to prepare; his habit of advising us *before* rather than *after* the event; his habit of requiring climactic scenes to demand multiple responses; his habit of squeezing each prepared situation for its last drop of dramatic effect before releasing it. These are samples only; but they and other habits to which this study draws attention evince the quality of an art that is deliberate, calculated, infinitely shrewd.

Preface. *Shakespeare's Comedies.* 1960.

[55] *L. C. Knights*

How should we read Shakespeare?

We start with so many lines of verse on a printed page which we read as we should read any other poem. We have to elucidate the meaning . . . and to unravel ambiguities; we have to estimate the kind and quality of the imagery and determine the precise degree of evocation of particular figures; we have to allow full weight to each word, exploring its 'tentacular roots', and to determine how it controls and is controlled by the rhythmic movement of the passage in which it occurs. In short, we have to decide exactly why the lines 'are so and not otherwise'.

As we read other factors come into play. The lines have a cumulative effect. 'Plot', aspects of 'character' and recurrent 'themes' —all 'precipitates from the memory'—help to determine our reaction at a given point. There is a constant reference backwards and forwards. But the work of detailed analysis continues to the last line of the last act. If the razor-edge of sensibility is blunted at any point we cannot claim to have read what Shakespeare wrote, however often our eyes may have travelled over the page. A play of Shakespeare's is a precise particular experience, a poem—and precision and particularity are exactly what is lacking in the greater part of Shakespeare criticism, criticism that deals with *Hamlet* or *Othello* in terms of abstractions that have nothing to do with the unique arrangement of words that constitutes these plays.

How Many Children Had Lady Macbeth? 1933. *Explorations.* 1946.

The Plays as Mirrors of Life

[56] *Maurice Morgann*

But it was not enough for *Shakespeare* to have formed his characters with the most perfect truth and coherence; it was further necessary that he should possess a wonderful facility of compressing, as it were, his own spirit into these images, and of giving alternate animation to the forms. This was not to be done *from without;* he must have *felt* every varied situation, and have spoken thro' the organ he had formed. Such an intuitive comprehension of things and such a facility, must unite to produce a *Shakespeare.* The reader will not now be surprised if I affirm that those characters in *Shakespeare,* which are seen only in part, are yet capable of being unfolded and understood in the whole; every part being in fact relative, and inferring all the rest. It is true that the point of action or sentiment, which we are most concerned in, is always held out for our special notice. But who does not perceive that there is a peculiarity about it, which conveys a relish of the whole? And very frequently, when no particular point presses, he boldly makes a character act and speak from those parts of the composition, which are *inferred* only, and not distinctly shewn. This produces a wonderful effect; it seems to carry us beyond the poet to nature itself, and gives an integrity and truth to facts and character, which they could not otherwise obtain: And this is in reality that art in *Shakespeare,* which being withdrawn from our notice, we more emphatically call *nature.* A felt propriety and truth from causes unseen, I take to be the highest point of Poetic composition. If the characters of *Shakespeare* are thus *whole,* and as it were original, while those of almost all other writers are mere imitation, it may be fit to consider them rather as Historic than Dramatic beings; and, when occasion requires, to account for their conduct from the *whole* of character, from general principles, from latent motives, and from policies not avowed.

An Essay on the Dramatic Character of Sir John Falstaff. (1774). 1777.

[57] *Mary Cowden Clarke*

The design has been, to trace the probable antecedents in the history of some of Shakespeare's women; to imagine the possible circumstances and influences of scene, event, and associate, surrounding the infant life of his heroines, which might have conduced to originate and foster those germs of character recognized in their maturity, as by him developed; to conjecture what might have been the first imperfect dawnings of that which he has shown us in the meridian blaze of perfection: and it was believed that such a design would combine much matter of interesting speculation, afford scope for pleasant fancy, and be productive of entertainment in the various narratives.

Preface. *The Girlhood of Shakespeare's Heroines.* Vol. I. 1850.

[58] *Alexander Pope*

His *Characters* are so much Nature her self, that 'tis a sort of injury to call them by so distant a name as Copies of her. Those of other Poets have a constant resemblance, which shews that they receiv'd them from one another, and were but multiplyers of the same image: each picture like a mock-rainbow is but the reflexion of a reflexion.

But every single character in *Shakespear* is as much an Individual, as those in Life itself; it is as impossible to find any two alike; and such as from their relation or affinity in any respect appear most to be Twins, will upon comparison be found remarkably distinct. To this life and variety of Character, we must add the wonderful Preservation of it; which is such throughout his plays, that had all the Speeches been printed without the very names of the Persons, I believe one might have apply'd them with certainty to every speaker.

Preface. *The Works of Shakespear*. 1725.

[59] *Samuel Johnson*

Shakespeare is above all writers, at least above all modern writers, the poet of nature; the poet that holds up to his readers a faithful mirrour of manners and of life. His characters are not modified by the customs of particular places, unpractised by the rest of the world; by the peculiarities of studies or professions, which can operate but upon small numbers; or by the accidents of transient fashions or temporary opinions: they are the genuine progeny of common humanity, such as the world will always supply, and observation will always find. His persons act and speak by the influence of those general passions and principles by which all minds are agitated, and the whole system of life is continued in motion. In the writings of other poets a character is too often an individual; in those of *Shakespeare* it is commonly a species.

★ ★ ★

Upon every other stage the universal agent is love, by whose power all good and evil is distributed, and every action quickened or retarded . . . But love is only one of many passions; and as it has no great influence upon the sum of life, it has little operation in the dramas of a poet, who caught his ideas from the living world, and exhibited only what he saw before him. He knew, that any other passion, as it was regular or exorbitant, was a cause of happiness or calamity.

★ ★ ★

Other dramatists can only gain attention by hyperbolical or aggravated characters, by fabulous and unexampled excellence or depravity, as the writers of barbarous romances invigorated the reader by a giant and a dwarf; and he that should form his expectations of human affairs from the play, or from the tale, would be equally deceived. *Shakespeare* has no heroes; his scenes are occupied only by men, who act and speak as the reader thinks that he should himself have spoken or acted on the same occasion: Even where the agency is supernatural the dialogue is level with life. Other writers disguise the most natural passions and most frequent incidents; so that he who contemplates them in the book will not know them in the world: *Shakespeare* approximates the remote, and familiarizes the wonderful; the event which he represents will not happen, but if it were possible, its effects would probably be such as he has assigned; and it may be said, that he has not only shewn human nature as it acts in real exigencies, but as it would be found in trials, to which it cannot be exposed.

This therefore is the praise of *Shakespeare*, that his drama is the mirrour of life; that he who has mazed his imagination, in following the phantoms which other writers raise up before him, may here be cured of his delirious extasies, by reading human sentiments in human language; by scenes from which a hermit may estimate the transactions of the world, and a confessor predict the progress of the passions.

Preface. *The Plays of William Shakespeare.* 1765.

[60] *Samuel Johnson*

Polonius is a man bred in courts, exercised in business, stored with observation, confident of his knowledge, proud of his eloquence, and declining into dotage. His mode of oratory is truly represented as designed to ridicule the practice of those times, of prefaces that made no introduction, and of method that embarrassed rather than explained. This part of his character is accidental, the rest is natural. Such a man is positive and confident, because he knows that his mind was once strong, and knows not that it is become weak. Such a man excels in general principles, but fails in the particular application. He is knowing in retrospect, and ignorant in foresight. While he depends upon his memory, and can draw from his repositories of knowledge, he utters weighty sentences, and gives useful counsel; but as the mind in its enfeebled state cannot be kept long busy and intent, the old man is subject to sudden dereliction of his faculties, he loses the order of his ideas, and entangles himself in his own thoughts, till he recovers the leading principle, and falls again into his former train. This idea of dotage encroaching upon wisdom, will solve all the phænomena of the character of *Polonius*.

The Plays of William Shakespeare. 1765. Vol. VIII.

[61] *Samuel Taylor Coleridge*

Shakespeare's characters, from Othello and Macbeth down to Dogberry and the Grave-digger, may be termed ideal realities. They are not the things themselves, so much as abstracts of the things, which a great mind takes into itself, and there naturalizes them to its own conception. Take Dogberry . . . He is not the creature of the day, to disappear with the day, but the representative and abstract of truth which must ever be true, and of humour which must ever be humorous.

★ ★ ★

In the plays of Shakespeare every man sees himself, without knowing that he does so: as in some of the phenomena of nature, in the mist of the mountain, the traveller beholds his own figure, but the glory round the head distinguishes it from a mere vulgar copy . . . So in Shakespeare: every form is true, everything has reality for its foundation; we can all recognise the truth, but we see it decorated with such hues of beauty, and magnified to such proportions of grandeur, that, while we know the figure, we know also how much it has been refined and exalted by the poet.

The Lectures of 1811–12. IX. Raysor II, 162–63.

[62] *James Russell Lowell*

As we study these [Homer, Dante, Goethe], we seem in our limited way to penetrate into their consciousness and to measure and master their methods; but with Shakespeare it is just the other way; the more we have familiarized ourselves with the operations of our own consciousness, the more do we find, in reading him, that he has been beforehand with us, and that, while we have been vainly endeavoring to find the door of his being, he has searched every nook and cranny of our own. While other poets and dramatists embody isolated phases of character and work inward from the phenomenon to the special law which it illustrates, he seems in some strange way unitary with human nature itself, and his own soul to have been the law and life-giving power of which his creations are only the phenomena. We justify or criticise the characters of others writers by our memory and experience, and pronounce them natural or unnatural; but he seems to have worked in the very stuff of which memory and experience are made, and we recognize his truth to Nature by an innate and unacquired sympathy, as if he alone possessed the secret of the "ideal form and universal mould," and embodied generic types rather than individuals. In this Cervantes alone has approached him; and Don Quixote and Sancho, like the men and women of Shakespeare, are the contemporaries of every generation, because they are not products of an artificial and transitory society, but because they are animated by the primeval and unchanging forces of that humanity which underlies and survives the forever-fickle creeds and ceremonials of the parochial corners which we who dwell in them sublimely call The World.

"Shakespeare Once More." *North American Review.* 1868. *Among My Books.* 1870.

[63] *Walter Raleigh*

The mistakes which beset our modern criticism of Shakespeare are not likely to be the mistakes of carelessness and undervaluation. We can hardly even join in Ben Jonson's confession, and say that we honour his memory "on this side idolatry." We are idolaters of Shakespeare, born and bred. Our sin is not indifference, but superstition—which is another kind of ignorance. In all the realms of political democracy there is no equality like that which a poet exacts from his readers. He seeks for no convertites nor worshippers, but records his ideas and impressions of life and society in order that the reader may compare them with his own. If the impressions tally, sympathy is born. If not, the courteous reader will yet find matter for thought. The indispensable preliminary for judging and enjoying Shakespeare is not knowledge of his history, not even knowledge of his works, but knowledge of his theme, a wide acquaintance with human life and human passion as they are reflected in a sensitive and independent mind. The poets, and but few others, have approached him from the right point of view, with the requisite ease and sincerity. There is no writer who has been so laden with the impertinences of prosaic enthusiasm and learned triviality. There is no book, except the Bible, which has been so misread, so misapplied, or made the subject of so many idle paradoxes and ingenuities. The most careless and casual lines in his plays have been twisted and squeezed in the hope that they will yield some medicinal secret. His poetry has been cut into minute indigestible fragments, and used like wedding-cake, not to eat, but to dream upon. The greatest poet of the modern world is at this day widely believed to have been also the most irrelevant, and to have valued the golden casket of his verse chiefly as a hiding-place for the odds and ends of personal gossip. These are the penalties to be paid by great poets when their works become fashionable.

Shakespeare. 1907. Chap. I.

[64] *Harold C. Goddard*

The critics who are continually bringing in the conventions of the Elizabethan stage, insisting above all things on a meticulously accurate text, or forever invoking the spirit of Shakespeare's time, are right and admirable in their reverence for history and fact and in their desire to get rid of "all this subjective business"—right and admirable, that is, up to a certain point. But beyond that point they are just indulging in another kind of subjective business of their own. For the objective business that is the object of their search is neither a whit better nor a whit worse than the subjective business that is the subject of their scorn. The two are extremes that meet. Suppose that in a drop of water an oxygen sect were to appear clamoring for the extinction of all this hydrogen business—or vice versa. It would be a parable of the factual critics. For what they leave out is one of the two constituents of life itself. What they forget is the dual character of the imagination.

Imagination is neither the language of nature nor the language of man, but both at once, the medium of communion between the two—as if the birds, unable to understand the speech of man, and man, unable to understand the songs of birds, yet longing to communicate, were to agree on a tongue made up of sounds they both could comprehend—the voice of running water perhaps or the wind in the trees. Imagination is the *elemental* speech in all senses, the first and the last, of primitive man and of the poets.

★ ★ ★

Poetry, the elemental speech, is like the elements. Its primary function is not to convey thought, but to reflect life. It shows man his soul, as a looking glass does his face. There hangs the mirror on the wall, a definite object, the same for all. Yet whoever looks into it sees not the mirror but himself. We all live in the same world, but what different worlds we see in it and make out of it: Caesar's, Jesus', Machiavelli's, Mozart's—yours and mine.

★ ★ ★

The reader with a poem before him is like a youth with life before him. In spite of all that the guides and drivers say, he must be faithful *to the text and to himself:* two lions at the gate of his adventure to keep him from wandering off into the desert of custom or the jungle of fancy. This is the answer to those who hold that opening the doors on individual interpretation is opening them on anarchy. If it is, we are to blame. It need not be. We read a poem as we live—at our risk. Though it may take its time about it, the world has a way of bringing up with a sharp jolt the man who attempts to substitute for its facts some private fancy. Fanciful interpretations of literature are doomed to as quick extinction. The text must be as sacred to the reader as his facts are to the scientist. He must discard instantly anything it contradicts. But he must be as ready to strike life into it, from his own experience, as a scientist must be fertile in hypotheses. And this is what the objective school of Shakespearean criticism forgets. How refreshing, when oppressed by the deposit of learning under which it sometimes threatens to bury Shakespeare, to remember a sentence of Emerson's: "A collector recently bought at public auction, in London, for one hundred and fifty-seven guineas, an autograph of Shakspeare: but for nothing a schoolboy can read *Hamlet,* and can detect secrets of highest concernment yet unpublished therein." What if that should cease to be true! What if someday the heart of Hamlet's mystery should be plucked out and whenever we went to the theater we could count not on seeing a new Hamlet as we do now but on seeing the one original and authentic Hamlet of "Shakespeare himself"! Would we care to attend the theater any longer? How right that Shakespeare's most masterly character should be his most baffling and protean one.

The Meaning of Shakespeare. 1951. Chap. I.

Unity and Chaos

[65] *Samuel Johnson*

The plots are often so loosely formed, that a very slight consideration may improve them, and so carelessly pursued, that he seems not always fully to comprehend his own design. He omits opportunities of instructing or delighting which the train of his story seems to force upon him, and apparently rejects those exhibitions which would be more affecting, for the sake of those which are more easy.

It may be observed, that in many of his plays the latter part is evidently neglected. When he found himself near the end of his work, and, in view of his reward, he shortened the labour to snatch the profit. He therefore remits his efforts where he should most vigorously exert them, and his catastrophe is improbably produced or imperfectly represented.

He had no regard to distinction of time or place, but gives to one age or nation, without scruple, the customs, institutions, and opinions of another, at the expence not only of likelihood, but of possibility.

★ ★ ★

His histories, being neither tragedies nor comedies, are not subject to any of their laws; nothing more is necessary to all the praise which they expect, than that the changes of action be so prepared as to be understood, that the incidents be various and affecting, and the characters consistent, natural, and distinct. No other unity is intended, and therefore none is to be sought.

In his other works he has well enough preserved the unity of action. He has not, indeed, an intrigue regularly perplexed and regularly unravelled: he does not endeavour to hide his design only to discover it, for this is seldom the order of real events, and *Shakespeare* is the poet of nature: But his plan has commonly what *Aristotle* requires, a beginning, a middle, and an end; one event is concatenated with another, and the conclusion follows by easy consequence. There are perhaps some incidents that might be spared, as in other poets there is much talk that only fills up time upon the stage; but the general system makes gradual advances, and the end of the play is the end of expectation.

To the unities of time and place he has shewn no regard . . .

★ ★ ★

Whether *Shakespeare* knew the unities, and rejected them by design, or deviated from them by happy ignorance, it is, I think, impossible to decide, and useless to enquire. We may reasonably suppose, that, when he rose to notice, he did not want the counsels and admonitions of scholars and criticks, and that he at last deliberately persisted in a practice, which he might have begun by chance. As nothing is essential to the fable, but unity of action, and as the unities of time and place arise evidently from false assumptions, and, by circumscribing the extent of the drama, lessen its variety, I cannot think it much to be lamented, that they were not known by him, or not observed: Nor, if such another poet could arise, should I very vehemently reproach him, that his first act passed at *Venice*, and his next in *Cyprus*. Such violations of rules merely positive, become the comprehensive genius of *Shakespeare*.

Preface. *The Plays of William Shakespeare*. 1765.

[66] *George Santayana*

We may observe in general that Shakespeare's genius shines in the texture of his poems rather than in their structure, in imagery and happy strokes rather than in integrating ideas. His poetry plays about life like ivy about a house, and is more akin to landscape than to architecture. He feels no vocation to call the stones themselves to their ideal places and enchant the very substance and skeleton of the world. How blind to him, and to Hamlet, are all ultimate issues, and the sum total of things how unseizable!

Introduction. *Hamlet*. The University Press Shakespeare, Renaissance Edition. XXX. 1908.

[67] *Samuel Taylor Coleridge*

A *unity of feeling* pervades the whole of his plays. In *Romeo and Juliet* all is youth and spring—it is youth with its follies, its virtues, its precipitancies; it is spring with its odours, flowers, and transiency:

—the same feeling commences, goes through, and ends the play. The old men, the Capulets and Montagues, are not common old men; they have an eagerness, a hastiness, a precipitancy—the effect of spring. With Romeo his precipitate change of passion, his hasty marriage, and his rash death, are all the effects of youth. With Juliet love has all that is tender and melancholy in the nightingale, all that is voluptuous in the rose, with whatever is sweet in the freshness of spring; but it ends with a long deep sigh, like the breeze of the evening. This unity of character pervades the whole of his dramas.

The Lectures of 1813–14. I. Raysor II, 265.

[68] *Samuel Taylor Coleridge*

The highest and the lowest characters are brought together [in the first scene of the *Tempest*], and with what excellence! Much of the genius of Shakespeare is displayed in these happy combinations—the highest and the lowest, the gayest and the saddest; he is not droll in one scene and melancholy in another, but often both the one and the other in the same scene. Laughter is made to swell the tear of sorrow, and to throw, as it were, a poetic light upon it, while the tear mingles tenderness with the laughter.

The Lectures of 1811–12. IX. Raysor II, 169–70.

[69] *James Russell Lowell*

With Shakespeare the plot is an interior organism, in Jonson an external contrivance. It is the difference between man and tortoise. In the one the osseous structure is out of sight, indeed, but sustains the flesh and blood that envelop it, while the other is boxed up and imprisoned in his bones.

"Shakespeare Once More." *North American Review*. 1868. *Amony My Books*. 1870.

Characters and Characterization

[70] *Ellen Terry*

I have tried five or six different ways of treating Portia, but the way I think best is not the one which finds the heartiest response from my audiences. Has there ever been a dramatist, I wonder, whose parts admit of as many different interpretations as do Shakespeare's? There lies his immortality as an acting force. For times change, and parts have to be acted differently for different generations. Some parts are not sufficiently universal for this to be possible, but every ten years an actor can reconsider a Shakespeare part and find new life in it for his new purpose and new audiences.

The Story of My Life. 1908. Chap. V.

[71] *Samuel Johnson*

His adherence to general nature has exposed him to the censure of criticks, who form their judgments upon narrower principles. *Dennis* and *Rhymer* think his *Romans* not sufficiently *Roman;* and *Voltaire* censures his kings as not completely royal. *Dennis* is offended, that *Menenius,* a senator of *Rome,* should play the buffoon; and *Voltaire* perhaps thinks decency violated when the *Danish* Usurper is represented as a drunkard. But *Shakespeare* always makes nature predominate over accident; and if he preserves the essential character, is not very careful of distinctions superinduced and adventitious. His story requires Romans or kings, but he thinks only on men. He knew that *Rome,* like every other city, had men of all dispositions; and wanting a buffoon, he went into the senate-house for that which the senate-house would certainly have afforded him. He was inclined to shew an usurper and a murderer not only odious but despicable, he therefore added drunkenness to his other qualities, knowing that kings love wine like other men, and that wine exerts its natural power upon kings. These are the petty cavils of petty minds; a poet overlooks the casual distinction of country and condition, as a painter, satisfied with the figure, neglects the drapery.

Preface. *The Plays of William Shakespeare.* 1765.

[72] *Maurice Morgann*

. . . There are certain qualities and capacities, which he seems to have considered as first principles; the chief of which are certain energies of courage and activity, according to their degrees; together with different degrees and sorts of sensibilities, and a capacity, varying likewise in the *degree*, of discernment and intelligence. The rest of the composition is drawn in from an atmosphere of surrounding things; that is, from the various influences of the different laws, religions and governments in the world; and from those of the different ranks and inequalities in society; and from the different professions of men, encouraging or repressing passions of particular sorts, and inducing different modes of thinking and habits of life; and he seems to have known intuitively what those influences in particular were which this or that original constitution would most freely imbibe, and which would most easily associate and coalesce. But all these things being, in different situations, very differently disposed, and those differences exactly discerned by him, he found no difficulty in marking every individual, even among characters of the same sort, with something peculiar and distinct.

An Essay on the Dramatic Character of Sir John Falstaff. (1774). 1777.

[73] *John Vyvyan*

In strict derivation, allegory means other-speak. Double-talk, one might be tempted to call it; and Shakespeare, like the poets of the Middle Ages, delights in subtle double-talk. In our own century we are unattuned to poetic allegory, and may think of allegorical figures as puppetry. There is a penalty for this: we sometimes fail to see allegory, unless it is so crude as to be a blemish, or unless a label, "This work is allegorical", has already been tied on.

To Shakespeare, allegory is not puppetry, but a deeper level of life; and he uses it frequently, where we are liable to miss it, in order that we may actually see the inner drama of his heroes' souls. This is one of the most significant elements of his art; and if it eludes us, we are losing his deepest thoughts. But it is easy for us to miss, partly because we are out of sympathy with it, and partly because Shakespeare uses it with great subtlety.

Many of his characters are dual: they are human beings and allegorical figures at the same time. And if we are not alerted to this, we may see nothing but the human being. When we try to analyse, completely, a Shakespearean character by psychological means, we run into trouble; because the allegorical aspect will not yield to this interpretation. Scenes, too, that are psychologically baffling, may be allegorically lucid; and when so considered, they fall into place.

Ophelia is a dual character of this kind: she is the girl we all know, and she is also an allegorical figure representing a quality in Hamlet's soul. When Hamlet speaks to her, he is sometimes talking to a girl, sometimes to an entity in himself, and often to both. As an allegorical figure, she is that point of love in Hamlet which is the centre of his true nobility; and therefore she coincides with his highest self, which he is about to fail, and is a symbol of the law of love, to which he cannot rise. Everything that happens to Ophelia is an allegory of what is taking place in Hamlet.

When he treated her—we know he once did—as a lover should treat his beloved, he was noble and could have been false to no man. When he has sworn to take revenge, but cannot do so until love has been cast out, we have those poignant scenes between them, when he is driving love from his soul and at the same time breaking her heart. When his nobility totters, she goes mad; when it is a ruin, she is drowned.

The Shakespearean Ethic. 1959. Chap. 4.

[74] *John Palmer*

[Shakespeare] has his characters alive and fully-formed in his mind. He takes for granted their primary qualities, which emerge, as it were, by accident. These characters are more than a sum of the traits which they exhibit. They do not come alive, feature by feature. They spring upon the stage in full career. They are not constructed; they enter upon the scene, men and women, rounded and complete in the imagination of the author, who assumes that his audience will recognise them for what they are as soon as they appear. They walk in upon us, each of them 'in his habit as he lived'. Shakespeare can thus exhibit them, if he chooses, behaving as men and women do, at odds with themselves, betraying inconsistencies and contradictions which no other dramatist has dared to permit in an equal degree. Taking the reality of Hamlet or Falstaff for granted, he can allow them to act out of character without destroying our belief in them but, on the contrary, increasing our sense of their human veracity. Hamlet, irresolute in action, courteous by nature and humane in disposition, surprises but in no way disconcerts us when he leads an attack upon a pirate ship, is gross with Ophelia or brutal in his references to the dead Polonius. Falstaff, a trained soldier of courage and resource, who at Shrewsbury leads his men into the thick of the battle where they are 'peppered', can yet find discretion the better part of valour and be exposed to ridicule as the man who ran away at Gadshill. Commentators on Shakespeare are puzzled by such inconsistencies and some critics have egregiously discovered them to be faults. But in no respect is Shakespeare's genius more manifest than in allowing his characters to act in ways which, at first sight and to the strictly logical mind, seem at variance with their essential qualities. It is worth noting that such apparent contradictions become more frequent as Shakespeare grows creatively more absolute. They are less notable in his political than in his comic characters and in his tragic characters they become master-strokes of delineation.

Political Characters of Shakespeare. 1945. Chap. I.

[75] *Robert Bridges*

The interest in a Shakespearean tragedy lies chiefly in the hero's conduct, and is greater as his conduct surprises while it satisfies: and from the constitution of things it is difficult to imagine a character or personality whose actions shall be at once consistent and surprising. The extreme of virtue may surprise; but Shakespeare never chose to depict men of whom the world was not worthy. Then there is the extreme of vice; and Shakespeare has surprised us with this in Iago and others; and he has surprised us, successfully or not, with monstrous forms of special qualities in Timon and in Coriolanus: but to sustain surprise in a worthy hero, he has sometimes had recourse to devices which are intended to baulk analysis. In order to attain the surprising, he will risk, or even sacrifice, the logical and consistent; and as such a flaw, if it were perceived, must ruin the interest, he is ready with abundant means to obscure the inconsistency. It seems to me that one method was to take advantage of uncertainty or confusion in motives or matters of fact lying partly or wholly outside the drama, which, if they were clearly conceived as determined one way or another, would confine the action within lesser lines. Some matter which, as it appears to us, might have happened as well one way as another, is purposely left half-determined: we are led to suppose that it happened one way, and if we are disturbed by conduct inconsistent with that surmise, we can shift our surmise, but only to be encountered by actions which drive us back upon it, or suggest another explanation. The pleasure attending our surprise gratifies us, and our critical faculty is quieted by the reflection that there must be a solution, and that it is natural enough that we should not hit upon it at once. This attitude of mind is further assured by the convincing verisimilitude and richness of Shakespeare's detail, as well as by the appearance of necessity which accompanies the presentation of action.

Some incongruity may well occur accidentally; and if extrascenic it may be difficult to avoid, and is to be found, I suppose, in the most classical Greek drama; but it is easy to see how it was forecast in the bare skeleton of such plays as the *Macbeth,* and *Measure for Measure.* Having found a story the actions of which were suitable, Shakespeare adopted them very much as they were, but remade the character of the actor. In the original story the actor would be known and judged by his actions: this, Shakespeare reverses by first introducing his hero as a man superior to his actions; his art being to create a kind of contrast between the two, which has, of course, no existence in the original tale; and his success depends on the power and skill with which this character is chosen and enforced upon the audience; for it is when their minds are preoccupied with his personality that the actions follow as unquestionable realities, and in the *Macbeth* even preordained and prophesied.

Not that there is anything illegitimate or even peculiar in this use of contrast: indeed if a worthy hero is to behave badly, he must be better than his actions, for he cannot be either equal or worse. And since the terms whereby we describe character are undefined, each several case must be considered on its own merits: there is no rule from which anything can be deduced beyond probabilities; and the probable is not what is desired, but the exceptional. Only it cannot be conceded that any character is capable of any action: there is a limit, and Shakespeare seems to delight in raiding across it. Consider the "opportunity" in the *Macbeth*. The hero's character having been elevated above his actions, their criminality is also increased; for in the history Macbeth kills Duncan in a soldier-like manner. But Shakespeare, choosing that Duncan shall be secretly murdered, makes Lady Macbeth represent the advent of Duncan to their castle as a favourable opportunity; and he knows that the audience, blinded by the material juxtaposition, will regard it as such. But to propose this dastardly violation of honour to Macbeth would, most probably, have stimulated his nobility and scared him from the crime however fully he might have been predetermined on it: yet Shakespeare, fortifying the position by Lady Macbeth's ambition and will, ventures to exhibit his hero as truly possessed by the proper shame and horror, but fascinated by the presentation which is deluding the audience.

★ ★ ★

The play of *Hamlet* may finally be taken in illustration of this view of Shakespeare's method. Why has there been such question whether Hamlet was mad or only feigning, unless it was Shakespeare's design to put his reason under suspicion? and does not the hypothesis of such a design reconcile all? The limit of madness is indefinable: to feign madness is no presumption in favour of sanity, and might itself be a kind of madness: again, if the conscious simulation led to an unconscious habit of acting insanely, how would this differ from the first degree of true madness, except in the possession of a healthy will in the background, which is precisely what Hamlet lacked? Something of this sort would seem, from Hamlet's excuse to Laertes, to have been his own view of his case. If we must choose between sane and insane, then the better opinion of the two, namely, that Hamlet was never more than "covering discretion with a cloak of folly," makes him guilty of the murder of Guildenstern and Rosencrantz,—which, moreover, is like a madman's unscrupulous action, inconsiderately and cunningly performed, and boasted of in full imaginative detail after;—his language to Ophelia has also to be excused, though that, even if it were unparalleled in Shakespeare, might possibly be defended as the extreme of self-repudiation in a proud, and perhaps somewhat cruel, nature safe-guarding itself from reproach by making the assumed mask impossible to be mistaken for truth. Again, why are we forbidden to know anything concerning his earlier relations with Ophelia, how long he had loved her, and how deeply? Why is even the date of that strange letter hopelessly obscured, unless it were that any one definite determination about it would expose or create a contradiction?

There must be mistakes in Shakespeare's work, ignorances and oversights in the writing, as there are misprints, false copyings, and perhaps fusion of incompatible versions: but the class of contradictions and obscurities which I have been noticing can hardly be ascribed to unconscious error. . . . [Shakespeare] had, as it were, a balance to maintain, and a fine sense of its equipoise: if one scale descends, he immediately throws something into the other, and though he may appear to be careless as to what he throws in, he only throws in such things as he knows he may be careless about. But an examination of those matters would tend to prove that he did not regard the reader as well as the audience of his plays.

"On The Influence Of The Audience." *The Works of William Shakespeare*, Stratford Town Edition, X. 1907.

[76] *Arthur Sewell*

Just as the *persona* which the music-hall comedian creates is the product of collaboration between himself and his audience, so it is with many of Shakespeare's characters. What vitality they have, and what consistency, does not come from within but from without, and it is not 'depth psychology' but a complex of social attitudes which gives them particular life. These characters have no private lives; they live in public, before an audience. This is obviously true about such a character as Launcelot Gobbo, but it is also true of Iago and Falstaff. Iago has that kind of actuality—and, except as a construction external to the play, no more—which comes from an audience. In his soliloquies he takes us into his confidence; he addresses us as though our estimate of men might be the same as his. He takes identity not from within but from without. Shakespeare never 'darted himself forth' into Iago; he conceived him, as the child-cowboy conceives the Indian, the necessary antagonist to that other character, Othello, who is conceived from within. Falstaff similarly has no private life. Falstaff must have his audience, and is, one may say, nobody when nobody is about. For, of course, we do not run away with Falstaff at Gadshill or counterfeit death at Shrewsbury; we watch him doing these things. It is almost true to say that while Shakespeare identified himself with Falstaff, as actor, he kept very much apart from him, as man. At most he does not assume the man; he assumes the attitude.

★ ★ ★

The characteristic moment in Shakespeare's presentation of the tragic character is the moment at which that character, looking to the future, says, 'To be or not to be', or 'Now might I do it pat', or 'If it were done when 'tis done'; and this is the moment of moral responsibility, not psychological determination. It is, indeed, the moment when the character seeks to make some settlement in his moral encounter with the universe, not the moment in which the climax comes in a whole chain of psychological motivation. Character is very much more than is revealed in a case-history, and, perhaps, something less. In drama, as in ethics, psychology is still the handmaid, not the mistress.

★ ★ ★

. . . in Shakespeare's plays, the essential process of character-creation is a prismatic breaking-up of the comprehensive vision of the play; and each element of vision, so separated out, is in itself a unique illumination, finding its individual fulfilment in character.

. . . in Shakespeare's mature plays even a minor character will enrich, diversify, and individually quicken the comprehensive view. Of that view he is the product, but in that view he is also an agent. The minor character is not merely a deduction from the theme of the play, related by a kind of dramatic geometry to the whole pattern. In him, as in a single brush-stroke in a picture, a moment of vision, a new angle of attitude, transforms to however small an extent, and lights up, the whole matter.

Character and Society in Shakespeare. 1951. Chap. I.

[77] *Samuel Taylor Coleridge*

In Shakespeare's females the sweet yet dignified feeling of all that *continuates* society, as sense of ancestry, of sex, etc. A purity inassailable by sophistry, because it does not rest on the analytic processes —but in feeling may be misinterpreted to the worst purposes—but in that sane equipoise of the faculties during which the feelings are representative of all past experience, not of the individual but of all those by whom she has been educated and of their predecessors *usque ad Evam.*

Lecture-Notes. 1813. Raysor I, 234.

[78] *William Hazlitt*

It is the peculiar excellence of Shakespear's heroines, that they seem to exist only in their attachment to others. They are pure abstractions of the affections. We think as little of their persons as they do themselves, because we are let into the secrets of their hearts, which are more important. We are too much interested in their affairs to stop to look at their faces, except by stealth and at intervals. No one ever hit the true perfection of the female character, the sense of weakness leaning on the strength of its affections for support, so well as Shakespear—no one ever so well painted natural tenderness free from affectation and disguise—no one else ever so well shewed how delicacy and timidity, when driven to extremity, grow romantic and extravagant; for the romance of his heroines (in which they abound) is only an excess of the habitual prejudices of their sex, scrupulous of being false to their vows, truant to their affections, and taught by the force of feeling when to forgo the forms of propriety for the essence of it. His women were in this respect exquisite logicians; for there is nothing so logical as passion. They knew their own minds exactly; and only followed up a favourite purpose, which they had sworn to with their tongues, and which was engraven on their hearts, into its untoward consequences. They were the prettiest little set of martyrs and confessors on record. —Cibber, in speaking of the early English stage, accounts for the want of prominence and theatrical display in Shakespear's female characters from the circumstance, that women in those days were not allowed to play the parts of women, which made it necessary to keep them a good deal in the back-ground. Does not this state of manners itself, which prevented their exhibiting themselves in public, and confined them to the relations and charities of domestic life, afford a truer explanation of the matter? His women are certainly very unlike stage-heroines; the reverse of tragedy-queens.

"Cymbeline." *Characters of Shakespear's Plays.* 1817.

[79] *Ellen Terry*

How many times Shakespeare draws fathers and daughters, and how little stock he seems to take of *mothers!* Portia and Desdemona, Cordelia, Rosalind and Miranda, Lady Macbeth, Queen Katherine and Hermione, Ophelia, Jessica, Hero, and many more are daughters of *fathers,* but of their mothers we hear nothing. . . . Of mothers of sons there are plenty of examples: Constance, Volumnia, the Countess Rousillon, Gertrude; but if there are mothers of daughters at all, they are poor examples, like Juliet's mother and Mrs. Page.

The Story of My Life. 1908. Chap. IX.

[80] *George Gordon*

I think the best division of the professional comic men in Shakespeare's plays—at any rate, the best division technically—would be this: (1) those who play with words; and (2) those who are played with by them—those, that is, who are sufficiently masters of the English language to make fun out of it; and those who are so mastered by it as to give fun unconsciously. . . . with one or two exceptions—Touchstone perhaps, at his best—I find the second, the helpless class, more amusing, and of a more lasting humour, than the first.

(1) In the first class come all the professional Fools, headed by Touchstone, with Feste, and such court-bred attendants as Moth—that 'tender juvenal'. In the same class, though touching on the second, come the men-servants, the roguish valets, like Speed, and Launce, and Launcelot. They see the fun well enough, but, sometimes, through illiterate ambition, they take a fall.

(2) In the second class come rustics like Costard, artisans like Bottom, and officials like Dogberry, Verges, and Dull. The amusement they cause is at their own expense. They are complacent, vain, and adorably stupid. Sometimes they achieve pure nonsense, than which nothing is more difficult to explain. . . . There is nothing in Shakespeare more certainly the work of genius than the *mettled* nonsense, the *complacent* nonsense, the perfectly contented and ideal inanity which Shakespeare, in some of these characters, has presented to us. Dogberry the head-constable—a person of some importance—who is sure that Borachio will be 'condemned to everlasting redemption'; who bids his company of the watch 'comprehend all vagrom men' and 'aspicious persons'; who believes that 'comparisons are odorous' and thinks a good many things 'most tolerable and not to be endured'; this, it has always been felt, is a considerable personage; but how much richer than even this Dogberry is the better, the less ambitious Dogberry, quietly and simply stating his mind in the language which God has given him.

Goodman Verges, sir, speaks a little off the matter: an old man, sir, and his wits are not so blunt, as, God help, I would desire they were; but, in faith, honest as the skin between his brows. . . .

Shakespearian Comedy and Other Studies. 1944. Chap. VIII.

[81] *Alfred Harbage*

Shakespeare's villains are not wholly villainous—even the fearful three of *King Lear.* Edmund has provocation for his deeds, and unlike his prototype, in the story of the Paphlagonian unkind king by Sidney, does not himself blind his father. Edmund is capable of pity, and dies attempting to do a kindness. This leaves Goneril and Regan as 'the only pictures of the . . . pure unnatural' in Shakespeare. But Regan is not so bad as Goneril, and thus shades off from black to dark-grey; and there are moments when we see eye to eye even with Goneril. In her objections to the riot of her father's train she at least acts understandably, and were it not for the exceptional nature of the situation would be wholly in the right. It requires an effort of the imagination on our part to side at this moment with Lear, who, in his curse upon his daughter's fertility, seems less sinned against than sinning. Goneril and Regan at first feel the need of self-justification—are not devoid of conscience. It is not until Act III, Scene 7, that they appear as hell-hounds. Sympathy with Lear in the interim from Act II has so taken possession of us that any touches of humanity in the daughters would now seem an irrelevance, and Shakespeare does not wastefully or confusingly include them. The earlier touches served their purpose. They distributed the onus of guilt between Lear and his daughters, and kept us alert measuring the rights of the case as it then appeared. Outside of *King Lear,* Shakespeare's blackest characters are King Richard the Third and Iago, but neither is a picture of pure malignance. The trigger-men in modern gangster films are more dreadful, more troll-like, and an Elmer Gantry is much more disgusting. Shakespeare the artist, unlike Lewis the moralist, declines to disgust. Richard and Iago, like Pecksniff and Squeers and Uriah Heep, are amusing devils—at least until the moment their deviltry bears fruit in human suffering. There is then little time left to loathe them. In the meanwhile, their very devotion to wickedness, their energy and vivacity, is exhilarating, and we are entertained by their actions as by the action in *Candide.* Cruelty cannot be made amusing, but neither Richard nor Iago seems enamored of cruelty so much as of self-expression. Richard wishes to dominate and Iago to be clever.

As They Liked It. 1947. Part I. Chap. IV.

[82] *W. H. Auden*

A distinction must be made between the villainous character–figures like Don John in *Much Ado,* Richard III, Edmund in *Lear,* Iachimo in *Cymbeline*–and the merely criminal character–figures like Duke Antonio in *The Tempest,* Angelo in *Measure for Measure,* Macbeth or Claudius in *Hamlet.* The criminal is a person who finds himself in a situation where he is tempted to break the law and succumbs to the temptation: he ought, of course, to have resisted the temptation, but everybody, both on stage and in the audience, must admit that, had they been placed in the same situation, they, too, would have been tempted. The opportunities are exceptional–Prospero, immersed in his books, has left the government of Milan to his brother, Angelo is in a position of absolute authority, Claudius is the Queen's lover, Macbeth is egged on by prophecies and heaven-sent opportunities, but the desire for a dukedom or a crown or a chaste and beautiful girl are desires which all can imagine themselves feeling.

The villain, on the other hand, is shown from the beginning as being a malcontent, a person with a general grudge against life and society. In most cases this is comprehensible because the villain has, in fact, been wronged by Nature or Society: Richard III is a hunchback, Don John and Edmund are bastards. What distinguishes their actions from those of the criminal is that, even when they have something tangible to gain, this is a secondary satisfaction; their primary satisfaction is the infliction of suffering on others, or the exercise of power over others against their will. Richard does not really desire Anne; what he enjoys is successfully wooing a lady whose husband and father-in-law he has killed. Since he has persuaded Gloucester that Edgar is a would-be parricide, Edmund does not need to betray his father to Cornwall and Regan in order to inherit. Don John has nothing personally to gain from ruining the happiness of Claudio and Hero except the pleasure of seeing them unhappy. Iachimo is a doubtful case of villainy. When he and Posthumus make their wager, the latter warns him:

> If she remain unseduced, you not making it appear otherwise, for your ill opinion and th'assault you have made on her chastity you shall answer me with your sword.

To the degree that his motive in deceiving Posthumus is simply physical fear of losing his life in a duel, he is a coward, not a villain; he is only a villain to the degree that his motive is the pleasure of making and seeing the innocent suffer. Coleridge's description of Iago's actions as "motiveless malignancy" applies in some degree to all the Shakespearian villains. The adjective *motiveless* means, firstly, that the tangible gains, if any, are clearly not the principal motive and, secondly, that the motive is not the desire for personal revenge upon another for a personal injury.

"The Joker in the Pack." *The Dyer's Hand and Other Essays.* 1962.

[83] *Bernard Spivack*

The majority of Shakespeare's criminals . . . are intelligible because they are dramatic portraits in conformity with the universal convention of human life under the impress of the culture of Renaissance England. Their actions and their feelings are consistent with their motives, and their motives are perspicuous either absolutely or in the terms of that culture. Desire satisfied and desire unsatisfied express their share in the elementary tragedy of human limitation. About them there is the individuality of free response to the circumstances in which they find themselves. Their criminality, in spite of problems of detail, is fundamentally lucid because it is conventionally human, because their relationship to crime is invariably moral.

Aaron, Richard, Don John, and Iago are not lucid because, beneath the drapery of conventional humanity which never fits them, they have nothing to do with the moral imperatives of human life. Their essential relationship to their crimes and to their victims is not moral but *artistic* . . .

★ ★ ★

All of them unmistakably announce themselves as possessors of a talent which they are about to display, and they make it perfectly clear in the course of their intrigues that what they are doing is being done for art's sake.

★ ★ ★

. . . whatever practical motives they express, they display in respect to them a nearly complete emotional indifference; for their whole action remains essentially an artistic demonstration that is not concerned with practical ends. Nor is there anything personal about their choice of victims. Not only are their motives extrinsic and verbal—grudging concessions to the convention of moral realism at work upon them—but their victims qualify as such by species, and it is only another concession to the same convention that these victims are detailed as particular persons who provoke revenge or stand in the way of ambition. If from the monologues of Iago and his kindred we subtract those formal expressions of cause which are mere draperies on the essential figure, we discover that their aggressions are directed against virtue and honor and that mixture of religious and secular values that defined the eminence of human life in Shakespeare's time. Ultimately their assault is upon unity and order and the piety of love in all its forms. . . .

Furthermore, the evil in the plays in which they appear is never really committed; it is only suffered. For the agents of evil are not moral; only their victims are. *Evil* is a word that describes the human and moral view of what they do. But since at bottom they are neither human nor moral, evil is for them solely an organic function and an artistic pleasure. They are aware of iniquity in the same way that a self-dedicated crusader is aware of the banner under which he gladly serves—as a standard to be advanced and planted on the highest ramparts of virtue. Their devotion is single and complete, their enormous energy and its direction constitutional. A total euphoria leaves in them no room for the slightest shred of conscience. Their monologues . . . are not simply overheard ruminations, but are, in fact, buoyant announcements of intention and triumphant declarations of achievement addressed directly to the audience. And if they maintain their original character to the end, as Richard III does not, the last scene finds them defiant, triumphant, and utterly careless of the "cunning cruelty" of the punishment in store. They are rigid, undeviating, monolithic, pursuing endlessly their single action and indulging endlessly their single emotion until they are stopped by superior physical force and thrown off the rails with their wheels still spinning in the air.

Finally, not only are they artists essentially; all of them are essentially one and the same artist, and their works all one work. For what are the actions of Aaron, Richard, Don John, and Iago except the fourfold repetition of a single stratagem whose meaning is immeasurably wider and deeper than the local details of four separate plots? It is not simply coincidence that Aaron, by contriving the rape of Lavinia, destroys virginity and defeats the consummation of chaste love in marriage; that Richard seduces Lady Anne out of the bonds of matrimonial piety that tied her to the memory of her dead husband; that the slander manipulated by Don John is an aggression against the values of chastity and matrimony; that Iago destroys the bond of love and marriage which, in the persons of Desdemona and Othello, unites transcendent virtues—love and purity with valor and magnanimity. Neither is it chance that all four gleefully demonstrate their skill in divorcing lover from lover, husband from wife, child from father, brother from brother, ruler from subject, friend from friend. Nor is it chance that they concentrate their wit and energy upon the art of making fools and victims out of human beings who express those values and relationships which defined for the Elizabethans the highest possibilities in human life—virtue, heroism, loyalty, love. Beneath the superficial differences of four separate plots there appears the strong outline of a single role four times repeated. We are witnessing four performances by the same craftsman. He may call himself Aaron, Richard, Don John, or Iago, and he may be more brilliant at one time than another; but his métier is undeviating, his style and theme unmistakable, his signature clear on all his works. He is an artist in dissimulation, seduction, and intrigue; and his purpose on the stage is to display his talent triumphantly at work against the affections, duties, and pieties which create the order and harmony of humane society. His speciality is the destruction of unity and love. His genius receives its affirmation from the existence of hate and disorder.

Shakespeare and the Allegory of Evil The History of a Metaphor in Relation to His Major Villains. 1958. Chap. II.

[84] *Alfred Harbage*

The stimulant effect of non-homogeneous characters may be briefly illustrated. Among plays such as Shakespeare's, *The Tempest* is not outstanding, and the first few hundred lines of the second act not especially remarkable. These lines pave the way for an averted assassination. There are six speaking characters: Alonso, the prospective victim; Gonzalo, his faithful minister, who will prevent the crime; Sebastian and Antonio, who will attempt it; and Adrian and Francisco, who will be mere pawns. To be prepared for their various actions we must be made acquainted with their 'characters.' Gonzalo must be shown as *good,* Sebastian and Antonio as *bad,* and Alonso as so overcome with grief for his lost son as to be momentarily defenseless. All quite easy—and, as we might readily imagine, quite uninteresting.

But in Shakespeare these characters all have an alloy. Gonzalo's goodness is a little egregious. He is kindly, but boringly optimistic, and importunate in his consolations which, as always in Shakespeare, are ill-received. Sebastian and Antonio are cynical and malicious, but they are clever and amusing. The weakness of Gonzalo they clearly perceive, and their comments upon him have a barb which he fumblingly attempts to counter. Gonzalo outlines his ideal commonwealth. Its weakness is that it reckons not with the defects of human nature. Sebastian and Antonio are aware of this weakness, the more so that they themselves are such people as would make a Utopia impossible. The pure and impractical is brought into juxtaposition with the practical and impure. As the scene progresses, we spectators find our own moral natures more and more involved. We have laughed a little at Gonzalo's virtue—have identified ourselves a little with the mockers and scorners. To the extent that we have done so we are implicated in their vice. Our debt to virtue has accrued sufficiently that it is no longer a matter of indifference that the assassination be averted: the crime in a measure would be ours.

As They Liked It. 1947. Chap. IV.

[85] *Samuel Taylor Coleridge*

Shakespeare never takes pains to make his characters win your esteem, but leaves it to the general command of the passions, and to poetic justice.

The Lectures of 1811–12. VII. Raysor II, 130.

Style

[86] *Samuel Johnson*

It will not easily be imagined how much *Shakespeare* excells in accommodating his sentiments to real life, but by comparing him with other authours . . . The theatre, when it is under any other direction, is peopled by such characters as were never seen, conversing in a language which was never heard, upon topicks which will never arise in the commerce of mankind. But the dialogue of this authour is often so evidently determined by the incident which produces it, and is pursued with so much ease and simplicity, that it seems scarcely to claim the merit of fiction, but to have been gleaned by diligent selection out of common conversation, and common occurrence.

Preface. *The Plays of William Shakespeare*. 1765.

[87] *Joseph Addison*

Can all the Trappings or Equipage of a King or Hero give *Brutus* half that Pomp and Majesty which he receives from a few Lines in *Shakespear?*

Spectator. No. 42. Wednesday, April 18, 1711.

[88] *John Dryden*

If Shakespeare be allowed, as I think he must, to have made his characters distinct, it will easily be inferred that he understood the nature of the passions: because it has been proved already that confused passions make undistinguishable characters: yet I cannot deny that he has his failings; but they are not so much in the passions themselves, as in his manner of expression: he often obscures his meaning by his words, and sometimes makes it unintelligible. I will not say of so great a poet, that he distinguished not the blown puffy style from true sublimity; but I may venture to maintain, that the fury of his fancy often transported him beyond the bounds of judgment, either in coining of new words and phrases, or racking words which were in use, into the violence of a catachresis.

Troilus and Cressida, or Truth found too late; a Tragedy: with a Preface containing the Grounds of Criticism in Tragedy. 1679. Ker I, 224.

[89] *Samuel Johnson*

Shakespeare engaged in dramatick poetry with the world open before him; the rules of the ancients were yet known to few; the publick judgment was unformed; he had no example of such fame as might force him upon imitation, nor criticks of such authority as might restrain his extravagance: He therefore indulged his natural disposition, and his disposition, as *Rhymer* has remarked, led him to comedy. In tragedy he often writes, with great appearance of toil and study, what is written at last with little felicity; but in his comick scenes, he seems to produce without labour, what no labour can improve. In tragedy he is always struggling after some occasion to be comick; but in comedy he seems to repose, or to luxuriate, as in a mode of thinking congenial to his nature. In his tragick scenes there is always something wanting, but his comedy often surpasses expectation or desire. His comedy pleases by the thoughts and the language, and his tragedy for the greater part by incident and action. His tragedy seems to be skill, his comedy to be instinct.

★ ★ ★

In tragedy his performance seems constantly to be worse, as his labour is more. The effusions of passion which exigence forces out are for the most part striking and energetick; but whenever he solicits his invention, or strains his faculties, the offspring of his throes is tumour, meanness, tediousness, and obscurity.

In narration he affects a disproportionate pomp of diction and a wearisome train of circumlocution, and tells the incident imperfectly in many words, which might have been more plainly delivered in few . . .

His declamations or set speeches are commonly cold and weak, for his power was the power of nature; when he endeavoured, like other tragick writers, to catch opportunities of amplification, and instead of inquiring what the occasion demanded, to show how much his stores of knowledge could supply, he seldom escapes without the pity or resentment of his reader.

★ ★ ★

But the admirers of this great poet have never less reason to indulge their hopes of supreme excellence, than when he seems fully resolved to sink them in dejection, and mollify them with tender emotions by the fall of greatness, the danger of innocence, or the crosses of love. He is not long soft and pathetick without some idle conceit, or contemptible equivocation. He no sooner begins to move, than he counteracts himself; and terrour and pity, as they are rising in the mind, are checked and blasted by sudden frigidity.

A quibble is to *Shakespeare,* what luminous vapours are to the traveller; he follows it at all adventures; it is sure to lead him out of his way, and sure to engulf him in the mire. It has some malignant power over his mind, and its fascinations are irresistible. Whatever be the dignity or profundity of his disquisition, whether he be enlarging knowledge or exalting affection, whether he be amusing attention with incidents, or enchaining it in suspense, let but a quibble spring up before him, and he leaves his work unfinished. A quibble is the golden apple for which he will always turn aside from his career, or stoop from his elevation. A quibble, poor and barren as it is, gave him such delight, that he was content to purchase it, by the sacrifice of reason, propriety and truth. A quibble was to him the fatal *Cleopatra* for which he lost the world, and was content to lose it.

Preface. *The Plays of William Shakespeare.* 1765.

[90] *Samuel Taylor Coleridge*

That Shakespeare has wit is indisputable, but it is not the same kind of wit as in other writers: his wit is blended with the other qualities of his works, and is, by its nature, capable of being so blended. It appears in all parts of his productions, in his tragedies, comedies, and histories: it is not like the wit of Voltaire, and of many modern writers, . . . whose wit consists in a mere combination of words; but in at least nine times out of ten in Shakespeare, the wit is produced not by a combination of words, but by a combination of images.

The Lectures of 1811–12. VI. Raysor II, 123–24.

[91] *Samuel Taylor Coleridge*

Shakespeare has evinced the power, which above all other men he possessed, that of introducing the profoundest sentiments of wisdom, where they would be least expected, yet where they are most truly natural. One admirable secret of his art is, that separate speeches frequently do not appear to have been occasioned by those which preceded, and which are consequent upon each other, but to have arisen out of the peculiar character of the speaker.

The Lectures of 1811–12. IX. Raysor II, 170.

[92] *G. B. Shaw*

What a pity it is that the people who love the sound of Shakespear so seldom go on the stage! The ear is the sure clue to him: only a musician can understand the play of feeling which is the real rarity in his early plays. In a deaf nation these plays would have died long ago. The moral attitude in them is conventional and secondhand: the borrowed ideas, however finely expressed, have not the overpowering human interest of those original criticisms of life which supply the rhetorical element in his later works. Even the individualization which produces that old-established British speciality, the Shakespearian "delineation of character," owes all its magic to the turn of the line, which lets you into the secret of its utterer's mood and temperament, not by its commonplace meaning, but by some subtle exaltation, or stultification, or slyness, or delicacy, or hesitancy, or what not in the sound of it. In short, it is the score and not the libretto that keeps the work alive and fresh; and this is why only musical critics should be allowed to meddle with Shakespear—especially early Shakespear.

"Poor Shakespear!" *The Saturday Review*. 2 February 1895. XXXIII, 25–26.

[93] *James Russell Lowell*

Shakespeare must have been quite as well aware of the provincialism of English as Bacon was; but he knew that great poetry, being universal in its appeal to human nature, can make any language classic, and that the men whose appreciation is immortality will mine through any dialect to get at an original soul. He had as much confidence in his home-bred speech as Bacon had want of it, and exclaims:—

Not marble nor the gilded monuments
Of princes shall outlive this powerful rhyme.

"Shakespeare Once More." *North American Review.* 1868. *Among My Books.* 1870.

[94] *John Crowe Ransom*

Let us regard Shakespeare as a fountain of language, from which was to flow and is yet to flow our peculiar English literature. More than any other writer, he laid down poetic strategies that suited the language, and one of his practices will be my present topic. It was good in his poetry, and it has determined the practice of other poets; it is surprisingly determining today, after the centuries of revolution in every department of life; and here, on a continent he never saw.

The specific usage which I have in mind as having been so fruitful is Shakespeare's way of compounding Latinical elements with his native English. I say his way of doing it; it is commonplace to bring Latinical words into English discourse, and was in Shakespeare's time; but not to do it in Shakespeare's way. He made it his frequent way only after he had come to maturity, but there are many instances of it. Thus Macbeth has Duncan's blood upon his hand and soliloquizes:

Will all great Neptune's ocean wash this blood
Clean from my hand? No, this my hand will rather
The multitudinous seas incarnadine,
Making the green one red.

We need not attribute much conscious Latinity to the first line; probably the public of Shakespeare's time had quite assimilated their Neptune, and indicated possession by the epithet they gave him; it is a folk locution rather than a literary one. So that, if we do not stop on this line, we may say that the four lines constitute a passage in native English, almost monosyllabic, broken by that Latinical explosion in the third line. The last line is specially primitive, having three strong accented words juxtaposed with some peril to the clear syntax; for we wonder, I think, whether to take *one* as going with *green* or with *red;* but a locution like *solid red* while explicit would be mildly Latinical, and it is apparently Shakespeare's idea to follow up the Latinical third line by about half a line of primitive language even with its natural disabilities.

The two big words do not represent Shakespeare's Latinity at its best but they are impressive enough. *Multitudinous* is *multitudo* plus *-ous* . . . Multitudinous has something to do with many-ness, but we cannot tell whether it means here that the seas are many, or that the seas have so many waters . . . we wonder if there may not be some idiomatic relation of *seas* to *multitudinous*. And *incarnadine* is one of those words from the Latin by way of the French, Latinical in the second degree. It is the French name of a pigment, here used by Shakespeare—probably for the first time—as a verb meaning to color to the shade of that pigment. But its proximity to *multitudinous* induces Latinity into our consciousness so that we stop and reflect upon its Latin meaning: to paint to the color of blood.

We can readily isolate from the later plays of Shakespeare many passages of three, four, or five lines each, having just about this architecture, and this poetic quality. They show a condensation of Latinical effect in a context of unusually pure English. And the Latinical words will seem fresh, the test being that we feel obliged to go back to the Latin to explore the full sense of them.

★ ★ ★

. . . I suggest . . . that the Latinical words were disappearing as such in the literature that was being written, but that Shakespeare's example more than any other one thing stopped the process. On this supposition, it was Shakespeare who preserved the life of Latin as a foreign language still held tributary to the borrowings of luxurious English writers. Without Shakespeare the Latinical words would probably have been lost. They would have been lost not by being dropped *out of* the language but by being dropped *into* it—as countless other foreign words have been lost within our capacious language and are now used over and over without any sense of their foreignness.

"On Shakespeare's Language." (A paper read at the Conference on the Heritage of the English-Speaking Peoples and Their Responsibility, at Kenyon College, October 5, 1946.) *Poems and Essays*. 1955.

[95] *James Russell Lowell*

In that secondary office of imagination, where it serves the artist, not as the reason that shapes, but as the interpreter of his conceptions into words, there is a distinction to be noticed between the higher and lower mode in which it performs its function. It may be either creative or pictorial, may body forth the thought or merely image it forth. With Shakespeare, for example, imagination seems immanent in his very consciousness; with Milton, in his memory. In the one it sends, as if without knowing it, a fiery life into the verse,

Sei die Braut das Wort,
Bräutigam der Geist;

[Bride be the word,
Bridegroom the spirit;]

in the other it elaborates a certain pomp and elevation. Accordingly, the bias of the former is toward over-intensity, of the latter toward over-diffuseness. Shakespeare's temptation is to push a willing metaphor beyond its strength, to make a passion over-inform its tenement of words; Milton cannot resist running a simile on into a fugue. One always fancies Shakespeare *in* his best verses, and Milton at the keyboard of his organ. Shakespeare's language is no longer the mere vehicle of thought, it has become part of it, its very flesh and blood. The pleasure it gives us is unmixed, direct, like that from the smell of a flower or the flavor of a fruit.

"Shakespeare Once More." *North American Review.* 1868. *Among My Books.* 1870.

[96] *George Rylands*

Coleridge tells us that the imaginative faculty reveals itself in the reconcilement of the general with the concrete, the idea with the image. Mediaeval literature employed personification and allegory to communicate intellectual concepts and states of mind. They thought in pictures: their books were frescoes, illuminated missals and stained glass. And for the Elizabethans the Cardinal Virtues, the Seven Deadly Sins, the Ages of Man, Death and Time were still pictorial figures. Graunde Amoure, False Report, Constrained Abstinence were as the lords and ladies of mediaeval chivalry. The mantle of Mercy is white, of Righteousness red, of Truth a sad green. As in Bunyan the abstract has the interest and vividness of the concrete. The mediaeval practice survives to some extent in Shakespeare; in his 'tickling Commodity' or 'the devil Lechery with his fat rump and potato finger' or, more submerged, in his fond use of the epithet 'envious'. But it is characteristic that Death the skeleton, so familiar in mediaeval art, is found in the history plays but is superseded by an Elizabethan bailiff; 'that fell sergeant death is strict in his arrest'. Personification is an artificial device and Shakespeare's method is more rapid and subtle. It is no longer a question of an abstract word with a capital letter and conventional attributes; the effect is obtained by a qualifying phrase, a verb or epithet. In Shakespeare, desire vomits, concealment feeds, corruption bubbles, fate hides in an auger hole, accident is shackled, description beggared, reason furs gloves, distinction puffs, liberty plucks justice by the nose, ambition shrinks through bad weaving, friendship's milky heart turns in less than two nights, valour preys on reason, impatience becomes a mad dog, injury is pity's gaoler, emulation hath a thousand sons. In the lines: "And silken dalliance in the wardrobe lies' or 'To lie in cold obstruction and to rot' we have the required reconcilement of the general with the concrete, of the idea with the image.

We can detect in this practice the influence of the Bible. The Old Testament, like Shakespeare, is full of images, metaphors and similes drawn from everyday life, and there are the same combinations of abstract and concrete. In the Bible, health is a faithful ambassador, poverty comes as one that travelleth, iniquity stops her mouth . . .

We must keep in mind also the terrific influx of Latinisms into the language about 1600 with which every writer was experimenting. In Shakespeare, as in Sir Thomas Browne, we have the Latinism and the native word, often a synonym, paired together, the first with intellectual, the second with physical associations; for example, exsufflicate and blown surmises, exterior and outward, inestimable and unvalued, malignant and turbaned Turk, the voice of occupation and the breath of garlic eaters, the inaudible and noiseless foot of time, catastrophe and heel of pastime, infinite and endless liar, earthy and abhorred commands. We frequently receive a treble effect. The Latin element is united with the Anglo-Saxon; the polysyllable with the monosyllable; the abstract with the concrete. Moral ideas, in which Shakespeare abounds, are visualised for the man in the street. Thus the thought that there is one justice for the rich and another for the poor becomes

> Plate sin with gold,
> And the strong lance of justice hurtless breaks;
> Arm it in rags, a pigmy's straw does pierce it,

and the simple truth, that 'the present eye praises the present object', is elaborated and varied by Ulysses, in thirty-five lines of personification and concrete imagery. Shakespeare's abstract words are neither the lords and ladies of mediaeval allegory nor the bogus deities of the eighteenth-century mode. *Nihil in intellectu quod non fuit prius in sensu.* [Nothing in thought that was not first in feeling.] One might indeed say that Shakespeare's body thought. It is to this simultaneous and harmonious working of all human faculties that the style of Shakespeare's greatest plays owes its strength.

"Shakespeare the Poet." *A Companion to Shakespeare Studies.* Ed. Harley Granville-Barker and G. B. Harrison. 1934.

[97] *Henry James*

There is that in The Tempest, specifically, though almost all indefinably, which seems to show us the artist consciously tasting of the first and rarest of his gifts, that of imaged creative Expression, the instant sense of some copious equivalent of thought for every grain of the grossness of reality; to show him as unresistingly aware, in the depths of his genius, that nothing like it had ever been known, or probably would ever be again known, on earth, and as so given up, more than on other occasions, to the joy of sovereign *science.*

★ ★ ★

The Tempest affects us, taking its complexity and its perfection together, as the rarest of all examples of literary art. There may be other things as exquisite, other single exhalations of beauty reaching as high a mark and sustained there for a moment, just as there are other deep wells of poetry from which cupfuls as crystalline may, in repeated dips, be drawn; but nothing, surely, of equal length and variety lives so happily and radiantly as a whole: no poetic birth ever took place under a star appointed to blaze upon it so steadily. The felicity enjoyed is enjoyed longer and more intensely, and the art involved, completely revealed, as I suggest, to the master, holds the securest revel.

Introduction. *The Tempest.* The University Press Shakespeare, Renaissance Edition. XVI. 1907.

Gallimaufry

Devices

[98] *Samuel Taylor Coleridge*

With the single exception of *Cymbeline* they [Shakespeare's first scenes] either place before us in one glance both the past and the future in some effect which implies the continuance and full agency of its cause, as in the feuds and party spirit of the servants of the two houses in the first scene of *Romeo and Juliet*, or in the degrading passion for shews and public spectacles, and the overwhelming attachment for the newest successful war-chief in the Roman people, already become a populace, contrasted with the jealousy of the nobles, in *Julius Caesar;* or they at once commence the action so as to excite a curiosity for the explanation in the following [scenes], as in the storm of the wind, the waves, and the boatswain in the *Tempest,* instead of anticipating our curiosity, as in most other first scenes and in too many other first *acts;* or they act, by contrast of diction suited to the characters, at once to heighten the effect and yet to give a naturalness to the language and rhythm of the principal characters, either as that of Prospero and Miranda, in the last instance, by the appropriate lowness of the style, or as in *King John* by the equally appropriate stateliness of state harangue or official narration, so that the after blank verse seems to belong to the rank and quality of the speakers and not to the poet; or they strike at once the key-note, give the predominant spirit of the play, as in the *Twelfth Night* and in *Macbeth;* or the first scene comprizes all these advantages at once, as in *Hamlet.*

Notes on the Tragedies. 1818. Raysor I, 41–42.

[99] *L. L. Schücking*

In ordinary life an utterance of a person made in order to draw attention to supposedly praiseworthy or reprehensible sides of his character allows us to infer his real character by way of indirect characterization; and we believe we can apply the same kind of reasoning to persons in a play, since we know that to recognize the good or evil in oneself, and even to go so far as to show them in the presence of others, requires special characteristics. Most interpreters following the traditional method have seen no difficulties here. Utterances of criminal personages in which they openly describe their deeds as wicked were unquestionably taken for Gospel truth and hardly ever regarded as serving as a means of indirect characterization. Lady Macbeth (I. v), looking at her own behaviour from an outside point of view, calls it 'cruelty', and describes her murderous intentions as 'fell'. A man like Iago, for example, terms his own behaviour villainy. ''Tis here, but yet confused', he says, after hatching the devilish plot of destroying Othello, his master; '*Knavery's* plain face is never seen till used' (II. i. c. 320). Cloten, in *Cymbeline,* the villain of the piece, quite glibly talks of the villainous orders he has given (III. v. 113). A person who is so little weighed down with the recognition of his own wickedness we usually style a cynic. This appellation might possibly fit a real rascal like Edmund in *King Lear,* who describes himself as 'rough and lecherous' (I. ii. 145). But this would be to regard these matters from an entirely erroneous point of view. This kind of self-characterization should not be considered as in any way an attempt at realism. . . . In the drama the villain is to be a villain, the noble character is to appear noble, from whichever side we look at them. This mode of representation has never been true to facts, neither in the Renaissance nor before; in all probability even Cain did not lack a very good reason for killing Abel (though this may not have been, as Byron asserts, his extreme dullness). The reason for this departure from reality is to be looked for in the careful regard which Shakespeare everywhere pays to the limited mental capacity of the public. The poet desires above all to avoid misapprehension of the main outlines of the action and the characters, to prevent the spectators from confusing the ethical values and from taking pleasure in the vices represented and the situations produced by them. In short, the public was an influential factor in determining the art-form.

We have long been accustomed, by a tacit agreement, not to take offence at this aspect of Shakespearian technique, but to regard it as a primitive trait, impossible nowadays, and therefore not exposed to misinterpretations. When the villains talk of their villainy we do not on that account consider them as cynics. Numerous critics of *Othello*, for example, find in certain speeches of Iago, in spite of the utterance cited above, an endeavour to palliate his wickedness, a thing which no cynic ever does. This kind of characterization turns out to be entirely traditional. Just in the same way the Jew of Malta, notwithstanding the very special reasons for his action, says of himself, on entering upon his villainous course: 'Now will I show myself to have more of the serpent than the dove; that is, more knave than fool.'

In this inquiry we are too apt to overlook the question that might be raised: What are we to think of utterances just the opposite of these, containing references to praiseworthy qualities? If Shakespeare's art-form is still so imperfect that it does not allow us, as we do nowadays, to interpret the calm description given by a person of his own baseness as a sign of cynicism, are we then forbidden to perceive in self-revelations regarding the possession of valuable moral qualities nothing but conceit, boastfulness, or arrogance? Here we may remember the ghost of Hamlet's father, who thinks himself so superior to his brother Claudius, a person 'whose natural gifts were poor to those of mine' (I. v. 51 *seq.*). This description in point of fact perfectly agrees with that which Hamlet gives of his father; nevertheless, spoken by the father himself, these words strike us as somewhat self-complacent. Did Shakespeare mean this? There does not seem to be any sense in thus showing up a weak side in the character of the ghost. Let us further consider the account which Prospero in *The Tempest* gives of himself, how he designates himself as

> the prime duke, being so reputed
> In dignity, and for the liberal arts
> Without a parallel. (I. ii. 73)

Cordelia, too, in *King Lear* may serve as an illustration. In the exposition she describes herself as wanting

> that glib and oily art
> To speak and purpose not, *since what I well intend,*
> *I'll do't before I speak.* . . .
> . . . [I lack] that *for which I am richer,*
> A still-soliciting eye, and such a tongue
> That I am glad I have not.

Here her air of knowing perfectly well what she is doing in presenting her advantages in their true light strikes a false note in the infinite harmony of her being, so that Kreyssig thinks he can discover a ring of something like 'sauciness' in 'the reply with which the daughter of the old Lear cannot quite disguise her race'. We may regard it as absolutely certain, however, that Shakespeare had not the slightest intention of endowing with any trait of vanity the touching figure of Cordelia, whom we see on other occasions, overpowered by her emotions, standing speechless, unable to articulate a word or even to produce a single sound.

Character Problems in Shakespeare's Plays. 1922. Chap. I.

[100] *Margaret Webster*

As with all his dramatic tools, Shakespeare takes it [the soliloquy] over as a ready-to-wear device by which the plot may be advanced and characters may tell the audience things which everybody else in the play already knows, while loquaciously announcing their own further intentions. As with his development of other technical devices, he soon makes of the soliloquy a far more eloquent weapon than that. The noble figureheads of *Henry VI* recite at us, much as they recite at each other. But Richard III uses the freedom of his monologues to much greater dramatic purpose; he takes us into his confidence with such assurance, such gleeful power, that we are his, villainy and all, right through the play. Even his use of the apostrophe

> Shine out, fair sun, till I have bought a glass,
> That I may see my shadow, as I pass,

emphasizes for us the self-appointed world in which Richard has his being, where no creature moves except in reflected light and nothing is absolute but his own will. We accept that this monstrous superman will recount to himself aloud his own schemes and celebrate his own triumphs for us to overhear, because none but we, in our all-knowing dimension, could possibly comprehend him. His soliloquies are a poetic extension of what Kipling reduced to the formula of every schoolboy in Stalky's, "I gloat! I gloat! hear me!"

By the time Shakespeare reaches Iago, the formula has changed; but still it is the villain who most needs the device of self-revelation, not the hero, who will command our emotional response without any such assistance. And again with Iago, Shakespeare is reveling in the mastery of such a man; he cannot get himself to hate Iago, and neither must we. The man has stature, in his own right; he is no piece of mechanism, part of the impersonal machinery of malice; if we were to think that, we should belittle Othello, and the tragedy of the play would be totally diminished. Iago's fascination for us lies just in that smooth, flawless functioning of the mind, which is yet so fatally flawed because it cannot conceive of a power greater than the power of the intellect. Edmund, in *King Lear,* is the play's chief soliloquizer. The dash and daring of his first outburst, his hand against all the smug conventions of society, his analysis of them so brilliantly specious, will carry us most unmorally with him throughout the play.

★ ★ ★

The soliloquy reaches its greatest flexibility and glory in *Hamlet,* where it is so apparently an integral part of the character Shakespeare was creating that any dissertation on its use would be redundant. He does not subsequently pursue this method of introspection because he is not writing another Hamlet. His later heroes, the men of action, Antony and Coriolanus, are in no need of it; and he has, by now, found twenty other ways of dealing with the establishment of a motive or the advancement of the story. Caliban will need it briefly, grumbling to himself as he sullenly trudges about his work; Autolycus will belong to the long line of liaison-commentators, his "Ha! what a fool Honesty is! and Trust, his sworn brother, a very simple gentleman!" chiming with the echo of Falstaff's soliloquy: "Well, 'tis no matter, honour pricks me on. Yea, but how if honour prick me off when I come on?"

Shakespeare Without Tears. 1942. Chap. 5.

[101] *W. B. Yeats*

I have been thinking a good deal about plays lately, and I have been wondering why I dislike the clear and logical construction which seems necessary if one is to succeed on the Modern Stage. It came into my head the other day that this construction, which all the world has learnt from France, has everything of high literature except the emotion of multitude. The Greek drama has got the emotion of multitude from its chorus, which called up famous sorrows, long-leaguered Troy, much-enduring Odysseus, and all the gods and heroes to witness, as it were, some well-ordered fable, some action separated but for this from all but itself. The French play delights in the well-ordered fable, but by leaving out the chorus it has created an art where poetry and imagination, always the children of far-off multitudinous things, must of necessity grow less important than the mere will. That is why, I said to myself, French dramatic poetry is so often a little rhetorical, for rhetoric is the will trying to do the work of the imagination. The Shakespearean Drama gets the emotion of multitude out of the sub-plot which copies the main plot, much as a shadow upon the wall copies one's body in the firelight. We think of *King Lear* less as the history of one man and his sorrows than as the history of a whole evil time. Lear's shadow is in Gloster, who also has ungrateful children, and the mind goes on imagining other shadows, shadows beyond shadow till it has pictured the world. In *Hamlet,* one hardly notices, so subtly is the web woven, that the murder of Hamlet's father and the sorrow of Hamlet are shadowed in the lives of Fortinbras and Ophelia and Laertes, whose fathers, too, have been killed. It is so in all the plays, or in all but all, and very commonly the sub-plot is the main plot working itself out in more ordinary men and women, and so doubly calling up before us the image of multitude.

"Emotion of Multitude." *The All Ireland Review.* April 11, 1903. *Ideas of Good and Evil.* 1903.

Decency

[102] *Samuel Johnson*

In his comick scenes he is seldom very successful, when he engages his characters in reciprocations of smartness and contests of sarcasm; their jests are commonly gross, and their pleasantry licentious; neither his gentlemen nor his ladies have much delicacy, nor are sufficiently distinguished from his clowns by any appearance of refined manners. Whether he represented the real conversation of his time is not easy to determine; the reign of *Elizabeth* is commonly supposed to have been a time of stateliness, formality and reserve, yet perhaps the relaxations of that severity were not very elegant. There must, however, have been always some modes of gayety preferable to others, and a writer ought to chuse the best.

Preface. *The Plays of William Shakespeare.* 1765.

[103] *Thomas Bowdler*

That Shakspeare is the first of dramatic writers will be denied by few, and I doubt whether it will be denied by any who have really studied his works, and compared the beauties which they contain with the very finest productions either of our own or of former ages. It must, however, be acknowledged, by his warmest admirers, that some defects are to be found in the writings of our immortal bard. The language is not always faultless. Many words and expressions occur which are of so indecent a nature as to render it highly desirable that they should be erased. Of these the greater part were evidently introduced to gratify the bad taste of the age in which he lived, and the rest may perhaps be ascribed to his own unbridled fancy. But neither the vicious taste of the age, nor the most brilliant effusons of wit, can afford an excuse for profaneness or obscenity; and if these could be obliterated, the transcendant genius of the poet would undoubtedly shine with more unclouded lustre. To banish every thing of this nature from his writings is the object of the present undertaking. It is the wish of the editor to render the plays of Shakspeare unsullied by any scene, by any speech, or, if possible, by any word that can give pain to the most chaste, or offence to the most religious of his readers.

⋆ ⋆ ⋆

I wish it were in my power to say of indecency as I have said of profaneness, that the examples of it are not very numerous. Unfortunately the reverse is the case. Those persons whose acquaintance with Shakspeare depends on theatrical representations, in which great alterations are made in the plays, can have little idea of the frequent recurrence in the original text, of expressions, which, however they might be tolerated in the sixteenth century, are by no means admissible in the nineteenth. Of these expressions no example can in this place be given. I feel it however incumbent on me to observe, in behalf of my favourite author, that in comparison with most of the contemporary poets, and with the dramatists of the seventeenth century, the plays of Shakspeare are remarkably decent; but it is not sufficient that his defects are trifling in comparison with writers who are highly defective. It certainly is my wish, and it has been my study, to exclude from this publication whatever is unfit to be read aloud by a gentleman to a company of ladies. I can hardly imagine a more pleasing occupation for a winter's evening in the country, than for a father to read one of Shakspeare's plays to his family circle. My object is to enable him to do so without incurring the danger of falling unawares among words and expressions which are of such a nature as to raise a blush on the cheek of modesty, or render it necessary for the reader to pause, and examine the sequel, before he proceeds further in the entertainment of the evening.

Preface. *The Family Shakspeare.* 1818.

[104] *Samuel Taylor Coleridge*

On looking through Shakespeare, offences against decency and manners may certainly be pointed out; but let us examine history minutely, and we shall find that this was the ordinary language of the time, and then let us ask, where is the offence? The offence, so to call it, was not committed wantonly, and for the sake of offending, but for the sake of merriment; for what is most observable in Shakespeare, in reference to this topic, is that what he says is always calculated to raise a gust of laughter, that would, as it were, blow away all impure ideas, if it did not excite abhorrence of them.

⋆ ⋆ ⋆

In Shakespeare there are a few gross speeches, but it is doubtful to me if they would produce any ill effect on an unsullied mind. . . . I appeal to the whole of Shakespeare's writings, whether his grossness is not the mere sport of fancy, dissipating low feelings by exciting the intellect, and only injuring while it offends?

The Lectures of 1811–12. VI. Raysor II, 125–27.

[105] *Samuel Taylor Coleridge*

The next character belonging to Shakespeare as Shakespeare, was the *keeping at all times the high road of life*. With him there were no innocent adulteries; he never rendered that amiable which religion and reason taught us to detest; he never clothes vice in the garb of virtue . . . his fathers were roused by ingratitude, his husbands were stung by unfaithfulness; the affections were wounded in those points where all may and all must feel.

The Lectures of 1813–14. I. Raysor II, 266.

[106] *Logan Pearsall Smith*

And then, too, there is Shakespeare's ribaldry—the bawdy jokes he is so fond of making. Luckily, it is only the specialist who knows how much ribaldry there is in Shakespeare's plays, how many passages which seem innocent enough are full of double-meanings. 'He can't mean that!' the shocked reader exclaims; but oh, my dear reader, he does mean it, and his meaning, if you are a nice-minded person, will make you blush all over. The late Poet Laureate tried to palliate the offence on the ground that Shakespeare was compelled against his will to season in this gross way the plays he wrote for his gross audience; but Robert Bridges did not explain the recondite improprieties which must have been far above the vulgar apprehension, and the indelicacies with which he spiced the sugared sonnets written for his private friends. A gross age, no doubt, but Sidney and Spenser wrote no sonnets of this kind. Even worse than this ithyphallic fun in which Shakespeare so plainly delighted, is the evidence of a more distressing kind of sex-preoccupation, by which, during a certain period of his life, he seems to have been obsessed. Lear's obscene railings against the mere fact of sex, which are quite inappropriate to his circumstances and situation, and in which he seems to scream and spit from horror, and Timon's even more terrible outbursts of sex-nausea, sound like the incoherent ravings of an unbalanced mind, driven to madness by a loathing for men and women in their natural intercourse together.

Difficult also to explain away is the moral callousness which Shakespeare often shows, not only in the physical atrocities he sometimes exhibits on the stage—the 'Out, vile jelly!' for instance, of Gloster's blinding—but in the moral outrages he perpetrates upon our feelings—the way he pardons, or rather ignores, unpardonable things; mates his heroines to dastards, and brings more than one of his plays by an ugly bed-trick to an ugly conclusion.[1]

[1] A list of the atrocities, the offences against taste, morals, and any kind of decent feeling, which are to be found in the canon of the Folio, and which are accepted as Shakespeare's work by his adorers, is enough to prove—if more proof were needed—what enormities the orthodox can swallow, apparently without a gulp, in their Sacred Writings. Otherwise the belief that Shakespeare wrote that disgusting record of more than beastly horror, *Titus Andronicus,* within a year or so of writing *A Midsummer Night's Dream,* would burst their brains; nor would they find it easy to digest Shakespeare's treatment of Joan of Arc in the scene (I *Henry VI,* V, iv) where the Maid of France, to escape burning, declares herself to be with child, first by one, and then by another of the French Princes. The wager of Posthumus about the chastity of Imogen, the slaughter of the unarmed Hector at the instigation of Achilles in *Troilus and Cressida,* and indeed the ugly degradation of all the Greek heroes in that magnificent but unpleasant play, would turn the stomachs of less devout readers. The marriage of Celia to that scoundrel Oliver, in *As You Like It,* and that of Hero to the despicable Claudio in *All's Well,* are bad enough, but as an outrage on our moral feelings few things in literature can equal the scene in the *Two Gentlemen of Verona,* where Valentine makes an outrageous and calm offer of Silvia, whom he loves, to the scoundrel whose attempt to outrage her he has just prevented. Shakespeare was apt to end off his plays, it is true, by any unscrupulous contrivance, but this plea can hardly be urged to palliate the cold-blooded rejection of Falstaff; and the only excuse which can be found for the degradation of that master-spirit into the poor dupe and buffoon of the *Merry Wives,* is to label as 'sentimentalists' those who do not like it.

It is impossible to get rid of the suspicion that of all great artists Shakespeare was the most completely devoid of all artistic conscience; that he was perfectly willing to make any sacrifice for the sake of stage-effect, money, and popular applause. One cannot but think of him and the other Elizabethan dramatists as being not unlike pastry-cooks who concoct their pies with little thought of anything but their sale to the customer of the day, and who are not in the least scrupulous about the ingredients they put into them.

On Reading Shakespeare. 1933. Chap. I.

Adaptability to Stage

[107] *Charles Lamb*

. . . to see Lear acted,—to see an old man tottering about the stage with a walking-stick, turned out of doors by his daughters in a rainy night, has nothing in it but what is painful and disgusting. We want to take him into shelter and relieve him. That is all the feeling which the acting of Lear ever produced in me. But the Lear of Shakspeare cannot be acted. The contemptible machinery by which they mimic the storm which he goes out in, is not more inadequate to represent the horrors of the real elements, than any actor can be to represent Lear: they might more easily propose to personate the Satan of Milton upon a stage, or one of Michael Angelo's terrible figures. The greatness of Lear is not in corporal dimension, but in intellectual: the explosions of his passion are terrible as a volcano: they are storms turning up and disclosing to the bottom that sea, his mind, with all its vast riches. It is his mind which is laid bare. This case of flesh and blood seems too insignificant to be thought on; even as he himself neglects it. On the stage we see nothing but corporal infirmities and weakness, the impotence of rage; while we read it, we see not Lear, but we are Lear,—we are in his mind, we are sustained by a grandeur which baffles the malice of daughters and storms; in the aberrations of his reason, we discover a mighty irregular power of reasoning, immethodized from the ordinary purposes of life, but exerting its powers, as the wind blows where it listeth, at will upon the corruptions and abuses of mankind. What have looks, or tones, to do with that sublime identification of his age with that of the *heavens themselves,* when in his reproaches to them for conniving at the injustice of his children, he reminds them that 'they themselves are old.' What gesture shall we appropriate to this? What has the voice or the eye to do with such things? But the play is beyond all art, as the tamperings with it shew: it is too hard and stony; it must have love-scenes, and a happy ending. It is not enough that Cordelia is a daughter, she must shine as a lover too. Tate has put his hook in the nostrils of this Leviathan, for Garrick and his followers, the showmen of the scene, to draw the mighty beast about more easily. A happy ending!—as if the living martyrdom that Lear had gone through,—the flaying of his feelings alive, did not make a fair dismissal from the stage of life the only decorous thing for him. If he is to live and be happy after, if he could sustain this world's burden after, why all this pudder and preparation,—why torment us with all this unnecessary sympathy? As if the childish pleasure of getting his gilt robes and sceptre again could tempt him to act over again his misused station—as if at his years, and with his experience, any thing was left but to die.

"On the Tragedies of Shakspeare considered with reference to their fitness for Stage Representation." *The Reflector.* No. IV. 1811.

[108] *Havelock Ellis*

I cannot at all admit that Shakespeare is unsuited for the stage. One has only to remember that it is the Romantic not the Classic stage. It is the function of the Shakespearian drama, and of the whole school of which Shakespeare is the supreme representative . . . to evoke a variegated vision of the tragi-comedy of life in its height and its depth, its freedom, and its wide horizon. This drama has for the most part little to do with the operation of the Fate which works itself out when a man's soul is in the stern clutch of Necessity. We are far here from Euripides and from Ibsen. Life is always a pageant here, a tragi-comedy, which may lean sometimes more to comedy, and sometimes more to tragedy, but has in it always, even in *Lear*, an atmosphere of enlarging and exhilarating gaiety.

Impressions and Comments. 1914. Entry of March 7, 1913.

Focus and Vision

General

[109] *Samuel Johnson*

His first defect is that to which may be imputed most of the evil in books or in men. He sacrifices virtue to convenience, and is so much more careful to please than to instruct, that he seems to write without any moral purpose. From his writings indeed a system of social duty may be selected, for he that thinks reasonably must think morally; but his precepts and axioms drop casually from him; he makes no just distribution of good or evil, nor is always careful to shew in the virtuous a disapprobation of the wicked; he carries his persons indifferently through right and wrong, and at the close dismisses them without further care, and leaves their examples to operate by chance. This fault the barbarity of his age cannot extenuate; for it is always a writer's duty to make the world better, and justice is a virtue independent on time or place.

Preface. *The Plays of William Shakespeare.* 1765.

[110] *John Dennis*

Shakespear has been wanting in the exact Distribution of Poetical Justice not only in his *Coriolanus,* but in most of his best Tragedies, in which the Guilty and the Innocent perish promiscuously; as *Duncan* and *Banquo* in *Mackbeth,* as likewise Lady *Macduffe* and her Children; *Desdemona* in *Othello; Cordelia, Kent,* and King *Lear,* in the Tragedy that bears his Name; *Brutus* and *Porcia* in *Julius Caesar,* and young *Hamlet* in the Tragedy of *Hamlet.* For tho' it may be said in Defence of the last, that *Hamlet* had a Design to kill his Uncle who then reign'd; yet this is justify'd by no less than a Call from Heaven, and raising up one from the Dead to urge him to it. The Good and the Bad then perishing promiscuously in the best of

Shakespear's Tragedies, there can be either none or very weak Instruction in them: For such promiscuous Events call the Government of Providence into Question, and by Scepticks and Libertines are resolv'd into Chance.

An Essay on the Genius and Writings of Shakespear. 1712. Letter I.

[111] *Samuel Taylor Coleridge*

Shakespeare always makes vice odious and virtue admirable . . .

The Lectures of 1811–12. Raysor II, 34.

[112] *John Palmer*

But the world in which Shakespeare's characters move is not a moral gymnasium. It is a world in which men and women reveal their hearts and minds, engage our sympathy and evoke our perpetual wonder at the intricate working of simple or subtle souls.

Political Characters of Shakespeare. 1945. Chap. III.

[113] *Nevill Coghill*

Dr. Johnson blamed Shakespeare for having in his plays too little regard for "morality". But if the kind of happiness to which all his Comedies travel is at all communicated to his readers and audiences, their imaginations, filled by that positive good, are themselves touched through happiness to goodness.

"The Basis of Shakespearian Comedy." (The substance of a lecture delivered in 1949 at Stratford-upon-Avon.) *Essays and Studies 1950.*

[114] *Edwin Arlington Robinson*

He gloomed and mumbled like a soul from Tophet,
His hands behind him and his head bent solemn.
"What is it now," said I,—"another woman?"
That made him sorry for me, and he smiled.
"No, Ben," he mused; "it's Nothing. It's all Nothing.
We come, we go; and when we're done, we're done.

Spiders and flies—we're mostly one or t'other—
We come, we go; and when we're done, we're done."
"By God, you sing that song as if you knew it!"
Said I, by way of cheering him; "what ails ye?"
"I think I must have come down here to think,"
Says he to that, and pulls his little beard;
"Your fly will serve as well as anybody,
And what's his hour? He flies, and flies, and flies,
And in his fly's mind has a brave appearance;
And then your spider gets him in her net,
And eats him out, and hangs him up to dry.
That's Nature, the kind mother of us all.
And then your slattern housemaid swings her broom,
And where's your spider? And that's Nature, also.
It's Nature, and it's Nothing. It's all Nothing.
It's all a world where bugs and emperors
Go singularly back to the same dust,
Each in his time; and the old, ordered stars
That sang together, Ben, will sing the same
Old stave tomorrow."

"Ben Jonson Entertains a Man from Stratford." *Drama.* Nov., 1915. *The Man Against the Sky.* 1916. Lines 280–305.

[115] *Walter Raleigh*

There is not a particle of evidence to show that Shakespeare held any views on the theory of the drama, or that the question was a live one in his mind. The species of play that he most affected in practice has been well described by Polonius; it is the "tragical-comical-historical-pastoral, scene individable, or poem unlimited." His first care was to get hold of a story that might be shaped to the needs of the theatre. It is possible, no doubt, for a dramatist, as it is for a novelist, to go another way to work. He may conceive living characters, and devise events to exhibit them; or he may start with a moral, a philosophy of life, an atmosphere, a sentiment, and set his puppets to express it. But Shakespeare kept to the old road, and sought first for a story. Some of his characters were made by his story, as characters are made by the events of life. Others he permits to intrude upon the story, as old friends, or new visitors, intrude upon a plan and disorder it. His wisdom of life grew, a rich incrustation, upon the events and situations of his fable. But the story came first with him,—as it came first with his audience, as it comes first with every child.

Shakespeare. 1907. Chap. V.

[116] *Samuel Taylor Coleridge*

Shakspeare never promulgates any party tenets. He is always the philosopher and the moralist, but at the same time with a profound veneration for all the established institutions of society, and for those classes which form the permanent elements of the state—especially never introducing a professional character, as such, otherwise than as respectable. If he must have any name, he should be styled a philosophical aristocrat, delighting in those hereditary institutions which have a tendency to bind one age to another, and in that distinction of ranks, of which, although few may be in possession, all enjoy the advantages. Hence, again, you will observe the good nature with which he seems always to make sport with the passions and follies of a mob, as with an irrational animal. He is never angry with it, but hugely content with holding up its absurdities to its face; and sometimes you may trace a tone of almost affectionate superiority, something like that in which a father speaks of the rogueries of a child.

Notes on the Comedies. *The Tempest.* Raysor I, 136.

[117] *Donald A. Stauffer*

Few readers can resist Shakespeare's sanity. He lives on so many levels at once, with such a spacious awareness, that his hopes and his speculations do not rouse suspicions that they are partial or forced. Shakespeare has been a Bible for skeptics and for believers, for those who live in the world and those who live in the spirit. The measure of his comprehensiveness is that he himself cannot be reduced to one of these tags or to any other. Yet his hopefulness, the resurgence of vital instinct, is remarkable. It shows in his open-handed creation of scores of living characters. It shows in his highest tragic theme: the conflict not between good and evil but between two goods, or between a mistaken and a valid desire for the good. It shows in the larger patterns of his development. And it explains why a poet who writes with such rich intensity can nevertheless create the impression of gentleness.

Shakespeare's World of Images. 1949. Chap. VII.

[118] *James Russell Lowell*

In estimating Shakespeare, it should never be forgotten, that, like Goethe, he was essentially observer and artist, and incapable of partisanship. . . . His business was with men as they were, not with man as he ought to be,—with the human soul as it is shaped or twisted into character by the complex experience of life, not in its abstract essence, as something to be saved or lost.

★ ★ ★

We may learn, to be sure, plenty of lessons from Shakespeare. We are not likely to have kingdoms to divide, crowns foretold us by weird sisters, a father's death to avenge, or to kill our wives from jealousy; but Lear may teach us to draw the line more clearly between a wise generosity and a loose-handed weakness of giving; Macbeth, how one sin involves another, and forever another, by a fatal parthenogenesis, and that the key which unlocks forbidden doors to our will or passion leaves a stain on the hand, that may not be so dark as blood, but that will not out; Hamlet, that all the noblest gifts of person, temperament, and mind slip like sand through the grasp of an infirm purpose; Othello, that the perpetual silt of some one weakness, the eddies of a suspicious temper depositing their one impalpable layer after another, may build up a shoal on which an heroic life and an otherwise magnanimous nature may bilge and go to pieces. All this we may learn, and much more, and Shakespeare was no doubt well aware of all this and more; but I do not believe that he wrote his plays with any such didactic purpose. He knew human nature too well not to know that one thorn of experience is worth a whole wilderness of warning,—that, where one man shapes his life by precept and example, there are a thousand who have it shaped for them by impulse and by circumstances. He did not mean his great tragedies for scarecrows, as if the nailing of one hawk to the barn-door would prevent the next from coming down souse into the hen-yard. No, it is not the poor bleaching victim hung up to moult its draggled feathers in the rain that he wishes to show us. He loves the hawk-nature as well as the hen-nature; and if he is unequalled in anything, it is in that sunny breadth of view, that impregnability of reason, that looks down all ranks and conditions of men, all fortune and misfortune, with the equal eye of the pure artist.

"Shakespeare Once More." *North American Review.* 1868. *Among My Books.* 1870.

[119] *Mark Van Doren*

It is literally true that while we read a play of Shakespeare's we are in it. We may be drawn in swiftly or slowly—in most cases it is swiftly—but once we are there we are enclosed. That is the secret, and it is still a secret, of Shakespeare's power to interest us. He conditions us to a particular world before we are aware that it exists; then he absorbs us in its particulars. We scarcely say to ourselves, this world exists; nor do we pause to note how consistent each thing in it is with every other. Our attention is on the details, which we take in as details should be taken in, one at a time. Meanwhile there is for us no other world. The great world is not forgotten—Shakespeare indeed knows best how to keep us reminded of its greatness—but it is here confined to a single mode of its being. He is not telling the whole truth in any play, nor does he do so in all of them together, nor could he have done so had he written ten thousand. But the piece of truth with which he is occupied at a given moment is for that moment eloquent both of itself and of the remainder. It seems to be all. It is satisfactory and complete. With each new line a play of Shakespeare's lights its own recesses, deepens its original hue, echoes, supports, and authenticates itself. The world is not there, but this part of it is so entirely there that we miss nothing; it is as if existence had decided to measure itself by a new standard. And the secret of that standard is shared with us. Shakespeare, who denies his reader nothing, denies him least of all the excitement of feeling that he is where things are simply and finally alive.

Only a remarkable artist could have done this, and only a remarkable man—a man, moreover, in whom the balance was well-nigh perfect between understanding and observation, between intellect and instinct, between vision and sight. It has long been recognized that his characters, while irreducibly individual, partake of that nature which belongs to all men, and seldom desert the types in whose terms they were conceived. Hamlet is young, melancholy, courteous, brilliant, and moral. Falstaff is old, fat, drunken, untruthful, and witty. None of those traits is new, and it would almost appear that nothing in either man had been invented by Shakespeare. Each, however, has his unique carriage and voice, and will not be mistaken for any other man on earth. He is first of all a member of the human race. After that he is himself, saying things which Shakespeare knows how to envelop in a silence so natural that for the time being we hear no other sound than that of his discourse. Yet the act of being himself never takes him beyond the range of our understanding. We hear him with our ears and we see him with our eyes, but he is most valuable to us because we can think about him with all the mind we possess. He is not that monstrous thing, an individual undefined, any more than Shakespeare's worlds are irresponsible constructions, or any more than Shakespeare's poetry is idiot-pure. Sometimes this poetry struts on cumbrous wings when it should go by foot, but seldom is it being written for its own sake, as if poetry were the most precious thing in the world. To Shakespeare it was apparently not that. The world was still more precious —the great one he never forgot, and the little one in which he knew how to imprison its voice and body. What he dealt in was existence, and his dealings were responsible, high-hearted, and humane. The reader who places himself in his hands will not be protected from any experience, but he will be safe from outrage because he will always know his bearings. What is supposed to happen in Shakespeare's plays does happen; and what has happened anywhere cannot be finally hated. Shakespeare loved the world as it is. That is why he understood it so well; and that in turn is why, being the artist he was, he could make it over again into something so rich and clear.

Introduction. *Shakespeare*. 1939.

[120] *Donald A. Stauffer*

Though Shakespeare expressed all gradations of romantic love, the largeness of his conception is best shown in his continual return to the idea that love is a quality of unshakable fidelity. He holds to this idea with such a peculiar consistency that he almost slights one of the abiding moral questions: what is right action in a conflict between loyalty and truth? He suspends his judgment—or more accurately, he judges on both sides—in the case of Falstaff versus Henry V. Troilus destroys himself by forcing himself to give up his love for Cressida in the face of fact. But for this question alone, Shakespeare seems ordinarily to have closed his mind passionately and beyond argument. Characteristically, he creates a melodramatic situation to show the fatal mistake of Enobarbus in abandoning his loyalty to follow his own interests. He selects or shapes material to persuade us that loyalty is rarely mistaken in its object and never mistaken in its nature. The procession of heroines—from Helena-and-Hermia and Juliet and Viola, to Desdemona and Cordelia and Cleopatra and Hermione—offer smiling reproach and eventual refuge to the fickleness and fever of the men. Love is a goddess, not a god; and being divine, she cannot change. Shakespeare might well say with Browning, "Our gifts once given must here abide." The turtledove is his symbol, not only because it loves absolute beauty in the phoenix, but because it represents in itself absolute devotion. The word "truth" becomes, then, almost the synonym for loyalty and love, and Shakespeare's moral discoveries may be reduced to the simple equation that love is truth.

Shakespeare's World of Images. 1949. Chap. VII.

[121] *Edward Hubler*

In the plays the most admirable characters are those who give themselves without reservation, and often the most poignant passages are those in which the freely given affection is betrayed. Hamlet is the world's best-loved tragic hero because in a sense he wears his heart upon his sleeve. He had idealized his mother, set his heart upon Ophelia, and made friends with Rosencranz and Guildenstern. Their betrayal of Hamlet's trust is one of the chief motives of the action of the play. Nor is his lovableness reduced by his recurrent savagery, which, in one way or another, is motivated by his devotion. He was cruel to his mother "only to be kind," and since he knew nothing more contemptible than a friendship based on policy, he sent his college friends to their deaths: "Why man, they did make love to this employment." Nor could Othello's tragedy have developed without the wholeness of his love. There is not a character giving his heart wholly—and it does not matter how imprudent the giving may be—who does not in a large measure win Shakespeare's admiration. Wholeheartedness is not only for Shakespeare's lovers; it is for husband and wife, father and daughter, mother and son, brothers, sisters, friends.

"The Young Man's Beauty." *The Sense of Shakespeare's Sonnets.* 1952.

[122] *Edward Hubler*

It is now common to think of the Elizabethan acceptance of Fortune as appropriate to the more primitive life of that era, as though we were now well on the way to getting things in hand. Shakespeare knew better. His works do not suggest that he was a determinist; one need not be a determinist in order to know the foolishness of a self-centered optimism. In his tragedies it is the villains who assume an unlimited freedom of the will; it is the heroes who come to know better. This is of course a matter of degree. The orthodox view of free will did not suppose that man's powers are uncircumscribed, nor did the fate which Hamlet and Othello came to accept deny all choice. There is rather a conviction of a partial fate, and it is allied to Shakespeare's detestation of . . . cool prudence . . . The self-contained man is doubly wrong: he denies his function, and in assuming his power to control, he denies his fate. If one is to live wisely on even a humble level, there must be some recognition of the operation of the unknowable: "Since why to love I can allege no cause." In Shakespeare's stories the recognition of the unknowable is often the beginning of wisdom. We may imagine that with him this attitude was a generalization from experience, though we can see its kinship to an older assumption which placed the beginning of wisdom in "the fear of the Lord."

"The Natural Fool of Fortune." *The Sense of Shakespeare's Sonnets.* 1952.

[123] *Edward Hubler*

Redemption through a knowledge of evil is at the heart of Shakespeare's deepest revelations of man. He presents it in pagan and Christian contexts. It may lead to repentance and confession, as with Hamlet's mother; or to repentance and prayer, as with Lear, even though Lear's gods are pagan gods; or it may lead a character to esteem honor and justice above salvation, as with Othello; or to a knowledge of evil without repentance, as with Macbeth. But it is the heart of the matter with all of them. In the dark lady sonnets, lust does not reveal its nature until after indulgence, and its slow repletion and recognition are one.

"Reputation and Knowledge of Good." *The Sense of Shakespeare's Sonnets.* 1952.

[124] *Geoffrey Bush*

Shakespeare's characters belong to time and the world; they have a natural constitution, natural passions, natural feeling, and natural reason. They are moved by excitements of their reason and their blood to share in the duties and pains and affections of natural life. In what they do and believe there is represented a deep involvement in persons and things; through this involvement Shakespeare's characters experience their profits and losses, and we are moved to pity and admiration by our understanding of the glories and mistakes of this involvement. Yet Shakespeare's characters are not wholly a part of the natural world. They are divided from their world; they are made to stand at one remove from their situation, and to undertake the effort of knowing and replying to the world. Their world, as it were, takes on an identity of its own; it has a shape and voice, and addresses those within it. The moral laws of nature and of nations, Hector says, "speak aloud." The Ghost speaks aloud to Hamlet, and in the storm Lear is addressed by the elements. And at their greatest moments Shakespeare's characters make their reply; at the end of the tragic progress it belongs not only to their suffering, but to their honor, that they stand apart from the world. They know the world and judge it, and they step forward to make their own address; they strike an attitude in the face of the world, and announce that they are natural fools, that "I am Bottom the weaver," or that "This is I, Hamlet the Dane."

It is at these moments that their involvement in nature becomes most complicated and precious. For to belong to nature is to be involved in an arrangement that at its most distant point, touches what is beyond things in themselves. There is "terror for that which is out of time," Mr. Sewell says, "and pity for that which is in time, and they make a single experience." This single experience is the end of Shakespeare's vision; it is, as it were, the Shakespearian moment. When Lear and Cordelia in prison will be God's spies, or when Hamlet tells Horatio that there is a special providence in the fall of a sparrow, moments seems to have been reached, at some remote limit of natural life, when there is made known the possibility of a settlement between the two aspects of nature.

It is not good, Bacon said, to remain too long in the theater; and having given his judgment of poetry Bacon turned to graver matters and would not stay for an answer. But Shakespeare's vision expresses itself through the words and gestures of the theater; it reaches toward a different advancement of our learning, a way of knowing and settling with the world by which we are drawn into the continuing action of poetry and the theater. What saddens us at Hamlet's death is that he has no more time to speak, and no further words with which to record his life; but it is a great comfort, and an argument of hope, that Horatio will report Hamlet and his cause aright. He will tell Hamlet's "story" in "this harsh world." In the equation between the world and the theater, it is Shakespeare's perception that life itself is a dramatic situation of address and reply, expressed most easily and naturally in the small globe of the stage. There is a profound commerce between our lives and the gestures of the theater; it is Hamlet's most glorious accomplishment to have made his life into a "story." Shakespeare's vision reaches toward a settlement with nature that in the deepest sense is a poetic and dramatic settlement: not a moment of certainty, the point in T. S. Eliot's *Four Quartets* when through the relinquishment of things in themselves we arrive at the still center of the turning world; but a moment when natural life is addressed by every voice, by things and by the meaning of things; when the possibilities of natural life go beyond even the power of words, and when it is right and proper that the rest is silence, and that Hamlet should say:

O, I could tell you—
But let it be.

Shakespeare and the Natural Condition. 1956. Chap. I.

Comedy

[125] *George Gordon*

Recall that romantic world in which Shakespeare is happiest—the world of his comedies and young people—that incomparable rainbow mixture of Old England and Utopia—and you will observe that most of these plays begin with some artificial seclusion or segregation from the world. The curtain goes up; and at once, or in a scene or two, the door is shut on ordinary life. Except in *The Comedy of Errors* and *The Merchant of Venice,* where the play opens on a public mart, hardly anybody goes to business in these Shakespearian latitudes, or seems to be obliged to get up at any particular time—

though, on the whole, except for the drinkers, all Shakespeare's people like the morning. The scene being staged for Love, it is essential that its young people should be idle, should have time on their hands. No enemy of Love like work! Everyone of importance lives on his or her estate; or in Arcadia—where there are no clocks, and everybody helps everybody else. It is a world of delicious make-believe: of Academes, Illyrias, and Forests of Arden—of seaside Bohemias or desert islands. Even when the scene is most real—when the postal address is known—it is still romantic and Utopian: for what, as we know, is Verona, what is Padua, but 'somewhere in Italy'? And Italy, to the Shakespearian young, was the Worldly Paradise, where a Lucentio might hopefully look for 'love in idleness'.

★ ★ ★

Long before the private Academes of Italy there were the monastic Academes of the religious, whose sign was the Cross; and the mixed monasteries of the worldly, in that mythical Garden of the Middle Ages whose sign was a flower—the Garden of the Rose. Perhaps the best model of all these aristocratic pleasure parties—these Colleges of *Thelēma*—of 'As You Like It'—is the Florentine Garden of Boccaccio, with its company of ladies and gentlemen telling their witty and courtly stories while the plague of life rumbled grimly outside. Shakespeare accepts the game with all its affectations, because they are *poetical* affectations; but of course he is not deceived. Even if the poetry comes first with him, he never forgets the work of Comedy. For what are they all, these charming lay societies, but attempts to reach Utopia on the cheap? I say, on the cheap, because what these attractive worldlings will not face, as Shakespeare well knew, is the *price* of Utopia. That price is constant, and is nothing less than a change of mind and heart. Shakespeare accepts these affectations—and when he has extracted the last ounce of poetry from them —but not till then—up goes his hand, crash goes the merry bomb of Comedy, and they are exploded in thin air. All he asks is a gentleman's park or a forest somewhere—and for three acts his young people walking about in it. If Life, which they believe they have eluded —if Life the traitor, with all its duties and responsibilities, is not already busy among them—Shakespeare will see to it that he finds a way in. Sooner or later, to these Young Utopians on the cheap, Shakespearian Comedy presents the bill.

★ ★ ★

Shakespeare, then, poetic as he is, does not neglect the work of Comedy. But it is said that he is too good-natured, too kind for Comedy.

Comedy has a mission, and in the interests of society must have the courage to be cruel, to use the lash. In the art of cruelty, and in whipcracking generally, it must be admitted that Shakespeare is defective. Not that he is without satire: he makes fun, of course, like all comedians, of the follies of his time: *Love's Labour's Lost,* it begins to be known and has always been suspected, is as topical as Gilbert's *Patience.* But hardly even of that rather exceptional play can it be said that satire, in the end, is its principal motive. Poetry and cheerfulness are always breaking in. One is conscious, from time to time, in many of the masterpieces of social Comedy, of the author as *censor morum,* as the representative of sane society, of *les honnêtes hommes,* flicking his whip, pinking his man. But we have, I make bold to say, no such feeling in reading Shakespeare: if his characters are corrected, the correction seems not to come from some external power: they seem to do it for one another. If exposures are made, it is still a family affair. Shakespeare's comedies, regarded purely as Comedy, present us with a holy war, conducted without malice or bloodshed on Egotism, Sentimentalism, Pedantry, and Self-importance: on precisely those weaknesses and follies, in short, which, without being criminal, make bad citizens and bad neighbours—tiresome husbands and tiresome wives—which make men and women unsociable, and unfit for the friendly purposes of life. They say to Life, these people, like peevish children, that they 'won't play', and are laughed by Shakespearian Comedy into the game.

★ ★ ★

What, then, to conclude, is the secret of Shakespeare's comedies: of their lasting beauty and power? It is no mystery. Their secret is the secret of Boccaccio's *Decameron.* As it has been said of that book, it is 'the secret of light and air'. A brilliant sunshine inundates and glorifies them. The spirit that inspires them is an absolute humanity unashamed and unafraid. You may sometimes be shocked by the language of your company; you may be shocked, but you will never be cold-shouldered. You may sometimes be incommoded by the diversity of your experience: but you are never melancholy, and you are never outcast. The World, which is the foundation of sanity, is always with you or near you. The World is made of Life and Hope: the Shakespearian Comedy is a portrait of the World. Boccaccio has been called 'the escape from Dante'. What is Shakespeare the 'escape from'? Shall I be accused of professional cynicism if I suggest that he is possibly the escape from his critics? Some of our modern analysts think that Shakespeare, in his comedies, might have gone deeper. The direction of his comedies, as of Boccaccio's stories, is rather to width than depth: but what is wrong with width? 'The world *is* wide, and its width supplies a kind of profundity in another dimension.'

Shakespearian Comedy and Others Studies. 1944. Chap. II.

[126] *S. C. Sen Gupta*

In comedy as well as in tragedy, he does not judge or unmask a character from without but reveals it from within. For him comedy is not the art of exposure but of exploration. He places his characters in certain situations in which they learn the deeper secrets of their own hearts. The new discovery proves that all their previous professions, however sincere, were unreal, because they were unaware of the profundities in their own characters. The simplest examples are the King and his lords in *Love's Labour's Lost* and Katharine in *The Taming of the Shrew,* all of whom came to realize that their characters are diametrically opposite to what they thought about themselves. Duke Orsino, who, till the discovery of Viola's sex, thought that he was in love with Olivia, finds that his heart has really been conquered by the page whom he was using as a mere go-between. Greater subtlety is seen in the portraiture of Benedick and Beatrice, who believed that they were immune against Cupid's shafts; they did not realize that the irresistible manner in which they were drawn to each other was itself an indication of dormant love, and when, by means of a trick, they are made to realize their mistake, they are not unmasked and exposed as are butts and gulls in ordinary comedies; their defeat is like a triumph, because it means the acknowledgement of the deepest instinct of humanity.

Shakespearian Comedy. 1950. Chap. III.

[127] *Geoffrey Bush*

In every play there is a moment of discovery and *anagnorisis,* when character and event stand self-exposed. In the histories and comedies, it is the moment when lovers remove their disguises and are recognized. There are only touches of natural adversity in the histories and comedies, and only a few facts that cannot be gathered into the image of perfection: fools, who refuse to be married, and

Falstaff, who refuses to be a member of an orderly commonwealth. Yet Falstaff and the idea of English kingship foreshadow the tragic collision between the fact and the image; the vision of the play is unable to cope with their encounter. The problem plays accept as their explicit theme the contradiction between these two aspects of experience: Ulysses and Hector and the Duke and Isabella are made to know and confront the fact of common natural weakness. At their most dramatic moments, they find themselves in a double situation, addressed by the world both as it is and as it ought to be. These are moments of intellectual anguish, when Angelo is torn between would and would not, and Isabella is at war " 'twixt will and will not." The cries of the lovers are discoveries that the dream of perfection and the fact of imperfection are bitterly divorced; they are cries not of the heart but of the mind: "this is, and is not, Cressid!"

Shakespeare and the Natural Condition. 1956. Chap. II.

[128] *Nevill Coghill*

Dante . . . saw the formula for Comedy as the pattern or picture of ultimate reality, and applied it to the state of the soul after death. That application may be extended to include life on earth; there was trouble in Eden, the knot was untied on Calvary, there is bliss in Heaven. The course of human life well-lived is a Comedy as defined. These realities, then unquestioned, could be figured in an earthly tale that followed the same pattern. Any human harmony achieved out of distress can awaken overtones of joy on higher planes. At least they imply an assertion that the harmonious is the normal, the attainable, that heaviness may endure for a night but joy cometh in the morning. Life is a union in love, not a battle of self-interest waged by the rules of an expedient ethic. Its greatest and characteristic triumph is positive joy, not a negative correction of vice and folly. The medieval formula for Comedy leads to the Beatific Vision, the Renaissance formula leads no further than the Day of Judgment, and is principally preoccupied with punishing the goats. The Christian vision sees love the cause and crown of life, the classical sees a useful morality, which will do to go on with. The best pagan faith offers Justice; Christianity, Mercy and Forgiveness.

In a spirit of conformity with these opposites stand the Comedies of Jonson and Shakespeare respectively. Almost all in Shakespeare are built up on a love-story, often indeed on a group of love-stories; lovers are united, faults are pardoned, enmities are reconciled. All this might be thought intolerably sentimental if it were merely a question of sentiment, not a whole and serious view of the real nature of life. Shakespeare's comic vision is not a sickly indulgence or "an escape from reality", but the firm assertion of basic harmony.

Out of this settled and traditional view he began early to create his "Comedy of the golden world" as it has been called. *A Midsummer Night's Dream* is its first full expression, and perhaps the most delicate. It is a picture of a world with no ill-will. If his comedies had never enlarged this picture to include the melancholy and the sinful, he might well be indicted of leading an escape from unpleasant facts into some Tudor Garden of the Rose. It is a proof how strongly he held to a view of life as harmony that he learnt later how to stretch Comedy to contain sorrow and evil, and yet to show them capable of resolution in love and joy. *Measure for Measure* and *The Winter's Tale* are the extreme examples of this vision and power.

"The Basis of Shakespearian Comedy." (The substance of a lecture delivered in 1949 at Stratford-upon-Avon.) *Essays and Studies 1950.*

[129] *W. H. Auden*

Comedy, on the other hand, is not only possible within a Christian society, but capable of a much greater breadth and depth than classical comedy. Greater in breadth because classical comedy is based upon the divison of mankind into two classes, those who have *arete* and those who do not, and only the second class, fools, shameless rascals, slaves, are fit subjects for comedy. But Christian comedy is based upon the belief that all men are sinners; no one, therefore, whatever his rank or talents, can claim immunity from the comic exposure and, indeed, the more virtuous, in the Greek sense, a man is, the more he realizes that he deserves to be exposed. Greater in depth because, while classical comedy believes that rascals should get the drubbing they deserve, Christian comedy believes that we are forbidden to judge others and that it is our duty to forgive each other. In classical comedy the characters are exposed and punished: when the curtain falls, the audience is laughing and those on stage are in tears. In Christian comedy the characters are exposed and forgiven: when the curtain falls, the audience and the characters are laughing together. Ben Jonson's comedies, unlike Shakespeare's, are classical, not Christian.

"The Globe." *The Dyer's Hand and Other Essays.* 1962.

[130] *Northrop Frye*

The Two Gentlemen of Verona is an orthodox New Comedy except for one thing. The hero Valentine becomes captain of a band of outlaws in a forest, and all the other characters are gathered into this forest and become converted. Thus the action of the comedy begins in a world represented as a normal world, moves into the green world, goes into a metamorphosis there in which the comic resolution is achieved, and returns to the normal world. The forest in this play is the embryonic form of the fairy world of *A Midsummer Night's Dream*, the Forest of Arden in *As You Like It*, Windsor Forest in *The Merry Wives of Windsor*, and the pastoral world of the mythical sea-coasted Bohemia in *The Winter's Tale*. In all these comedies there is the same rhythmic movement from normal world to green world and back again. Nor is this second world confined to the forest comedies. In *The Merchant of Venice* the two worlds are a little harder to see, yet Venice is clearly not the same world as that of Portia's mysterious house in Belmont, where there are caskets teaching that gold and silver are corruptible goods, and from whence proceed the wonderful cosmological harmonies of the fifth act. In *The Tempest* the entire action takes place in the second world, and the same may be said of *Twelfth Night*, which, as its title implies, presents a carnival society, not so much a green world as an evergreen one. The second world is absent from the so-called problem comedies, which is one of the things that makes them problem comedies.

The green world charges the comedies with a symbolism in which the comic resolution contains a suggestion of the old ritual pattern of the victory of summer over winter. This is explicit in *Love's Labor's Lost*. In this very masque-like play, the comic contest takes the form of the medieval debate of winter and spring. In *The Merry Wives of Windsor* there is an elaborate ritual of the defeat of winter, known to folklorists as "carrying out Death," of which Falstaff is the victim; and Falstaff must have felt that, after being thrown into the water, dressed up as a witch and beaten out of a house with curses, and finally supplied with a beast's head and singed with candles while he said, "Divide me like a brib'd buck, each a haunch," he had done about all that could reasonably be asked of any fertility spirit.

The association of this symbolism with the death and revival of human beings is more elusive, but still perceptible. The fact that the heroine often brings about the comic resolution by disguising herself as a boy is familiar enough. In the Hero of *Much Ado About Nothing* and the Helena of *All's Well That Ends Well,* this theme of the withdrawal and return of the heroine comes as close to a death and revival as Elizabethan conventions will allow. The Thaisa of *Pericles* and the Fidele of *Cymbeline* are beginning to crack the conventions, and with the disappearance and revival of Hermione in *The Winter's Tale,* who actually returns once as a ghost in a dream, the original nature-myth of Demeter and Proserpine is openly established. The fact that the dying and reviving character is usually female strengthens the feeling that there is something maternal about the green world, in which the new order of the comic resolution is nourished and brought to birth. However, a similar theme which is very like the rejuvenation of the *senex* so frequent in Aristophanes occurs in the folklore motif of the healing of the impotent king on which *All's Well That Ends Well* is based, and this theme is probably involved in the symbolism of Prospero.

★ ★ ★

This world of fairies, dreams, disembodied souls, and pastoral lovers may not be a "real" world, but, if not, there is something equally illusory in the stumbling and blinded follies of the "normal" world, of Theseus' Athens with its idiotic marriage law, of Duke Frederick and his melancholy tyranny, of Leontes and his mad jealousy, of the Court Party with their plots and intrigues. The famous speech of Prospero about the dream nature of reality applies equally to Milan and the enchanted island. We spend our lives partly in a waking world we call normal and partly in a dream world which we create out of our own desires. Shakespeare endows both worlds with equal imaginative power, brings them opposite one another, and makes each world seem unreal when seen by the light of the other. He uses freely both the heroic triumph of New Comedy and the ritual resurrection of its predecessor, but his distinctive comic resolution is different from either: it is a detachment of the spirit born of this reciprocal reflection of two illusory realities. We need not ask whether this brings us into a higher order of existence or not, for the question of existence is not relevant to poetry.

We have spoken of New Comedy as Aristotelian, Old Comedy as Platonic and Dante's *commedia* as Thomist, but it is difficult to suggest a philosophical spokesman for the form of Shakespeare's comedy. For Shakespeare, the subject matter of poetry is not life, or nature, or reality, or revelation, or anything else that the philosopher builds on, but poetry itself, a verbal universe. That is one reason why he is both the most elusive and the most substantial of poets.

"The Argument of Comedy." *English Institute Essays, 1948.* 1949.

[131] *John Vyvyan*

FIRST: We are shown a soul containing the principles of strength which will enable it to pass the coming tests.

SECOND: The voice or voices of the higher Self, which will help the hero in his temptations, are characterized for us.

THIRD: There is a test or temptation scene, in which the hero triumphs, because he is true to the Self and faithful to Love.

FOURTH: There is a confirmatory experience, tending towards inner sovereignty or lordship of the soul.

FIFTH and SIXTH: There is a second test, and a second confirmation.

SEVENTH: The act of creative mercy, including self-forgiveness.

EIGHTH: An experience of enlightenment.

NINTH: The symbolic union of love.

The Shakespearean Ethic. 1959. Chap. 16.

[132] *George Gordon*

. . . it is sometimes complained that Shakespeare in his comedies is careless of his women: that having first made them attractive, he gives some of them, in the end, very doubtful husbands. Well, there is no doubt something it. Proteus and Julia, Oliver and Celia, Claudio and Hero, Bertram and Helena, Angelo and Mariana: it is impossible to be happy about such alliances as these, or to think that the dramatist was very fastidious when he made them. But we must not ask too much. Every dramatist in this matter is to be regarded as an embarrassed parent with a bevy of marriageable daughters—proud to have arranged some good matches, and particularly that especially suitable one for the Beauty of the family—but heartily glad to have them all settled somehow: to have them, as we say, 'off his hands'.

Shakespearian Comedy and Other Studies. 1944. Chap. VII.

History

[133] *Samuel Taylor Coleridge*

Let no man blame his son for learning history from Shakespeare.

The Lectures of 1811–12. Raysor II, 32.

[134] *Walter Pater*

The irony of kingship—average human nature, flung with a wonderfully pathetic effect into the vortex of great events; tragedy of everyday quality heightened in degree only by the conspicuous scene which does but make those who play their parts there conspicuously unfortunate; the utterance of common humanity straight from the heart, but refined like other common things for kingly uses by Shakespeare's unfailing eloquence: such, unconsciously for the most part, though palpably enough to the careful reader, is the conception under which Shakespeare has arranged the lights and shadows of the story of the English kings, emphasising merely the light and shadow inherent in it, and keeping very close to the original authorities, not simply in the general outline of these dramatic histories but sometimes in their very expression. Certainly the history itself, as he found it in Hall, Holinshed, and Stowe, those somewhat picturesque old chroniclers who had themselves an eye for the dramatic "effects" of human life, has much of this sentiment already about it. What he did not find there was the natural prerogative—such justification, in kingly, that is to say, in exceptional, qualities, of the exceptional position, as makes it practicable in the result. It is no *Henriade* he writes, and no history of the English people, but the sad fortunes of some English kings as conspicuous examples of the ordinary human condition. As in a children's story, all princes are in extremes. Delightful in the sunshine above the wall into which chance lifts the flower for a season, they can but plead somewhat more touchingly than others their everyday weakness in the storm. Such is the motive that gives unity to these unequal and intermittent contributions toward a slowly evolved dramatic chronicle . . .

"Shakespeare's English Kings." *Scribner's Magazine*. April, 1889. *Appreciations*. 1889.

[135] *John Masefield*

Shakespeare's mind seems to brood on the idea, that our tragical Kings failed because they did not conform to a type somewhat lower than themselves. It may be said that Henry V conforms to type, having the qualities that impress the bourgeoisie: he is a success. Henry VI does not conform to type, having the qualities of the Christian mystic: he is stabbed in the Tower. Edward IV conforms to type, having the qualities that win the commonalty: he is a success. Richard II does not conform to type, being a man of nerves: he is done to death at Pomfret. King John does not conform to type, having more mind than capacity, more imagination than character: he is poisoned at Swinstead. (Or did he indulge too far in peaches and new cider?)

"King John." *William Shakespeare.* 1954.

[136] *Edward Dowden*

But the most important influence exercised by his dramatic studies in English history upon the mind of Shakspere was that they engaged his imagination in an inquiry into the sources of power and of weakness, of success and of failure in a man's dealing with the positive, social world. They kept constantly before Shakspere's mind the problem, "How is a man to obtain a mastery of the actual world, and in what ways may be fail of such mastery?" This was a subject in which Shakspere had a personal interest, for he was himself resolved, as far as in him lay, not to fail in this material life of ours, but rather, if possible, to be for his own needs a master of events. The portraits of English kings from King John to King Henry V. are a series of studies of weakness and of strength for the attaining of kingly ends. To fail is the supreme sin. Worse almost than criminality is weakness, except that crime besides being crime, is itself a certain kind of weakness. Henry VI. is a timid saint; it were better that he had been a man. Does his timid saintliness serve him in the place of energy of thought and will, or secure him from a miserable overthrow? It is important to observe the fundamental difference which exists between the series of English historical plays and the great series of tragedies, beginning with Hamlet, ending with Timon of Athens, in which Shakspere embodied his ripest experience of life. In the historical plays the question which inevitably comes forward again and again is this, "By what means shall a man attain the noblest practical success in the objective world?" In the great tragedies the problem is a spiritual one. It is still the problem of failure and success. But in these tragedies success means not any practical achievement in the world, but the perfected life of the soul; and failure means the ruin of the life of a soul through passion or weakness, through calamity or crime.

Shakspere, His Mind and Art. 1874. Chap. II.

[137] *Lily B. Campbell*

If we are to talk in terms of cycles, then, we cannot ignore the fact that the completion of a cycle depends upon following a path to the original starting point. If the First Folio editors rightly attributed the ten plays to Shakespeare, he wrote of two cycles of history: from the seizing of the crown by Henry IV to its loss by "the third heir," Henry VI; and from the seizing of the crown from Henry VI by Edward IV to its loss by "the third heir," Richard III. Whether or not Shakespeare did write the plays dealing with this second cycle of history, it is clear that in *Richard II, Henry IV,* and *Henry V* he saw the developing pattern of the cycle, from usurpation to usurpation, for he wrote in the epilogue to *Henry V:*

> Henry the Sixth, in infant bands crown'd King
> Of France and England, did this king succeed;
> Whose state so many had the managing,
> That they lost France and made his England bleed:
> Which oft our stage hath shown; and, for their sake,
> In your fair minds let this acceptance take.

But though the sequence of plays is important to the moral patterning of history, each of the Shakespeare histories serves a special purpose in elucidating a political problem of Elizabeth's day and in bringing to bear upon this problem the accepted political philosophy of the Tudors. And as I turn to the study of these individual plays, I wish to stress two points in particular. First, Shakespeare chose for his histories kings who had already been accepted as archetypes and who had been used over and over again to point particular morals. Second, Shakespeare, like all other writers who used history to teach politics to the present, cut his cloth to fit the pattern, and the approach to the study of his purposes in choosing subjects and incidents from history as well as in his altering the historical fact is best made with current political situations in mind. It is on the assumption that history repeats itself that political mirrors of history can be utilized to explain the present. But it does not repeat itself in every detail, and while the larger outlines of historical fact must be preserved to be convincing, the details are often altered to make them more reminiscent of the present.

Shakespeare's "Histories" Mirrors of Elizabethan Policy. 1947. Chap. XI.

Tragedy

[138] *Herman Melville*

. . . this blackness it is that furnishes the infinite obscure of his back-ground,—that back-ground, against which Shakspeare plays his grandest conceits, the things that have made for Shakspeare his loftiest but most circumscribed renown, as the profoundest of thinkers . . . Through the mouths of the dark characters of Hamlet, Timon, Lear, and Iago, he craftily says, or sometimes insinuates the things, which we feel to be so terrifically true, that it were all but madness for any good man, in his own proper character, to utter, or even hint of them. Tormented into desperation, Lear, the frantic king, tears off the mask, & speaks the sane madness of vital truth.

"Hawthorne and His Mosses." *The Literary World*. 17 August 1850.

[139] *W. B. Yeats*

All perform their tragic play,
There struts Hamlet, there is Lear,
That's Ophelia, that Cordelia;
Yet they, should the last scene be there,
The great stage curtain about to drop,
If worthy their prominent part in the play,
Do not break up their lines to weep.
They know that Hamlet and Lear are gay;
Gaiety transfiguring all that dread.

"Lapis Lazuli." (1936). *The London Mercury*. March, 1938. *New Poems*. 1938. Lines 9–17.

[140] *A. C. Bradley*

The tragic hero with Shakespeare, then, need not be 'good,' though generally he is 'good' and therefore at once wins sympathy in his error. But it is necessary that he should have so much of greatness that in his error and fall we may be vividly conscious of the possibilities of human nature. Hence, in the first place, a Shakespearean tragedy is never, like some miscalled tragedies, depressing. No one ever closes the book with the feeling that man is a poor mean creature. He may be wretched and he may be awful, but he is not small. His lot may be heart-rending and mysterious, but it is not contemptible. The most confirmed of cynics ceases to be a cynic while he reads these plays. And with this greatness of the tragic hero (which is not always confined to him) is connected, secondly, what I venture to describe as the centre of the tragic impression. This central feeling is the impression of waste. With Shakespeare, at any rate, the pity and fear which are stirred by the tragic story seem to unite with, and even to merge in, a profound sense of sadness and mystery, which is due to this impression of waste. 'What a piece of work is man,' we cry; 'so much more beautiful and so much more terrible than we knew! Why should he be so if this beauty and greatness only tortures itself and throws itself away?' We seem to have before us a type of the mystery of the whole world, the tragic fact which extends far beyond the limits of tragedy. Everywhere, from the crushed rocks beneath our feet to the soul of man, we see power, intelligence, life and glory, which astound us and seem to call for our worship. And everywhere we see them perishing, devouring one another and destroying themselves, often with dreadful pain, as though they came into being for no other end. Tragedy is the typical form of this mystery, because that greatness of soul which it exhibits oppressed, conflicting and destroyed, is the highest existence in our view. It forces the mystery upon us, and it makes us realise so vividly the worth of that which is wasted that we cannot possibly seek comfort in the reflection that all is vanity.

Shakespearean Tragedy. 1904. Lect. I.

[141] *John Vyvyan*

First: We are shown a soul, in many respects noble, but with a fatal flaw, which lays it open to a special temptation.

SECOND: The "voices" of the coming temptation are characterized for us, so that we may have no doubt that they will persuade to evil.

THIRD: There is a temptation scene, in which the weak spot of the hero's soul is probed, and the temptation is yielded to.

FOURTH: We are shown an inner conflict, usually in the form of a soliloquy, in which the native nobility of the hero's soul opposes the temptation, but fails.

FIFTH AND SIXTH: There is a second temptation and a second inner conflict, of mounting intensity, with the result that the hero loses the kingship of his own soul.

SEVENTH: The tragic act, or act of darkness.

EIGHTH: The realization of horror.

NINTH: Death.

The Shakespearean Ethic. 1959. Chap. I.

[142] *Arthur Sewell*

The tragic situation in an elementary form is to be found in the discomfitures that attend Shylock, Malvolio, and perhaps Falstaff. Each of these characters is faced by or brought to a situation for which his previous address to the world had never covenanted. To meet this situation that address must be transformed, and it must be transformed from within. They are thrown on resources within themselves and they are, for the time, alone. Hatred, wit, self-love have lost their outside sources of sustenance. They no longer serve. In addition, however, there has been induced in us an attitude to the character which is as much at a loss in the new situation as the character's own address to life. We, too, had never covenanted for this moment, and whereas, before, these characters had largely drawn their identity from our attitudes to them, we are suddenly called upon to share with them, in sympathy, their attitude to life. Only by becoming one with Shylock can we know what Shylock must do now; and so it is with Falstaff and Malvolio. For the manner in which we have hitherto regarded these characters has become irrelevant. The social attitude is asked to give way to something to which we can scarcely give a name, 'without it be compassion'. The social attitude, however, does not so easily accommodate itself, and we can give to these persons in their misfortune little more than that less significant pity which we give to unlucky people in real life.

Character and Society in Shakespeare. 1951. Chap. IV.

[143] *Brents Stirling*

As we follow the protagonists in their fated careers a common quality of withdrawal into self seems to distinguish them. This quality is rarely sentimental, but it is always willful or perverse. Richard II withdraws to mirror-worship and expresses it in pageants of defeat and martyrdom; Brutus becomes self-sufficient in ritual which enables him to abide the role of conspirator and executioner; Othello follows the same course, emphasizing as did Brutus the motive of hateless sacrifice; Hamlet rejects the world as a sterile promontory, proceeds to stress motives of privacy with the alien antic, and becomes engrossed in testing his capacity for balanced passion; Macbeth is not merely withdrawn but is translated into "brainsickly" raptness; Antony, the most naturalistic of the major figures becomes detached in sensuality; Lear, Timon, and Coriolanus all retreat into egoism, and Lear is the only one of the three who "returns."

So far it would appear simply that Shakespeare's tragic heroes isolate themselves from other men. But this simple truth can be our starting point in considering the form, the manner, of the isolation as it appears in plays we have studied. Retreat into self is generally marked by ceremonial: pageant, ritual, incantation, or play-acting, either singly or in combination. The return of the outer world is often presented as a breaking of the ceremonial spell. Richard II's last pageant is the deposition scene during which he compels Bolingbroke to join him in holding the crown and calls for the symbolic looking glass that he may better witness his own fall. His shattering of the glass ends the pose, and the scene turns to realism. The ritual withdrawal of Brutus is ended by Antony in a mock-ritual and a depiction of the sacrifice, the dish carved for the gods, in the very guise which Brutus disavowed—the carcass hewn for hounds. Othello's retirement into self, also climaxed in a sacrifice, is suddenly ended by Emilia in Shakespeare's most dramatic clash between the formal and realistic planes of being. Macbeth's incantatory retreat into darkness, sleep, and raptness is at its height in the episode of Duncan's murder, and the drunken porter breaks the spell with comic symbols of contradiction.

★ ★ ★

Naturally, the use of ritual or other artifice in the expression of withdrawal does not fit the whole of Shakespearian tragedy, but it is both characteristic and prominent. What does this mean?

★ ★ ★

Without wishing to complicate Shakespeare's "moral universe," I suggest that he knew the idea of tragedy to be capable of tragic misuse, that he saw the elevation to tragic dignity of an erring protagonist as something which could be turned into the elevation of error itself. It is just this transformation which most of the heroes attempt for themselves. As Richard II invents his pageants of martyrdom, as Brutus and Othello enter upon rites of self-justification, as Macbeth incants the spell of his own helplessness before evil, each in effect composes spurious tragedy for himself, casts himself as a fated victim bound to do evil which is not really evil because it is made beautiful with gesture, intonation, and invocation. This is not the tragedy Shakespeare composes but a delusion of tragedy entertained by the protagonist; it is the false tragic sense which emerges as false upon appearance of the genuine, for as the true vision becomes clear the untrue is formulated and rejected.

Unity in Shakespearian Tragedy. 1956. Chap. XI.

[144] *Geoffrey Bush*

In *Othello, Timon of Athens,* and *Coriolanus,* our encounter with the aspects of natural life is seen as an encounter with our own natures and with the larger natural arrangement of affection and pity. Bacon wrote that "Nature is often hidden; sometimes overcome; seldom extinguished." The tragic defeat of Othello and Timon and Coriolanus is the consequence of their extinguishing what is natural in themselves and their separation of themselves from the natural arrangement. They have a natural nobility; they are honorable men; but they reject natural feeling to commit themselves unnaturally to absolutes and to what seems to be the perfect shape of action and belief. "It is the cause, it is the cause," Othello says; he is dedicated, like Angelo, to what he thinks is an absolute justice beyond natural affection. "The middle of humanity thou never knewest," Apemantus says to Timon, "but the extremity of both ends." Timon is committed first to one extreme and then to its opposite; and Coriolanus' mother tells her son: "You are too absolute." They are three absolutists, pledged to certainties and conclusions that are sadly mistaken. They repudiate their natural allegiance to the things of the world; they embrace pride, "Justice," or a "contempt of nature." They separate themselves from the world that gives them being, and the result is suicide and the death of the heart.

Shakespeare and the Natural Condition. 1956. Chap. III.

[145] *Willard Farnham*

It is rare spirits deeply tainted that Shakespeare places at the center of his last tragic world. The faults given them to make them men are not only great enough to "wage equal" with their virtues but are also pervasive, and yet these spirits are noble. Their nobility . . . is one of life's mysteries, for it seems to issue from ignoble substance.

★ ★ ★

No one of them is a doer of duty, like Brutus or Hamlet, or an unselfish repenter for wrong done, like Othello or Lear. Macbeth has a conscience that brings him to despair at the end of his tragic course, but . . . this conscience leaves something to be desired because, like himself, it is deeply flawed. Each of these heroes has faulty substance reaching to the very center of his character. Timon's glowing love for his fellow men turns out to be in reality a form of selfishness, for as soon as he learns that his fellows have never had love for him, but only love for his money, this glowing love becomes searing hate. Macbeth gives himself to evil in order to gain worldly position, and gives himself completely, realizing that he does so. Antony knows that Cleopatra is destructive of his honor as a man and a soldier, and at the opening of his tragedy we find him breaking his "strong Egyptian fetters" so that he will not lose himself in dotage; but he quickly chooses that these fetters shall be forged again, and there is then no more question of his leaving Cleopatra. Coriolanus, the warrior artistocrat, is so thoroughly blinded by regard for himself that he embraces treason, the crime *par excellence* for a warrior aristocrat bred to fight for his state. Coriolanus embraces treason not once, but twice, and yet he never comes to know what treason really is. It is plain that these four heroes are self-centered individualists.

In the last tragic world there is less of the medieval drama of good and evil than in the middle tragic world. In *Timon* and *Antony and Cleopatra* there are no villains, and the heroes are so much bent upon involving themselves in tragedy through the flaws in their characters that they seem to need no villains to help in the work of entanglement. In *Coriolanus* the tribunes and Aufidius take on villainous roles when they work against the hero underhandedly, but Coriolanus also seems to need no help in making his tragic end certain. In *Macbeth,* however, the witches, who are greater than merely human villains in the hierarchy of evil, do villain's work upon the hero and are by no means a supernumerary part of the tragedy. Of these four plays, *Macbeth* alone presents a fearsome struggle between representatives of good and representatives of evil that is reminiscent of *Othello and Lear.* Yet this is a struggle with a difference. It is to be remembered that in *Othello* and *Lear* the heroes are never truly brought over to the side of evil, though in their confusion they for a time join its ranks. In *Macbeth* the soul of the deeply flawed hero is securely won by evil at the beginning of the action.

Timon, Macbeth, Antony, and Coriolanus all have a power, such as the heroes of the middle tragic world do not have, to draw from us reactions that vary widely between profound antipathy and profound sympathy. Along with sympathy they can inspire admiration. Each, because of his deeply flawed nature, can compel from some of us severe condemnation. Each, despite his deeply flawed nature, can compel from others of us high praise. Probably in most who observe their tragedies, antipathy and sympathy for these heroes tend to be strangely mixed and any admiration for them tends to be tempered by a knowledge that it cannot easily be explained. There is nobility to be found in Timon, Macbeth, Antony, and Coriolanus, but in the main it seems inseparable from their flaws, and an admirer of that nobility may wonder whether he is not admiring the flaws themselves even while he sees that they are flaws.

★ ★ ★

Shakespeare seems willing to make it hard for us to admire, even while he asks us to admire, these tragic individualists who as they impel themselves toward catastrophe are totally self-absorbed, Timon and Coriolanus blindly, Antony and Cleopatra wilfully. All are children of folly. All are at times made ridiculous, and all are frequently enough subjected to ridicule at the hands of associates. . . . But when we do admire these children of folly, we remember that though they are ridiculed in their dramas, they are also praised, and praised in no mean terms. Taints and honors "wage equal" with them, and despite their faults they are counted rare spirits.

Shakespeare's Tragic Frontier The World of His Final Tragedies. 1950. Chap. I.

[146] *James Russell Lowell*

In the modern tragedy [as opposed to the Greek], certainly in the four greatest of Shakespeare's tragedies, there is still something very like Destiny, only the place of it is changed. It is no longer above man, but in him; yet the catastrophe is as sternly foredoomed in the characters of Lear, Othello, Macbeth, and Hamlet as it could be by an infallible oracle. In Macbeth, indeed, the Weird Sisters introduce an element very like Fate; but generally it may be said that with the Greeks the character is involved in the action, while with Shakespeare the action is evolved from the character. In the one case, the motive of the play controls the personages; in the other, the chief personages are in themselves the motive to which all else is subsidiary.

"Shakespeare Once More." *North American Review*. 1868. *Among My Books*. 1870.

[147] *John Palmer*

Shakespeare might well have said of all his tragedies: In my end is my beginning. He moves to a point determined from the outset by the inexorable play of character and circumstance, and yet contrives to make every step towards his conclusion seem like the adventure of a free spirit. He thus reproduces with fidelity the ultimate paradox of life itself, namely a constant opposition of free-will with necessity.

Political Characters of Shakespeare. 1945. Chap. V.

[148] *John Lawlor*

But in one great respect the modern and the Elizabethan are not far apart. 'Happiness' as 'but the occasional episode in a general drama of pain' may not be unshakeable doctrine. But it is very like life as human beings encounter it in every age. So the older serious drama, 'tragedie' and tragedy alike, may still speak to us with the note of the authentic. Men must endure; the necessity of playing the Stoic; even the lesson of fortitude rubricated for us in the old tragedy of 'blood will have blood'—all seem to us to partake of the real. Pathos is certainly a dominant characteristic of Elizabethan imagining—the presentation of man as in some measure doomed. But, equally, we are never far from the resolution that if man is tied to a stake then he must 'fight the course'. Thus apparent opposites meet. The strength of Shakespearian tragic work in particular is that it offers no easily established relationship between what we are and what we must endure. It, least of all, need fear any diminution of power over a modern audience. The freedom of the tragic chooser is no mere doctrine for philosophical scrutiny; rather, Shakespeare's penetration into the mind of his choosers is part of the evidence on which any doctrine of choice in the real world must be founded.

The Tragic Sense in Shakespeare. 1960. Chap. IV.

[149] *H. B. Charlton*

Shakespearian tragedy is profoundly spiritual, and yet in no real sense is it at all religious. To say that it is entirely humanist is to invite a misunderstanding of its scope. It is almost completely confined to life as the human experience of living. In its whole ambit, it takes life as a manifestation of the phenomena which are the substance of morality. But it is occupied with life as life is lived in a universe wherein mightier forces than those of man are perpetually exerting their powers in shaping the lot of mankind. These are the vast circumambient mysteries. In their ways, they are too inscrutable to be resolved into any but the simplest and vaguest theological formulary, and their complicity in making man's destiny is so indirect and so remote that, as divinities, they have no assessable or definable rôle in the overt plan of Shakespeare's tragedies. Nor does that plan presuppose or promise ampler and more gratifying revelation of the nature of God or of the gods. At farthest, it vaguely apprehends that the ultimate arbiters cannot be hostile to man's search for goodness, though they leave to man himself the immense rigour of the strife. Shakespeare's abiding interest is in the absorbing spectacle of this effort. His preoccupation is moral, and not religious. In his normal day-to-day existence, there is no reason to suspect that Shakespeare was not a good Elizabethan Anglican: but the ideal world in which he moved when he was imaginatively excited was the world of man and of morality, not that of the gods and of theology.

Yet Shakespeare's moral world is not inconsistent with a universe capable of being apprehended religiously. At all events, and without distorting its outlines, hosts of men have fitted it into their own sectarian dogmas. Predominantly, however, Shakespeare's major concern is that of the humanist. But it is that of a humanist whose imaginative grasp is wider than his rational comprehension, and who therefore is always too conscious of the elusive mystery of things ever to be a consistent rationalist or even to be professedly an agnostic. For he has an unswerving faith. It is faith in the mysterious spirit of man.

Shakespearian Tragedy. 1948. Chap. VIII.

[150] *W. H. Auden*

To the Greeks, suffering and misfortune are signs of the displeasure of the gods and must therefore be accepted by men as mysteriously just. One of the commonest kinds of suffering is to be compelled to commit crimes, either unwittingly, like the parricide and incest of Oedipus, or at the direct command of a god, like Orestes. These crimes are not what we mean by sins because they are against, not with, the desire of the criminal. But in Shakespeare, suffering and misfortune are not in themselves proofs of Divine displeasure. It is true that they would not occur if man had not fallen into sin, but, precisely because he has, suffering is an inescapable element in life—there is no man who does not suffer—to be accepted, not as just in itself, as a penalty proportionate to the particular sins of the sufferer, but as an occasion for grace or as a process of purgation. Those who try to refuse suffering not only fail to avoid it but are plunged deeper into sin and suffering. Thus, the difference between Shakespeare's tragedies and comedies is not that the characters suffer in the one and not in the other, but that in comedy the suffering leads to self-knowledge, repentance, forgiveness, love, and in tragedy it leads in the opposite direction into self-blindness, defiance, hatred.

The audience at a Greek tragedy are pure spectators, never participants; the sufferings of the hero arouse their pity and fear, but they cannot think, "Something similar might happen to me," for the whole point in a Greek tragedy is that the hero and his tragic fate are exceptional. But all of Shakespeare's tragedies might be called variations on the same tragic myth, the only one which Christianity possesses, the story of the unrepentant thief, and anyone of us is in danger of re-enacting it in his own way. The audience at a tragedy of Shakespeare's, therefore, has to be both a spectator and a participant, for it is both a feigned history and a parable.

"The Globe." *The Dyer's Hand and Other Essays.* 1962.

[151] *Arthur Sewell*

In the comedies, where the social sense was lightly but assuredly—and not so lightly in the so-called 'dark' comedies—affirmed, the Comic Muse was regulative. It corrected with a smile, with a touch of irony, and (as in *Twelfth Night*) with a little melancholy, the modest assaults made on social order and social decorum . . .

In the histories, even where disorder most threatens, we have a sure expectation that it will not triumph, and the order that will shortly be established always presides over our attitudes and hopes. The ideal of political order remains constant in the histories, and in terms of that ideal vision and character are formed. Vision remains itself and character undergoes no transforming change. Our attitudes are never at a loss, and when Henry V comes into his kingdom we know that at last we are where we had hoped to be.

In the comedies and the histories there is never any real doubt about the world-picture into which the characters must be fitted, and in terms of which the characters find identity. And in so far as this world-picture involves also a world beyond this world, it may be said that that other world is the Christian universe; but Shakespeare's concern in these plays is secular and social, and his vision scarcely comprehends the play of forces beyond the stage of Time. It is not in terms of the play of such metaphysical forces that character must be apprehended. There is little in the comedies that the Comic Muse cannot deal with: in the histories there is little that the Prince cannot take into account.

In the great tragedies, however, just as there is change and development within the character, so also is there change and development within the vision of the play. So far as character is concerned, the pattern of the tragedies has often been remarked upon. The hero is confronted by a situation with which the organization of his being is unable to cope. He loses his moral bearings; he is at a loss; his whole personality seems to disintegrate more and more wilfully towards destruction. In the end, chastened and changed, he is absolute for death. But there is also a parallel, perhaps an underlying, development of vision accompanying this process in character. This development reveals itself in a change in our attitudes, although it concerns something more than attitude. . . . In the tragedies the hero undergoes an experience which puts all our previous attitudes into question and which exacts from us, as from him, a transformation of vision which can accommodate and appropriate the new and uncovenanted experience.

If the tragic heroes could be apprehended in terms of the temporal and secular world, social and political judgements would be adequate to deal with them. The great Shakespearian tragedies, however, are what they are just because social and political judgements (though never wholly abrogated) tend to break down. Consequently we must say of Hamlet, Macbeth, Othello, and King Lear that in some part of their natures they belong not to the temporal world but to a world beyond the world, a universe outside time, and that in this way we must apprehend them. In other words, vision, fulfilling itself in these characters, is no longer contained within society, legal, moral, or political, but seeks, as it were, to transcend society, to judge the social judgement, to bring society and its judgements *sub specie aeternitatis.* So—Macbeth is a villain; but when Duncan lies dead in the next room we think not of the murder but of the horror of Macbeth's realization that he shall sleep no more. He is for the moment like a soul in hell, and this is hell, nor is he out of it, and we know a little more about hell because Macbeth has had a glimpse of it. These tragedies, then, all imply a metaphysical world in which what matters is not what men do to society but what they do to themselves. This is the major vision which seeks to fulfil itself in the tragic heroes.

Character and Society in Shakespeare. 1951. Chap. IV.

[152] *Bernard Spivack*

Although Iago is essentially an amoral figure, we fail to grasp the deepest moral *consequence* of his action upon his victims unless we can appreciate the full meaning of his assault upon the "holy cords" that express Shakespeare's vision of the Good that suffers destruction in all his great tragedies. They are the bonds that knit nature, human society, and the cosmos into hierarchic order and unity and create the divinely ordained harmony of the universe. In the little world of men they are those ties of duty, piety, and humane affection which give a religious meaning to all domestic and social relationships, for in Shakespeare "religion" frequently has this wider sense. Our typical modern view, by comparison, is fragmentary and limited. Having lost the vision of a spiritual destiny, we read into love and morality no higher purpose than private happiness inside the pitiful span of mortal life, create an exclusive secular absolute to define the meaning of society and the state, and display the desperate tendency to equate salvation with romantic love. Shakespeare's vision, by contrast, has a profound metaphysical reach. Everywhere in his plays, but particularly in his great tragedies, human behavior on every level of life and in every kind of relationship receives its moral definition from its adherence or lack of adherence to the spiritual harmony and order of the universe. It is all religion.

Filial piety, matrimonial love, fraternal loyalty, and the immutable social degrees under God's royal regent are spiritual alliances that express man's conformity with the divinely established order of the cosmos and create the health and happiness—the very possibility in fact—of human society . . .

The metaphysical range of his moral vision is the main literal and imaginative cargo of the great tragedies, controlling their origin and direction to a degree that still escapes us. The evil in each of them is much broader than simply the violation of private love and natural fealty between person and person. In each a great bond of piety, electric with cosmic meaning, is ruptured; the religious foundations of society are shaken and the universe is racked with disorder. A brother's murder, the unfaithfulness of a wife to the memory of her dead husband, filial ingratitude, the assassination of a king by his subject, the presumed adultery of a wife with her husband's friend—these are acts with infinite repercussion in the poet's ethical imagination. They violate the nature of man, the nature of society, the nature of the universe. It is in this deep sense that they all receive their great condemnation as *unnatural* acts. They are, in fact, all one crime. Their distinguishing details as separate malefactions dissolve and merge into a single large affront to the unity and harmony of the world. The bias of Shakespeare's choice for his great tragic themes and the depth of treatment he brings to them are a double consequence of his vision that evil in its greatest magnitude expresses division and disorder. This single burden of all the great tragedies, a meaning deeper than the actual deed of fraud or bloody violence, unites all their separate and literal crimes into a vision of metaphysical evil, single and undifferentiated.

Shakespeare and the Allegory of Evil The History of a Metaphor in Relation to His Major Villains. 1958. Chap. II.

[153] *Geoffrey Bush*

At the moment of death the secular vision of nature can go no further. There are no more natural causes or natural meanings; the philosophy of things as they are has nothing more to tell us. But it is at this moment that the religious vision turns to the second aspect of nature, a continuance beyond time and death, "spirituall, intelligible and the unchangeable beginning of motion and rest, or rather the vertue, efficient, the preserving cause of all things." Spenser looks toward another stage of certainty, and a time when no more change shall be; the religious argument proposes another way to be saved. There is hope of a different kind of knowledge, that does indeed carry blessings with it. And in *Hamlet* and *King Lear* there are suggestions of this further knowledge: there are hints that the tragic journey may convey the mind toward a manner of understanding that redeems the distress attaching to persons and things. There is something in Hamlet's story more than natural, if philosophy could find it out; the approach of the Ghost, A. C. Bradley says, is "a reminder or a symbol of the connexion of the limited world of ordinary experience with the vaster life of which it is but a partial appearance." So at the end, at Horatio's benediction, "we have an intimation of the same character, and a reminder that the apparent failure of Hamlet's life is not the ultimate truth concerning him." In the histories and comedies we look toward a perfect image of success; in *Othello* and *Macbeth* we witness total defeats. At the end of *Hamlet* and *King Lear* we reach moments that seem beyond success or failure. It seems, at the death of Hamlet and Lear, that nothing is here for tears; the vision passes beyond suffering and natural misfortune, until it is comforting and right that Hamlet will have no more to do with this harsh world, and that Kent should say at the death of Lear: "O, let him pass!" At Colonus, Oedipus prays: "Grant me then, goddesses, passage from life at last." Something of this thought is in our minds at the end of *Hamlet* and *King Lear;* there are phrases and intonations suggesting that all may be well, and that "To die, now," as Oedipus tells his daughters, "would not be so terrible."

Shakespeare and the Natural Condition. 1956. Chap. V.

[154] *Kenneth Muir*

The generalizations which have been made about Shakespearian tragedy—even those in Bradley's brilliant introductory chapter—do not seem to me to be very helpful, since the differences between one play and another are more significant than the resemblances. The sense of waste, for example, is apparent in all the tragedies, but the kind of waste differs greatly from play to play. We may discern a tragic flaw—a dram of eale—in all the tragic heroes, but there is such a difference between the flaw in Romeo and that in Richard III, or between that in Hamlet and that in Macbeth, that it becomes a difference in kind. Or, again, Professor G. R. Elliott's statement that all the tragic heroes fall through pride can be justified only on theological grounds. We must, as Mr. J. C. Maxwell says, 'grant artistic autonomy to the individual work'.

All the alterations which have been made in adapting Shakespeare to suit the tastes of later ages, and all the generalizations which have been imposed on his work, have been caused by timidity. The adaptors and the critics have shrunk from the appalling clarity of Shakespeare's vision. They have wanted to pretend that evil does not have certain inevitable consequences, so they have married Edgar to Cordelia, and restored Lear to his throne; or they have pretended that Othello was not really jealous, or that Iago is merely an abstraction; or they have denied Shakespeare's negative capability and turned him into a stoic or an Hegelian whose thesis and antithesis lead to a comfortable synthesis. But Shakespeare always refused to impose an ideological pattern on his material: the only pattern that emerges is an artistic one. As a poet he was primarily concerned with imposing order on chaos, with extracting the maximum of significance from the situation with which he was dealing. He might, if the material allowed, show that crime does not pay, or reveal that pride is destructive and self-love suicidal. But such morals are not imposed on his material: they emerge as the simple facts of life. He holds, as it were, a mirror up to nature.

"Shakespeare and the Tragic Pattern." Annual Shakespeare Lecture of the British Academy, 1958.

Romance

[155] *E. K. Chambers*

The chief difficulty in the theory, which traces the characteristics of Shakespeare's last dramatic manner to the imitation of Beaumont and Fletcher, seems to me to lie in its failure to account for the profound change of spiritual mood which underlies the transition from tragedy to romance. For years the soul of Shakespeare had trodden the abyss of vexed and gloomy speculation. From the questionings of *Macbeth* he had passed to the denials of *King Lear,* and had seen love of woman as the scourge of the world in *Antony and Cleopatra,* and honour of man as the mask of the egoist in *Coriolanus.* The last echo of the Titanic denunciation is in the half incoherent mutterings of *Timon of Athens;* and then, tentatively at first in *Pericles,* but fully and without hesitation in *Cymbeline,* comes this entirely new utterance, the expression of a mind at peace with itself and ready to accept the ordering of things with the contented optimism of an unembarrassed faith. *Cymbeline* is, as it were, a palinode to *King Lear.* The radiant whiteness of Cordelia, impotent of old to make head against the forces of evil, revisits earth again in Imogen, and broods like a dove over a *dénouement* in which unspotted purity and simple honesty come in the ultimate issue, after much vexation, to their own. The unanswered cosmic problems are laid aside, or take on new colours in the light of a regained faith. Life, which the purged eye once scanned with a splendid despair, is now seen only through a golden haze of sentiment. The broken harmonies are resolved before the close. . . .

I hope to give all credit to the critical principle which bids us remember that Shakespeare, in addition to being a great poet, was also an expert and adroit stage-manager. But I do not find it possible to ascribe so fundamental a metamorphosis to a mere desire to rival others in exploiting a dramatic convention, which had proved congenial to the easy temper of Anne of Denmark or the chivalrous instincts of the young Prince Henry. Surely to adopt such a theory would be to refuse a spiritual content alike to the tragedies and to the romances, and to see nothing either in *Hamlet* or in *The Tempest* but the product of an inventive brain intent on penny-knaves' delight. There must be more in it than this. The profound cleavage in Shakespeare's mental history about 1607–1608 must have been due to some spiritual crisis the nature of which it is only possible dimly to conjecture; some such process as that which in the psychology of religion bears the name of conversion; or perhaps some sickness of the brain which left him an old man, freed at last from the fever of speculation and well disposed to spend the afternoon of life in unexacting and agreeable dreams. This latter hypothesis would help also to explain the marked change of style which accompanies the change of dramatic purpose in the romances. In these complicated and incoherent periods, in these softened and unaccentuated rhythms, in these tender and evanescent beauties, I find less a deliberate attempt to reduce the declamation of the stage to the colloquial dialogue of daily life, than the natural outcome of relaxed mental energies, shrinking from the effort after the wrought and nervous rhythms of the past.

Introduction. *Cymbeline.* Red Letter Shakespeare. 1907. *Shakespeare: A Survey.* 1925.

[156] *Louis MacNeice*

Autolycus

In his last phase when hardly bothering
To be a dramatist, the Master turned away
From his taut plots and complex characters
To tapestried romances, conjuring
With rainbow names and handfuls of sea-spray
And from them turned out happy Ever-afters.

Eclectic always, now extravagant,
Sighting his matter through a timeless prism
He ranged his classical bric-à-brac in grottos
Where knights of Ancient Greece had Latin mottoes
And fishermen their flapjacks—none should want
Colour for lack of an anachronism.

A gay world certainly though pocked and scored
With childish horrors and a fresh world though
Its mainsprings were old gags—babies exposed,
Identities confused and queens to be restored;
But when the cracker bursts it proves as you supposed—
Trinket and moral tumble out just so.

Such innocence—In his own words it was
Like an old tale, only that where time leaps
Between acts three and four there was something born
Which made the stock-type virgin dance like corn
In a wind that having known foul marshes, barren steps,
Felt therefore kindly towards Marinas, Perditas . . .

Thus crystal learned to talk. But Shakespeare balanced it
With what we knew already, gabbing earth
Hot from Eastcheap—Watch your pockets when
That rogue comes round the corner, he can slit
Purse-strings as quickly as his maker's pen
Will try your heartstrings in the name of mirth.

O master pedlar with your confidence tricks,
Brooches, pomanders, broadsheets and what-have-you,
Who hawk such entertainment but rook your client

And leave him brooding, why should we forgive you
Did we not know that, though more self-reliant
Than we, you too were born and grew up in a fix?

Collected Poems. 1949.

[157] *Arthur Sewell*

The harmony between what had once been seen as opposites—between that Reason which makes for order and those appetites which enable continuance—is the major reconciliation, amongst so many others, in the Romances.

Character and Society in Shakespeare. 1951. Chap. VI.

[158] *E. M. W. Tillyard*

Examining the bare plots rather than the total impression of the last three plays, we find in each the same general scheme of prosperity, destruction, and re-creation. The main character is a King. At the beginning he is in prosperity. He then does an evil or misguided deed. Great suffering follows, but during this suffering or at its height the seeds of something new to issue from it are germinating, usually in secret. In the end this new element assimilates and transforms the old evil. The King overcomes his evil instincts, joins himself to the new order by an act of forgiveness or repentance; and the play issues into a fairer prosperity than had first existed.

Shakespeare's Last Plays. 1938. Chap. II.

[159] *Patrick Cruttwell*

. . . if we look at these [last] plays not from the viewpoint of afterwards, but as Shakespeare came to them himself, from what he had written before them and not knowing what was to come after, it will not be as an end, but as a new beginning, that we shall see them. They have many of the signs of an artist who is feeling his way towards a new use of his medium; they are experimental. There is never in them the kind of uncertainty found in the problem-plays, springing from a real confusion about life and values; the values here are as firm as in the great tragedies: but there *is* an exhilarating quality of surprise and searching and discovery. If Shakespeare had lived, if he had continued to write, these plays might be seen as "bridge-poems" in his career as the *Second Anniversarie* in Donne's; what they would have led to we must try to decide from themselves.

★ ★ ★

What Shakespeare seems to have been moving towards was a kind of dramatic poetry quite unlike anything he had written before. It would have lived in the world of allegory and symbolism, but behind it, giving it backbone and force, would have been a lifetime of experience. It would have been less concerned with human beings as such, and more with human passions in their pure states: virtues and vices, good and evil, "the two contrary states of the human soul" (in Blake's phrase). This is the general point at which a parallel with Donne's *Anniversaries* might be legitimately made. Both Shakespeare and Donne had worked through a pre-occupation with real (i.e., particular, individual) experience towards a poetry which attempts to distil an essence out of the experience and also to transcend it.

★ ★ ★

A quality common to all these plays is one that might be called *extremeness*. Half-tones and qualifications are missing; this is a poetry, as it were, of primary colours.

★ ★ ★

So with all the characters (that word, with its suggestion of "reality", is not the word for them): that these are absolutes and not real people, can be seen by the fact that their behaviour, however inconsistent—and it is hopelessly inconsistent—with their natures as described, is not regarded as in any way demanding a change in one's verdict on their natures. Victorian critics were wont to sigh heavily over the fate of poor Imogen, united to such an unworthy husband as Posthumus; the truth is that he is not meant to be in the least unworthy: on the contrary, he is presented as the one man in the world who *is* worthy of her. He is perfect good, for a time corrupted and almost ruined by the perfect, and monstrous, evil of Iachimo. And when Leontes' jealousy has done its work, killing his son and (as he thinks) killing also his wife, Paulina breaks off her bitter reproaches with words which a modern reader is apt to feel can only be taken as ironic—"he is toucht to th' Noble heart." But ironic they are not: he *is* "noble", always has been, and always will be. Noble, but corrupted: which makes the corruption more dreadful. So, too, the death of his son is explained as caused by the same, inherent nobleness . . . To complain, as commonsense would, that a small boy does not go into a decline and die because his parents quarrel, would clearly be as irrelevant as to object that Elizabeth Drury [whose early death Donne memorialized in "The Second Anniversarie"] had hardly had time to practise the virtue of chastity. The death of Mamillius is not the death of a small boy; it is the death of innocence. The death of Elizabeth Drury is not (in the poem) the death of a girl; it is the death of goodness.

In these plays, one feels that the meaning which Shakespeare is striving to express lies almost beyond the capacity of a drama filled only with human "characters": hence the monstrous, in Caliban and almost in Cloten—who is virtually a monster, a "thing", not a man, as the first scene describes him.[1] This quality of monstrousness enters even into others, not in themselves hideous or evil. Evil invades them like a spirit—uninvited, it seems, by anything in their "characters"; as the age would have put it, they seemed "possessed". No other plays of Shakespeare render evil with quite the same kind of unmotivated purity as these do; the evil of Claudius and Iago, in contrast, was seen as entirely human and explainable. The remorse of Claudius, Iago's explanations of his own motives (whether we credit them or not), put their evil within the scope of human experience, comprehensible both by something outside and by something within themselves; but Leontes' jealousy, Iachimo's challenge and treachery, and Posthumus' crediting of his story, have motives so flimsy that they can, and in practice must, be disregarded. What is more dwelt on in these plays, and rendered with far greater force, than in any of the earlier work, is evil as a corrupter of the mind and imagination—of the soul, in fact. This aspect of it did, of course, exist, and exist very strongly, in earlier plays, as in the evil of Macbeth; but there the imaginative corruption is much more adequately, more realistically, balanced by actual events: what Macbeth *does* is good enough motive for what he *feels.* The jealousy of Leontes and Posthumus, so ill-based in fact, releases a flood of foul imaginings whose extraordinary physical violence seems completely disproportionate to what set it going, to the "nobility" of the men who pour it out, and to the loves which it defiles. They seem to throw themselves, at once and eagerly, as if this were what they really wanted, into a nightmare

[1] Iachimo also is thus described: "slight thing of Italy".

of obscenity . . . Though it seems unjustified, for these plays as for any of Shakespeare's work, to use theological terms or to fancy that Shakespeare thought in such terms, one does feel that here is being presented a "state" rather than a human being: the state of damnation, as its victims present the state of blessedness. The pure evil of these imaginings is put beside the pure good of the women who are falsely accused. . . .

The Shakespearean Moment and Its Place in the Poetry of the 17th Century. 1954. Chap. 3.

II. The Individual Plays

All's Well That Ends Well

[160] *Samuel Johnson*

I cannot reconcile my heart to *Bertram;* a man noble without generosity, and young without truth; who marries *Helen* as a coward, and leaves her as a profligate: when she is dead by his unkindness, sneaks home to a second marriage, is accused by a woman whom he has wronged, defends himself by falshood, and is dismissed to happiness.

The Plays of William Shakespeare. 1765. Vol. III.

[161] *Samuel Taylor Coleridge*

I cannot agree with the solemn abuse which the critics have poured out upon Bertram . . . He was a young nobleman in feudal times, just bursting into manhood, with all the feelings of pride of birth and appetite for pleasure and liberty natural to such a character so circumstanced. Of course he had never regarded Helena otherwise than as a dependant in the family; and of all that which she possessed of goodness and fidelity and courage, which might atone for her inferiority in other respects, Bertram was necessarily in a great measure ignorant. And after all, her *primâ facie* merit was the having inherited a prescription from her old father the Doctor, by which she cures the King,—a merit, which supposes an extravagance of personal loyalty in Bertram to make conclusive to him in such a matter as that of taking a wife. Bertram had surely good reason to look upon the king's forcing him to marry Helena as a very tyrannical act. Indeed, it must be confessed that her character is not very delicate, and it required all Shakspeare's consummate skill to interest us for her; and he does this chiefly by the operation of the other characters,—the Countess, Lafeu, &c. We get to like Helena from their praising and commending her so much.

Table-Talk. 1835. Raysor II, 356-57.

[162] *John Masefield*

The play is undoubtedly about a woman who twice puts the man whom she loves into an intolerable position, which nothing but a King can end by intolerable edict. Few can read, or see, the play with any hope of the possibility of happiness in a couple so married.

William Shakespeare. 1954.

[163] *M. C. Bradbrook*

Bertram is very young, perhaps seventeen or eighteen at most, left without a father's direction and highly conscious of his position. He is handsome, courageous, winning in manners; but also an inveterate liar. Yet the Elizabethan code of honour supposed a gentleman to be absolutely incapable of a lie. To give the lie was the deadliest of insults, not to be wiped out but in blood. Honour was irretrievably lost only by lies or cowardice; a gentleman, as Touchstone remembered, swore by his troth, as a knight by his honour. Crimes of violence were less dishonourable: the convicted liar was finished socially. Bassanio, though he thinks of a lie at the end, to get himself out of an awkward situation, does not utter it.

Bertram's fall is due to ill company: Parolles, or Words, another character of Shakespeare's own invention, is perceived in the end by Bertram himself to be the Lie incarnate, a fact which everyone else has known from the beginning. He is that principal danger of noble youth, the flatterer and misleader, the base companion against whom all books of behaviour issued lengthy warning. The relation of Bertram and Parolles resembles that which every one except Prince Hal takes to exist between himself and Falstaff. Parolles claims to be both courtier and soldier but his courtship is entirely speech, as his soldiership is entirely dress. Even the clown calls him knave and fool to his face; he is ready to play the pander, and at the end he crawls to the protection of old Lafeu, the first to detect and, with provocative insults, to 'uncase' him.

The model of a perfect courtier is set before the young man by the King, in a 'mirror' or portrait of his father.

★ ★ ★

By making his social climber a woman Shakespeare took a good deal of the sting out of the situation. The question of blood and descent versus native worth was an ancient subject of debate on the stage: indeed the first secular play to survive, *Fulgens and Lucres,* deals with precisely this matter. Here the lady's verdict was given for the worthy commoner against the degenerate nobleman. Though noble descent was prized as giving a disposition to virtue, and the opportunity of good education and good examples, yet 'one standard commonplace on nobility took shape; that lineage was not enough, but that the son of a noble house should increase and not degrade the glory of his ancestors'.[8]

Hellen has been conscious throughout of her humble station, and has urged the Countess that though she loves Bertram she would not have him till she should deserve him (I. 3. 199). Before and after marriage she thinks of Bertram as her 'master' as well as her lord, a title Parolles will not give him. It was within the power of the King to confer honour where he chose; and Hellen had already been ennobled in a superior way by being marked out as the instrument of Heaven towards the King's recovery.

★ ★ ★

The customary formula when presenting young people to each other in such circumstances was, 'Can you like of this man?', 'Can you like of this maid?', in other words, can you make a harmonious marriage? Love was not expected. If Bertram is thought to show peculiar delicacy in demanding passion as the basis of marriage, he removes all such notions at the end of the play by his alacrity in accepting Lafeu's daughter, a match which the King had planned since their childhood. In the original story, Beltramo protests his unwillingness but he does not defy the King, nor does he recant as Bertram so abjectly does under the King's threats, protesting that he now sees Hellen to be ennobled by the royal choice. The King's fury, far more reasonable than old Capulet's when Juliet exercises a right of rejection, depends on his, and everyone else's conviction that Hellen is 'vertuous' and the special favourite of heaven. Not

[8] H. T. Price. "Mirror-Scenes in Shakespeare," *J. Q. Adams Memorial Studies,* ed. J. McManaway and others. 1948.

only his king but his mother accepts it. That Bertram should misprize her is not in keeping with the decorum of the play. This is not *Romeo and Juliet;* it is written upon quite different premises, the social premises which that play so pointedly omits. And Bertram has no precontract; for his vamped-up excuse in the fifth act that he was really in love with Mademoiselle Lafeu is patently one of his fibs. He dislikes Hellen on social, not personal grounds. He is being wilful; and in running away after the marriage ceremony, he is evading obligations which are imposed by the Church as well as the State, as Diana does not fail to recall to him (4. 2. 12–13).

Shakespeare and Elizabethan Poetry. 1952. Chap. X.

[164] *Katherine Mansfield*

The First Lord is worth attending to. One would have thought that his speeches and those of the Second Lord would have been interchangeable; but he is a very definite, quick-cut character. Take, for example, the talk between the two in Act IV Scene III. The Second Lord asks him to let what he is going to tell dwell darkly with him.

First Lord: 'When you have spoken it, 'tis dead, and I am the grave of it.'

And then his comment:

'How mightily sometimes we make us comforts of our losses.'

And this is most excellent:

'The web of our life is of a mingled yarn, good and ill together; our virtues would be proud if our faults whipped them not; and our faults would despair if they were not cherished by our virtues.'

I like the temper of that extremely–and does it not reveal the man? Disillusioned and yet–amused–worldly, and yet he has feeling. But I see him as–quick, full of life, and marvellously at his ease with his company, his surroundings, his own condition, and the whole small, solid earth. He is like a man on shipboard who is inclined to straddle just to show (but not to *show off*) how well his sea-legs serve him. . . .

The Clown–'a shrewd knave and an unhappy'–comes to tell the Countess of the arrival of Bertram and his soldiers.

'Faith, there's a dozen of 'em, with delicate fine hats, and most courteous feathers, that bow and nod the head at every man.'

In that phrase there is all the charm of soldiers on prancing, jingling, dancing horses. It is a veritable little pageant. With what an air the haughty (and intolerable) Bertram wears his two-pile velvet patch—with what disdain his hand in the white laced French glove tightens upon the tight rein of his silver charger. Wonderfully sunny, with a little breeze. And the Clown, of course, sees the humour of this conceit. . . .

Parolles is a lovable creature, a brave little cock-sparrow of a ruffian.

. . . 'I am now sir, muddied in Fortune's mood, and smell somewhat strong of her strong displeasure.'

I must say Helena is a terrifying female. Her virtue, her persistence, her pegging away after the odious Bertram (and disguised as a pilgrim—so typical!) and then telling the whole story to that *good* widow-woman! And that tame fish Diana. As to lying in Diana's bed and enjoying the embraces meant for Diana—well, I know nothing more sickening. It would take a respectable woman to do such a thing. The worst of it is I can so well imagine . . . for instance acting in precisely that way, and giving Diana a present afterwards. *What* a cup of tea the widow and D. must have enjoyed while it was taking place, or did D. at the last moment want to cry off the bargain? But to forgive such a woman! Yet Bertram would. There's an espèce de mothers-boyisme in him which makes him stupid enough for anything.

The Old King is a queer old card—he seems to have a mania for bestowing husbands. As if the one fiasco were not enough, Diana has no sooner explained herself than he begins:

> 'If thou be'st yet a fresh uncropped flower
> Choose thou thy husband, and I'll pay thy dower.'

I think Shakespeare must have seen the humour of that. It just—at the very last moment of the play, puts breath into the old fool.

Journal of Katherine Mansfield. 1921. Ed. J. Middleton Murry. 1954.

Antony and Cleopatra

[165] *Samuel Taylor Coleridge*

The highest praise or rather form of praise, of this play which I can offer in my own mind, is the doubt which its perusal always occasions in me, whether it is not in all exhibitions of a giant power in its strength and vigor of maturity, a formidable rival of the *Macbeth*,

Lear, Othello, and *Hamlet. Feliciter audax* is the motto for its style comparatively with his other works, even as it is the general motto of all his works compared with those of other poets. Be it remembered too, that this happy valiancy of style is but the representative and result of all the material excellencies so exprest.

This play should be perused in mental contrast with Romeo and Juliet;—as the love of passion and appetite opposed to the love of affection and instinct. But the art displayed in the character of Cleopatra is profound in this, especially, that the sense of criminality in her passion is lessened by our insight into its depth and energy, at the very moment that we cannot but perceive that the passion itself springs out of the habitual craving of a licentious nature, and that it is supported and reinforced by voluntary stimulus and sought-for associations, instead of blossoming out of spontaneous emotion.

Notes on the Tragedies. Raysor I, 86.

[166] *G. B. Shaw*

Shakespear's Antony and Cleopatra must needs be as intolerable to the true Puritan as it is vaguely distressing to the ordinary healthy citizen, because, after giving a faithful picture of the soldier broken down by debauchery, and the typical wanton in whose arms such men perish, Shakespear finally strains all his huge command of rhetoric and stage pathos to give a theatrical sublimity to the wretched end of the business, and to persuade foolish spectators that the world was well lost by the twain.

"Better than Shakespear?" Preface. *Three Plays for Puritans.* 1900. IX. xxx–xxxi.

[167] *Willard Farnham*

In writing the closing scenes of *Antony and Cleopatra* Shakespeare pays his compliments in two directions with marked evenhandedness, now to the tradition that Cleopatra was really moved to end her life by concern for herself and her honor, and now to the tradition that she was really moved to do so by love for Antony. His evenhandedness can be exasperating to anyone bent upon determining whether his Cleopatra does or does not die as one of Cupid's saints; he takes and uses effectively almost everything to be found in either tradition.

★ ★ ★

Obviously, an advocate who would have Shakespeare's Cleopatra enrolled in the catalogue of Cupid's saints can made a case for canonization. Having many times previously sworn her love for Antony, she dies with that "Husband, I come" and that "O Antony!" upon her lips. It may be argued that these words, spoken at the moment when she would naturally reveal whatever lies deepest in her heart, show that her love for Antony has come to be the center of her being. She seems to think of herself as winning the right to call Antony husband by demonstrating, in the face of defeat and threatened dishonor, the courage to make a Roman exit from life such as he has made. She visualizes Antony as rousing himself in the next world to praise her "noble act" and mock the "luck of Caesar."

But, just as obviously, a Devil's advocate can make a case against canonization. Cleopatra seems to have thought of escaping Caesar's triumph by suicide before Antony gives her his Roman example of suicide. Before Antony dies she seems quite capable of deciding her fate independently. After he dies she prolongs her stay in the world that he has deserted, and she ends that stay only after she is absolutely certain that Caesar plans to lead her in triumph. As she makes her decision to end her life, she says nothing of a desire to rejoin Antony or a desire to do what Antony would approve, but talks only of being noble to herself. It seems that the self to which she is to be noble means far more to her than her children, and we may therefore all the more readily believe that it means more than Antony. As for the "Husband, I come" and the "O Antony!" of the death scene, it may be effectively argued by the heartless critic that in these words an ever-histrionic Cleopatra is dramatizing her exit from the world with a fine show of sentiment.

Perhaps it is the Devil's advocate who in the way of reason can make the better case. He has an advantage in that he argues from both words and actions of Cleopatra's, not merely from words, as his opponent does.

But by following reason coldly the Devil's advocate may arrive at a condemnation of Cleopatra that Shakespeare will not support. The beauty and sublimity of the poetry given to her upon more than one occasion when she speaks of what Antony means to her must be felt and duly taken into account by the critic if the Cleopatra whom he judges is to remain Shakespeare's. This beauty and this sublimity are parts of a certain splendor lent by Shakespeare to his heroine which persistently refuses to be written off as in every way false. If we are to understand that the love of Cleopatra for Antony, like her character, continues to be deeply flawed to the end of her life, we are nevertheless to understand that, like her character, it has its measure of nobility. If Cleopatra never comes to have a love for Antony to match his love for her, she at least comes to have magnificent visions of what it would be like to achieve such a love, and her climactic vision leads her to call him husband as she dies.

Shakespeare seems to have done his poetic best to make us feel that the full achievement of Cleopatra in love is a dark matter, dark perhaps even to her, but that though she very possibly does not attain to a noble constancy in love, she does attain to a noble aspiration in love. Also, Shakespeare seems to have done his poetic best to make us sense in the "immortal longings" of Cleopatra a paradox to cap the other paradoxes in her character—a paradox which gives her the visions of a daughter of the game at the same time that it gives her those of a constant wife.

Shakespeare's Tragic Frontier The World of His Final Tragedies. 1950. Chap. IV.

[168] *Harold S. Wilson*

Against all this is arrayed the power of the West, the greatness of Rome as represented in the heir of Julius Caesar, calm, cold, judicious, ruthlessly efficient, far too astute to be beguiled either through his own vices or through trusting other men, a Caesar greater than Julius Caesar if success is the measure of greatness—as many think; a man who is lucky because he never forgets himself, never makes a mistake, never shows weakness, never yields an inch; a man who loves his sister Octavia because she is part of his own grandeur, because, even though she becomes the wife of Antony and loves him, she remains Caesar's sister, and everything that is Caesar's must be inviolate, sacred, the gaze and wonder of the world; a man who is terrible because he seems invincible, to himself as to us. He is apparently without scruple—he would delude Cleopatra with his seeming magnanimity and consideration for her dignity, to exhibit her in triumph on his return to Rome, if he could; little concerned with "honour," which Antony holds so high, he never considers Antony's challenge seriously, never thinks of an obligation of generosity to his foes—like Achilles in *Troilus and Cressida,* except that Achilles is a savage while Octavius is highly civilized, dignified, kingly, not without understanding of the greatness of Antony and of what his love for Cleopatra means, but utterly without love himself, unless for himself. Yet even self-love hardly seems a clue to Octavius, for self-love should signify vanity and he appears to have none. Rather, he has a god-like impersonality, an unassailable sense of righteousness in his dealings with Antony, a god-like singleness of purpose. There is no apparent irony in the portrait of Octavius; and we see that he *can* make his power prevail, that he *is* invincible. We know that the historical Octavius was not so great a man as Julius Caesar, and Shakespeare surely knew this, too; but it did not suit his dramatic purpose in this play to make Octavius fully understandable, with human weaknesses as well as formidable strength. He remains an enigmatic figure, implacable, menacing, cold, as the historical Octavius doubtless was; but a power rather than a person, a function of the developing action, the nemesis of Antony and Cleopatra, the tragic measure of their human limitation.

⋆ ⋆ ⋆

That the love of Antony and Cleopatra cannot prevail against the ambition of Caesar is the tragic theme of the play. But the greatness of their love shines forth the more clearly because the antagonist who defeats them, though shrewd, ruthless, lucky, and exceedingly formidable, is so obviously without a shred of the generosity, the heroic humanity, the careless grandeur of the lovers. Foolish mortals they are, and the gods punish them for their folly; but theirs is the kind of human dignity that the gods respect. The qualities of Octavius, we may recognize with chagrin, are the virtues that make for success in this world; but there need be no bitterness in the recognition, for we see likewise how paltry is the world of Octavius, as paltry as the man who wins it, whose unheroic measure is sufficiently indicated by the attempt to imagine him succeeding Antony as the lover of Cleopatra.

On the Design of Shakespearian Tragedy. University of Toronto Press, 1957. Chap. VI.

[169] *Harley Granville-Barker*

We do not, as we have noted, see the re-uniting of the lovers; we find her at a nagging match with Enobarbus, and turned, with her Antony, to something very like a shrew. And if to the very end she stays for him an unguessed riddle, 'cunning past man's thought,' there is much in which Shakespeare is content to leave her so for us—thereby to manifest her the more consummately. By what twists of impulse or of calculation is she moved through the three fateful days of swaying fortune? How ready was she to 'pack cards' with Caesar? What the final betrayal amounted to, that sent Antony raging after her, Shakespeare, it may be said, could not tell us, because he did not know; and her inarticulate terror at this point may therefore show us his stagecraft at its canniest. But in retrospect all this matters dramatically very little; what does matter is that as we watch her she should defy calculation.

It is futile, we know, to apply the usual moral tests to her, of loyalty, candour, courage. Yet because she shamelessly overacts her repentance for her share in that first defeat it by no means follows that she feels none. She lends an ear to Thidias, and the message to Caesar sounds flat treason; this is the blackest count against her. But soft speech costs nothing, and perhaps it was Caesar who was to be tricked. Can we detect, though, a new contempt for Antony as she watches him, his fury glutted by the torment of the wretched envoy? She might respect him more had he flogged her instead! Is there in the sadly smiling

Not know me yet?

with which she counters his spent reproach, and in her wealth of protest, something of the glib falsity of sated passion? Next morning she buckles on his armour and bids him good-bye like a happy child; but, his back turned:

He goes forth gallantly. That he and Caesar might
Determine this great war in single fight!
Then, Antony—! But now—?

It is a chilling postscript.

She is like Antony in this at least—and it erects them both to figures of heroic size—that she has never learnt to compromise with life, nor had to reconcile her own nature's extremes. To call her false to this or to that is to set up a standard that could have no value for her. She is true enough to the self of the moment; and, in the end, tragically true to a self left sublimated by great loss. The passionate woman has a child's ardours and a child's obliterating fears, an animal's wary distrust; balance of judgment none, one would say. But often, as at this moment, she shows the shrewd scepticism of a child.

Prefaces to Shakespeare. Second Series. 1930.

[170] *Maynard Mack*

Macbeth and *King Lear,* like *Othello* earlier, are dark plays, filled with actions taking place in what can only be called "dramatic" as well as literal night, a dark night of the soul engulfed by evil. *Antony and Cleopatra,* on the other hand, is a bright play. *Macbeth* and *King Lear,* too, are savage—if one fully responds to them, terrifying. There is no savagery in *Antony and Cleopatra;* it is moving, exhilarating, even exalting, but contains nothing that should tear an audience to tatters. The humor of *Macbeth* and *King Lear* is either grim or pitiful: a drunken porter at the gate of hell, a court jester shivering on a stormy heath. The humor of *Antony and Cleopatra* is neither grim nor pitiful, although sometimes acrid enough. Cleopatra is given qualities that make her a very unqueenly queen: she lies, wheedles, sulks, screams, and makes love, all with equal abandon. Antony is given qualities that make him in some senses more like an elderly playboy than a tragic hero. We are encouraged by Shakespeare in this play to disengage ourselves from the protagonists, to feel superior to them, even to laugh at them, as we rarely are with earlier tragic persons.

Against laughter, however, the playwright poises sympathy and even admiration. Tawdry though he has made these seasoned old campaigners in love and war, he has also magnified and idealized them, to the point at which their mutual passion becomes glorious as well as cheap. Antony, the play tells us, has "infinite virtue," Cleopatra "infinite variety." He is the "triple pillar of the world," she is the "day o' th' world." He seems a "plated Mars," she more beautiful than Venus. His guardian spirit is called "unmatchable," she is called a "lass unparalleled." He descends from the god Hercules, she from the moon-goddess Isis. She sees him as the sun and moon, lighting this "little O, th' earth"; Charmian sees her as the "Eastern star." When Antony cries Ho! "Like boys unto a muss, kings would start forth"; Cleopatra has a hand that "kings Have lipped, and trembled kissing." When Antony will swear an oath, he cries, "Let Rome in Tiber melt and the wide arch Of the ranged empire fall!" When Cleopatra will swear, she cries, "Melt Egypt into Nile! and kindly creatures Turn all to serpents." Antony, about to die, thinks of death as a continuing amour with Cleopatra: "Where souls do couch on flowers, we'll hand in hand, And with our sprightly port make the ghosts gaze." When Cleopatra is about to die, she sees death in the same transcendent terms: "Go, fetch My best attires. I am again for Cydnus, To meet Mark Antony."

★ ★ ★

[Of Enobarbus's portrait of Cleopatra]

This is clearly not a portrait of a mere intriguing woman, but a kind of absolute oxymoron: Cleopatra is glimpsed here as a force like the Lucretian Venus, whose vitality resists both definition and regulation. Yet enveloped as she is by Enobarbus's mocking tones, wise and faintly world-weary, calculating amusedly the effects of his words on these uninitiated Romans, she remains the more a trollop for that. His reliable anti-romanticism undercuts the picture he draws of her, and at the same time confirms it, because it comes from him.

The ambiguity of these lines extends to almost everything in the play. In the world the dramatist has given his lovers, nothing is stable, fixed, or sure, not even ultimate values; all is in motion. Seen from one point of view, the motion may be discerned as process, the inexorable march of causes and effects, exemplified in Antony's fall and epitomized by Caesar in commenting to Octavia on the futility of her efforts to preserve the peace: "But let determined things to destiny Hold unbewailed their way." Seen from another angle, the motion reveals itself as flux, the restless waxing and waning of tides, of moons, of human feeling. Especially of human feeling. Antony pursued Brutus to his death, we are reminded by Enobarbus, yet wept when he found him slain. So within the play itself Caesar weeps, having pursued Antony to his death; and Antony, desiring that Fulvia die, finds her "good, being gone"; and Enobarbus, seeking some way to leave his master, is heart-struck when he succeeds; and the Roman populace, always fickle, "Like to a vagabond flag upon the stream, Goes to and back, lackeying the varying tide, To rot itself with motion."

In such a context, it is not surprising that the lovers' passion is subject to vicissitudes, going to and back in ever more violent oscillations of attraction and recoil. . . . It is likewise not surprising that the play's structure should reflect, in its abrupt and numerous shifts of scene, so marked a quality of its leading characters—their emotional and psychological vacillation. Though these shifts have also met with criticism, some finding in them a serious threat to unity, they are easily seen in the theatre to be among the dramatist's means of conveying to us an awareness of the competing values by which the lovers, and particularly Antony, are torn.

★ ★ ★

Are we to take the high-sounding phrases which introduce us to this remarkable love affair in the play's first scene as amorous rant? . . . Or is there a prophetic resonance in that reference to "new heaven, new earth," which we are meant to remember when Cleopatra, dreaming of a transcendent Antony . . . consigns her baser elements to "baser life"? Does the passion of these two remain a destructive element to the bitter end, doomed like all the feeling in the play "to rot itself with motion"? Or, as the world slips from them, have they a glimmering of something they could not have earlier understood, of another power besides death "Which shackles accidents and bolts up change"? Is it "paltry to be Caesar," as Cleopatra claims, since "Not being Fortune, he's but Fortune's knave"? Or is it more paltry to be Antony, and, as Caesar sees it, "give a kingdom for a mirth," as well as, eventually, the world?

To such questions, *Antony and Cleopatra,* like life itself, gives no clear-cut answers. Shakespeare holds the balance even, and does not decide for us who finally is the strumpet of the play, Antony's Cleopatra, or Caesar's Fortune, and who, therefore, is the "strumpet's fool." Those who would have it otherwise, who are "hot for certainties in this our life," as Meredith phrased it, should turn to other authors than Shakespeare, and should have been born into some other world than this.

Introduction. *Antony and Cleopatra.* The Pelican Shakespeare. 1960.

As You Like It

[171] *Edward Dowden*

Shakspere, when he wrote this idyllic play, was himself in his Forest of Arden. He had ended one great ambition—the historical plays—and not yet commenced his tragedies. It was a resting-place. He sends his imagination into the woods to find repose. Instead of the courts and camps of England, and the embattled plains of France, here was this woodland scene, where the palmtree, the lioness, and the serpent are to be found; possessed of a flora and fauna that flourish in spite of physical geographers. There is an open-air feeling throughout the play. The dialogue, as has been observed, catches freedom and freshness from the atmosphere. "Never is the scene within-doors, except when something discordant is introduced to heighten as it were the harmony."* After the trumpet-tones of

*C. A. Brown. *Shakespeare's Autobiographical Poems,* p. 283.

Henry V. comes the sweet pastoral strain, so bright, so tender. Must it not be all in keeping? Shakspere was not trying to control his melancholy. When he needed to do that, Shakspere confronted his melancholy very passionately, and looked it full in the face. Here he needed refreshment, a sunlight tempered by forest-boughs, a breeze upon his forehead, a stream murmuring in his ears.

Shakspere, His Mind and Art. 1874. Chap. II.

[172] *Mrs. Jameson*

Everything about Rosalind breathes of "youth and youth's sweet prime." She is fresh as the morning, sweet as the dew-awakened blossoms, and light as the breeze that plays among them. She is as witty, as voluble, as sprightly as Beatrice; but in a style altogether distinct. In both, the wit is equally unconscious; but in Beatrice it plays about us like the lightning, dazzling but also alarming; while the wit of Rosalind bubbles up and sparkles like the living fountain, refreshing all around. Her volubility is like the bird's song; it is the outpouring of a heart filled to overflowing with life, love, and joy, and all sweet and affectionate impulses. She has as much tenderness as mirth, and in her most petulant raillery there is a touch of softness—"By this hand it will not hurt a fly!" As her vivacity never lessens our impression of her sensibility, so she wears her masculine attire without the slightest impugnment of her delicacy. Shakespeare did not make the modesty of his women depend on their dress, as we shall see further when we come to Viola and Imogen. Rosalind has in truth "no doublet and hose in her disposition." How her heart seems to throb and flutter under her page's vest! What depth of love in her passion for Orlando! whether disguised beneath a saucy playfulness, or breaking forth with a fond impatience, or half betrayed in that beautiful scene where she faints at the sight of his 'kerchief stained with his blood! Here her recovery of her self-possession—her fears lest she should have revealed her sex—her presence of mind, and quick-witted excuse—

I pray you, tell your brother how well I counterfeited—

and the characteristic playfulness which seems to return so naturally with her recovered senses,—are all as amusing as consistent. Then how beautifully is the dialogue managed between herself and Orlando! how well she assumes the airs of a saucy page, without throwing off her feminine sweetness! How her wit flutters free as air over every subject! With what a careless grace, yet with what exquisite propriety!

"Rosalind." *Characteristics of Women, Moral, Poetical, and Historical.* 1832. Vol. I.

[173] *G. B. Shaw*

The popularity of Rosalind is due to three main causes. First, she only speaks blank verse for a few minutes. Second, she only wears a skirt for a few minutes. . . . Third, she makes love to the man instead of waiting for the man to make love to her—a piece of natural history which has kept Shakespear's heroines alive, whilst generations of properly governessed young ladies, taught to say "No" three times at least, have miserably perished.

"Toujours Shakespear." *The Saturday Review.* 5 December 1896. XXIV, 282–83.

[174] *G. B. Shaw*

Rosalind is not a complete human being: she is simply an extension into five acts of the most affectionate, fortunate, delightful five minutes in the life of a charming woman. And all the other figures in the play are cognate impostures. Orlando, Adam, Jaques, Touchstone, the banished Duke, and the rest play each the same tune all through. This is not human nature or dramatic character; it is juvenile lead, first old man, heavy lead, heavy father, principal comedian, and leading lady, transfigured by magical word-music.

"At Several Theatres." *The Saturday Review.* 9 October 1897. XXV, 220–21.

[175] *S. C. Sen Gupta*

The peculiarity of Touchstone is that he is nothing if not a critic. He has been called a philosopher, but has no positive philosophy. Critical by temperament, he has had the training of a professional jester whose business it is to flout the world. He possesses a sharp insight and also a capacity for searching analysis, and it is this intellectual acumen which makes him critical of human absurdities in all spheres of life. He knows the weaknesses of courtiers whom he satirizes with relentless thoroughness. He is acquainted with their pomposity, their extravagance, and their cowardice. With his remarkable command of the grotesque, he easily reduces all exuberance to absurdity. His keen sense of humour does not spare even Rosalind whenever she transgresses the bounds of normality. . . . His comic sense is so acute and pervasive that it not only brings out the ludicrous element in the fantastic vagaries of love-lorn maidens or forsworn knights but reveals a core of absurdity even in the most normal and universal thing, the passage of time (II.vii.20–28). Poets discover the source of beauty in everything; Touchstone, whose gifts are the reverse of the poetical, travesties all that he comes across so that from his point of view life appears to be essentially ludicrous and grotesque. That is what makes him both a critic and a clown.

Shakespearian Comedy. 1950. Chap. V.

[176] *J. B. Priestley*

Jaques and Touchstone stand in somewhat similar relation to the rest of the company. They are "the critics," detached from the main action, observing, mocking. Whatever departs from sincerity receives a flick of the whip from them; or, if you will, they supply the chorus to the piece; one, the sad-suited gentleman, this somewhat eighteenth-century figure with his exquisite sensibility and his lack of real warm human sympathy, plays the part of cynical-sentimental-moralistic chorus; the other, motleying for more than mere beef and ale, an embassy from the Spirit of Comedy, supplies the comic chorus. But while these two seem to run together most of the way, Touchstone parodying to Jaques' applause, there is a very real and very important difference in their respective attitudes. Motley is a better critic than Melancholy. He is a better critic because, unlike Jaques, he does not completely detach himself from his fellow mortals but identifies himself with them; he does not say, in effect, "What beasts you are!" but "What fools we are!"; and so, like a true comic genius, he is universal. He does not stand entirely apart, but plays the courtier and the pastoral lover like the rest, only taking care that everything he does shall be plunged into his own atmosphere of exaggeration and absurdity; he parodies humanity, which looked at from one angle is fundamentally ridiculous, in his own activities and in his own person; and he does this not simply because he is a Fool, a professional humorist, but also because he is by temperament and inclination a kind of comic philosopher. In this leafy republic of Arden, with its moralising gentlemen, rhyming lovers, passionate shepherds, where so many moods and whims are being dandled throughout the long golden days, the Comic Spirit, scenting profitable negotiations, has established its embassy, and Touchstone, full-dressed in his motley, is the ambassador.

★ ★ ★

The relation between Touchstone and his stolid mistress is really nothing but the reverse side, the unpoetical, comic, gross side, of the relation between Orlando and Rosalind, all ardour and bloom and young laughter, beyond the reach of disillusion. Shake them up together and out of them both could be fashioned the actual relations between most men and women in this world; and Shakespeare, who knew most things, knew this too, and so gave us both sides of the question. By the time he came to create Touchstone, his comic relief had become something more than buffoonery flung in at random, it had become comment, criticism.

"Touchstone." *The English Comic Characters.* 1925.

Coriolanus

[177] *William Hazlitt*

Shakespear has in this play shewn himself well versed in history and state-affairs. *Coriolanus* is a store-house of political commonplaces. Any one who studies it may save himself the trouble of reading Burke's Reflections, or Paine's Rights of Man, or the Debates in both Houses of Parliament since the French Revolution or our own. The arguments for and against aristocracy or democracy, on the privileges of the few and the claims of the many, on liberty and slavery, power and the abuse of it, peace and war, are here very ably handled, with the spirit of a poet and the acuteness of a philosopher. Shakespear himself seems to have had a leaning to the arbitrary side of the question, perhaps from some feeling of contempt for his own origin; and to have spared no occasion of baiting the rabble. What he says of them is very true: what he says of their betters is also very true, though he dwells less upon it.—The cause of the people is indeed but little calculated as a subject for poetry: it admits of rhetoric, which goes into argument and explanation, but it presents no immediate or distinct images to the mind, 'no jutting frieze, buttress, or coigne of vantage' for poetry 'to make its pendant bed and procreant cradle in.' The language of poetry naturally falls in with the language of power. The imagination is an exaggerating and exclusive faculty: it takes from one thing to add to another: it accumulates circumstances together to give the greatest possible effect to a favourite object. The understanding is a dividing and measuring faculty: it judges of things not according to their immediate impression on the mind, but according to their relations to one another. The one is a monopolising faculty, which seeks the greatest quantity of present excitement by inequality and disproportion; the other is a distributive faculty, which seeks the greatest quantity of ultimate good, by justice and proportion. The one is an aristocratical, the other a republican faculty. The principle of poetry is a very anti-levelling principle. It aims at effect, it exists by contrast. It admits of no medium. It is everything by excess. It rises above the ordinary standard of sufferings and crimes. It presents a dazzling appearance. It shows its head turretted, crowned, and crested. Its front is gilt and blood-stained. Before it 'it carries noise, and behind it leaves tears.' It has its altars and its victims, sacrifices, human sacrifices. Kings, priests, nobles, are its train-bearers, tyrants and slaves its executioners.—'Carnage is its daughter.'—Poetry is right-royal. It puts the individual for the species, the one above the infinite many, might before right. A lion hunting a flock of sheep or a herd of wild asses is a more poetical object than they; and we even take part with the lordly beast, because our vanity or some other feeling makes us disposed to place ourselves in the situation of the strongest party. So we feel some concern for the poor citizens of Rome when they meet together to compare their wants and grievances, till Coriolanus comes in and with blows and big words drives this set of 'poor rats,' this rascal scum, to their homes and beggary before him. There is nothing heroical in a multitude of miserable rogues not wishing to be starved, or complaining that they are like to be so: but when a single man comes forward to brave their cries and to make them submit to the last indignities, from mere pride and self-will, our admiration of his prowess is immediately converted into contempt for their pusillanimity. The insolence of power is stronger than the plea of necessity. The tame submission to usurped authority or even the natural resistance to it has nothing to excite or flatter the imagination: it is the assumption of a right to insult or oppress others that carries an imposing air of superiority with it. We had rather be the oppressor than the oppressed. The love of power in ourselves and the admiration of it in others are both natural to man: the one makes him a tyrant, the other a slave. Wrong dressed out in pride, pomp, and circumstance, has more attraction than abstract right.

★ ★ ★

The care of the state cannot, we here see, be safely entrusted to maternal affection, or to the domestic charities of high life. The great have private feelings of their own, to which the interests of humanity and justice must courtesy. Their interests are so far from being the same as those of the community, that they are in direct and necessary opposition to them; their power is at the expense of *our* weakness; their riches of *our* poverty; their pride of *our* degradation; their splendour of *our* wretchedness; their tyranny of *our* servitude. If they had the superior knowledge ascribed to them (which they have not) it would only render them so much more formidable; and from Gods would convert them into Devils. The whole dramatic moral of *Coriolanus* is that those who have little shall have less, and that those who have much shall take all that others have left. The people are poor; therefore they ought to be starved. They are slaves; therefore they ought to be beaten. They work hard; therefore they ought to be treated like beasts of burden. They are ignorant; therefore they ought not to be allowed to feel that they want food, or clothing, or rest, that they are enslaved, oppressed, and miserable. This is the logic of the imagination and the passions; which seek to aggrandize what excites admiration and to heap contempt on misery, to raise power into tyranny, and to make tyranny absolute; to thrust down that which is low still lower, and to make wretches desperate: to exalt magistrates into kings, kings into gods; to degrade subjects to the rank of slaves, and slaves to the condition of brutes.

Characters of Shakespear's Plays. 1817.

[178] *B. Ifor Evans*

The contrast of the language of *Coriolanus* with that of *Antony and Cleopatra* is striking. Instead of magnificence and variety unending, there is what seems at first sight a flatness or aridity. The easiest explanation would be to suggest some creative exhaustion, as if Shakespeare had used up the resources of his imaginative association in *Antony and Cleopatra,* and now moved, with a drab bareness, through the later play. To judge thus would be to consider too severely, for the theme of *Coriolanus* is itself more intellectual, and constitutes a continual argument, into which the personal elements are allowed to intrude only to the extent to which they can modify the political theme. It would be as false to condemn the language of *Coriolanus* as being something left over from *Antony and Cleopatra,* as negative and inadequate, as it would be to condemn the later poetry of W. B. Yeats because it did not possess the obviously melodious qualities of his earlier lyrics. *Antony and Cleopatra* is based on a personal theme, made supremely more impressive because the whole of the world depends on the private actions and passions of the protagonist, but *Coriolanus* is a political theme and the personal relations intrude only to define and emphasise the nature of the political characters. Out of that contrast arises the difference in the language of the two plays.

The Language of Shakespeare's Plays. 1952. Chap. XII.

[179] *John Palmer*

'Coriolanus', as we have seen, is more exclusively concerned with politics than any other play he ever wrote. The politics are nevertheless in the last analysis incidental. Shakespeare is intent on persons, not on public affairs. His interest, when he writes of Coriolanus, as when he writes of Brutus or Henry or Richard, is in a human character who happens also to be a politician. There are more politics to be found in his plays than in those of any other dramatic writer. We invariably find, however, that his theme, as it takes shape and moves to a climax, is not essentially a political problem but the adventure of a human spirit. We discover, in fact, that Shakespeare, who wrote more genuinely political plays than any other dramatist before or since, is only indirectly concerned with the political principles and ideas in which they abound. Hazlitt refers to the arguments in 'Coriolanus' for and against aristocracy and democracy. There are no such arguments. There are only aristocrats and democrats. He refers to power and the abuse of it. There is no discussion of this problem. There is only a proud man who assumes the right to despise persons of a lesser breed. And, when the climax of the play is reached, we find that Shakespeare is presenting a conflict, not between private inclination and public duty, not between the merits of peace and war, not between party-feeling and patriotism, not between the privileges of the few and the claims of the many—not in fact between any of the political opposites mentioned by Hazlitt—but between the stubborn self-regarding pride of Caius Marcius Coriolanus and the promptings of great Nature which make it impossible for him to disregard a mother's intercession. If, as Hazlitt suggests, we were to read 'Coriolanus' as a substitute for Burke's 'Reflections' or Paine's 'Rights of Man' we should expect the climax of the play to be a grand confrontation of the aristocratic and popular parties; we should look for a statement of the principles at issue on both sides and a dramatic conflict between qualified representatives of those principles who knew what they were fighting for and loved what they knew. But Shakespeare gives us instead Menenius and First Citizen; a fable of the belly and its members from an old gentleman more conversable with the buttock of the night than with the forehead of the morning; some typical knavery on the part of a group of senators and a brace of tribunes; a few simple, good-natured men in the street who are disconcerted by a government which tries to obtain their support by equivocation and moved to a not unreasonable indignation against it by the leaders of the opposition. Here are politics but they appear as men walking. 'Coriolanus' is not the dramatisation of a political thesis. It is not a play in which the supreme conflict is one of political principle.

Political Characters of Shakespeare. 1945. Chap. V.

[180] *Algernon Charles Swinburne*

It is from first to last, for all its turmoil of battle and clamour of contentious factions, rather a private and domestic than a public or historical tragedy. As in *Julius Caesar* the family had been so wholly subordinated to the state, and all personal interests so utterly dominated by the preponderance of national duties, that even the sweet and sublime figure of Portia passing in her 'awful loveliness' was but as a profile half caught in the background of an episode, so here on the contrary the whole force of the final impression is not that of a conflict between patrician and plebeian, but solely that of a match of passions played out for life and death between a mother and a son. The partisans of oligarchic or democratic systems may wrangle at their will over the supposed evidences of Shakespeare's prejudice against this creed and prepossession in favour of that: a third bystander may rejoice in the proof thus established of his impartial indifference towards either: it is all nothing to the real point in hand. The subject of the whole play is not the exile's revolt, the rebel's repentance, or the traitor's reward, but above all it is the son's tragedy. The inscription on the plinth of this tragic statue is simply to Volumnia Victrix.

A Study of Shakespeare. 1880. "Third Period; Tragic and Romantic."

[181] *John Palmer*

Marcius, if you examine the scene [V.iii.] attentively, does not succumb to his mother's arguments but, again, to the rough edge of her tongue. In both scenes she appeals in vain to his reason and good sense. Then, giving him up as hopeless, she makes as though she would leave him to his own devices, with the result that he immediately collapses. This is a fundamental trait in the character of our hero. He is essentially the splendid oaf who has never come to maturity. His vanity in the field, his insolence to persons outside his own particular set, his intolerance of anything outside his special code of honour are more characteristic of an adolescent than a grown man. It is this, in fact, that makes his conduct, which would be intolerable in a responsible adult, so far acceptable as to qualify him for the part of a tragic hero.

Political Characters of Shakespeare. 1945. Chap. V.

[182] *Harold C. Goddard*

Coriolanus has often been taken as a political treatise in dramatic form. Its subject, in that case, is the struggle between the ruling and the oppressed classes, and Coriolanus himself is a typical tory who prefers the privileges of his class to the good of his country, as tories have been prone to do from time out of mind. It sounds plausible, but it will not do. Tories there are in this play—and a class struggle—but Coriolanus is not one of them. His one speech on custom—

Custom calls me to't.
What custom wills, in all things should we do't,
The dust on antique time would lie unswept,
And mountainous error be too highly heapt
For truth to o'er-peer,

—is sufficient to disqualify him once for all. And as for loyalty to his class, he comes to hate the members of it who acquiesced in his banishment worse, if anything, than the plebeians and their tribunes who engineered it. A comparison with its source will show that Plutarch's *Life of Coriolanus* fills the prescription of a plebeian-patrician treatise far better than Shakespeare's tragedy. It may be a political play, but its scheme is not so simple as that.

An opposite view holds that Shakespeare here, as usual, is just portraying an interesting and tragic individual. The fact that the background happens to be political is unimportant. But surely the politics of the play is far more than background, anything but incidental. The point is that Shakespeare does not divorce his politics from his general science of human nature, as we so often do. The children of this world are still in our generation wiser than the children of light, and it has been the tragedy of the twentieth century that the latter left it to the former to discover before they did that politics is just a branch of psychology—and to put that discovery to diabolical use. . . . Shakespeare was naturally unacquainted with twentieth-century psychiatry. Yet, whether by instinct or wisdom, what he sets down in this play with clinical precision is a case of not wholly normal mother-son relationship (the sort of thing that some critics have wrongly found in *Hamlet*). Until this is analyzed, it is futile to say anything about the politics of the play in the narrower sense.

★ ★ ★

A Mother like Volumnia would be a liability to any boy. She was the most unfortunate of mothers for such a rare and sensitive child as Caius Marcius evidently was. Whoever fancies him a young ruffian spoiling from the first for a fight must revise his picture. His mother herself says that, when he was yet "tender-bodied," he was so comely that, when she took him abroad, he was the focus of all eyes. Congenitally he must have been closer to a young poet than a young warrior. True, he grows up to be a prodigy of physical strength. "What an arm he has!" says one of Aufidius' servants. "He turned me about with his finger and his thumb as one would set up a top." But his grace is just as much stressed as his strength. It must have been more that of Helios than of Hephaestus, whatever it became under his mother's tutelage. The fact seems to be that Volumnia, who was a widow, played father as well as mother to her son and made the most of the double docility that comes from a child's natural affection for his mother and reverence for his father. Indeed, she was far more father than mother to him. What wonder that, beginning in his infancy, she could shape him into anything she liked! Praise for any audacity on his part seems to have been her main instrument, and praise can be as fatal to youth as blame. Who has not seen a child awkward and embarrassed at being openly commended in the presence of others?—and the finer the child's instincts the more marked the self-consciousness. Caius Marcius must have been like that, and retains as a man something of the same feeling:

> My mother,
> Who has a charter to extol her blood,
> When she does praise me grieves me.

His hatred of boasting or of hearing his own bravery lauded is generally diagnosed as inverted pride. It may be partly that, but it is much more the native modesty of a man who on instinct feels that "whatever praises itself but in the deed, devours the deed in the praise." And so, when we hear how the crude Volumnia ground her own ax on this sensitive boy, we are reminded of Blake's design, *Aged Ignorance,* in which an old dotard with a huge pair of scissors is clipping off the psyche-like wings of a boy who is struggling to escape. "The vilest abortionist," says Bernard Shaw in the same vein, "is he who attempts to mould a child's character." By that rule Volumnia qualifies as vilest of the vile. She all but succeeds in turning into a Hercules a child who evidently no more resembled Hercules by nature than Hamlet did in his own estimation. Furthermore, Hamlet was a grown man before his father set out to convert him to the doctrine of blood. And his father was then only a ghost. What chance, comparatively, had the infant Marcius against this portentous mother-father of flesh and blood? The man Coriolanus seems expressly drawn to record the results of the martial indoctrination of childhood.

★ ★ ★

Why did Coriolanus loathe the mob—not with the philosophic contempt of an Emerson nor with the defensive shrinking of a Debs, but with a positive and fierce abhorrence?

We hate—in that way—what we fear. And the more unconscious the fear the more intense the hatred. Coriolanus hated the mob because, without knowing it, he feared it. Why should he, of all men, fear it? Not physically at all, and not politically in any high degree. He feared it imaginatively and symbolically. To see this is to see into the very heart of the man.

Coriolanus is built on an antithesis, a figure and an anti-figure: mankind as a mass versus mankind as an organism. The ancient companion metaphors of the body politic and of man as a little kingdom identify the appetites and the slave class as the lowest strata, respectively, of the mind and of mankind. The slave becomes for this reason the inevitable symbol of the animal nature, and, conversely, the animal instincts are, psychologically, slaves. Hence emerges the symbolical equation *beast=mob=passion.* The mob *is* passion. The passions *are* a mob. It is so in mythology, it is so in dreams, it is so in poetry. The imaginative literature of all ages offers examples. In modern times the Russian classics, written under the czarist despotism, offer particularly striking ones.

When Anna Karenina, against her highest instincts, gives way to her lower ones with Vronsky, her dreams are haunted by a dirty unkempt peasant who clearly embodies for Tolstoy both her own lower nature and the class in Russia that Anna's class has injured. (We hate what we have hurt.) In *The Brothers Karamazov* the little peasant whom Ivan treads on and abandons in the snow before his interview with the devil, but whom he picks up and helps after his better instincts have conquered his worser ones, is a veritable barometer of Ivan's spiritual condition. And Chekhov's stories abound in the same symbolism.

Now *Coriolanus* is based on precisely these images. Marcius himself, molded from infancy by his mother, becomes a warrior against the fine grain of his nature. But offensive war is founded on the passions: on lust, on greed, on pride, and on revenge. In strict proportion to the violence his soul has undergone is the violence of Coriolanus' unconscious detestation of his lower nature. But being nothing of a psychologist, he projects his hatred of that lower nature into the mass of mankind, and sees it as a monster. The nauseous odor of it which he can never forget is the measure of his loathing for himself. The emotion it elicits goes far beyond the unpleasant reaction that the unpleasant smell itself might warrant.

That we may not miss his point, Shakespeare makes Coriolanus make it himself, though of course he does not realize what he is saying:

> For the mutable, rank-scented many, let them
> Regard me as I do not flatter, and
> *Therein behold themselves.*

A mob without gazing at a mob within. Each is looking in a glass.

What wonder that they hate each other! And the final proof that this diagnosis is correct is the fact that it is the word "traitor" that explodes Coriolanus as a match does a keg of powder. It touches the sorest spot in his soul, for he has been a traitor, not to Rome, but to himself in obeying his mother and not *it*.

The Meaning of Shakespeare. 1951. Chap. XXXII.

Cymbeline

[183] *E. M. W. Tillyard*

The tragic events (for which Cymbeline's original error is ultimately responsible) are curiously apt to end in insignificance, while the new existence into which the tragic action issues is, as any recognisable and convincing way of life, a pallid and bloodless affair. By making an intellectual abstract of the plot we may convince ourselves that Cymbeline is regenerate at the end of the play; but from reading the play we can only say that he fails to stir our imagination and that his regeneration is a thing quite dead.

★ ★ ★

Imogen is at times a human being, at times a Griselda of the medieval imagination. Nor is it any use trying to regard her as primarily the one or the other, and her aberrations from her primary rôle as the exceptions. Once she has had the boy's disguise imposed on her, she loses all possibility of dignity as a human being; and in her part as Griselda she is too weakly portrayed to be significant as a symbol. We may enjoy her isolated splendours, her outbursts of true human feeling, or the lovely poetry that passes her lips, but as a great character we must simply give her up.

Shakespeare's Last Plays. 1938. Chap. II.

[184] *G. B. Shaw*

All I can extract from the artificialities of the play is a double image—a real woman *divined* by Shakespear without his knowing it clearly, a natural aristocrat, with a high temper and perfect courage, with two moods—a childlike affection and wounded rage; and an idiotic paragon of virtue produced by Shakespear's *views* of what a woman ought to be, a person who sews and cooks, and reads improving books until midnight, and "always reserves her holy duty," and is anxious to assure people that they may trust her implicitly with their spoons and forks, and is in a chronic state of suspicion of improper behavior on the part of other people (especially her husband) with abandoned females.

★ ★ ★

Imogen is an impulsive person, with quick transitions, absolutely frank self-expression, and no half affections or half forgiveness. The moment you abuse anyone she loves, she is in a rage: the moment you praise them she is delighted. It is quite easy for Iachimo to put her out of countenance by telling her that Posthumus has forgotten her; but the instant he makes the mistake of trying to gratify her by abusing him—"that runagate"—he brings down the avalanche. It is just the same with Cloten: she is forbearing with him until he makes the same mistake. And Iachimo has nothing to do but praise Posthumus, and lay the butter on thick, and she is instantly as pleased as Punch, and void of all resentment. It is this that makes her pay him the extra special compliment of offering to take the chest into her own bedroom . . .

Ellen Terry and Bernard Shaw. A Correspondence. Ed. Christopher St. John. 1932. Letters of 6 and 8 September 1896.

[185] *Harley Granville-Barker*

But what possesses Iachimo, we ask, who can turn Posthumus round his finger, to make such a crassly blundering approach to Imogen that he comes within an ace of being thrown neck and crop from the Court? The answer is an index to the man, and shows no more inconsistency in him than goes to make him a living character, not, as he might have been—as the Queen is—a mere joint in the mechanism of the plot. It is an illuminating inconsistency. He has a keen eye for a man's weaknesses; they are food for his cynicism and a sop to his vanity. But the ways of such honest innocence as Imogen's are without the range of his understanding. For, even if we must acknowledge it, we cannot understand what we do not believe in.

Prefaces to Shakespeare. Second Series. 1930.

[186] *William Witherle Lawrence*

It is of the highest importance to distinguish the two different kinds of "romance" in *Cymbeline.* There is, on the one hand, a strong fairy-tale element in the play; the Guiderius-Arviragus plot has often been compared with the *märchen* of *Little Snow-White and the Dwarfs.* But this idyllic rustic material is in sharp contrast to the main plot. There the romantic conventions are of a very definite sort, as far removed from *Blue Beard* at one end as from *Pilgrim's Progress* at the other. They are the conventions of court life, which may be studied, mingled with other material, in such plays as *Philaster,* the *Maid's Tragedy, Thierry and Theodoret,* conventions which were a survival of the Middle Ages, which had been an outgrowth and an accompaniment of the feudal system, and which were, in somewhat altered form, in the height of fashion in Shakespeare's time. They had been modified by Renaissance views of conduct, derived from Italian and classical sources, and by changes in the popular attitude towards moral questions. The Elizabethans were not ready to accept the adulterous love condoned by the twelfth and thirteenth centuries. Their treatment of the Troilus-Cressida story makes that clear. But they clung passionately to externals, and their romantic observances were full of the absurdities so characteristic of the Middle Ages.

So the wager in *Cymbeline,* in its fantastic exaggeration of confidence in Imogen's virtue, is at once thoroughly mediaeval and thoroughly Elizabethan. This old theme, hallowed by centuries of story-telling, happened to fit to a nicety, through its very extravagances, the spirit of sixteenth century chivalry. In the light of mediaeval knightly observances Posthumus Leonatus emerges fully vindicated in the making of the wager; his was the only conduct possible for the perfect knight and lover.

★ ★ ★

. . . modern readers and playgoers do not find the acts and expressions of Posthumus heroic. They do not share the peculiar view of chivalric obligation which sways him in the wager-scene, and they do not believe that virtue which flies in the face of common-sense remains virtue. They have learned a more humane tradition for the punishment of the woman taken in adultery. And they demand in a hero more consistency, more use of his wits, more emotional restraint. The ravings of Posthumus, his rapid fluctuations of purpose, disgust Anglo-Saxons of today, bred to repress their deepest feelings. Moreover, Posthumus has to bear all the heavier burden of reprobation because the misfortunes of Imogen are due to his conduct. Every reader of the play loves this radiant and spirited girl; what more natural than to dislike the husband who makes her suffer? "Womanish tears" and "wild acts" may be pardoned in Romeo, who sacrifices everything for Juliet, but not in Posthumus, who makes Imogen herself the sacrifice. It will probably make little difference to remind people that Posthumus has justification for his course of action; they will continue to think just as meanly of him. Perhaps they are right. We are all familiar with the way in which "good" persons in real life, with virtue on their side, and a valid reason for every act, can make the innocent suffer. We wish that Posthumus had thought more of Imogen and less of social correctness. We wish, in short, that he were a man with modern notions, instead of an Elizabethan with medieval ideas still dogging him. But we must remember that the judgments which we pass on him today are probably harsher than those of the men who beheld his figure on the stage under the gray and shifting skies of London three hundred years ago.

Shakespeare's Problem Comedies. 1931. Chap. V.

Hamlet

[187] *Matthew Arnold*

To the common public 'Hamlet' is a famous piece by a famous poet, with crime, a ghost, battle, and carnage; and that is sufficient. To the youthful enthusiast 'Hamlet' is a piece handling the mystery of the universe, and having thru-out cadences, phrases, and words full of divinest Shakesperian magic; and that, too, is sufficient. To the pedant, finally, 'Hamlet' is an occasion for airing his psychology; and what does pedant require more? But to the spectator who loves true and powerful drama, and can judge whether he gets it or not, 'Hamlet' is a piece which opens, indeed, simply and admirably, and then: "The rest is puzzle"!

The reason is, apparently, that Shakespere conceived this play with his mind running on Montaigne, and placed its action and its hero in Montaigne's atmosphere and world. What is that world? It is the world of man viewed as a being *ondoyant et divers,* balancing and indeterminate, the plaything of cross-motives and shifting impulses, swayed by a thousand subtle influences, physiological and pathological. Certainly the action and hero of the original Hamlet story are not such as to compel the poet to place them in this world and no other, but they admit of being placed there, Shakespere resolved to place them there, and they lent themselves to his resolve. The resolve once taken to place the action in this world of problem, the problem became brightened by all the force of Shakespere's faculties, of Shakespere's subtlety. 'Hamlet' thus comes at last to be not a drama followed with perfect comprehension and profoundest emotion, which is the ideal for tragedy, but a problem soliciting interpretation and solution.

It will never, therefore, be a piece to be seen with pure satisfaction by those who will not deceive themselves. But such is its power and such is its fame that it will always continue to be acted, and we shall all of us continue to go and see it.

"Hamlet Once More." *Pall Mall Gazette.* Dec. 6, 1884. *Letters of an Old Playgoer.* 1919. Chap. V.

[188] *George Santayana*

The impression of utter gloom which the plot leaves when taken, so to speak, realistically, as if it were a picture of actual existences, is not the impression it leaves when we take it as lyric poetry, as music, as an abstract representation of sundry moods and loyalties traversing a noble mind. The world which is set before us may be grotesque and distracted; but we are not asked to be interested in that world. Had Hamlet himself been interested in it, he would have acted more rationally. It was not intelligence or courage that he lacked; it was practical conviction or sense for reality. Had he possessed this he would have turned his wits and sympathies towards improving the given situation, as he turns them towards improving the player's art. In truth he cared nothing for the world; man pleased him not, no, nor woman, neither; and we may well abandon to its natural confusion a dream in which we do not believe. Had Hamlet tried to justify his temperament by expressing it in a philosophy, he would have been an idealist. He would have said that events were only occasions for exercising the spirit; they were nothing but imagined situations meant to elicit a certain play of mind. If a man's comments had been keen, if his heart had been tender, if his will had been upright and pure, the rest was nothing. The world might feign to be mad and put on an antic disposition; it was sane enough if it fulfilled its purpose and gave a man an opportunity to test his own mettle. Those idiocies and horrors which he lived among would have been in truth the flights of angels that bore him to his rest. At any rate, express it how we will, the sympathetic reader will instinctively feel that he should pass over lightly the experience which the play depicts and carry away from it only the moral feeling, the spiritual sentiment, which it calls forth in the characters. As the poet himself thought a violent and somewhat absurd fable not unworthy to support his richest verse and subtlest characterisations, so we must take the fabric of destiny, in this tragedy and in that, too, which we enact in the world, as it happens to be, and think the moral lights that flicker through it bright enough to redeem it.

Introduction. *Hamlet.* The University Press Shakespeare, Renaissance Edition. XXX. 1908.

[189] *Geoffrey Bush*

There are stories, Gilbert Murray says, "deeply implanted in the memory of the race." There is "something in us which leaps at the sight of them, a cry of the blood which tells us we have known them always." One of these is the story of revenge, the story of Hamlet and Orestes. And there is, I think, a deeper correspondence, between the plot of revenge and Christian history; they share the same threefold story, the original goodness of nature, its violation, and the hope of a remedy through the intervention of a figure whose actions seem more than natural. The Red Cross Knight is a revenger; he brings redemption to the King and Queen of Eden; and in Hamlet there is suggested something of the folly and madness and ultimate divinity of those who suffer and die to set right the world, passing through nature to eternity. The room of Memory in *The Faerie Queene* holds records of ancient stories that are never forgotten; and perhaps from some buried memory of the race, some cellarage of the mind, came this interchange in Marston's *Malcontent:*

> *Orestes,* beware *Orestes.*
> Out beggar.
> I once shall rise,
> Thou rise?
> I at the resurrection.

There is some quality in the revenge plot that involves it in religious matters; there is some liaison between the brutality of revenge and the violence of sanctification. Revenge, Bacon said, is a kind of wild justice; and the chorus in *Agamemnon* cry out that "grace comes somehow violent." Hamlet and Orestes are not religious redeemers; yet there are contradictions about them that approach the paradoxes of religion. Their revenge is both an act of horror and an apotheosis; it is a descent into barbarism and a leap into sanctity; it is an act of extremity that represents the contradictions inherent in any human action performed in the context of the world and what is beyond the world. It may be that in the story of revenge Elizabethan drama reached after its most religious statement; and that in Hamlet's revenge Shakespeare found means to picture the violence and pain that attend those moments when our secular lives are crossed by grace.

Shakespeare and the Natural Condition. 1956. Chap. V.

[190] *James Russell Lowell*

All through the play we get the notion of a state of society in which a savage nature has disguised itself in the externals of civilization . . . Historically, at the date of Hamlet, the Danes were in the habit of burning their enemies alive in their houses, with as much of their family about them as might be to make it comfortable. Shakespeare seems purposely to have dissociated his play from history by changing nearly every name in the original legend. The motive of the play —revenge as a religious duty—belongs only to a social state in which the traditions of barbarism are still operative, but, with infallible artistic judgment, Shakespeare has chosen, not untamed Nature, as he found it in history, but the period of transition, a period in which the times are always out of joint, and thus the irresolution which has its root in Hamlet's own character is stimulated by the very incompatability of that legacy of vengeance he has inherited from the past with the new culture and refinement of which he is the representative.

"Shakespeare Once More." *North American Review.* 1868. *Among My Books.* 1870.

[191] *Harold S. Wilson*

We may conclude that Shakespeare does not wish to make explicit the status of the Ghost (carefully avoids doing so, in fact, by beclouding the issue) further than to suggest (1) that the Ghost functions in a context of Christian significance, coming from a realm of the after-life that Christians believe in, whether hell or purgatory; (2) that the Ghost enjoins upon his son a "duty" which a professing Christian must regard as a grave sin, the sin of personal vengeance forbidden by Scripture; (3) that Hamlet, in his overwrought excitement and for the moment, accepts the obligation imposed by the Ghost without trying to understand what warrant he has for so doing.

Later on, Hamlet will try to understand that warrant, passionately, searchingly. This is an essential part of the play's design and of its perennial fascination: the nightmarish uncertainty of Hamlet's predicament, an uncertainty for which he is hardly to be blamed. It is his very scrupulousness of conscience that makes him uncertain of the apparition he has seen.

On the Design of Shakespearian Tragedy. 1957. Chap. II.

[192] *John Masefield*

Hamlet is the most baffling of the great plays, because it is about baffling: that is the theme: Hamlet is baffled because, being wise, he finds the wise course difficult to decide upon.

A murder has been done, blood calls for vengeance: something from outside life urges Hamlet to take vengeance, but his wisdom does not admit vengeance, it seeks justice, and cannot see its way to justice; however necessary justice may be. Hamlet's indecision, or inaction, baffles that power outside life that urges him to take vengeance. The play is a confusion or welter of promptings to kill and seekings for a righter course than killing.

All through the play there is the uneasiness of something trying to get done, something from outside life trying to get into life, but baffled always because the instrument chosen is, himself, a little outside life, as the wise must be. This baffling of the purpose of the dead leads to a baffling of the living, and, at last, to something like an arrest of life, a deadlock, in which each act, however violent, makes the obscuring of life's purpose greater.

★ ★ ★

The society is created with Shakespeare's fullest power. It is not an image of the world in little, like the world of the late historical plays. It is an image of the world as intellect is made to feel it. It is a society governed by the enemies of intellect, by the sensual and the worldly, by deadly sinners and the philosophers of bread and cheese. The King is a drunken, incestuous murderer, who fears intellect. The Queen is a false woman, who cannot understand and has betrayed intellect. Polonius is a counsellor who suspects intellect. Ophelia is a doll without intellect. Laertes is a boor who destroys intellect. The courtiers are parasites who flourish on the decay of intellect. Fortinbras, bright and noble, marching to the drum to win a dunghill, gives a colour to the folly. The only friends of the wise man are Horatio, the school-fellow, and the leader of a cry of players.

The task set by the dead is a simple one, but to a delicate mind any violent act involves not only a large personal sacrifice of ideal, but a tearing-up by the roots of half the order of the world. Wisdom is founded upon justice; but justice, to the wise man, is more a scrupulous quality in the mind than the doing of expedient acts upon sinners. Hamlet is neither "weak" nor "unpractical", as so many call him. What he hesitates to do may be necessary, or even just, as the world goes, but it is a defilement of personal ideals, difficult for a wise mind to justify. It is so great a defilement, and a world so composed is so great a defilement, that death seems preferable to action and existence alike.

William Shakespeare. 1954.

[193] *Robert Bridges*

Hamlet himself would never hav been aught to us, or we
to Hamlet, wer't not for the artful balance whereby
Shakespeare so gingerly put his sanity in doubt
without the while confounding his Reason.

The Testament of Beauty. 1929. Lines 577–80.

[194] *Anonymous*

Now I am come to mention *Hamlet*'s Madness, I must speak my Opinion of our Poet's Conduct in this Particular. To conform to the Ground-work of his Plot, *Shakespeare* makes the young Prince feign himself mad. I cannot but think this to be injudicious; for so far from Securing himself from any Violence which he fear'd from the Usurper, which was his Design in so doing, it seems to have been the most likely Way of getting himself confin'd, and consequently, debarr'd from an Opportunity of Revenging his Father's Death, which now seem'd to be his only Aim; and accordingly it was the

Occasion of his being sent away to *England.* Which Design, had it taken effect upon his Life, he never could have revenged his Father's Murder. To speak Truth, our Poet, by keeping too close to the Ground-work of his Plot, has fallen into an Absurdity; for there appears no Reason at all in Nature, why the young Prince did not put the Usurper to Death as soon as possible, especially as *Hamlet* is represented as a Youth so brave, and so careless of his own Life.

The Case indeed is this: Had *Hamlet* gone naturally to work, as we could suppose such a Prince to do in parallel Circumstances, there would have been an End of our Play. The Poet therefore was obliged to delay his Hero's Revenge; but then he should have contrived some good Reason for it.

Some Remarks on the Tragedy of Hamlet Prince of Denmark. 1736.

[195] *Samuel Johnson*

Of the feigned madness of *Hamlet* there appears no adequate cause, for he does nothing which he might not have done with the reputation of sanity. He plays the madman most, when he treats *Ophelia* with so much rudeness, which seems to be useless and wanton cruelty.

Hamlet is, through the whole play, rather an instrument than an agent. After he has, by the stratagem of the play, convicted the King, he makes no attempt to punish him, and his death is at last effected by an incident which *Hamlet* has no part in producing.

The Plays of William Shakespeare. 1765. Vol. VIII.

[196] *George Santayana*

Those who have maintained that Hamlet is really mad had this partial justification for their paradox, that Hamlet is irrational. He acts without reflection, as he reflects without acting. At the basis of all his ingenuity and reasoning, of his nimble wit and varied feeling, lies this act of inexplicable folly: that he conceals his discovery, postpones his vengeance before questioning its propriety, and descends with no motive to a grotesque and pitiful piece of dissimulation. This unreason is not madness, because his intellect remains clear, his discourse sound and comprehensive; but it is a sort of passionate weakness and indirection in his will, which mocks its own ends, strikes fantastic attitudes, and invents elaborate schemes of action useless for his declared purposes. The psychology of Hamlet is like that which some German metaphysicians have attributed to their Spirit of the World, which is the prey to its own perversity and to what is called romantic irony, so that it eternally pursues the good in a way especially designed never to attain it. In Hamlet, as in them, beneath this histrionic duplicity and earnestness about the unreal, there is a very genuine pathos. Such brilliant futility is really helpless and sick at heart. The clouded will which plays with all these artifices of thought would fain break its way to light and self-knowledge through this magic circle of sophistication. It is the tragedy of a soul buzzing in the glass prison of a world which it can neither escape nor understand, in which it flutters about without direction, without clear hope, and yet with many a keen pang, many a dire imaginary problem, and much exquisite music.

Introduction. *Hamlet.* The University Press Shakespeare. Renaissance Edition. XXX. 1908.

[197] *J. Dover Wilson*

We are driven . . . to conclude with Loening, Bradley, Clutton-Brock and other critics that Shakespeare meant us to imagine Hamlet suffering from some kind of mental disorder throughout the play. Directly, however, such critics begin trying to define the exact nature of the disorder, they go astray. Its immediate origin cannot be questioned; it is caused, as we have seen, by the burden which fate lays upon his shoulders. We are not, however, at liberty to go outside the frame of the play and seek remoter origins in his past history. It is now well known, for instance, that a breakdown like Hamlet's is often due to seeds of disturbance planted in infancy and brought to evil fruition under the influence of mental strain of some kind in later life. Had Shakespeare been composing *Hamlet* to-day, he might conceivably have given us a hint of such an infantile complex. But he knew nothing of these matters and to write as if he did is to beat the air. We may go further. It is entirely misleading to attempt to describe Hamlet's state of mind in terms of modern psychology at all, not merely because Shakespeare did not think in these terms, but because—once again—Hamlet is a character in a play, not in history. He is part only, if the most important part, of an artistic masterpiece, of what is perhaps the most successful piece of dramatic illusion the world has ever known. And at no point of the composition is the illusion more masterly contrived than in this matter of his distraction.

What Happens in Hamlet. 1935. Chap. VI.

[198] *George Lyman Kittredge*

The necessity for some device like the play within the play is due to the failure of Hamlet's assumed madness to achieve its purpose. In the old saga and in Belleforest, Hamlet feigns madness for self-protection. It is made perfectly clear that the King can kill him at any moment, and that he refrains only because he cannot satisfy himself that the boy is in his right mind. He tries to entrap him into some act that will prove his sanity, but in vain. Hamlet is too shrewd for him and carries through his pretence of insanity until at last he finds the moment for a terrible revenge. Thus his pretended madness, like the deferred vengeance, was an essential element in the saga and the old play. How the old play accounted for it, it is idle to conjecture. In Shakespeare's drama, however, Hamlet's motive for acting the madman is obvious. We speak unguardedly in the presence of children and madmen, for we take it for granted that they will not listen or will not understand; and so the King or the Queen (for Hamlet does not know that his mother is ignorant of her husband's crime) may say something that will afford the evidence needed to confirm the testimony of the Ghost. The device is adopted on the spur of the moment (i, 5, 169ff.), and, once adopted, it must be maintained. But it is unsuccessful. The King is always on his guard, and the Queen is not an accomplice.

Introduction. *Hamlet.* 1939.

[199] *Anonymous*

HAMLET's Speech upon seeing the King at Prayers, has always given me great Offence. There is something so very Bloody in it, so inhuman, so unworthy of a Hero, that I wish our Poet had omitted it. To desire to destroy a Man's Soul, to make him eternally miserable, by cutting him off from all hopes of Repentance; this surely, in a

Christian Prince, is such a Piece of Revenge, as no Tenderness for any Parent can justify. To put the Usurper to Death, to deprive him of the Fruits of his vile Crime, and to rescue the Throne of *Denmark* from Pollution, was highly requisite: But there our young Prince's Desires should have stop'd, nor should he have wished to pursue the Criminal in the other World, but rather have hoped for his Conversion, before his putting him to Death; for even with his Repentance, there was at least Purgatory for him to pass through, as we find even in a virtuous Prince, the Father of *Hamlet*.

Some Remarks on the Tragedy of Hamlet Prince of Denmark, 1736.

[200] *George Lyman Kittredge*

Shakespeare is face to face with an exacting problem. He has brought his two main personages together in such a way that it is impossible for Hamlet to strike, though the opportunity is ideal, and though it is, in theory, his sacred duty to kill his uncle as soon as he can. How is he to extricate his characters from the situation in which he has deliberately involved them?

Manifestly it is out of the question for Hamlet to give the real reason for sheathing his sword; for that would be to make him repudiate the traditional code to which he still subscribes, though he has outgrown its literal savagery. The only excuse or pretext for inaction now must consist in his persuading himself that, after all, the moment is *not* favourable; and there is but one way in which he can so persuade himself—by proving that, if he strikes now, his vengeance will be ineffectual. Hence we have the diabolical outburst which prompted Dr. Johnson's famous comment: 'This speech, in which Hamlet is not content with taking blood for blood, but contrives damnation for the man that he would punish, is too horrible to be read or to be uttered.'

But these diabolical sentiments are not Hamlet's sentiments. He does not really postpone his uncle's death in order that he may consign him to perdition. The speech is merely a pretext for delay. The problem is not, 'Why does Hamlet entertain such infernal sentiments?' but rather, 'How happens it that such a pretext occurs to him?' And the answer is obvious: Because the views in question accord with an old-established convention with regard to adequate revenge. With this convention the Elizabethan audience was familiar, and it made allowance accordingly; for language means only what it is meant to mean by the speaker and what it is understood to mean by the hearer.

Introduction. *Hamlet*. 1939.

[201] *Samuel Taylor Coleridge*

[Shakespeare] intended to pourtray a person, in whose view the external world, and all its incidents and objects, were comparatively dim, and of no interest in themselves, and which began to interest only, when they were reflected in the mirror of his mind. Hamlet beheld external things in the same way that a man of vivid imagination, who shuts his eyes, sees what has previously made an impression on his organs.

The poet places him in the most stimulating circumstances that a human being can be placed in. He is the heir apparent of a throne; his father dies suspiciously; his mother excludes her son from his throne by marrying his uncle. This is not enough; but the Ghost of the murdered father is introduced, to assure the son that he was put to death by his own brother. What is the effect upon the son?—instant action and pursuit of revenge? No: endless reasoning and hesitating—constant urging and solicitation of the mind to act, and as constant an escape from action; ceaseless reproaches of himself for sloth and negligence, while the whole energy of his resolution evaporates in these reproaches. This, too, not from cowardice, for he is drawn as one of the bravest of his time—not from want of forethought or slowness of apprehension, for he sees through the very souls of all who surround him, but merely from that aversion to action, which prevails among such as have a world in themselves.

★ ★ ★

Anything finer than this conception, and working out of a great character, is merely impossible. Shakespeare wished to impress upon us the truth, that action is the chief end of existence—that no faculties of intellect, however brilliant, can be considered valuable, or indeed otherwise than as misfortunes, if they withdraw us from, or render us repugnant to action, and lead us to think and think of doing, until the time has elapsed when we can do anything effectually. In enforcing this moral truth, Shakespeare has shown the fulness and force of his powers: all that is amiable and excellent in nature is combined in Hamlet, with the exception of one quality. He is a man living in meditation, called upon to act by every motive human and divine, but the great object of his life is defeated by continually resolving to do, yet doing nothing but resolve.

The Lectures of 1811–12. XII. Raysor II, 192–93, 197–98.

[202] *Katherine Mansfield*

Coleridge on Hamlet. 'He plays that subtle trick of pretending to act only when he is very near being what he acts.'

. . . So do we all begin by acting and the nearer we are to what we would be the more perfect our *disguise.* Finally there comes the moment when *we are no longer acting;* it may even catch us by surprise. We may look in amazement at our no longer borrowed plumage. The two have merged; that which we put on has joined that which was; acting has become action. The soul has accepted this livery for its own after a time of trying on and approving.

To act . . . to see ourselves in the part—to make a larger gesture than would be ours in life—to declaim, to pronounce, to even exaggerate. To persuade ourselves? Or others? To put ourselves in heart? To do more than is necessary in order that we may accomplish ce qu'il faut.

And then Hamlet is lonely. The solitary person always acts.

But I could write a thousand pages about Hamlets.

Mad Scene. If one looks at it with a cold eye is really very poor. It depends entirely for its effect upon wispy Ophelia. The cardboard King and Queen are of course only lookers-on. They don't care a halfpenny. I think the Queen is privately rather surprised at a verse or two of her songs. . . . And who can believe that a solitary violet withered when that silly fussy old pomposity died? And who can believe that Ophelia really loved him, and wasn't thankful to think how peaceful breakfast would be without his preaching?

The Queen's speech after Ophelia's death is exasperating to one's sense of poetic truth. If no one saw it happen—if she wasn't found until she was drowned, how does the Queen know how it happened? Dear Shakespeare has been to the Royal Academy . . . for his picture.

Journal of Katherine Mansfield. 1921. Ed. J. Middleton Murry. 1954.

[203] *James Russell Lowell*

. . . there is a kind of genealogical necessity in the character,—a thing not altogether strange to the attentive reader of Shakespeare. Hamlet seems the natural result of the mixture of father and mother in his temperament, the resolution and persistence of the one, like sound timber wormholed and made shaky, as it were, by the other's infirmity of will and discontinuity of purpose. In natures so imperfectly mixed it is not uncommon to find vehemence of intention the prelude and counterpoise of weak performance, the conscious nature striving to keep up its self-respect by a triumph in words all the more resolute that it feels assured beforehand of inevitable defeat in action.

★ ★ ★

It is an inherent peculiarity of a mind like Hamlet's that it should be conscious of its own defect. Men of his type are forever analyzing their own emotions and motives. They cannot do anything, because they always see two ways of doing it. They cannot determine on any course of action, because they are always, as it were, standing at the cross-roads, and see too well the disadvantages of every one of them. It is not that they are incapable of resolve, but somehow the band between the motive power and the operative faculties is relaxed and loose. The engine works, but the machinery it should drive stands still. The imagination is so much in overplus, that thinking a thing becomes better than doing it, and thought with its easy perfection, capable of everything because it can accomplish everything with ideal means, is vastly more attractive and satisfactory than deed, which must be wrought at best with imperfect instruments, and always falls short of the conception that went before it. "If to do," says Portia in the *Merchant of Venice*,—"if to do were as easy as to know what 't were good to do, chapels had been churches, and poor men's cottages princes' palaces." Hamlet knows only too well what 't were good to do, but he palters with everything in a double sense: he sees the grain of good there is in evil, and the grain of evil there is in good, as they exist in the world, and, finding that he can make these feather-weighted accidents balance each other, infers that there is little to choose between the essences themselves. He is of Montaigne's mind, and says expressly that "there is nothing good or ill, but thinking makes it so." He dwells so exclusively in the world of ideas that the world of facts seems trifling, nothing is worth the while; and he has been so long objectless and purposeless, so far as actual life is concerned, that, when at last an object and an aim are forced upon him, he cannot deal with them, and gropes about vainly for a motive outside of himself that shall marshall his thoughts for him and guide his faculties into the path of action. He is the victim not so much of feebleness of will as of an intellectual indifference that hinders the will from working long in any one direction.

He wishes to will, but never wills. His continual iteration of resolve shows that he has no resolution. He is capable of passionate energy where the occasion presents itself suddenly from without, because nothing is so irritable as conscious irresolution with a duty to perform. But of deliberate energy he is not capable; for there the impulse must come from within, and the blade of his analysis is so subtile that it can divide the finest hair of motive 'twixt north and northwest side, leaving him desperate to choose between them. The very consciousness of his defect is an insuperable bar to his repairing it; for the unity of purpose, which infuses every fibre of the character with will available whenever wanted, is impossible where the mind can never rest till it has resolved that unity into its component elements, and satisfied itself which on the whole is of greater value. A critical instinct so insatiable that it must turn upon itself, for lack of something else to hew and hack, becomes incapable at last of originating anything except indecision. It becomes infallible in what *not* to do.

★ ★ ★

Hamlet . . . is always studying himself. This world and the other, too, are always present to his mind, and there in the corner is the little black kobold of a doubt making mouths at him. He breaks down the bridges before him, not behind him, as a man of action would do; but there is something more than this. He is an ingrained sceptic; though his is the scepticism, not of reason, but of feeling, whose root is want of faith in himself. . . . Hamlet doubts everything. He doubts the immortality of the soul, just after seeing his father's spirit, and hearing from its mouth the secrets of the other world. He doubts Horatio even, and swears him to secrecy on the cross of his sword, though probably he himself has no assured belief in the sacredness of the symbol. He doubts Ophelia, and asks her, "Are you honest?" He doubts the ghost, after he has had a little time to think about it, and so gets up the play to test the guilt of the king.

★ ★ ★

[Hamlet's irony] is not like the irony of Timon, which is but the wilful refraction of a clear mind twisting awry whatever enters it,—or of Iago, which is the slime that a nature essentially evil loves to trail over all beauty and goodness to taint them with distrust: it is the half-jest, half-earnest of an inactive temperament that has not quite made up its mind whether life is a reality or no, whether men were not made in jest, and which amuses itself equally with finding a deep meaning in trivial things and a trifling one in the profoundest mysteries of being, because the want of earnestness in its own essence infects everything else with its own indifference. If there be now and then an unmannerly rudeness and bitterness in it, as in the scenes with Polonius and Osrick, we must remember that Hamlet was just in the condition which spurs men to sallies of this kind: dissatisfied, at one neither with the world nor with himself, and accordingly casting about for something out of himself to vent his spleen upon. But even in these passages there is no hint of earnestness, of any purpose beyond the moment; they are mere cat's-paws of vexation, and not the deep-raking ground-swell of passion, as we see it in the sarcasm of Lear.

"Shakespeare Once More." *North American Review.* 1868. *Among My Books.* 1870.

[204] *G. B. Shaw*

Mr Forbes Robertson is essentially a classical actor . . . What I mean by classical is that he can present a dramatic hero as a man whose passions are those which have produced the philosophy, the poetry, the art, and the statecraft of the world, and not merely those which have produced its weddings, coroners' inquests, and executions. And that is just the sort of actor that Hamlet requires. . . . Hamlet is not a man in whom "common humanity" is raised by great vital energy to a heroic pitch, like Coriolanus or Othello. On the contrary, he is a man in whom the common personal passions are so superseded by wider and rarer interests, and so discouraged by a degree of critical self-consciousness which makes the practical efficiency of the instinctive man on the lower plane impossible to him, that he finds the duties dictated by conventional revenge and ambition as disagreeable a burden as commerce is to a poet. Even his instinctive sexual impulses offend his intellect; so that when he meets the woman who excites them he invites her to join him in a bitter and scornful criticism of their joint absurdity, demanding "What should such fellows as I do crawling between heaven and earth?" "Why wouldst thou be a breeder of sinners?" and so forth, all of which is so completely beyond the poor girl that she naturally thinks him mad. And, indeed, there is a sense in which Hamlet is insane; for he trips over the mistake which lies on the threshold of intellectual self-consciousness: that of bringing life to utilitarian or Hedonistic tests, thus treating it as a means instead of an end. Because Polonius is "a foolish prating knave," because Rosencrantz and Guildenstern are snobs, he kills them as remorselessly as he might kill a flea, shewing that he has no real belief in the superstitious reason which he gives for not killing himself . . . go and watch Mr Forbes Robertson's Hamlet seizing delightedly on every opportunity for a bit of philosophic discussion or artistic recreation to escape from the "cursed spite" of revenge and love and other common troubles; see how he brightens up when the players come; how he tries to talk philosophy with Rosencrantz and Guildenstern the moment they come into the room; how he stops on his country walk with Horatio to lean over the churchyard wall and draw out the gravedigger whom he sees singing at his trade; how even his fits of excitement find expression in declaiming scraps of poetry; how the shock of Ophelia's death relieves itself in the fiercest intellectual contempt for Laertes's ranting, whilst an hour afterwards, when Laertes stabs him, he bears no malice for that at all, but embraces him gallantly and comradely; and how he dies as we forgive everything to Charles II for dying, and makes "the rest is silence" a touchingly humorous apology for not being able to finish his business. See all that; and you have seen a true classical Hamlet. . . .

And please observe that this is not a cold Hamlet. He is none of your logicians who reason their way through the world because they cannot feel their way through it: his intellect is the organ of his passion: his eternal self-criticism is as alive and thrilling as it can possibly be.

"Hamlet." *The Saturday Review.* 2 October 1897. XXV, 211–13.

[205] *Ernest Jones*

Extensive studies of the past half century, inspired by Freud, have taught us that a psychoneurosis means a state of mind where the person is unduly, and often painfully, driven or thwarted by the "unconscious" part of his mind, that buried part that was once the infant's mind and still lives on side by side with the adult mentality that has developed out of it and should have taken its place. It signifies *internal* mental conflict. We have here the reason why it is impossible to discuss intelligently the state of mind of anyone suffering from a psychoneurosis, whether the description is of a living person or an imagined one, without correlating the manifestations with what must have operated in his infancy and is *still operating*. That is what I propose to attempt here.

For some deep-seated reason, which is to him unacceptable, Hamlet is plunged into anguish at the thought of his father being replaced in his mother's affections by someone else. It is as if his devotion to his mother had made him so jealous for her affection that he had found it hard enough to share this even with his father and could not endure to share it with still another man. Against this thought, however, suggestive as it is, may be urged three objections. First, if it were in itself a full statement of the matter, Hamlet would have been aware of the jealousy, whereas we have concluded that the mental process we are seeking is hidden from him. Secondly, we see in it no evidence of the arousing of an old and forgotten memory. And, thirdly, Hamlet is being deprived by Claudius of no greater share in the Queen's affection than he had been by his own father, for the two brothers made exactly similar claims in this respect—namely, those of a loved husband. The last-named objection, however, leads us to the heart of the situation. How if, in fact, Hamlet had in years gone by, as a child, bitterly resented having had to share his mother's affection even with his own father, had regarded him as a rival, and had secretly wished him out of the way so that he might enjoy undisputed and undisturbed the monopoly of that affection? If such thoughts had been present in his mind in childhood days they evidently would have been "repressed," and all traces of them obliterated, by filial piety and other educative influences. The actual realization of his early wish in the death of his father at the hands of a jealous rival would then have stimulated into activity these "repressed" memories, which would have produced, in the form of depression and other suffering, an obscure aftermath of his childhood's conflict. This is at all events the mechanism that is actually found in the real Hamlets who are investigated psychologically.

The explanation, therefore, of the delay and self-frustration exhibited in the endeavour to fulfil his father's demand for vengeance is that to Hamlet the thought of incest and parricide combined is too intolerable to be borne. One part of him tries to carry out the task, the other flinches inexorably from the thought of it. How fain would he blot it out in that "bestial oblivion" which unfortunately for him his conscience contemns. He is torn and tortured in an insoluble inner conflict.

Hamlet and Oedipus. 1949. Chap. III.

[206] *Elmer Edgar Stoll*

So far are Shakespeare's other heroes removed from the infection that they are, all of them, great of heart, bold in deed, even strong and lithe of limb, as today no hero need be. They are worthies, champions, tall men of their hands. Othello, as he bids his uncle let him come forth, cries, "I have made my way through more than twenty times your stop"; old Lear, in his last hours, kills Cordelia's executioner; Macbeth, Antony, and Coriolanus perform prodigies of valour single-handed in the field. And just such, we have seen, is Hamlet. He dauntlessly follows the Ghost; he welcomes the perilous sport of the expedition to England; and when pitted against them hand to hand, he is more than a match for his antagonists,—whether struggling on the platform, killing the spy in the bedchamber, boarding the pirate ship, grappling in the grave, or fencing and stabbing and wrestling the cup at the end. These are the "acts and events greater and more heroical," which in tragedy Elizabethan dramatic taste required. Indeed, the dramatist seems to have deliberately suppressed or avoided much of what might remind us of the student or scholar. The original Hamlet, probably, was as pedantic, and talked as much Latin, as old Hieronimo. In Quarto 1 he appears twice with a book in his hand, in Quarto 2 but once. And Hamlet once seems to make a distinction, and speaks to Horatio of "your philosophy" as if it were he that was the student rather than himself. No one calls him a scholar save Ophelia, who at the same time calls him a courtier and soldier; and no one scorns him or condescends to him . . . as a bookish, dreamy, impractical person, though one might expect the King, Polonius, or at least Laertes to do it. He is a student of the Renaissance, taking to his sword as readily as to his inkhorn and book,—indeed in all Shakespeare who takes to his sword more readily? Even before the slaughter at the end, Hamlet might well have rubbed his eyes and cried out with Candide: "Hélas! mon Dieu! je suis le meilleur homme du monde et voilà déjà trois hommes que je tue." And at the end, though he envies Laertes his reputation as a fencer, he awaits the combat with confidence—a confidence fully warranted by the event. "You will lose this wager, my lord"— "I do not think so . . . I shall win at the odds." He does better than that—he has more "hits" to his credit than Laertes—and, when what began in play ends up in grim earnest, he has killed two enemies, to their one. Why should a dreamy weakling, a melancholy doubter or cynic, one broken in will or hopelessly engulfed in thought, be made so healthy and sturdy—so formidable—a man of this world?

Now Shakespeare is, in his method, emphatic and unmistakable; and if he had suddenly resolved to abandon heroic romance, and undertake a novel—a psychological—type of character, such as Hamlet has, in the last century, been understood to be, he would have tried to make him as different as possible from his other characters—make him really a Werther, an Aprile, or, say, a Romeo who kept his sword like a dancer and shunned danger and death. Instead, he has, save for the delay, given him all the stout qualities of the others. Instead, he has kept for him all the stout qualities he had had in Kyd. How, then, could an audience detect the difference, if a difference there was meant to be? And to indicate a difference that the audience could not detect, Shakespeare, of course, was not the man to have lifted a finger. He was not painting pictures that were never to be seen, not shooting arrows into the air. He was writing plays which plain and common people were expected to like, and in order to like them, of course, must understand. How naturally—and how differently from us—they understood the play now in question we have learned already.

Hamlet: An Historical and Comparative Study. 1919.

[207] *J. Dover Wilson*

There is nothing slovenly in *Hamlet,* whatever may be said about some other of his plays. The more one contemplates it the more flawless and subtle does its technique appear. What, then, is the general impression which Shakespeare, by means of the devices we have been examining, strove to give of Hamlet's character? Surely it is simply the impression which three centuries of spectators (apart from critics and readers, who treat the play as a book, as a novel or a chapter of history) have always received, viz. that of a great, an almost superhuman, figure tottering beneath a tragic burden too heavy even for his mighty back; or, if you will, of a genius suffering from a fatal weakness and battling against it, until in the end it involves him in the catastrophe which is at once his liberation and his atonement.

Finally, this compound of overwhelmingly convincing humanity and psychological contradiction is the greatest of Shakespeare's legacies to the men of his own quality. No "part" in the whole repertory of dramatic literature is so certain of success with almost any audience, and is yet open to such a remarkable variety of interpretation. There are as many Hamlets as there are actors who play him; and

Bernhardt has proved that even a woman can score a success. Of a rôle so indeterminate in composition almost any version is possible; with a character so fascinating and so tremendous in outline hardly any impersonator can fail.

What Happens in Hamlet. 1935. Chap. VI.

[208] *Harold S. Wilson*

The ever-present suggestion of the sickness that afflicts all Denmark, emphasized and reiterated in the imagery of the play, of the human guilt of Claudius and Gertrude, of Polonius and Laertes, of Hamlet's father and of Hamlet himself, of the blind striving and repeated frustration of their human wills and purposes, is countered by the emergent theme of an over-ruling Providence which shapes the action towards a climax none of the actors foresees, a climax in which justice at length prevails, the land is purged of its sickness, the kingdom of Denmark restored to pristine health.

★ ★ ★

Hamlet, at length, through the agony of his frustration, comes to recognize his true role as the instrument of justice rather than the dispenser of it; and he learns how to accept what comes, quietly, humbly, with manly resolution rather than with the assortment of heroic poses that had earlier beguiled him, and that beguile Laertes, in his callowness, to the end.

★ ★ ★

. . . the soliloquies are masterly studies of Hamlet's self-absorption, of the half-conscious dramatization of himself by a young man entangled in a serious dilemma, a young man possessed of the highest intellectual gifts, but egotistical and self-centred with the single-minded concentration, the innocent intensity that is possible only in youth, and that, in its customary unawareness of itself, is hardly ever offensive. This is why Hamlet is so hard upon Ophelia; youth is quite merciless in its judgments when labouring under a sense of wrong; it is not Hamlet's attachment to his mother and his sense of outrage at Gertrude's betrayal of his ideal, great though this is, that he vents upon Ophelia; it is his sense of outrage at *Ophelia,* that she could place obedience to her father before her love for him. Hell hath no fury like a young man scorned; and Shakespeare shows us this trait of his hero, among many others, if we will but see it, in the Nunnery scene and elsewhere.

It is a sign of Hamlet's genius that he can be half-ashamed of the glimpses he catches of himself, as he unpacks his heart with words; yet he cannot quite help himself; and we must not expect him, in his agitation, to tell us what really ails him. The soliloquies are dramatic and ironical, with an irony that is implicit and eloquent in the very extravagances of Hamlet's rhetoric. Shakespeare has fully learned, by this time, how to avoid all comment in his tragedies, not simply the overt comment of a prologue but also the comment of a choral character like the Prince in *Romeo and Juliet*. We must puzzle out Hamlet's predicament for ourselves; and we must have our wits about us as we do so, for he is not a simple character. But if we follow him closely through the play, we may see how he grows up; how at length he abandons all his rhetorical posturings, his operatic arias; how he changes from a youth—a youth of genius, but still a youth—into a man.

On the Design of Shakespearian Tragedy. 1957. Chap. II.

[209] *Maynard Mack*

The crucial evidence of Hamlet's new frame of mind, as I understand it, is the graveyard scene. Here, in its ultimate symbol, he confronts, recognizes, and accepts the condition of being man. It is not simply that he now accepts death, though Shakespeare shows him accepting it in ever more poignant forms: first, in the imagined persons of the politician, the courtier, and the lawyer, who laid their little schemes "to circumvent God," as Hamlet puts it, but now lie here; then in Yorick, whom he knew and played with as a child; and then in Ophelia. This last death tears from him a final cry of passion, but the striking contrast between his behavior and Laertes's reveals how deeply he has changed.

Still, it is not the fact of death that invests this scene with its peculiar power. It is instead the haunting mystery of life itself that Hamlet's speeches point to, holding in its inscrutable folds those other mysteries that he has wrestled with so long. These he now knows for what they are, and lays them by. The mystery of evil is present here—for this is after all the universal graveyard, where, as the clown says humorously, he holds up Adam's profession; where the scheming politician, the hollow courtier, the tricky lawyer, the emperor and the clown and the beautiful young maiden, all come together in an emblem of the world; where even, Hamlet murmurs, one might expect to stumble on "Cain's jawbone, that did the first murther." The mystery of reality is here too—for death puts the question, "What is real?" in its irreducible form, and in the end uncovers all appearances: "Is this the fine of his fines and the recovery of his recoveries, to have his fine pate full of fine dirt?" "Now get you to my lady's chamber, and tell her, let her paint an inch thick, to this favor she must come." Or if we need more evidence of this mystery, there is the anger of Laertes at the lack of ceremonial trappings, and the ambiguous character of Ophelia's own death. "Is she to be buried in Christian burial when she wilfully seeks her own salvation?" asks the gravedigger. And last of all, but most pervasive of all, there is the mystery of human limitation. The grotesque nature of man's little joys, his big ambitions. The fact that the man who used to bear us on his back is now a skull that smells; that the noble dust of Alexander somewhere plugs a bunghole; that "Imperious Caesar, dead and turn'd to clay, Might stop a hole to keep the wind away." Above all, the fact that a pit of clay is "meet" for such a guest as man, as the gravedigger tells us in his song, and yet that, despite all frailties and limitations, "That skull had a tongue in it and could sing once."

After the graveyard and what it indicates has come to pass in him, we know that Hamlet is ready for the final contest of mighty opposites. He accepts the world as it is, the world as a duel, in which, whether we know it or not, evil holds the poisoned rapier and the poisoned chalice waits; and in which, if we win at all, it costs not less than everything. I think we understand by the close of Shakespeare's *Hamlet* why it is that unlike the other tragic heroes he is given a soldier's rites upon the stage. For as William Butler Yeats once said, "Why should we honor those who die on the field of battle? A man may show as reckless a courage in entering into the abyss of himself."

"The World of *Hamlet*." *The Yale Review*. XLI. 1952.

[210] *Arthur Sewell*

Hamlet is not a challenge to our psychological ingenuity; it is a challenge to the faith we seek to live by. The puzzle and the explanation both lie in our common predicament; that action is imperative for man, but that all action whatsoever involves man in evil.

Character and Society in Shakespeare. 1951. Chap. III.

Henry IV

[211] *Samuel Johnson*

None of *Shakespeare's* plays are more read than the first and second parts of *Henry* the fourth. Perhaps no authour has ever in two plays afforded so much delight. The great events are interesting, for the fate of kingdoms depends upon them; the slighter occurrences are diverting, and, except one or two, sufficiently probable; the incidents are multiplied with wonderful fertility of invention, and the characters diversified with the utmost nicety of discernment, and the profoundest skill in the nature of man.

The prince, who is the hero both of the comick and tragick part, is a young man of great abilities and violent passions, whose sentiments are right, though his actions are wrong; whose virtues are obscured by negligence, and whose understanding is dissipated by levity. In his idle hours he is rather loose than wicked, and when the occasion forces out his latent qualities, he is great without effort, and brave without tumult. The trifler is roused into a hero, and the hero again reposes in the trifler. The character is great, original, and just.

Piercy is a rugged soldier, cholerick, and quarrelsome, and has only the soldier's virtues, generosity and courage.

But *Falstaff* unimitated, unimitable *Falstaff*, how shall I decribe thee? Thou compound of sense and vice; of sense which may be admired but not esteemed, of vice which may be despised, but hardly detested. *Falstaff* is a character loaded with faults, and with those faults which naturally produce contempt. He is a thief, and a glutton, a coward, and a boaster, always ready to cheat the weak, and prey upon the poor; to terrify the timorous and insult the defenceless. At once obsequious and malignant, he satirises in their absence those whom he lives by flattering. He is familiar with the prince only as an agent of vice, but of this familiarity he is so proud as not only to be supercilious and haughty with common men, but to think his interest of importance to the duke of *Lancaster*. Yet the man thus corrupt, thus despicable, makes himself necessary to the prince that despises him, by the most pleasing of all qualities, perpetual gaiety, by an unfailing power of exciting laughter, which is the more freely indulged, as his wit is not of the splendid or ambitious kind, but consists in easy escapes and sallies of levity, which make sport but raise no envy. It must be observed that he is stained with no enormous or sanguinary crimes, so that his licentiousness is not so offensive but that it may be borne for his mirth.

The moral to be drawn from this representation is, that no man is more dangerous than he that with a will to corrupt, hath the power to please; and that neither wit nor honesty ought to think themselves safe with such a companion when they see *Henry* seduced by *Falstaff*.

The Plays of William Shakespeare. 1765. Vol. IV.

[212] *Maurice Morgann*

We all like *Old Jack;* yet, by some strange perverse fate, we all abuse him, and deny him the possession of any one single good or respectable quality. There is something extraordinary in this: It must be a strange art in *Shakespeare* which can draw our liking and good will towards so offensive an object. He has wit, it will be said; chearfulness and humour of the most characteristic and captivating sort. And is this enough? Is the humour and gaiety of vice so very captivating? Is the wit, characteristic of baseness and every ill quality capable of attaching the heart and winning the affections? Or does not the apparency of such humour, and the flashes of such wit, by more strongly disclosing the deformity of character, but the more effectually excite our hatred and contempt of the man? And yet this is not our *feeling* of *Falstaff's* character. When he has ceased to amuse us, we find no emotions of disgust; we can scarcely forgive the ingratitude of the Prince in the new-born virtue of the King, and we curse the severity of that poetic justice which consigns our old good-natured delightful companion to the custody of the *warden,* and the dishonours of the *Fleet*.

★ ★ ★

. . . whilst we look upon *Falstaff* as a character of the like nature with that of *Parolles* or of *Bobadil,* we . . . preserve for him a great degree of respect and good-will, and yet feel the highest disdain and contempt of the others, tho' they are all involved in similar situations. The reader, I believe, would wonder extremely to find either *Parolles* or *Bobadil* possess himself in danger: What then can be the cause that we are not at all surprized at the gaiety and ease of *Falstaff* under the most trying circumstances; and that we never think of charging *Shakespeare* with departing, on this account, from the truth and coherence of character? Perhaps, after all, the *real* character of *Falstaff* may be different from his *apparent* one; and possibly this difference between reality and appearance, whilst it accounts at once for our liking and our censure, may be the true point of humour in the character, and the source of all our laughter and delight.

★ ★ ★

To me . . . it appears that the leading quality in *Falstaff's* character, and that from which all the rest take their colour, is a high degree of wit and humour, accompanied with great natural vigour and alacrity of mind. This quality so accompanied, led him probably very early into life, and made him highly acceptable to society; so acceptable, as to make it seem unnecessary for him to acquire any other virtue. Hence, perhaps, his continued debaucheries and dissipations of every kind.—He seems, by nature, to have had a mind free of malice or any evil principle; but he never took the trouble of acquiring any good one. He found himself esteemed and beloved with all his faults; nay *for* his faults, which were all connected with humour, and for the most part, grew out of it. As he had, possibly, no vices but such as he thought might be openly professed, so he appeared more dissolute thro' ostentation. To the character of wit and humour, to which all his other qualities seem to have conformed themselves, he appears to have added a very necessary support, *that* of the profession of a *Soldier*. He had from nature, as I presume to say, a spirit of boldness and enterprise; which in a Military age, tho' employment was only occasional, kept him always above contempt, secured him an honourable reception among the Great, and suited best both with his particular mode of humour and of vice. Thus living continually in society, nay even in Taverns, and indulging himself, and being indulged by others, in every debauchery; drinking, whoring, gluttony, and ease; assuming a liberty of fiction, necessary perhaps to his wit, and often falling into falsity and lies, he seems to have set, by degrees, all sober reputation at defiance; and finding eternal resources in his wit, he borrows, shifts, defrauds, and even robs, without dishonour.—Laughter and approbation attend his greatest excesses; and being governed visibly by no settled bad principle or ill design, fun and humour account for and cover all. By degrees, however, and thro' indulgence, he acquires bad habits, becomes an humourist, grows enormously corpulent, and falls into the infirmities of age; yet never quits, all the time, one single levity or vice of youth, or loses any of that chearfulness of mind, which had enabled him to pass thro' this course with ease to himself and delight to others; and thus, at last, mixing youth and age, enterprize and corpulency, wit and folly, poverty and expence, title and buffoonery, innocence as to purpose, and wickedness as to practice; neither incurring hatred by bad principle, or contempt by Cowardice, yet involved in circumstances productive of imputation in both; a butt and a wit, a humourist and a man of humour, a touchstone and a laughing stock, a jester and a jest, has Sir *John Falstaff*, taken at that period of his life in which we see him, become the most perfect Comic character that perhaps ever was exhibited.

★ ★ ★

Whatever there may be of dishonour in *Falstaff's* conduct, he neither does or says any thing on this occasion [the battle at Shrewsbury] which indicates terror or disorder of mind: On the contrary, this very act is a proof of his having all his wits about him, and is a stratagem, such as it is, not improper for a buffoon, whose fate would be singularly hard, if he should not be allowed to avail himself of his Character when it might serve him in most stead. We must remember, in extenuation, that the executive, the destroying hand of *Douglas* was over him: *'It was time to counterfeit, or that hot termagant Scot had paid him scot and lot too.'* He had but one choice; he was obliged to pass thro' the ceremony of dying either in jest or in earnest; and we shall not be surprized at the event, when we remember his propensities to the former.—Life (and especially the life of *Falstaff*) might be a jest; but he could see no joke whatever in dying: To be chopfallen was, with him, to lose both life and character together: He saw the point of honour, as well as every thing else, in ridiculous lights, and began to renounce its tyranny.

★ ★ ★

. . . he is a character made up by *Shakespeare* wholly of incongruities;—a man at once young and old, enterprizing and fat, a dupe and a wit, harmless and wicked, weak in principle and resolute by constitution, cowardly in appearance and brave in reality; a knave without malice, a lyar without deceit; and a knight, a gentleman, and a soldier, without either dignity, decency, or honour: This is a character, which, though it may be decompounded, could not, I believe, have been formed, nor the ingredients of it duly mingled upon any receipt whatever: It required the hand of *Shakespeare* himself to give to every particular part a relish of the whole, and of the whole to every particular part;—alike the same incongruous, identical *Falstaff*, whether to the grave Chief Justice he vainly talks of his youth, and offers to *caper for a thousand;* or cries to Mrs. *Doll*, *'I am old,*

I am old,' though she is seated on his lap, and he is courting her for busses.

★ ★ ★

There is in truth no such thing as totally demolishing *Falstaff;* he has so much of the invulnerable in his frame that no ridicule can destroy him; he is safe even in defeat, and seems to rise, like another *Antaeus,* with recruited vigour from every fall; in this as in every other respect, unlike *Parolles* or *Bobadil:* They fall by the first shaft of ridicule, but *Falstaff* is a butt on which we may empty the whole quiver, whilst the substance of his character remains unimpaired. His ill habits, and the accidents of age and corpulence, are no part of his essential constitution; they come forward indeed on our eye, and solicit our notice, but they are second natures, not *first;* mere shadows, we pursue them in vain; *Falstaff* himself has a distinct and separate subsistence; he laughs at the chace, and when the sport is over, gathers them with unruffled feather under his wing. . .

An Essay on the Dramatic Character of Sir John Falstaff. (1774). 1777.

[213] *J. B. Priestley*

Shakespeare—it cannot be repeated too often—shows us what happened, what was inevitable under such circumstances and with such characters, and leaves the situation to make its own impression. And our attitude towards it is determined by our cast of mind. This is why the critics have differed so widely. If we are romantic Hotspurs or solemn Lancasters, we shall rejoice that the air is now cleared of its Falstaffian malodours, that honour and responsibility and the like have now the stage to themselves. Behind the bent, receding back of Sir John, we shall read a little moral lesson, as Gervinus does. If, on the other hand, we delight in sack and sugar, mirth and ease, and revel in the unfamiliar sense of freedom that is the very atmosphere of Falstaff, compared with which the world into which Henry enters, the world of statecraft and battle, is something forbiddingly angular and hard, then the end of the play will leave us resentful or depressed, as if we had been present at a piece of rank injustice. And if we can enter, with sympathy, into both worlds, but find ourselves torn between them, knowing that they are incompatible, that we cannot have our cake and eat it, then we shall be neither complacent nor resentful but will find ourselves at once quickened, by our dramatic sympathy, and yet thoughtful, dubious, touched by the old irony of things.

★ ★ ★

Falstaff owes his predominant position among comic figures to the fact that in him there meet the clown that delights the crowd, who love a person to laugh at; and the subtle character that engages the philosopher, who loves a person to laugh with. The first is a tribute to Shakespeare as a writer for his own theatre, the second is a tribute to his power of subtle characterisation, and the whole figure, displaying so many facets as the lights of different intelligences flash upon him and never failing to win your laughter and applause whatever your idea of the comic may be, is an example of his creator's amazing dramatic genius. He sets Falstaff walking and talking down the centuries, and though they may be ages of reason or ages of romance, they call for the biggest arm-chair, place him in their midst, and will not let him go.

★ ★ ★

There is no mystery, as some critics would have us suppose, about the appeal of such comic characters as Falstaff. Their crimes and vices, such as they are (and they are never very grave), have little or no effect upon us; they are so distant from us that we can regard them without moral indignation; it is not *our* sack they drink nor *our* money they borrow or steal or "convey"; it is no more possible to work ourselves up into a state of moral indignation over them than it is for us to grow angry at the thought of all the bandits existing in the remoter provinces of China, or tearful over the sexual laxity of the aborigines. On the other hand, though such fellows do not borrow *our* money and get drunk in *our* houses, so that their little weaknesses do not trouble us, it is for us, in the last resort, that these amusing rascals go through their various antics; their depredations are distant in time and space, but their jokes are here and now. Thus we can afford to be indulgent and to encourage them. It is often forgotten that Falstaff, after all, stands for something that is good in itself. He is the embodiment of masculine comradeship, ease, and merriment. He turns the whole world into the smoking-room of a club. He is the supreme example of the clubbable man.

★ ★ ★

Compared with him, we are all slaves. Out of his incongruous self and the incongruity that he is quick to perceive everywhere, he has contrived to build up a kingdom of his own, a Cloud-Cuckoodom, that exists in its own right and has its own consistency. There, all the restraints of this life are only so many little playthings; old father antic the law is our butt; we have no secrets and can never be disillusioned; we are the triumphant supper-party behind the scenes of life; the curse of Adam has been blown away. Throned in this kingdom, Falstaff is seemingly invulnerable; what would be weaknesses to other men become sources of strength to him; every predicament, every crisis, is but the beginning of a fresh triumph; every arrow shot from the bow of circumstance he catches in his hand and suddenly twists into some ludicrous shape, only to waken more laughter; he has frankly entertained the animal in himself, banishing the solemn dreams of our species in order to do so, and now, behold, the animal is no longer there—for he is throned like a god, enjoying a freedom, a dominion over the sad necessities, compared with which our common existence is a term in the galleys. What does it matter that he is old and fat and every thirsty and reduced to begging from old women, that his name is tarnished and his reputation an evil odour among the godly? He has escaped from the machinery of our moral and social order, does not obey or even recognise its rules, but has long since passed into his own kingdom, there attended by a host of fiery, nimble, and delectable shapes, born of fancy and sack. All our criticism passes him by. And so inward and searching is his humour, his mind so free from all common subterfuges and disguises, that however we may point to his devotion to sack, his great belly, his ancient lechery, his gross, palpable, open lies, we cannot laugh *at* him because he has everywhere forestalled us, pointed the way, and laughed first himself, so that willy-nilly we are compelled to laugh *with* him and thus enter his own kingdom. He seems to have accepted all the facts, he has not buried away a single impulse, and would appear to have achieved what all men wish to achieve, a synthesis, and so become master of life. Small wonder that he seems invulnerable.

"Falstaff and His Circle." *The English Comic Characters.* 1925.

[214] *C. L. Barber*

Hal's final expulsion of Falstaff appears . . . to carry out an impersonal pattern, not merely political but ritual in character. After the guilty reign of Bolingbroke, the prince is making a fresh start as the new king. At a level beneath the moral notions of a personal reform, we can see a nonlogical process of purification by sacrifice—the sacrifice of Falstaff. The career of the old king, a successful usurper whose conduct of affairs has been sceptical and opportunistic, has cast doubt on the validity of the whole conception of a divinely-ordained and chivalrous kingship to which Shakespeare and his society were committed. And before Bolingbroke, Richard II had given occasion for doubts about the rituals of kingship in an opposite way, by trying to use them magically. Shakespeare had shown Richard assuming that the symbols of majesty should be absolutes, that the names of legitimate power should be transcendently effective regardless of social forces. Now both these attitudes have been projected also in Falstaff; he carries to comically delightful and degraded extremes both a magical use of moral sanctions and the complementary opportunistic manipulation and scepticism. So the ritual analogy suggests that by turning on Falstaff as a scapegoat, as the villagers turned on their Mardi Gras, the prince can free himself from the sins, the "bad luck," of Richard's reign and of his father's reign, to become a king in whom chivalry and a sense of divine ordination are restored.

Shakespeare's Festive Comedy. A Study of Dramatic Form and Its Relation to Social Custom. 1959. Chap. VIII.

[215] *John F. Danby*

The rejection of Falstaff by Hal is an allegory. Behind that allegory is the concrete world of Elizabeth and her England. The twin forces in the sixteenth century state—each one needing the other, both in an uneasy state of counterpoise, capable of clashing as well as collaborating—were Appetite and Authority. In the rejection scene Hal and my Lord Chief Justice stand for Authority; Falstaff is Appetite, wonderfully enlarged, marvellously self-confident, a 'bolting hutch of beastliness', naïve and unashamed. Authority in Elizabeth's world lived and was sustained by Appetite. It could not have lasted in the world of Appetite, however, if it had not been strong. Authority therefore was, in the end, Power. Power was needed in the Tudor world (as in Henry V's) to centralize, organize, canalize, concentrate, and sometimes curb Appetite; to check it and give it more adequate goals—Spanish treasure fleets instead of merchant men on Gadshill, the Grand Lease of the Prince Bishop's coal mines instead of Mistress Quickly's bed linen. Falstaff's world is a symbol of the unofficial side of Elizabeth's reign. There was always also the official sphere of order and ceremony and decorum the buccaneer and entrepreneur readily fell in with. But the real work of the realm was done on the high seas by the buccaneers, in the coal mines and salt-beds and glass and brass manufactories by the entrepreneur: an unofficial realm Elizabeth could only recognize in private, when the attention of the rest of Europe was distracted elsewhere.

The high life of Elizabeth's monopolist-courtiers we see in *Henry IV, Part I,* when Hotspur and Glendower are quarrelling over the carving-up of the Kingdom. The unvarnished version is Falstaff and his retainers at their shady business. Appetite monstrous and unabashed, as plausible as it is unlimited, strides through London and the English countryside in Falstaff's person. The protective camouflage of the official world he does not need. His cynicism, as Bradley points out, pierces to the bottom of truth, honour, law, patriotism, duty, courage, war, religion. And everything at bottom, he sees—as the machiavel does—is self-preservation: 'What, ye rogues, young men must live.' His is the vitality and consciencelessness of Hawkins on the high seas. Hal, as Authority, is Elizabeth. Elizabeth had her unruly brigandage which nourished, supported, and sometimes clumsily clashed with her 'Order'—Drakes who flouted her with her silent permission, Essexes who presumed too far on the strength of the Queen's favour and met with sudden rebuff. Hal throws off Falstaff in order to be a more effective King: Elizabeth put away the flesh to be all the more effectively the Virgin Queen. Elizabeth's asceticism, of course, had its limits. Love of pomp, display, flattery, and money she indulged to the full. Hal's moral stance also has its limits, the limits of the necessity to be strong in possession of his throne, and the original limits of his entire manoeuvre to make reformation a means rather than an end:

> My reformation, glitt'ring o're my fault,
> Shall show more goodly, and attract more eyes,
> Than that which hath no foyle to set it off.
> Ile so offend, to make offence a skill,
> Redeeming time when men thinke least I will.

★ ★ ★

Hal and Falstaff, then, go together. They are to be accepted together, or rejected together. Certainly Hal's rejection of Falstaff must not be regarded as more significant than his long association with the rogue. It need not even be regarded as a final rejection. Prof. Dover Wilson has laboured successfully to show that Hal in the rejection scene is not being so hard on the old man as less percipient critics have led us to believe. There is also Falstaff's last word on the business (which Prof. Dover Wilson does not take so seriously as other parts of the text):

> Master Shallow, do not you grieve at this: I shall be sent for in private to him: Looke you, he must seeme thus to the world: fear not your advancement: I will be the man yet, that shall make you great. . . . This that you heard, was but a colour.
>
> (2 *Henry* IV, V, v.)

Such a 'colour' would be very credible to 'an Elizabethan audience'. It was Elizabeth's own way of dealing with her brigandage.

Analysis leaves us, then, with symbols of Power and Appetite as the keys to the play's meaning: Power and Appetite, the two sides of Commodity. The world is disunited and corrupt at heart. Corruption and disunity spread, too, through the whole body politic. The England depicted in *Henry IV, Part 1* and *2* is neither ideally ordered nor happy. It is an England, on the one side, of bawdy-house and thieves'-kitchen, of waylaid merchants, badgered and bewildered Justices, and a peasantry wretched, betrayed, and recruited for the wars; an England, on the other side, of the chivalrous wolf-pack of Hotspur and Douglas, and of state-sponsored treachery in the person of Prince John—the whole presided over by a sick King, hag-ridden by conscience, dreaming of a Crusade to the Holy Land as M. Remorse thinks of slimming and repentance. Those who see the world of *Henry IV* as some vital, joyous Renaissance England must go behind the facts Shakespeare presents. It is a world where to be normal is to be anti-social, and to be social is to be anti-human. Humanity is split in two. One half is banished to an underworld where dignity and decency must inevitably submerge in brutality and riot. The other half is restricted to an over-world where the same dignity and decency succumb to heartlessness and frigidity.

Shakespeare's Doctrine of Nature. 1949. Part II. Chap. I.

[216] *W. H. Auden*

Seeking for an explanation of why Falstaff affects us as he does, I find myself compelled to see *Henry IV* as possessing, in addition to its overt meaning, a parabolic significance. Overtly, Falstaff is a Lord of Misrule; parabolically, he is a comic symbol for the supernatural order of Charity as contrasted with the temporal order of Justice symbolized by Henry of Monmouth.

* * *

Falstaff speaks of himself as if he were always robbing travelers. We see him do this once—incidentally, it is not Falstaff but the Prince who is the instigator—and the sight convinces us that he never has been and never could be a successful highwayman. The money is restolen from him and returned to its proper owners; the only sufferer is Falstaff himself who has been made a fool of. He lives shamelessly on credit, but none of his creditors seems to be in serious trouble as a result. The Hostess may swear that if he does not pay his bill, she will have to pawn her plate and tapestries, but this is shown to be the kind of exaggeration habitual to landladies, for in the next scene they are still there. What, overtly, is dishonesty becomes, parabolically, a sign for a lack of pride, humility which acknowledges its unimportance and dependence upon others.

Then he rejoices in his reputation as a fornicator with whom no woman is safe alone, but the Falstaff on stage is too old to fornicate, and it is impossible to imagine him younger. All we see him do is defend a whore against a bully, set her on his knee and make her cry out of affection and pity. What in the real world is promiscuous lust, the treatment of other persons as objects of sexual greed, becomes in the comic world of play a symbol for the charity that loves all neighbors without distinction.

★ ★ ★

Falstaff's neglect of the public interest in favor of private concerns is an image for the justice of charity which treats each person, not as a cipher, but as a unique person. The Prince may justly complain:

> I never did see such pitiful rascals

but Falstaff's retort speaks for all the insulted and injured of this world:

> Tut tut—good enough to toss, food for powder, food for powder. They'll fit a pit as well as better. Tush, man, mortal men, mortal men. . . .

These are Falstaff's only acts: for the rest, he fritters away his time, swigging at the bottle and taking no thought for the morrow. As a parable, both the idleness and the drinking, the surrender to immediacy and the refusal to accept reality, become signs for the Unworldly Man as contrasted with Prince Hal who represents worldliness at its best.

★ ★ ★

Falstaff never really does anything, but he never stops talking, so that the impression he makes on the audience is not of idleness but of infinite energy. He is never tired, never bored, and until he is rejected he radiates happiness as Hal radiates power, and this happiness without apparent cause, this untiring devotion to making others laugh becomes a comic image for a love which is absolutely self-giving.

★ ★ ★

The Christian God is not a self-sufficient being like Aristotle's First Cause, but a God who creates a world which he continues to love although it refuses to love him in return. He appears in this world, not as Apollo or Aphrodite might appear, disguised as man so that no mortal should recognize his divinity, but as a real man who openly claims to be God. And the consequence is inevitable. The highest religious and temporal authorities condemn Him as a blasphemer and a Lord of Misrule, as a Bad Companion for mankind. Inevitable because, as Richelieu said, "The salvation of States is in this world," and history has not as yet provided us with any evidence that the Prince of this world has changed his character.

"The Prince's Dog." *The Dyer's Hand and Other Essays.* 1962.

[217] *G. B. Shaw*

Everything that charm of style, rich humor, and vivid natural charterization can do for a play are badly wanted by Henry IV, which has neither the romantic beauty of Shakespear's earlier plays nor the tragic greatness of the later ones. One can hardly forgive Shakespear quite for the worldly phase in which he tried to thrust such a Jingo hero as his Harry V down our throats. The combination of conventional propriety and brute masterfulness in his public capacity with a low-lived blackguardism in his private tastes is not a pleasant one. No doubt he is true to nature as a picture of what is by no means uncommon in English society, an able young Philistine inheriting high position and authority, which he holds on to and goes through with by keeping a tight grip on his conventional and legal advantages, but who would have been quite in his place if he had been born a gamekeeper or a farmer. We do not in the first part of Henry IV see Harry sending Mrs Quickly and Doll Tearsheet to the whipping-post, or handing over Falstaff to the Lord Chief Justice with a sanctimonious lecture; but he repeatedly makes it clear that he will turn on them later on, and that his self-indulgent good-fellowship with them is consciously and deliberately treacherous. His popularity, therefore, is like that of a prizefighter: nobody feels for him as for Romeo or Hamlet. Hotspur, too, though he is stimulating as ginger cordial is stimulating, is hardly better than his horse; and King Bolingbroke, preoccupied with his crown exactly as a miser is preoccupied with his money, is equally useless as a refuge for our affections, which are thus thrown back undivided on Falstaff, the most human person in the play, but none the less a besotted and disgusting old wretch. And there is neither any subtlety nor (for Shakespear) much poetry in the presentation of all these characters. They are labelled and described and insisted upon with the roughest directness; and their reality and their humor can alone save them from the unpopularity of their unlovableness and the tedium of their obviousness. Fortunately, they offer capital opportunities for interesting acting. Bolingbroke's long discourse to his son on the means by which he struck the imagination and enlisted the snobbery of the English people gives the actor a chance comparable to the crafty early scenes in Richelieu. Prince Hal's humor is seasoned with sportsmanlike cruelty and the insolence of conscious mastery and contempt to the point of occasionally making one shudder. Hotspur is full of energy; and Falstaff is, of course, an unrivalled part for the right sort of comedian. Well acted, then, the play is a good one in spite of there not being a single tear in it. Ill acted—O heavens!

"Henry IV." *The Saturday Review*. 16 May 1896. XXIV, 134–35.

[218] *Edward Hubler*

Doll Tearsheet, the girl on call at Mistress Quickly's tavern, is so minor a character that everything she says and everything which is said about her could be printed on a page or two. Commentators and actresses alike prefer to think of her as pure trollop, thus simplifying the act of comprehension and making the task of the actress easier than Shakespeare intended it to be. I hope that I do not seem to bestow on Doll Tearsheet any considerable dignity. She is, of course, the most common of mortals; but she is not simply a type. Shakespeare established her commonness in the beginning. "What pagan may that be?" asks the Prince when she is first mentioned. And the Page replies, "A proper gentlewoman, sir; and a kinswoman of my master's." The Prince is not deceived: "Even such kin as the parish heifers are to the town bull." Nothing that follows belies the guess, and the estimate of her character is confirmed on her first entrance, made after having drunk too much canary, "a marvelous searching wine" which "perfumes the blood e're one can say, 'What's this?' " Her conversation demonstrates that in all truth she is as "common as the way between St. Alban's and London." Shakespeare never pampers her. When we last see her she is being dragged off to prison for being what she is. Nor does he patronize her. He allows her a kind of wit and abundant animal spirits (the whore in modern literature is generally anemic) and although her tact is not what it should be, she means well: "I'll be friends with thee, Jack: thou art going to the wars; and whether I shall ever see thee again or no, there is nobody cares." It is comedy, but it is not farce. There is a humanity which the actress would do well to remember. Shakespeare's feeling for Doll is written in the lines. It cannot be abstracted, and it must not be ignored. She is the embodiment of warm and tawdry humanity, and she is *also* a trollop. If in our love of categories we think of her as only a trollop and fail to distinguish her from her sisters, we shall reduce Shakespeare's sketch to a stereotype.

There is no word for the point of view embodied here. "Rabelaisian" will not do, for the gusto it implies suggests a commitment absent from Shakespeare. "Elizabethan" and "Shakespearean" indicate but do not define the view so free from both bravado and apology. Sometimes we read that Shakespeare's view is naïve, but nothing could be further from the truth. Shakespeare is not naïve; it is simply that he is not sophisticated. He is not afraid of the commonplace, and he can accept the simple without condescension. In one of his sonnets he lists the things which displease him most, and among them he places "simple truth miscall'd simplicity." He is not Olympian, though no writer ever had more reason to be. He is not neutral. One understands the temptation to find him so, but it will not do. No writer's view of life was ever less a priori than Shakespeare's. He came to conclusions about life, but first he saw it. And what is more remarkable is that there are so many areas of his observation which his point of view does little to color. His tenderness does not trap him into sentimentality; his wit never serves as protective coloring, sophisticating the thrust of emotion to an easy obliquity. In the sonnets to the dark lady he accepts the passion, and, later, the remorse. "Everyone," wrote Aldous Huxley long ago . . . "feels a little Christian now and then, especially after an orgy." This is precisely the sort of awareness Shakespeare did *not* have; it diminishes both the Christianity and the orgy. One of the greatest aspects of Shakespeare's art (no other writer has it to a like degree) is his ability to give us contrasting things without the slightest diminution of either.

"Shakespeare and the Unromantic Lady." *The Sense of Shakespeare's Sonnets.* 1952.

Henry V

[219] *Elmer Edgar Stoll*

As a king, Henry is made to suit the Globe; as a man, to suit the English people. How English he is,—so practical, sportsmanlike, moral and pious; so manly and stalwart, and yet free and easy; so self-assertive and yet modest and generous; so fierce against his enemies, and yet merciful towards women and the weak; so serious, and yet simple and humorous; and so bluff and downright, and hearty and genuine, in the avowal of his love. And how instinctively an English audience must have taken to him! His wildness in youth gave him an added flavor, as it did to Richard the Lion-hearted before him and to Edward VII since; and his skill at leapfrog—a game which had not yet passed over into the hands of boys any more than had hopscotch, played, in their wigs, by Hogarth and his middle-aged friends, in the eighteenth century—fitted him even then to be a hero in this land of sport. The wooing scene itself, in which he refers to this and other accomplishments, must have been enough to float the play. If there is anything that the English take to, it is the unconventional and plain-spoken, especially when combined with humor and genuine affection at the core. "A character" the combination is called, as you find it throughout English literature, from Dekker down to Fielding and Dickens. And this character has the further charm of a king and soldier trying—and yet scorning—to be a suitor; unconventional in part because he cannot help it, in part because he would not help it if he could; wooing, and overruling, a conventional and coquettish princess, in a language that he cannot speak and she will not understand. All that is simple and English, all that is affected and French, and all that is mannish and womanish, too, comes out in the lively encounter between them; and how hugely an English audience must have been tickled with the contrast!

Poets and Playwrights. 1930. Chap. II.

[220] *Walter Pater*

Henry the Fourth . . . is presented, of course, in general outline, as an impersonation of "surviving force:" he has a certain amount of kingcraft also, a real fitness for great opportunity. But still true to his leading motive, Shakespeare, in *King Henry the Fourth,* has left the high-water mark of his poetry in the soliloquy which represents royalty longing vainly for the toiler's sleep; while the popularity, the showy heroism, of Henry the Fifth, is used to give emphatic point to the old earthy commonplace about "wild oats." The wealth of homely humour in these plays, the fun coming straight home to all the world, of Fluellen especially in his unconscious interview with the king, the boisterous earthiness of Falstaff and his companions, contribute to the same effect. The keynote of Shakespeare's treatment is indeed expressed by Henry the Fifth himself, the *greatest* of Shakespeare's kings.—"Though I speak it to you," he says *incognito,* under cover of night, to a common soldier on the field, "I think the king is but a man, as I am . . ." And, in truth, the really kingly speeches which Shakespeare assigns to him, as to other kings weak enough in all but speech, are but a kind of flowers, worn for, and effective only as personal embellishment. They combine to one result with the merely outward and ceremonial ornaments of royalty, its pageantries, flaunting so naively, so credulously, in Shakespeare, as in that old medieval time.

"Shakespeare's English Kings." *Scribner's Magazine.* April, 1889. *Appreciations.* 1889.

[221] *William Hazlitt*

Henry V is a very favourite monarch with the English nation, and he appears to have been also a favourite with Shakespear, who labours hard to apologise for the actions of the king, by shewing us the character of the man, as 'the king of good fellows.' He scarcely deserves this honour. He was fond of war and low company:—we know little else of him. He was careless, dissolute, and ambitious;—idle, or doing mischief. In private, he seemed to have no idea of the common decencies of life, which he subjected to a kind of regal licence; in public affairs, he seemed to have no idea of any rule of right or wrong, but brute force, glossed over with a little religious hypocrisy and archiepiscopal advice. His principles did not change with his situation and professions. His adventure on Gadshill was a prelude to the affair of Agincourt, only a bloodless one; Falstaff was a puny prompter of violence and outrage, compared with the pious and politic Archbishop of Canterbury, who gave the king *carte blanche,* in a genealogical tree of his family, to rob and murder in circles of latitude and longitude abroad—to save the possessions of the church at home. This appears in the speeches in Shakespear, where the hidden motives that actuate princes and their advisers in war and policy are better laid open than in speeches from the throne or woolsack. Henry, because he did not know how to govern his own kingdom, determined to make war upon his neighbours. Because his own title to the crown was doubtful, he laid claim to that of France. Because he did not know how to exercise the enormous power, which had just dropped into his hands, to any one good purpose, he immediately undertook (a cheap and obvious resource of sovereignty) to do all the mischief he could. Even if absolute monarchs had the wit to find out objects of laudable ambition, they could only 'plume up their wills' in adhering to the more sacred formula of the royal prerogative, 'the right divine of kings to govern wrong,' because will is only then triumphant when it is opposed to the will of others, because the pride of power is only then shewn, not when it consults the rights and interests of others, but when it insults and tramples on all justice and all humanity. Henry declares his resolution 'when France is his, to bend it to his awe, or break it all to pieces'—a resolution worthy of a conqueror, to destroy all that he cannot enslave; and what adds to the joke, he lays all the blame of the consequences of his ambition on those who will not submit tamely to his tyranny. Such is the history of kingly power, from the beginning to the end of the world . . .

Henry V, it is true, was a hero, a king of England, and the conqueror of the king of France. Yet we feel little love or admiration for him. He was a hero, that is, he was ready to sacrifice his own life for the pleasure of destroying thousands of other lives: he was a king of England, but not a constitutional one, and we only like kings according to the law; lastly, he was a conqueror of the French king, and for this we dislike him less than if he had conquered the French people. How then do we like him? We like him in the play. There he is a very amiable monster, a very splendid pageant. As we like to gaze at a panther or a young lion in their cages in the Tower, and catch a pleasing horror from their glistening eyes, their velvet paws, and dreadless roar, so we take a very romantic, heroic, patriotic, and poetical delight in the boasts and feats of our younger Harry, as they appear on the stage and are confined to lines of ten syllables; where no blood follows the stroke that wounds our ears, where no harvest bends beneath horses' hoofs, no city flames, no little child is butchered, no dead men's bodies are found piled on heaps and festering the next morning—in the orchestra!

Characters of Shakespear's Plays. 1817.

[222] *W. B. Yeats*

To pose character against character was an element in Shakespeare's art, and scarcely a play is lacking in characters that are the complement of one another, and so, having made the vessel of porcelain Richard II., he had to make the vessel of clay Henry V. He makes him the reverse of all that Richard was. He has the gross vices, the coarse nerves, of one who is to rule among violent people, and he is so little 'too friendly' to his friends that he bundles them out of doors when their time is over. He is as remorseless and undistinguished as some natural force, and the finest thing in his play is the way his old companions fall out of it broken-hearted or on their way to the gallows; and instead of the lyricism which rose out of Richard's mind like the jet of a fountain to fall again where it had risen, instead of that phantasy too enfolded in its own sincerity to make any thought the hour had need of, Shakespeare has given him a resounding rhetoric that moves men, as a leading article does today. His purposes are so intelligible to everybody that everybody talks of him as if he succeeded, although he fails in the end, as all men great and little fail in Shakespeare, and yet his conquests abroad are made nothing by a woman turned warrior, and that boy he and Katherine were to 'compound,' 'half French, half English,' 'that' was to 'go to Constantinople and take the Turk by the beard,' turns out a Saint and loses all his father had built up at home and his own life.

Shakespeare watched Henry V. not indeed as he watched the greater souls in the visionary procession, but cheerfully, as one watches some handsome spirited horse, and he spoke his tale, as he spoke all tales, with tragic irony.

"At Stratford-on-Avon." *The Speaker.* May 11, 18, 1901. *Ideas of Good and Evil.* 1903.

Henry VI

[223] *Algernon Charles Swinburne*

In this play [Part I] . . . more decisively than in *Titus Andronicus,* we find Shakespeare at work (so to speak) with both hands—with his left hand of rhyme, and his right hand of blank verse. The left is loth to forego the practice of its peculiar music; yet, as the action of the right grows freer and its touch grows stronger, it becomes more and more certain that the other must cease playing, under pain of producing mere discord and disturbance in the scheme of tragic harmony. We imagine that the writer must himself have felt the scene of the roses to be pitched in a truer key than the noble scene of parting between the old hero and his son on the verge of desperate battle and certain death. This is the last and loftiest farewell note of rhyming tragedy; still, in *King Richard II.* and in *Romeo and Juliet* it struggles for a while to keep its footing, but now more visibly in vain.

A Study of Shakespeare. 1880. "First Period: Lyric and Fantastic."

King John

[224] *John Masefield*

As a study of an Englishman, the Bastard can be recommended to foreign diplomatists, but they should be warned that public schools have somewhat changed the type. He is a robust, hearty person, contemptuous of the weak, glad to be a king's bastard, making friends with women (his own mother one of them) with a trusty, good-humoured frankness, fond of fighting, extremely able when told what to do, fond of plain measures—the plainer the better, an honest servant, easily impressed by intellect when found in high place on his own side, but utterly incapable of perceiving intellect in a foreigner, fond of those sorts of humour which generally lead to blows, extremely just, very kind when not fighting, fond of the words "fair play", and nobly and exquisitely moved to deep, true poetical feeling by a cruel act done to something helpless and little.

William Shakespeare. 1954.

Julius Caesar

[225] *John Dennis*

I conceive, that every Tragedy, ought to be a very Solemn Lecture, inculcating a particular Providence, and shewing it plainly protecting the Good, and chastizing the Bad, or at least the Violent; and that, if it is otherwise, it is either an empty Amusement, or a scandalous and pernicious Libel upon the Government of the World. The killing of *Julius Caesar* in *Shakespear,* is either a Murder, or a Lawful Action; if the killing *Caesar* is a Lawful Action, then the killing of *Brutus* and *Cassius* is downright Murder; and the Poet has been guilty of polluting the Scene, with the Blood of the very Best and Last of the *Romans.* But if the killing of *Caesar* is Murder, and *Brutus* and *Cassius* are very justly punish'd for it, then Shakespear is, on the other Side, answerable for introducing so many Noble *Romans,* committing, in the Face of an Audience, a very horrible Murder, and only punishing Two of them; which Proceeding gives an Occasion to the People, to draw a dangerous Inference from it, which may be destructive to Government, and to Human Society.

The Epistle Dedicatory. *The Advancement and Reformation of Modern Poetry.* 1701.

[226] *G. B. Shaw*

Shakespear, who knew human weakness so well, never knew human strength of the Caesarian type. His Caesar is an admitted failure: his Lear is a masterpiece. The tragedy of disillusion and doubt, of the agonized struggle for a foothold on the quicksand made by an acute observation striving to verify its vain attribution of morality and respectability to Nature, of the faithless will and the keen eyes that the faithless will is too weak to blind: all this will give you a Hamlet or a Macbeth, and win you great applause from literary gentlemen; but it will not give you a Julius Caesar. Caesar was not in Shakespear, nor in the epoch, now fast waning, which he inaugurated.

"Better than Shakespear?" Preface. *Three Plays for Puritans.* 1900. IX, xxxii.

[227] *Donald A. Stauffer*

But is it not possible, on the contrary, to think of Caesar as obsessed with the idea of the soul of the state, which he calls "Caesar," making a series of quick appraisals and decisions, and sensitive to all the forces and factions in Rome except care for his own personal safety? He dismisses the soothsayer: should a governor heed portents? He decides not to attend the Senate, at Calpurnia's entreaties: is this not a husband's generous gesture? When Decius presents the problem as a choice between a wife's whims and the business of state, between fear and fortitude, who would have him fail as a ruler to set the state before family comfort? He places the petition of Trebonius ahead of the personal warning of Artemidorus. His last long speech is an eloquent defense of his constancy in statecraft against the flattery of Metellus Cimber, the exhortations of Cassius, Cinna and Decius, and the friendship of Brutus. In his few huddled and hurried appearances, he yet has time for shrewd appraisals of Cassius and Antony, and special glancing words that show how affairs stand between him and Brutus, or Caius Ligarius, or Trebonius, or the unnamed Soothsayer. He listens to everyone, is aware of everyone. Nowhere does Shakespeare make Caesar's sensitivity to opinion clearer than in the account of how popular sentiment caused him, though personally ambitious, to refuse the crown—as if "he was very loath to lay his fingers off it." He swooned after this great refusal, but before he fell down, says Casca, "when he perceiv'd the common herd was glad he refus'd the crown, he pluck'd me ope his doublet and offer'd them his throat to cut."

May not this be a picture of the ideal governor, disregarding his own desires and fears, acting for the good of Rome as he conceives it, speaking the famous "Cowards die many times before their deaths" with the voice of Rome to quell his own personal tremors, and building above his weaknesses the conception of the impersonal Caesar, unshaken, unseduced, unterrified? Unless Caesar is seen as more than a person in this play, then his name should never have been given to a tragedy in which he appears, unghosted, in only three scenes, and speaks in a mere hundred and fifty lines. His body lies in full view on the stage during two scenes, each of which is considerably longer than the sum of the lines Caesar speaks in the entire play. Stage pictures and silence may point a moral.

Shakespeare's World of Images. 1949. Chap. IV.

[228] *Hazelton Spencer*

Structurally the drama is so open to objection that its effectiveness on stage evidently arises from other considerations. In lieu of his usual method of close-packed compression, Shakespeare often skips. The major episodes are vigorously executed, but they fail to form a steady progression. Perhaps an uncut text gave more links and transitions. The quarrel scene is played up because it affords fine scope for the two leading actors, but it assumes a prominence out of all proportion. The piece obviously breaks in two in the middle. Our interest in Brutus does more to bridge the gap than Caesar's ghost does. Shakespeare fails to cast the historical facts in the revenge-tragedy mold, or else deliberately chooses not to. Neither Antony nor Octavius becomes that appealing figure, the sorely tried avenger consecrated to a great task. They remain Antony and Octavius, famous persons from the pages of Roman history. Nor is Brutus much more satisfactory. He is not the hero-villain whose fall inspires awe, nor the eager hero who fully commands our sympathy. For one thing, Caesar dwarfs him at first. For another, Shakespeare's touch is less sure than usual; he seems not quite certain what to make of Brutus. No doubt in "This was the noblest Roman of them all" he formulates the impression he wishes to leave with us. But we have also seen Brutus through the eyes of Cassius, and there is more than a hint of the stuffed shirt about him. Shaw calls him the perfect Girondin, doomed by the coarser Antony and Octavius, "who at least knew the difference between life and rhetoric." Cassius is the best piece of character drawing—the genuine radical and drive-wheel of revolution. Antony is for the company's "juvenile"—a straight and surefire rôle, embellished with splendid recitatives and arias.

The Art and Life of William Shakespeare. 1940. Chap. 6.

[229] *William Hazlitt*

Shakespear has in this play and elsewhere shown the same penetration into political character and the springs of public events as into those of every-day life. For instance, the whole design of the conspirators to liberate their country fails from the generous temper and overweening confidence of Brutus in the goodness of their cause and the assistance of others. Thus it has always been. Those who mean well themselves think well of others, and fall a prey to their security. That humanity and honesty which dispose men to resist injustice and tyranny render them unfit to cope with the cunning and power of those who are opposed to them. The friends of liberty trust to the professions of others, because they are themselves sincere, and endeavour to reconcile the public good with the least possible hurt to its enemies, who have no regard to anything but their own unprincipled ends, and stick at nothing to accomplish them. Cassius was better cut out for a conspirator. His heart prompted his head. His watchful jealousy made him fear the worst that might happen, and his irritability of temper added to his inveteracy of purpose, and sharpened his patriotism. The mixed nature of his motives made him fitter to contend with bad men. The vices are never so well employed as in combating one another. Tyranny and servility are to be dealt with after their own fashion: otherwise, they will triumph over those who spare them, and finally pronounce their funeral panegyric, as Antony did that of Brutus.

Characters of Shakespear's Plays. 1817.

[230] *John Palmer*

Brutus has precisely the qualities which in every age have rendered the conscientious liberal ineffectual in public life. His convictions required him to take the lead in a political conspiracy which, for its success, called for great agility of mind, a deft and callous adjustment of means to ends, acceptance of the brutal consequences which attend an act of violence, and insight into the motives of men less scrupulous and disinterested than himself. In all these respects he was deficient. Brutus, plotting the assassination of Caesar, did violence to his character, entered into association with men whom he did not understand and involved himself in events which he was unable to control. He committed himself to a course of action which could only be justified by principles which had ceased to be valid for the society in which he lived and which entangled him in unforeseen consequences with which he was unable to cope.

★ ★ ★

[Cassius] is the familiar type of politician who plumes himself on being a 'realist' and stoutly affects to base his political conduct on the meanest of motives. The implication that Brutus would do well to avoid politics altogether—for it is meet that noble minds keep ever with their likes—is equally characteristic. It expresses just that blend of admiration and contempt felt by the practical man of affairs for the man of principle.

★ ★ ★

The lean and hungry Cassius gives place to the gamesome Antony;

the man who thinks too much to the sanguine opportunist who hardly thinks at all but responds to the mood of the moment. Brutus, the man of sentiment, is now to be contrasted with Antony, the man of passion, and we are soon to realise that passion in politics can be as effective as sentiment is unavailing. Antony uses his private grief to inflame the emotions of the crowd. He is that most effectively mischievous of orators who can blend an emotion sincerely felt with a nicely calculated appeal to the feelings of his audience. Giving free rein to a personal passion he at the same time plays upon the passion of the mob. His blood may be at fever heat, but he keeps a cool head. Above all, he understands the common man and can put himself into immediate sympathy with those about him. He has no political convictions, no programme either of reaction or reform. He intends to save himself and to avenge his friend. He is the politician to whom politics will never be more than a game and who of his own choice would never have concerned himself seriously with public affairs. He is the political amateur who in time of peace excels in sport and revels long o' nights, and who, in time of war, goes into battle as into a stadium.

★ ★ ★

These two [funeral] orations cannot be too closely studied. There is a complete political character in each of them. Brutus speaks from the pathetic conviction that he has only to state a case honestly and clearly to the people; the people will be convinced and thereafter remain steadfast in their opinion. It is the fallacy of a liberal-minded politician, who assumes that men in the mass are governed by reason and who ignores the conscious self-interest or, what is even more potent, the irrational impulse of the crowd. It is the tragic error of a civilised man, who believes that it is only necessary to prove, for example, that war is unprofitable or a policy intellectually absurd in order to bring everlasting peace to the nations and Utopia to the individual. Brutus gives to this conviction a form which is marvellously appropriate. He makes no appeal to the emotions of his audience. His speech consists of a series of terse, antithetical sentences, conveying precisely the idea he has in mind. It is Euclidean in its logic, Tacitean in its tidiness and brevity. It requires from those who listen a close, consecutive attention. Brutus might be addressing an academy of science, a congress of philosophers, an audience of literary exquisites, capable of appreciating an exposition in which every sentence contributes to the formal symmetry of the rhetorical design.

Political Characters of Shakespeare. 1945. Chap. I.

[231] *Richard G. Moulton*

The passion in the play of *Julius Caesar* gathers around the conspirators, and follows them through the mutations of their fortunes. If however we are to catch the different parts of the action in their proper proportions we must remember the character of these conspirators, and especially of their leaders Brutus and Cassius. These are actuated in what they do not by personal motives but by devotion to the public good and the idea of republican liberty; accordingly in following their career we must not look too exclusively at their personal success and failure. The exact key to the movement of the drama will be given by fixing attention upon the *justification of the conspirators' cause* in the minds of the audience; and it is this which is found to rise gradually to its height in the centre of the play, and from that point to decline to the end. I have pointed out in the preceding study how the issue at stake in *Julius Caesar* amounts to a conflict between the outer and inner life, between devotion to a public enterprise and such sympathy with the claims of individual humanity as is specially fostered by the cultivation of the inner nature. The issue is reflected in words of Brutus already quoted:

> The abuse of greatness is, when it disjoins
> Remorse from power.

Brutus applies this as a test to Caesar's action, and is forced to acquit him: but is not Brutus here laying down the very principle of which his own error in the play is the violation? The assassin's dagger puts Brutus and the conspirators in the position of power; while 'remorse' —the word in Shakespearean English means human sympathy—is the due of their victim Caesar, whose rights to justice as a man, and to more than justice as the friend of Brutus, the conspirators have the responsibility of balancing against the claims of a political cause. These claims of justice and humanity are deliberately ignored by the stoicism of Brutus, while the rest of the conspirators are blinded to them by the mists of political enthusiasm; this outraged human sympathy asserts itself after Caesar's death in a monstrous form in the passions of the mob, which are guided by the skill of Antony to the destruction of the assassins. Of course both the original violation of the balance between the two lives and the subsequent reaction are equally corrupt. The stoicism of Brutus, with its suppression of the inner sympathies, arrives practically at the principle—destined in the future history of the world to be the basis of a yet greater crime—that it is expedient that one man should die rather than that a whole people should perish. On the other hand, Antony trades upon the fickle violence of the populace, and uses it as much for personal ends as for vengeance. This demoralisation of both the sides of character is the result of their divorce. Such is the essence of this play if its action be looked at as a whole; but it belongs to the movement of dramatic passion that we see the action only in its separate parts at different times. Through the first half of the play, while the justification of the conspirators' cause is rising, the other side of the question is carefully hidden from us; from the point of the assassination the suppressed element starts into prominence, and sweeps our sympathies along with it to its triumph at the conclusion of the play.

Shakespeare as a Dramatic Artist. 1885. Chap. IX.

[232] *Harold S. Wilson*

This is the design, then, of political events and their outcome which Shakespeare presents to us in the play. The human ideal of liberty is incompatible with the limits of human wisdom, the human capacity of self-knowledge and self-rule. This fact is tragic for the noble-minded idealist like Brutus and for the great statesman like Caesar; and it is tragic for the state, for each member of it has his share of responsibility in the catastrophe, from Caesar and Brutus, Caesar's supporters and Brutus's supporters, on down to the humblest of the Roman mob, who make holiday when Caesar triumphs over the sons of Pompey and would indifferently accept Caesar or Brutus for their king.

On the Design of Shakespearian Tragedy. 1957. Chap. IV.

King Lear

[233] *Samuel Taylor Coleridge*

The strange, yet by no means unnatural, mixture of selfishness, sensibility, and habit of feeling derived from and fostered by the particular rank and usages of the individual; the intense desire to be intensely beloved, selfish, and yet characteristic of the selfishness of a loving and kindly nature—a feeble selfishness, self-supportless and leaning for all pleasure on another's breast; the selfish craving after a sympathy with a prodigal disinterestedness, contradicted by its own ostentation and the mode and nature of its claims; the anxiety, the distrust, the jealousy, which more or less accompany all selfish affections, and are among the surest contradistinctions of mere fondness from love, and which originate Lear's eager wish to enjoy his daughter's violent professions, while the inveterate habits of sovereignty convert the wish into claim and positive right, and the incompliance with it into crime and treason;—these facts, these passions, these moral verities, on which the whole tragedy is founded, are all prepared for, and will to the retrospect be found implied in, these first four or five lines of the play. They let us know that the trial is but a trick; and that the grossness of the old king's rage is in part the natural result of a silly trick suddenly and most unexpectedly baffled and disappointed.

★ ★ ★

. . . in [Edmund's] own presence his own father takes shame to himself for the frank avowal that he is his father—has "blushed so often to acknowledge him that he is now braz'd to it." He hears his mother and the circumstances of his birth spoken of with a most degrading and licentious levity—described as a wanton by her own paramour, and the remembrance of the animal sting, the low criminal gratifications connected with her wantonness and prostituted beauty assigned as the reason why "the whoreson must be acknowledged." This, and the consciousness of its notoriety—the gnawing conviction that every shew of respect is an effort of courtesy which recalls while it represses a contrary feeling—this is the ever-trickling flow of wormwood and gall into the wounds of pride, the corrosive virus which inoculates pride with a venom not its own, with envy, hatred, a lust of that power which in its blaze of radiance would hide the dark spots on his disk, [with] pangs of shame personally undeserved and therefore felt as wrongs, and a blind ferment of vindictive workings towards the occasions and causes, especially towards a brother whose stainless birth and lawful honors were the constant remembrancers of *his* debasement, and were ever in the way to prevent all chance of its being unknown or overlooked and forgotten.

Notes on the Tragedies. Raysor I, 55–57.

[234] *Donald A. Stauffer*

The old theme that love can create love is given one last twist in a startling intimation. The opening subject of the play was heartless laughter at the bastard Edmund and the sport at his making,

Edmund, lonely exile from the world, fights society with its own weapons and its own rules for the survival of the fittest. Now the wheel has come full circle. Dying—since selfish interests are no longer relevant—he observes the passing time; knowing that his own life is passing, he even forgives the unknown man who has dealt him the deathstroke. He hears Edgar's tale of his ministering to the father who has wronged him, and muses: "This speech of yours hath mov'd me, And shall perchance do good." He hears of the deaths of Goneril and Regan, and the theme of unity reappears in this harsh key: "I was contracted to them both. All three Now marry in an instant." And again:

Yet Edmund was belov'd.

The theme of love is here distorted, the four little words carry complicated emotions, but they give Edmund at least a pitiful moment of assuagement. The slave is for a moment free. Shakespeare knew how imperfect a mirror man is for his own ideals, and might have said with Dante: "The eternal light always kindles love; and if anything your love should lead astray, it is not without some gleam, ill understood, that still shines through." However it may be, from whatever mixed motives of altruism and personal passion, Edmund suddenly attempts to repeal his writ upon the lives of Lear and Cordelia. "I pant for life," he says, a remark as significant in the symbolic as the literal world. "Some good I mean to do, Despite of mine own nature." And despite his own nature, warped by the evil of others and his own counter-evil, he repents in a moment, and by this action is an exile no longer, but a man within the brotherhood of men. It is the last miracle in the play, except for the resurrection of Cordelia in the mind of the desolated Lear. The tragedy generates miracles through misery. But the miracles are no less true than the misery; and the gods, kind and avenging, seek to give losses their remedies.

Shakespeare's World of Images. 1949. Chap. V.

[235] *Samuel Taylor Coleridge*

Kent [is] the nearest to perfect goodness of all Shakespeare's characters, and yet the most *individualized.*

★ ★ ★

The Steward . . . [is] the only character of utter unredeemable *baseness* in Shakespeare.

★ ★ ★

The deepest tragic notes are often struck by a half sense of an impending blow. The Fool's conclusion of this act [I] by a grotesque prattling seems to indicate the dislocation of feeling that has begun and is to be continued.

★ ★ ★

What can I say of this scene [the blinding of Gloucester]? My reluctance to think Shakespeare wrong, and yet—

Notes on the Tragedies. Raysor I, 61–62, 64, 66.

[236] *Robert Bechtold Heilman*

The blinding of Gloucester might well be gratuitous melodrama but for its being imbedded in a field of meanings centered in the concept of *seeing:* references, whether literal or figurative, to the act of seeing, to things seen (sights), to the conditions of seeing (darkness and light), and to the means of seeing (eyes) persist throughout the play. This sight pattern relentlessly brings into play the problem of seeing, and what is always implied is that the problem is one of insight, of the values which determine how one sees.

This Great Stage Image and Structure in King Lear. 1948. Chap. I.

[237] *Robert Bechtold Heilman*

Shakespeare so qualifies and amplifies *reason in madness* that he avoids having, at one polar extreme, a mere surrealistic laudation of lunacy. Along with Lear's burning knowledge we must take the insight of the Fool and Edgar, which is an essential part of the madness pattern. Madness becomes, then, not merely clinical insanity but the whole realm of what is, from the conventional point of view, mental and worldy incompetence. Shakespeare takes three very "unlikely specimens," as the world might view them—a crazy old man long told that he is in his dotage, a Fool who may be clever but is probably unbalanced and is certainly a no-account, a naïve young man who manages so ill that he can save himself only by becoming an outcast bedlam—and makes them, as far as the reflective and imaginative world is concerned, his three wise men. Lear's interpretative union of symbolic patterns, the Fool's keen perceptions of fact and imaginative inferences from fact, and Edgar's gnomic observations constitute, certainly not a formal philosophic commentary on experience, but a very solid aggregation of wisdom about it. That it should come from the humble, the scorned, and the exiled produces almost a Christian transvaluation of the values of Lear's pagan world. This is Shakespeare's central paradox, by which he unites the other paradoxes into an inclusive paradox: the blind see, the naked survive, and wisdom belongs to the mad. By these paradoxes he presents the dilemma of the World: humanity must live in it, and wishes to do well in it, yet the better man does in it, the more likely he seems to come to ultimate grief. To have little and to be outside the sphere of the great seem the surest way to salvation.

What of the other side? Shakespeare presents madness not merely as psychologically "realistic"; he goes far beyond this and presents madness, which in one sense is a negation of all values, as itself containing value. But since we are quite evidently not to be told that this value is absolute, we look immediately for the contrapuntal statement; since Shakespeare is a master of the world of polarities, we automatically seek the alternative necessary to the tension of the play. At one pole, we find *reason in madness;* at the other, indeed, is *madness in reason.* Here we come to a balancing set of paradoxes. We have already seen the ironic contrast between the blind who come to insight, and the sharp-seeing who see so complacently well that more escapes their eyes than they know. We have seen, too, the paradox of the wild animals who are destroyed, and of those in proud array who have neither warmth nor protection. They are the wise in the world, and they have their own kind of madness.

This Great Stage Image and Structure in King Lear. 1948. Chap. VIII.

[238] *John Middleton Murry*

What is fairly plain to me is that this vision of humanity self-destroyed by its own animality was one that Shakespeare's imagination did not dominate into a drama, as he was wont to do. It may be said that *King Lear* is the drama into which he dominated it. In which case, I reply that there is a difference in kind between *King Lear* and the tragedies with which it is generally ranked, and to which it is forcibly assimilated. That this difference in kind was due to some essential intractability in the material itself, I can readily allow. But to speak of imaginative mastery in *King Lear* in the same sense in which it can be applied to *Hamlet,* or *Othello* or *Macbeth* or *Antony and Cleopatra,* or even *Coriolanus,* is to me impossible.

Here, I feel, was a vision which Shakespeare did not master; and by that I mean that the Imagination in him did not master it. It may have been a vision which took possession of him, in a sense essentially the same as that in which the Gospel and Christian tradition speak of a man being possessed by the devil. 'An ounce of civet, good apothecary, to sweeten my imagination!' is, to my ear, the voice of the man through whom *King Lear* was uttered. And there is a vital difference between such possession and the spontaneous self-abeyance which is the attitude of Imagination. A man imagines, we have said, with his whole being. A man possessed, as Shakespeare may have been possessed, during the writing of *King Lear,* by the vision that is continually breaking forth in it, cannot imagine with his whole being. It is his wholeness of being which is incessantly being destroyed.

To use such terms as these, *King Lear* impresses me as a constant struggle of Imagination against Possession—a struggle in which, in the main, the Imagination is defeated. And Possession does not make for poetry. The 'mad' scenes of *King Lear* have been overestimated in this regard. In texture and expressiveness they are, on the whole, inferior to what Shakespeare had elsewhere achieved. To my sense, the lapse of creative vigour in them is palpable; and I am inclined to suspect that some such impression is the solid basis of the traditional romantic theory that the difficulty which is always found in making the mad scenes convincing on the stage is due to their very magnificence. The conception is too 'titanic', the poetry too 'sublime'.

I do not feel that. On the contrary, I believe that many of the scenes are evidently the work not so much of a tired, as of a divided man—and a man divided in the sense I have tried to indicate: intermittently possessed by a vision that is inimical to the spontaneity of Imagination. Probably this enduring impression of mine could be expressed in terms more congruous with critical tradition by saying that Shakespeare's conception was so tremendous that his art broke under the strain. But, in the first place, that is not how I feel it; and, in the second—even if such a notion were intrinsically credible to me, which it is not—it would make it impossible to explain how *King Lear* came to be followed by *Coriolanus* and *Antony and Cleopatra.* I can conceive, without difficulty, that these plays followed a period of obsession and possession by a vision of life which Shakespeare himself felt and knew could not be final; but I cannot conceive that, if Shakespeare had felt that this vision, while it lasted, was ultimate, the sequel would have been *Coriolanus* and *Antony and Cleopatra.*

The distinction may be hard to establish objectively, but it is very real to me. It is indeed the difference between the tragic and the diseased vision of life; or again, it is the difference between a despair which engulfs the whole man, and a despair which some part of the man refuses to acknowledge. It seems to me that much of *King Lear* derives from an exaggeration, or exploitation of partial despair. It is a kind of enforced utterance, in a period when—from the ideal point of view—silence was more wholesome and more natural.

A poet of genius creates not how he should, but how he can. I am not saying that it would have been better if Shakespeare had not written *King Lear;* and I wish to safeguard myself in advance against a misinterpretation so preposterous. I am merely demurring to the almost inveterate habit of Shakespeare criticism with regard to the play, which is to represent it as the sublime and transcendent culmination of a 'tragic period'. It is not that, to my mind, at all. It does not belong to the same order as *Hamlet, Othello* and *Macbeth;* or as *Coriolanus* and *Antony and Cleopatra.* It is, in that sequence, an anomaly. Compared to them, it is lacking in imaginative control, it is lacking in poetic 'intensity'. It belongs rather to a group of plays —to which *Timon* and *Troilus* belong—which are the work of a man struggling with an obsession. Amongst these plays it is, indubitably, supreme; but it is with them that it belongs.

Shakespeare. 1936. Chap. XVI.

[239] *Algernon Charles Swinburne*

[Lear] is by far the most Æschylean of his works; the most elemental and primaeval, the most oceanic and Titanic in conception. He deals here with no subtleties as in *Hamlet,* with no conventions as in *Othello:* there is no question of 'a divided duty' or a problem half insoluble, a matter of country and connection, of family or of race; we look upward and downward, and in vain, into the deepest things of nature, into the highest things of providence; to the roots of life, and to the stars; from the roots that no God waters to the stars which give no man light; over a world full of death and life without resting-place or guidance.

But in one main point it differs radically from the work and the spirit of Æschylus. Its fatalism is of a darker and harder nature. To Prometheus the fetters of the lord and enemy of mankind were bitter; upon Orestes the hand of heaven was laid too heavily to bear; yet in the not utterly infinite or everlasting distance we see beyond them the promise of the morning on which mystery and justice shall be made one; when righteousness and omnipotence at last shall kiss each other. But on the horizon of Shakespeare's tragic fatalism we see no such twilight of atonement, such pledge of reconciliation as this. Requital, redemption, amends, equity, explanation, pity and mercy, are words without a meaning here.

As flies to wanton boys are we to the gods;
They kill us for their sport.

Here is no need of the Eumenides, children of Night everlasting; for here is very Night herself.

The words just cited are not casual or episodical; they strike the keynote of the whole poem, lay the keystone of the whole arch of thought.

A Study of Shakespeare. 1880. "Third Period: Tragic and Romantic."

[240] *Arthur Sewell*

King Lear is the play in which Shakespeare returns once again to see man as a human soul, not in opposition to society, not rejecting society, but finding in society the sphere of fulfilment. Order is now seen, for the first time, and perhaps imperfectly, 'not merely negative, but creative and liberating'. It is a vision of society very different from that discovered in *Othello*. In *Othello* we cannot suppose that society is ever moral or good. Othello and Iago die, but future Othellos will find themselves betrayed in Venice, and future Iagos will still prey upon its profligates. In *King Lear* the conflict is no longer apprehended as a conflict between the individual and society; the conflict is now within society itself. Disorder in the human soul is both the agent and the product of disorder in society. Social order is the condition, as it is the resultant, of sweet and affirmative being, without which man relapses into a beastly and self-destructive individualism.

★ ★ ★

. . . it is not a merely secular society in which these characters are conceived to have their being. Nor, on the other hand, do I think it can be said (even through allegory) to be a society understood in terms of Christian theology. Nevertheless, to put the matter quite simply, we certainly get the impression in the play that the characters are imagined not only as members of each other but also as members of a Nature which is active both within themselves and throughout the circumambient universe. Man is nowhere so certainly exhibited as a member of all organic creation and of the elemental powers. Man's membership of society is more than legal, is more than political, because it is subtended in a wider membership, in which plants and animals, the wind and the thunder, are also included. And is it too extravagant to suggest that this natural universe is, in the earlier part of the play, peopled not only by men but also by beings of a primitive pagan belief—by Hecate, by Apollo, by Jupiter, by 'the gods'; and that the dominion of these beings is, in the action of the play, superseded? Is it, indeed, too extravagant to suggest that in the play we have a veritable change in dispensation? That, at any rate, is the impression given as the imagery changes and one store of images gives way to another. What the final dispensation is, however, it is difficult to determine, for Shakespeare seems not to specify it. The most we can say is that, like the promise of rain in Mr. T. S. Eliot's *The Waste Land,* there are moments and images towards the end of *King Lear* which give promise of grace and benediction.

Character and Society in Shakespeare. 1951. Chap. V.

[241] *Samuel Johnson*

The injury done by *Edmund* to the simplicity of the action is abundantly recompensed by the addition of variety, by the art with which he is made to co-operate with the chief design, and the opportunity which he gives the poet of combining perfidy with perfidy, and connecting the wicked son with the wicked daughters, to impress this important moral, that villany is never at a stop, that crimes lead to crimes, and at last terminate in ruin.

But though this moral be incidentally enforced, *Shakespeare* has suffered the virtue of *Cordelia* to perish in a just cause, contrary to the natural ideas of justice, to the hope of the reader, and, what is yet more strange, to the faith of chronicles. . . . A play in which the wicked prosper, and the virtuous miscarry, may doubtless be good, because it is a just representation of the common events of human life: but since all reasonable beings naturally love justice, I cannot easily be persuaded, that the observation of justice makes a play worse; or, that if other excellencies are equal, the audience will not always rise better pleased from the final triumph of persecuted virtue.

In the present case the publick has decided. *Cordelia,* from the time of *Tate,* has always retired with victory and felicity. And, if my sensations could add any thing to the general suffrage, I might relate, that I was many years ago so shocked by *Cordelia*'s death, that I know not whether I ever endured to read again the last scenes of the play till I undertook to revise them as an editor.

The Plays of William Shakespeare. 1765. Vol. VI.

[242] *W. H. Auden*

In *King Lear,* Shakespeare attempts to show absolute love and goodness, in the person of Cordelia, destroyed by the powers of this world, but the price he pays is that Cordelia, as a dramatic character, is a bore.

If she is not to be a fake, what she says cannot be poetically very impressive nor what she does dramatically very exciting.

> What shall Cordelia speak? Love and be silent.

In a play with twenty-six scenes, Shakespeare allows her to appear in only four, and from a total of over three thousand three hundred lines, he allots to her less than ninety.

"The Prince's Dog." *The Dyer's Hand and Other Essays.* 1962.

[243] *A. C. Bradley*

. . . the touch of reconciliation that we feel in contemplating the death of Cordelia is not due, or is due only in some slight degree, to a perception that the event is true to life, admissible in tragedy, and a case of a law which we cannot seriously desire to see abrogated.

What then is this feeling, and whence does it come? I believe that we shall find that it is a feeling not confined to *King Lear,* but present at the close of other tragedies; and that the reason why it has an exceptional tone or force at the close of *King Lear,* lies in that very peculiarity of the close which also—at least for the moment—excites bewilderment, dismay, or protest. The feeling I mean is the impression that the heroic being, though in one sense and outwardly he has failed, is yet in another sense superior to the world in which he appears; is, in some way which we do not seek to define, untouched by the doom that overtakes him; and is rather set free from life than deprived of it. Some such feeling as this—some feeling which, from this description of it, may be recognised as their own even by those who would dissent from the description—we surely have in various degrees at the deaths of Hamlet and Othello and Lear, and of Antony and Cleopatra and Coriolanus. It accompanies the more prominent tragic impressions, and, regarded alone, could hardly be called tragic. For it seems to imply (though we are probably quite unconscious of the implication) an idea which, if developed, would transform the tragic view of things. It implies that the tragic world, if taken as it is presented, with all its error, guilt, failure, woe and waste, is no final reality, but only a part of reality taken for the whole, and, when so taken, illusive; and that if we could see the whole, and the tragic facts in their true place in it, we should find them, not abolished, of course, but so transmuted that they had ceased to be strictly tragic,—find, perhaps, the suffering and death counting for little or nothing, the greatness of the soul for much or all, and the heroic spirit, in spite of failure, nearer to the heart of things than the smaller, more circumspect, and perhaps even 'better' beings who survived the catastrophe. The feeling which I have tried to describe, as accompanying the more obvious tragic emotions at the deaths of heroes, corresponds with some such idea as this.[1]

Now this feeling is evoked with a quite exceptional strength by the death of Cordelia. It is not due to the perception that she, like Lear, has attained through suffering; we know that she had suffered and attained in his days of prosperity. It is simply the feeling that what happens to such a being does not matter; all that matters is what she is. How this can be when, for anything the tragedy tells

[1] It follows from the above that, if this idea were made explicit and accompanied our reading of a tragedy throughout, it would confuse or even destroy the tragic impression. So would the constant presence of Christian beliefs. The reader most attached to these beliefs holds them in temporary suspension while he is immersed in a Shakespearean tragedy. Such tragedy assumes that the world, as it is presented, is the truth, though it also provokes feelings which imply that this world is not the whole truth, and therefore not the truth.

us, she has ceased to exist, we do not ask; but the tragedy itself makes us feel that somehow it is so. And the force with which this impression is conveyed depends largely on the very fact which excites our bewilderment and protest, that her death, following on the deaths of all the evil characters, and brought about by an unexplained delay in Edmund's effort to save her, comes on us, not as an inevitable conclusion to the sequence of events, but as the sudden stroke of mere fate or chance. The force of the impression, that is to say, depends on the very violence of the contrast between the outward and the inward, Cordelia's death and Cordelia's soul. The more unmotived, unmerited, senseless, monstrous, her fate, the more do we feel that it does not concern her. The extremity of the disproportion between prosperity and goodness first shocks us, and then flashes on us the conviction that our whole attitude in asking or expecting that goodness should be prosperous is wrong; that, if only we could see things as they are, we should see that the outward is nothing and the inward is all.

And some such thought as this (which, to bring it clearly out, I have stated, and still state, in a form both exaggerated and much too explicit) is really present through the whole play. Whether Shakespeare knew it or not, it is present. I might almost say that the 'moral' of *King Lear* is presented in the irony of this collocation:

> *Albany.* The gods defend her!
> *Enter Lear with Cordelia dead in his arms.*

The 'gods,' it seems, do *not* show their approval by 'defending' their own from adversity or death, or by giving them power and prosperity. These, on the contrary, are worthless, or worse; it is not on them, but on the renunciation of them, that the gods throw incense. They breed lust, pride, hardness of heart, the insolence of office, cruelty, scorn, hypocrisy, contention, war, murder, self-destruction. The whole story beats this indictment of prosperity into the brain. Lear's great speeches in his madness proclaim it like the curses of Timon on life and man. But here, as in *Timon,* the poor and humble are, almost without exception, sound and sweet at heart, faithful and pitiful. And here adversity, to the blessed in spirit, is blessed. It wins fragrance from the crushed flower. It melts in aged hearts sympathies which prosperity had frozen. It purges the soul's sight by blinding that of the eyes. Throughout that stupendous Third Act the good are seen growing better through suffering, and the bad worse through success. The warm castle is a room in hell, the storm-swept heath a sanctuary. The judgment of this world is a lie; its goods, which we covet, corrupt us; its ills, which break our bodies, set our souls free;

> Our means secure us, and our mere defects
> Prove our commodities.

Let us renounce the world, hate it, and lose it gladly. The only real thing in it is the soul, with its courage, patience, devotion. And nothing outward can touch that.

Shakespearean Tragedy. 1904. Lect. VIII.

[244] *William Empson*

Fool [in V. iii: "And my poor fool is hanged!"] has been taken as a kindly reference to the otherwise unrecorded fate of the clown, and this has a renewed attraction for our modern hard-boiled school, who regard it as a bit of tidying-up pushed in as a belated afterthought. The line breaks out as a wail after a tedious ten lines by Albany about rewards and punishments for the nobles, and even before that Lear was only dropping brief irrelevancies to Kent. His mind might have wandered to the clown; he believes that "Caius" is dead too. However, this interpretation of the word would make the sentence contradict the movement of thought that it introduces, and must therefore be wrong; the passage is in verse, whereas random wanderings are always in prose. The argument is that other creatures are alive but not Cordelia, and the whole impulse of the speech is concentrated on her. On the other hand the N. E. D. theory that *fool* was used as a term of affection should not be carried to the point of thinking that this use excluded the normal meaning of the word. It seems extraordinarily out of place to describe Cordelia. In fact, the word seems likely to puzzle the audience whichever way round you take it. One must suppose, as Bradley did, that his mind has wandered so far that he no longer distinguishes the two; but this should not be softened into "a very old man failing to distinguish two of his children". The Fool has not been required after the storm scenes, because the mad king has taken over his functions completely. But Lear is now thrown back into something like the storm phase of his madness, the effect of immediate shock, and the Fool seems to him part of it. The only affectionate dependent he had recently has been hanged, and the only one he had then was the Fool; the point is not that they are alike—it is shocking because they are so unalike—but that he must be utterly crazy to call one by the name of the other. Presumably the audience was meant to accept it as mere raving and thereby get the right poetical effect; it is meant to recall the whole background of clownery which is what he has discovered about the world. (And no doubt, if you deduce that the Fool was hanged too, that is consistent with the tone of the play; but Lear was not likely to have inquired.) I do not pretend to know how to fix an equation onto such a use. But I think there is another touch of the same process (in the mind of Shakespeare, if not of Lear) when he says:

Never, never, never, never, never!
Pray you, undo this button. Thank you, sir.

The last time he talked about unbuttoning was when he tore off his clothes to be like the naked beggar, in search of the rockbottom which is the worst. There is no worst; the only rockbottom he can find is the grave, and it is a release. In the next two lines he dies of a passion of joy at the false belief that Cordelia has recovered.

"Fool in *Lear.*" *Sewanee Review.* Spring, 1949. *The Structure of Complex Words.* 1951.

[245] *A. C. Bradley*

His shattered mind passes from the first transports of hope and despair, as he bends over Cordelia's body and holds the feather to her lips, into an absolute forgetfulness of the cause of these transports. This continues so long as he can converse with Kent; becomes an almost complete vacancy; and is disturbed only to yield, as his eyes suddenly fall again on his child's corpse, to an agony which at once breaks his heart. And . . . though he is killed by an agony of pain, the agony in which he actually dies is one not of pain but of ecstasy. Suddenly, with a cry represented in the oldest text by a four-times repeated 'O,' he exclaims:

Do you see this? Look on her, look, her lips,
Look there, look there!

These are the last words of Lear. He is sure, at last, that she *lives:* and what had he said when he was still in doubt?

She lives! if it be so,
It is a chance which does redeem all sorrows
That ever I have felt!

To us, perhaps, the knowledge that he is deceived may bring a culmination of pain: but, if it brings *only* that, I believe we are false to Shakespeare, and it seems almost beyond question that any actor is false to the text who does not attempt to express, in Lear's last accents and gestures and look, an unbearable *joy*.

Shakespearean Tragedy. 1904. Lect. VIII.

Love's Labour's Lost

[246] *Walter Pater*

The merely dramatic interest of the piece is slight enough; only just sufficient, indeed, to form the vehicle of its wit and poetry. The scene —a park of the King of Navarre—is unaltered throughout; and the unity of the play is not so much the unity of a drama as that of a series of pictorial groups, in which the same figures reappear, in different combinations but on the same background. It is as if Shakespeare had intended to bind together, by some inventive conceit, the devices of an ancient tapestry, and give voices to its figures.

⋆ ⋆ ⋆

It is this foppery of delicate language, this fashionable plaything of his time, with which Shakespeare is occupied in *Love's Labours Lost*. He shows us the manner in all its stages; passing from the grotesque and vulgar pedantry of Holofernes, through the extravagant but polished caricature of Armado, to become the peculiar characteristic of a real though still quaint poetry in Biron himself, who is still chargeable even at his best with just a little affectation. As Shakespeare laughs broadly at it in Holofernes or Armado, so he is the analyst of its curious charm in Biron; and this analysis involves a delicate raillery by Shakespeare himself at his own chosen manner.

⋆ ⋆ ⋆

Biron is the perfect flower of this manner:

> A man of fire-new words, fashion's own knight:

—as he describes Armado, in terms which are really applicable to himself. In him this manner blends with a true gallantry of nature, and an affectionate complaisance and grace. He has at times some of its extravagance or caricature also, but the shades of expression by which he passes from this to the "golden cadence" of Shakespeare's own most characteristic verse, are so fine, that it is sometimes difficult to trace them. What is a vulgarity in Holofernes, and a caricature in Armado, refines itself with him into the expression of a nature truly and inwardly bent upon a form of delicate perfection, and is accompanied by a real insight into the laws which determine what is exquisite in language, and their root in the nature of things. He can appreciate quite the opposite style—

> In russet yeas, and honest kersey noes;

he knows the first law of pathos, that

> Honest plain words best suit the ear of grief.

He delights in his own rapidity of intuition; and, in harmony with the half-sensuous philosophy of the Sonnets, exalts, a little scornfully, in many memorable expressions, the judgment of the senses, above all slower, more toilsome means of knowledge, scorning some who fail to see things only because they are so clear:

> So ere you find where light in darkness lies,
> Your light grows dark by losing of your eyes:—

as with some German commentators on Shakespeare. Appealing always to actual sensation from men's affected theories, he might seem to despise learning; as, indeed, he has taken up his deep studies partly in sport, and demands always the profit of learning in renewed enjoyment. Yet he surprises us from time to time by intuitions which could come only from a deep experience and power of observation; and men listen to him, old and young, in spite of themselves. He is quickly impressible to the slightest clouding of the spirits in social intercourse, and has his moments of extreme seriousness: his trial-task may well be, as Rosaline puts it—

> To enforce the pained impotent to smile.

But still, through all, he is true to his chosen manner: that gloss of dainty language is a second nature with him: even at his best he is not without a certain artifice: the trick of playing on words never deserts him; and Shakespeare, in whose own genius there is an element of this very quality, shows us in this graceful, and, as it seems, studied, portrait, his enjoyment of it.

"Love's Labours Lost." (1878). *Macmillan's Magazine.* Dec., 1885. *Appreciations.* 1889.

[247] *C. L. Barber*

The final joke is that in the end "Love" does not arrive, despite the lords' preparations for a triumphal welcome. That the play should end without the usual marriages is exactly right, in view of what it is that is released by its festivities. Of course what the lords give way to is, in a general sense, the impulse to love; but the particular form that it takes for them is a particular sort of folly—what one could call the folly of amorous masquerade, whether in clothes, gestures, or words. It is the folly of acting love and talking love, without being in love. For the festivity releases, not the delights of love, but the delights of expression which the prospect of love engenders—though those involved are not clear about the distinction until it is forced on them; the clarification achieved by release is this recognition that love is not wooing games or love talk. And yet these sports are not written off or ruled out; on the contrary the play offers their delights for our enjoyment, while humorously putting them in their place.

Shakespeare's Festive Comedy A Study of Dramatic Form and Its Relation to Social Custom. 1959. Chap. 5.

Macbeth

[248] *A. C. Bradley*

A Shakespearean tragedy, as a rule, has a special tone or atmosphere of its own, quite perceptible, however difficult to describe. The effect of this atmosphere is marked with unusual strength in *Macbeth*. It is due to a variety of influences which combine with those just noticed, so that, acting and reacting, they form a whole; and the desolation of the blasted heath, the design of the Witches, the guilt in the hero's soul, the darkness of the night, seem to emanate from one and the same source. This effect is strengthened by a multitude of small touches, which at the moment may be little noticed but still leave their mark on the imagination. We may approach the consideration of the characters and the action by distinguishing some of the ingredients of this general effect.

Darkness, we may even say blackness, broods over this tragedy. It is remarkable that almost all the scenes which at once recur to memory take place either at night or in some dark spot. The vision of the dagger, the murder of Duncan, the murder of Banquo, the sleep-walking of Lady Macbeth, all come in night-scenes. The Witches dance in the thick air of a storm, or, 'black and midnight hags,' receive Macbeth in a cavern. The blackness of night is to the hero a thing of fear, even of horror; and that which he feels becomes the spirit of the play. The faint glimmerings of the western sky at twilight are here menacing: it is the hour when the traveller hastens to reach safety in his inn, and when Banquo rides homeward to meet his assassins; the hour when 'light thickens,' when 'night's black agents to their prey do rouse,' when the wolf begins to howl, and the owl to scream, and withered murder steals forth to his work. Macbeth bids the stars hide their fires that his 'black' desires may be concealed; Lady Macbeth calls on thick night to come, palled in the dunnest smoke of hell. The moon is down and no stars shine when Banquo, dreading the dreams of the coming night, goes unwillingly to bed, and leaves Macbeth to wait for the summons of the little bell. When the next day should dawn, its light is 'strangled,' and 'darkness does the face of earth entomb.' In the whole drama the sun seems to shine only twice; first, in the beautiful but ironical passage where Duncan sees the swallows flitting round the castle of death; and, afterwards, when at the close the avenging army gathers to rid the earth of its shame. Of the many slighter touches which deepen this effect I notice only one. The failure of nature in Lady Macbeth is marked by her fear of darkness; 'she has light by her continually.' And in the one phrase of fear that ecapes her lips even in sleep, it is of the darkness of the place of torment that she speaks.

The atmosphere of Macbeth, however, is not that of unrelieved blackness. On the contrary, as compared with *King Lear* and its cold dim gloom, *Macbeth* leaves a decided impression of colour; it is really the impression of a black night broken by flashes of light and colour, sometimes vivid and even glaring.

Shakespearean Tragedy. 1904. Lect. IX.

[249] *Theodore Spencer*

One of the most remarkable things about Shakespeare is that although he uses the same materials for the achievement of size and universality in his great tragedies, he creates in each a distinctive and particular world. In *Macbeth,* as in *King Lear,* the individual, the state, and external nature are seen as interrelated parts of a single whole, so that a disturbance in one disturbs the others as well—and yet the atmosphere and tone of the two plays are very different; we may say that *Lear* is a play that opens out, whereas *Macbeth* is a play that closes in. Lear's sufferings end in release, but Macbeth, in the course of his career, becomes trapped by his own crimes, until he sees himself, at the end, as a captured animal:

> They have tied me to a stake; I cannot fly,
> But bear-like I must fight the course,
>
> (v, 7, 1)

In *Macbeth* there is nothing like the purgation of King Lear. As the action of *King Lear* progresses the main character *loses* his bad qualities; in the course of *Macbeth,* the main character *develops* them. This is something new. Iago, for example, does not become increasingly evil as the play goes on; he is thoroughly and completely bad from the beginning. But Macbeth *grows* into evil; that is why those critics are right who describe the play as a more intense study of evil than any other. Unlike *King Lear* it portrays, not the whitening, but the blackening of a soul.

Shakespeare and the Nature of Man. 1942. Chap. VI.

[250] *L. C. Knights*

Macbeth is a statement of evil. I use the word 'statement' (unsatisfactory as it is) in order to stress those qualities that are 'non-dramatic', if drama is defined according to the canons of William Archer or Dr. Bradley. It also happens to be poetry, which means that the apprehension of the whole can only be obtained from a lively attention to the parts, whether they have an immediate bearing on the main action or 'illustrate character', or not. Two main themes, which can only be separated for the purpose of analysis, are blended in the play—the themes of the reversal of values and of unnatural disorder. And closely related to each is a third theme, that of the deceitful appearance, and consequent doubt, uncertainty and confusion. All this is obscured by false assumptions about the category 'drama'; *Macbeth* has greater affinity with *The Waste Land* than with *The Doll's House.*

★ ★ ★

I have called *Macbeth* a statement of evil; but it is a statement not of a philosophy but of ordered emotion. This ordering is of course a continuous process (hence the importance of the scrupulous analysis of each line), it is not merely something that happens in the last

Act corresponding to the dénouement or unravelling of the plot. All the same, the interests aroused are heightened in the last Act before they are finally 'placed', and we are given a vantage point from which the whole course of the drama may be surveyed in retrospect. There is no formula that will describe this final effect. It is no use saying that we are 'quietened', 'purged' or 'exalted' at the end of *Macbeth* or of any other tragedy. It is no use taking one step nearer the play and saying we are purged, etc., because we see the downfall of a wicked man or because we realize the justice of Macbeth's doom whilst retaining enough sympathy for him or admiration of his potential qualities to be filled with a sense of 'waste'. It is no use discussing the effect in abstract terms at all; we can only discuss it in terms of the poet's concrete realization of certain emotions and attitudes.

How Many Children Had Lady Macbeth? 1933. *Explorations.* 1946.

[251] *Roy Walker*

The kingdom in *Macbeth* shadows forth the kingdom of heaven on earth, obscured for a time by the blanket of the dark but never sundered from heaven. The tragedy is focused on the destruction of awareness of the kingdom of heaven within and the attempt of the human vassals of evil to usurp the divine-temporal kingship. But Malcolm and Donalbain, Fleance and Macduff, the pious English King and Siward, the rebellious thanes and the anonymous Old Man, the slain Banquo and Macduff's little son, are all conscious in some degree of being the children of Saint Columba, citizens of a kingdom of which the great bond they dimly read is carried in their own souls. Hamlet is noble despite his world; the world is noble despite Macbeth. If the central tragic figures reflect the spiritual experiences of the poet, we may say that the desperate misanthropy of *Hamlet* has become the agonised *mea culpa* of *Macbeth.* The tempest-tossed ship has rounded the sterile promontory, and as the storm of evil abates a little the shores of Prospero's magic island are already distantly visible to the pilot's prophetic eye.

Introduction. *The Time Is Free A Study of Macbeth.* 1949.

[252] *Cleanth Brooks*

The clothed daggers and the naked babe—mechanism and life—instrument and end—death and birth—that which should be left bare and clean and that which should be clothed and warmed—these are facets of two of the great symbols which run throughout the play. They are not the only symbols, to be sure; they are not the most obvious symbols: darkness and blood appear more often. But with a flexibility which must amaze the reader, the image of the garment and the image of the babe are so used as to encompass an astonishingly large area of the total situation. And between them—the naked babe, essential humanity, humanity stripped down to the naked thing itself, and yet as various as the future—and the various garbs which humanity assumes, the robes of honor, the hypocrite's disguise, the inhuman "manliness" with which Macbeth endeavors to cover up his essential humanity—between them, they furnish Shakespeare with his most subtle and ironically telling instruments.

The Well Wrought Urn Studies in the Structure of Poetry. 1947. Chap. II.

[253] *Thomas De Quincey*

All action in any direction is best expounded, measured, and made apprehensible, by reaction. Now apply this to the case in *Macbeth.* Here . . . the retiring of the human heart, and the entrance of the fiendish heart was to be expressed and made sensible. Another world has stept in; and the murderers are taken out of the region of human things, human purposes, human desires. They are transfigured: Lady Macbeth is 'unsexed;' Macbeth has forgot that he was born of woman; both are conformed to the image of devils; and the world of devils is suddenly revealed. But how shall this be conveyed and made palpable? In order that a new world may step in, this world must for a time disappear. The murderers, and the murder must be insulated—cut off by an immeasurable gulf from the ordinary tide and succession of human affairs—locked up and sequestered in some deep recess; we must be made sensible that the world of ordinary life is suddenly arrested—laid asleep—tranced—racked into a dread armistice; time must be annihilated; relation to things without abolished; and all must pass self-withdrawn into a deep syncope and suspension of earthly passion. Hence it is, that when the deed is done, when the work of darkness is perfect, then the world of darkness passes away like a pageantry in the clouds: the knocking at the gate is heard; and it makes known audibly that the reaction has commenced; the human has made its reflux upon the fiendish; the pulses of life are beginning to beat again; and the re-establishment of the goings-on of the world in which we live, first makes us profoundly sensible of the awful parenthesis that had suspended them.

O mighty poet! Thy works are not as those of other men, simply and merely great works of art; but are also like the phenomena of nature, like the sun and the sea, the stars and the flowers; like frost and snow, rain and dew, hail-storm and thunder, which are to be studied with entire submission of our own faculties, and in the perfect faith that in them there can be no too much or too little, nothing useless or inert—but that, the farther we press in our discoveries, the more we shall see proofs of design and self-supporting arrangement where the careless eye had seen nothing but accident!

"On the Knocking at the Gate in 'Macbeth.'" *The London Magazine.* October 1823.

[254] *Samuel Taylor Coleridge*

Lady Macbeth, like all in Shakespeare, is a class individualized:—of high rank, left much alone, and feeding herself with day-dreams of ambition, she mistakes the courage of fantasy for the power of bearing the consequences of the realities of guilt. Hers is the mock fortitude of a mind deluded by ambition; she shames her husband with a superhuman audacity of fancy which she cannot support, but sinks in the season of remorse, and dies in suicidal agony.

Notes on the Tragedies. Raysor I, 72.

[255] *Harold S. Wilson*

Macbeth's fear is a complex thing to understand, or for an actor to interpret adequately. It is not the fear that is cowardice, timidity, or cravenness. Macbeth, in one sense, is a very brave man, or perhaps we should say, a very bold one. His fear is partly self-distrust, partly bewilderment; perhaps, though it is always a dangerous thing to do, we should read between the lines and say, as many commentators would, that despite Macbeth's concentration in words on the immediate consequences he does also fear the ultimate consequences of his crime, his soul's damnation. And yet, it does not seem as if Shakespeare meant precisely this. Surely he would have made it plainer, if he had. It is a subtler thing which constitutes the chief fascination that the play exercises upon us—this fear Macbeth feels, a fear not fully defined, for him or for us, a terrible anxiety that is a sense of guilt without becoming (recognizably, at least) a sense of sin. It is not a sense of sin because he refuses to recognize such a category; and, in his stubbornness, his savage defiance, it drives him on to more and more terrible acts. Macbeth is the sort of man who keeps telling himself he is exceptional, that he can do the impossible. He will not recognize or submit to his own fears, his own scruples. He tries to be entirely self-sufficient and will not face the all but overwhelming evidence of his insufficiency. He is a Faust who denies the ultimate source of his fear, of his despair.

★ ★ ★

And so Macbeth becomes lonelier and more hopeless:

> And that which should accompany old age,
> As honour, love, obedience, troops of friends,
> I must not look to have. . . .
>
> Tomorrow, and tomorrow, and tomorrow
> Creeps in this petty pace from day to day
> To the last syllable of recorded time. . . .

This is his tragedy, this utter and complete disenchantment, this dull disgust with life, this disappointment—this, and his continual fear. He does not fear hell, we might say, because he *is* in hell: "Why, this is hell, nor am I out of it"; though his vitality will not quite let him give up. He keeps trying to delude himself with hopes and defiances he knows to be vain, and the result is that he begins "to be aweary of the sun." He is tied to the stake, by his own hands; he knows he is like the bear that will be baited to death by the dogs. Yet he never submits. And this terrible effort of human will, the more terrible in a man of Macbeth's mighty imagination, is in its way heroic.

On the Design of Shakespearian Tragedy. 1957. Chap. III.

[256] *G. R. Elliott*

The question as to the central meaning of this drama turns upon the difference, not commonly recognized by the modern secular mind, between the true charity, which is *justly and righteously kind,* and that inadequate sort of charity which is the *milk* of human-kindness. The word milk, here as elsewhere in Shakespeare's works, is ambiguous: it may denote either nourishment or weakness, chiefly the latter in the case of Macbeth. But he is very typical; his conduct evinces both the potential value and the tragic limitation of that fellow-feeling, that human-kindness, which most people have most of the time. Ordinarily it serves to cement human society; but this cement melts very quickly, and for most persons surprisingly, in the heat of selfish interests. In vivid contrast is the virtuous charity of King Duncan, so carefully shown by the dramatist in the first Act. Unlike Macbeth, Duncan is not proudly conscious of his own kindness; in him it is a subordinate and nourishing constituent of the true charity. This king bears his faculties meekly and is clear in his great office, gentle but firm, mercifully just. He has the manly meekness that inherits the earth in the sense that it alone can transform human society into a real human family. And Shakespeare, with beautiful art, makes the spirit of Duncan persist throughout the play after his death, to become victorious at the close.

★ ★ ★

The whitest feature of Macbeth . . . is that, like his wife and unlike a multitude of other sinners, he does not strive to cloak his wickedness with conventional religiosity. Many a tyrant in pagan and Christian times, including Henry Eighth, has succeeded in conceiving his evil doings as in the main condoned by the gods or God. But Macbeth, with all his imagination, never imagines that. In the close of the play, for the first time in his career, he has to hear himself utterly condemned to his face for his wickedness: two noble gentlemen, Young Siward and Macduff, representing a wide range of human society, tell him plainly and strongly that he has become a servant of hell and the devil. And he does not utter a single word in repudiation of that verdict. So that our sense of uplift at the end of this tragedy is due in no small measure to the fact that Macbeth has at least the grace not to claim for his doings any tinge of Grace. And in this respect he adumbrates a characteristic of Shakespeare himself, who continually in his works shows up the hollowness and black deceptiveness of a merely conventional, egoistic piety.

Introduction. *Dramatic Providence in Macbeth A Study of Shakespeare's Tragic Theme of Humanity and Grace.* 1958.

Measure for Measure

[257] *Donald A. Stauffer*

As with the other comedies of this period of dead center, the play fails as a stage-play because it does not fully translate into credible drama Shakespeare's strong temporary predilections for moral philosophy. The prying and tampering of the Duke arouses some incredulity and resentment when he is considered as a human character. Yet considered as the king-piece in a moral game of chess, his power and impregnable calm is justifiable. His philosophic rôle is forgotten if the play is viewed dramatically as a tragedy with an incompatible comic ending tacked on. After the great clean-up campaign, the disappointed audience is hardly left with a bigger and better Vienna. Raw human nature has not been changed, the brothels still concoct their unsavory stews, and the only difference might appear to be that the two finest natures have "become much more the better for being a little bad." It is not easy for the common reader, and it may not have been easy for Shakespeare, to accept disillusioned laxity and overripe tolerance as final answers to emotional struggles and conflicting ideals. In this first major crisis in his writing career, Shakespeare has marked down all his goods and is selling them at a loss. His sense of mercy and forgiveness seems based on the desperate belief that the human materials he is working with are in the main shoddy and flimsy.

Shakespeare's World of Images. 1949. Chap. IV.

[258] *Samuel Taylor Coleridge*

Measure for Measure is the single exception to the delightfulness of Shakspeare's plays. It is a hateful work, although Shakspearian throughout. Our feelings of justice are grossly wounded in Angelo's escape. Isabella herself contrives to be unamiable, and Claudio is detestable.

Table-Talk. 1835. Raysor II, 352.

[259] *Walter Bagehot*

We agree with Hazlitt, that this play seems to be written, perhaps more than any other, *con amore,* and with a relish; and this seems to be the reason why, notwithstanding the unpleasant nature of its plot, and the absence of any very attractive character, it is yet one of the plays which take hold on the mind most easily and most powerfully. Now the entire character of Angelo, which is the expressive feature of the piece, is nothing but a successful embodiment of the pleasure, the malevolent pleasure, which a warm-blooded and expansive man takes in watching the rare, the dangerous and inanimate excesses of the constrained and cold-blooded. One seems to see Shakespeare, with his bright eyes and his large lips and buoyant face, watching with a pleasant excitement the excesses of his thin-lipped and calculating creation, as though they were the excesses of a real person. It is the complete picture of a natural hypocrite, who does not consciously disguise strong impulses, but whose very passions seem of their own accord to have disgusised themselves and retreated into the recesses of the character, yet only to recur even more dangerously when their proper period is expired, when the will is cheated into security by their absence, and the world (and, it may be, the 'judicious person' himself) is impressed with a sure reliance in his chilling and remarkable rectitude.

"Shakespeare—the Man." *Prospective Review*. August 1853. *Literary Studies*. 1879.

[260] *Walter Pater*

. . . the reader will note the vivid reality, the subtle interchange of light and shade, the strongly contrasted characters of this group of persons, passing across the stage so quickly. The slightest of them is at least not ill-natured: the meanest of them can put forth a plea for existence . . . they are never sure of themselves, even in the strong tower of a cold unimpressible nature: they are capable of many friendships and of a true dignity in danger, giving each other a sympathetic, if transitory, regret—one sorry that another "should be foolishly lost at a game of tick-tack." Words which seem to exhaust man's deepest sentiment concerning death and life are put on the lips of a gilded, witless youth; and the saintly Isabella feels fire creep along her, kindling her tongue to eloquence at the suggestion of shame. In places the shadow deepens: death intrudes itself on the scene, as among other things "a great disguiser," blanching the features of youth and spoiling its goodly hair, touching the fine Claudio even with its disgraceful associations. As in Orcagna's fresco at Pisa, it comes capriciously, giving many and long reprieves to Barnardine, who has been waiting for it nine years in prison, taking another thence by fever, another by mistake of judgment, embracing others in the midst of their music and song. The little mirror of existence, which reflects to each for a moment the stage on which he plays, is broken at last by a capricious accident; while all alike, in their yearning for untasted enjoyment, are really discounting their days, grasping so hastily and accepting so inexactly the precious pieces. The Duke's quaint but excellent moralising at the beginning of the third act does but express, like the chorus of a Greek play, the spirit of the passing incidents. To him in Shakespeare's play, to a few here and there in the actual world, this strange practical paradox of our life, so unwise in its eager haste, reveals itself in all its clearness.

The Duke disguised as a friar, with his curious moralising on life and death, and Isabella in her first mood of renunciation, a thing "ensky'd and sainted," come with the quiet of the cloister as a relief to this lust and pride of life: like some grey monastic picture hung on the wall of a gaudy room, their presence cools the heated air of the piece. For a moment we are within the placid conventual walls, whither they fancy at first that the Duke has come as a man crossed in love, with Friar Thomas and Friar Peter, calling each other by their homely, English names, or at the nunnery among the novices, with their little limited privileges, where

> If you speak you must not show your face,
> Or if you show your face you must not speak.

Not less precious for this relief in the general structure of the piece, than for its own peculiar graces is the episode of Mariana, a creature wholly of Shakespeare's invention, told, by way of interlude, in subdued prose. The moated grange, with its dejected mistress, its long, listless, discontented days, where we hear only the voice of a boy broken off suddenly in the midst of one of the loveliest songs of Shakespeare, or of Shakespeare's school, is the pleasantest of many glimpses we get here of pleasant places—the fields without the town, Angelo's garden-house, the consecrated fountain. . . . Again it is a picture within a picture, but with fainter lines and a greyer atmosphere: we have here the same passions, the same wrongs, the same continuance of affection, the same crying out upon death, as in the nearer and larger piece, though softened, and reduced to the mood of a more dreamy scene.

"Measure for Measure." *Fortnightly Review*. Nov., 1874. *Appreciations*. 1889.

[261] *R. W. Chambers*

Isabel then, as Shakespeare sees her and asks us to see her, would frankly, joyously, give her life to save Claudio: and, let there be no mistake about it, '*greater love hath no man than this*'. And now

Claudio is asking for what she cannot give, and she bursts out in agony. Have the critics never seen a human soul or a human body in the extremity of torment? Physical torture Isabel thinks she could have stood without flinching. She has said so to Angelo:

> The impression of keen whips I'ld wear as rubies,
> And strip myself to death, as to a bed
> That longing have been sick for, ere I'ld yield
> My body up to shame.

To suppose that Shakespeare gave these burning words to Isabel so that we should perceive her to be selfish and cold, is to suppose that he did not know his job. The honour of her family and her religion are more to her than mere life, her own or Claudio's.

★ ★ ★

Isabel is the most vehement of the three. Sisterly technique has its own rules; there is a peculiar freedom about the talk of those who have known each other from babyhood. And Isabel can use arguments outside the range of Beatrice or Lady Macbeth. Don't forget that Escalus, when he first pleaded for Claudio, remembered his 'most noble father'. Isabel had exclaimed, when she first found Claudio firm,

> there my father's grave
> Did utter forth a voice.

And now she cries,

> Heaven shield my mother play'd my father fair.

Isabel appeals to the passion which, in an Elizabethan gentleman, may be presumed to be stronger than the fear of death—pride in his gentle birth and in the courage which should mark it. Don't people see that there are things about which we cannot argue calmly? The fierceness of Isabel's words is the measure of the agony of her soul. 'The fortress which parleys, the woman who parleys, is lost.' I grant that, at the end of a lifetime's training, a saint like Thomas More could smile on his daughter when she tempted him, 'What, Mistress Eve?' But the young martyrs are apt to be more stern, whether it be Cordelia or Antigone, the spitfire St. Eulalia, or St. Juliana putting the fear of death upon the Devil. And it is our fault if we don't see that Isabel is suffering martyrdom none the less because her torment is mental, not physical.

One of the most significant of Shakespeare's alterations of his original is to make the heroine a 'votarist of St. Clare'. At the root of the movement of St. Francis and St. Clare was the intense remembrance of the sufferings of Christ, in atonement for the sins of the whole world—the 'remedy' of which Isabel in vain reminds Angelo. Isabel, as a novice, is testing herself to see whether she is called to that utter renunciation which is the life of the 'poor Clare'. Whether she remains in the Convent or no, one who is contemplating such a life can no more be expected to sell herself into mortal sin, than a good soldier can be expected to sell a stronghold entrusted to him.

"The Jacobean Shakespeare and *Measure for Measure.*" Annual Shakespeare Lecture of the British Academy. 1937.

[262] *Arthur Sewell*

The world of the play is not really the world of human souls. It is true that in the last act there is some play with the notions of penitence and forgiveness; the Law is threatened and then remitted. But the play is called *Measure for Measure,* and the deeper seriousness of penitence and forgiveness are uneasily accommodated in the treatment of such a theme. The final concern of the play is not with redemption or with grace but with the Law, and when the Law seems at the end of the play to be abrogated it is surely an error to suppose that its place has been taken by a covenant of grace. For the Law, in fact, is not abrogated. The marriages imposed—Angelo's as much as Lucio's—are salutary, not blessed. This so-called forgiveness, this remission of the Law, is in some ways more terrible than the rigour of the law suspended; for it implies that lust may, after all, be bridled as well by marriage as by death. Angelo's marriage is not very different from Lucio's; it is not, surely, the marriage of a man who has undergone a 'saving experience'. It is a marriage which will conserve (and perhaps continuate) the society to which both Angelo and Lucio belong.

Character and Society in Shakespeare. 1951. Chap. IV.

[263] *Francis Fergusson*

The Duke has displeased many critics, who report either that he is not a character at all, but merely a *deus ex machina,* or else that he is a liar, weakling and hypocrite. The Duke is puzzling, and perhaps ultimately not quite successful. But it is certain that he is the center of the play, and the clue to its intention and its peculiar style. Shakespeare . . . made the Duke both a character within the play who takes a crucial part in the struggle, and at the same time a sort of stage director, who because of his power and wisdom can start and control the action as though from the wings. . . .

★ ★ ★

The Duke . . . wishes to *teach* Vienna the properties of government. That is the clue of his action in the play, and also to his *régisseur*'s action outside the play: he wishes to show London the properties of government in the experimental situation of Vienna.

If the Duke is understood as a teacher, his supposed deviousness and hypocrisy is explained, for he is a very modest and empirical kind of teacher. . . . He anticipates our progressive educators, who maintain that one can really learn only "by doing." . . . When the Duke departs and leaves Angelo in charge, he sets the city a practical problem in government. The city unfolds the properties of government by trying all the wrong moves; and the Duke is at hand to reinforce the painful lessons in his counsel to Isabella or to Claudio, and at last by the order which, as temporal ruler, he can impose. . . .

Most students of *Measure for Measure* find the first three acts the best. It is there that we most unmistakably recognize poetry, drama, the natural movement and variety of life as in Shakespeare's greatest tragedies. And it is there that the Duke takes the least active part. Having set the stage for a tragedy by handing his city over to the tyrannical perfectionist Angelo, he merely observes, and explains in secrecy to the characters whose suffering might bear fruit in wisdom.

Shakespeare and the Duke clearly intended this effect, as the first part of their demonstration. They wished to show to Vienna, and to London in the mirror of Vienna, a tragedy in the making: a city hopelessly divided between the doctrinaire perfectionism of Angelo and Isabella, the innocent sensuality of Claudio, and the cynical sophistication of Lucio, the whole placed against a background of the weaknesses, fears and darkness of routine human nature as we see it in any corrupt old city. The nascent tragedy which results is wonderfully suggestive for us also. I see in it a theme like Yeats's "The centre cannot hold, / Mere anarchy is loosed upon the world." The Duke, with his wisdom and power, represents the missing center. Angelo and Isabella, with their ambitious intellectuality, represent revolutionary or counterrevolutionary forces, which change their policies but not their narrow power drives, as they struggle in the dark and empty center. . . .

In this nascent tragedy Lucio is the counterpart of the Duke, and thus throws a great deal of light upon him. Lucio has a talent for chaos as great as the Duke for wisdom or the central order. Shakespeare uses Lucio in the first two acts as the chief reflector of the action, to use Henry James's valuable term: it is through Lucio's intelligent and faithless eyes that we grasp what is going on. . . .

At the end of the play Lucio is the only character whom the Duke cannot really forgive. Shall we say that Lucio has insight without integrity? Or that he represents treachery, which Shakespeare, like Dante, hates above all other sins? Or that he is only a trimmer like Rosencrantz and Guildenstern, a "private of fortune," neither for good nor for evil but only for his trivial self? However that may be, Lucio has things his own way in the first half of the play, encouraging the unregenerate appetites of all the characters, using his imagination in the service of darkness, while the Duke keeps his true power hidden. But in the middle of Act III the Duke begins to take an active part, and thenceforth Lucio is out of his depth and can no longer interpret the action for us. The tragedy is arrested on the very brink of catastrophe, and the end of the play presents the mystery of justice and mercy in a way undreamed of in Lucio's philosophy.

★ ★ ★

The Duke starts to intervene when he proposes the bed-trick to Isabella. In Act IV his plans proceed with great speed. The timing is close, and the language is prose, as though Shakespeare by this change of rhythm, this sudden deflation and sobriety in speech, were warning us that playtime is over, the citizens have been given their head long enough, and now we must pay attention to matters of a different kind of seriousness. I find this change of key successful: there is poetic power in the sequence in the prison, at night, with the Duke working against time to avert catastrophe and accept his sober responsibility for his flock. But the act is very brief, a modulation from the nascent tragedy of the first three acts to the complex demonstration of Act V. Just before abandoning his role as Friar, the Duke warns us what to expect in the final part of his play: "By cold gradation and well-balanced form," he says, "we shall proceed with Angelo."

It has often been maintained that Act V is a mere perfunctory windup of the plot, in which Shakespeare himself had no real interest. I am sure that on the contrary it is composed with the utmost care, and in perfect consistency with the basis of the whole play—this quite apart from the question whether one *likes* it or not. It is indeed so beautifully composed that it could almost stand alone. Perhaps we should think of it as a play within a play, presenting the theme of justice and mercy in another story and in another and colder tone. But the new story—that of the Duke's intervention and demonstration—was implicit from the first; and the new cold, intellectual tone may be understood as underneath the more richly poetic manner of the first three acts.

We are invited to watch this last act with a kind of double vision: from the front of the house, and at the same time from the wings, where we can see the actors getting ready to pretend to be what they are not. For, like the Duke, we know what they are; and moreover we have seen the Duke's backstage preparations for the final play. This final public play, unrolling before us and the supposedly ignorant Duke, is in the form of a series of trials. The first begins with Isabella's desperate complaint of Angelo, and ends when her suit is rejected on the basis of the evidence then publicly available: the wild improbability of her story, and Angelo's fine reputation and dignified manner. The second trial starts when the Duke leaves Angelo and Escalus to try Isabella for her supposed lying slander, and it ends when the Duke returns in his Friar disguise as a witness, and is suddenly revealed as the Duke when Lucio pulls off his hood. The third part ends both trials: the Duke, now revealed as both judge and witness, metes out justice to all, but on the assumption which we know to be false, that Claudio is dead. Notice that up to this point the trials and judgments have obeyed the strictest reasoned conception of justice, and the facts insofar as they could be found under the frightened and passionate lies in which they had been hidden. The Duke has been following a Mosaic regularity, and he has also been acting like that image of justice as a woman with bandaged eyes, a pair of scales in one hand and a sword in the other. He has been pretending to rely, not upon his concrete vision, but upon reportable "facts" and his abstract measuring-machine. But in the final act of this playlet the Duke as it were drops the bandage from his eyes, confesses what he can really see, starting with the fact that Claudio is alive. He then tempers or proportions justice with mercy, abstract reason with his perception of the analogical relationships between real people, in whom truth and error, sin and grace, are mingled in ways which mathematics cannot compute.

"Philosophy and Theatre in *Measure for Measure*." (A lecture given at Harvard University, March 22, 1951.) *Kenyon Review*. Winter, 1952. *The Human Image in Dramatic Literature*. 1957. Part II.

The Merchant of Venice

[264] *Harley Granville-Barker*

The Merchant of Venice is a fairy tale. There is no more reality in Shylock's bond and the Lord of Belmont's will than in Jack and the Beanstalk.

Shakespeare, it is true, did not leave the fables as he found them. This would not have done; things that pass muster on the printed page may become quite incredible when acted by human beings, and the unlikelier the story, the likelier must the mechanism of its acting be made. Besides, when his own creative impulse was quickened, he could not help giving life to a character; he could no more help it than the sun can help shining. So Shylock is real, while his story remains fabulous; and Portia and Bassanio become human, though, truly, they never quite emerge from the enchanted thicket of fancy into the common light of day. Aesthetic logic may demand that a story and its characters should move consistently upon one plane or another, be it fantastic or real. But Shakespeare's practical business, once he had chosen these two stories for his play, was simply so to charge them with humanity that they did not betray belief in the human beings presenting them, yet not so uncompromisingly that the stories themselves became ridiculous.

★ ★ ★

Shakespeare keeps character within the bounds of story with great tact; but such a character as this that has surged in his imagination asks more than such a story to feed on. Hence, partly at least, the new theme of Jessica and her flight, which will give Shylock another and more instant grudge to satisfy. It is developed with strict economy. Twenty-one lines are allowed to Jessica and Launcelot, another twenty or so to her lover and their plans; then, in a scene not sixty long, Shylock and his household are enshrined. As an example of dramatic thrift alone this is worth study. The parting with Launcelot: he has a niggard liking for the fellow, is even hurt a little by his leaving, touched in pride too, and shows it childishly.

> Thou shalt not gormandize
> As thou hast done with me. . . .

But he can at least pretend that he parts with him willingly and makes some profit by it. The parting with Jessica, which we of the audience know to be a parting indeed; that constant calling her by name, which tells us of the lonely man! He has looked to her for everything, has tasked her hard, no doubt; he is her gaoler, yet he trusts her, and loves her in his extortionate way. Uneasy stranger that he is within these Venetian gates; the puritan, who, in a wastrel world, will abide by law and prophets! So full a picture of the man does the short scene give that it seems hardly possible we see no more of him than this between the making of the bond and the climacteric outbreak of passion upon Jessica's loss and the news of Antonio's ruin.

* * *

Portia. Art thou contented, Jew? What doest thou say?
Shylock. I am content.

With the three words of submission the swung pendulum of the drama comes to rest. And for the last of him we have only

I pray you give me leave to go from hence;
I am not well. Send the deed after me,
And I will sign it.

Here is the unapproachable Shakespeare. 'I am not well.' It nears banality and achieves perfection in its simplicity. And what a completing of the picture of Shylock! His deep offence has been to human kindness; he had scorned compassion and prayed God himself in aid of his vengeance. So Shakespeare dismisses him upon an all but ridiculous appeal to our pity, such as an ailing child might make that had been naughty; and we should put the naughtiness aside. He passes out silently, leaving the gibing Gratiano the last word, and the play's action sweeps on without pause. There can be no greater error than to gerrymander Shylock a strenuously 'effective exit'—and most Shylocks commit it. From the character's point of view the significant simplicity of that

I am not well.

is spoilt; and from the point of view of the play the technical skill with which Shakespeare abstracts from his comedy this tragic and dominating figure and avoids anti-climax after is nullified.

Prefaces to Shakespeare. Second Series. 1930.

[265] *Bernard Spivack*

I hate him for he is a Christian;
But more for that in low simplicity
He lends out money gratis . . .

[I.iii.43–45]

We are perhaps a little too comparative today in our religions and too comfortable in our economic Zion to receive from such an avowal the import it had for its own time. Its equivalent effect might come to a middle-class audience in some Midwest city if a caricatured villain of a commissar turned to the front seats in order to say of the hero, "I hate him because he believes in God, and even more because he believes in human liberty and free enterprise."

Shakespeare and the Allegory of Evil The History of a Metaphor in Relation to His Major Villains. 1958. Chap. XII.

[266] *John Middleton Murry*

Shylock is both the embodiment of an irrational hatred, and a credible human being. He is neither of these things to the exclusion of the other. And if we ask how can that be? the only answer is that it is so. This was Shakespeare's way of working. If we choose, we may say that there are in the story primitive elements which he could not wholly assimilate to his own conception; but such an explanation, in *The Merchant of Venice* as in *Hamlet,* brings us against the fact that the dramatic impression made by these plays is the impression of an artistic whole. And, indeed, it seems more probable that Shakespeare did not deal in 'conceptions' of the kind that are often attributed to him. He set himself in successive attempts to infuse a general impression of credibility into an old story, and to secure from his audience no more, and no less, than 'that willing suspension of disbelief which constitutes poetic faith'.

One cannot too often emphasize the nature of Shakespeare's dramatic 'method'. It was not chosen by him, neither was it imposed upon his reluctant genius; it was simply the condition of the work he had chosen to do. The situation was given; necessarily, therefore, the 'characters' in a certain primitive sense—much the same sense in which we can speak of 'characters' in a nursery-story like Cinderella or Robin Hood or a Punch and Judy show. They are simply the necessary agents for that situation or that story. Shakespeare proceeded to endow them with poetic utterance, and with character in a quite different sense. He did what he could to make them credible human beings to himself. He gave them, so far as was possible, humanly plausible motives for their acts and situations, although these were often in fact prior to humane psychology. In a word, the method of Shakespeare's drama consists, essentially, in the humanization of melodrama. And each of those terms must have real validity for the Shakespeare critic who is to avoid ascending or descending into some private universe of his own and calling it Shakespeare.

★ ★ ★

Antonio and his friends are unconscious. They do not realize any more than did the average decent man of Shakespeare's day, that their morality is essentially no finer than Shylock's, or rather that Shylock's is the logical consequence of their own. Because they are unconscious, they are forgiven; where Shylock, being conscious, cannot be. And that is true to life. Logic in morality is intolerable and inhuman, and Antonio's escape from Shylock's revenge by a legal quibble is poetic justice. The impediment of logic and law is broken down by logic and law, and the stream of human life—ordinary, approximate, unconscious, instinctive human life—can flow on. The decency of an age and an average prevails over the design of an isolated bitterness.

There is a morality in *The Merchant of Venice,* though it is not of the formulable kind; nor is it a morality on the level of the deepest insights expressed in the play. Shylock's incrimination of 'Christian' society, Portia's appeal to Christian mercy—these are overtones, as it were caught from the celestial spheres.

> Sit Jessica. Look how the floor of heaven
> Is thick inlaid with patines of bright gold:
> There's not the smallest orb which thou beholdest
> But in his motion like an angel sings
> Still quiring to the young-eyed cherubims;
> Such harmony is in immortal souls;
> But whilst this muddy vesture of decay
> Doth grossly close us in, we cannot hear it.
>
> (V. i. 58–65)

No one distinctly hears that harmony in the play: and it would be fatal if they did. For this play was never intended to vex us with thoughts beyond the reaches of our souls, but 'to give some shadow of satisfaction to the mind of man in these points where the nature of things doth deny it'.

Shakespeare. 1936. Chap. IX.

[267] *C. L. Barber*

The key question in evaluating the play is . . . whether the baffling of Shylock is meaningful or simply melodramatic. Certainly the plot, considered in outline, seems merely a prodigal's dream coming true: to have a rich friend who will set you up with one more loan so that you can marry a woman both beautiful and rich, girlishly yielding and masterful; and on top of that to get rid of the obligation of the loan because the old money bags from whom your friend got the money is proved to be so villainous that he does not deserve to be paid back! If one adds humanitarian and democratic indignation at anti-semitism, it is hard to see, from a distance, what there can be to say for the play: Shylock seems to be made a scapegoat in the crudest, most dishonest way. One can apologize for the plot, as Middleton Murry and Granville-Barker do, by observing that it is based on a fairy-story sort of tale, and that Shakespeare's method was not to change implausible story material, but to invent characters and motives which would make it acceptable and credible, moment by moment, on the stage. But it is inadequate to praise the play for delightful and poetic incoherence. Nor does it seem adequate to say, as E. E. Stoll does, that things just do go this way in comedy, where old rich men are always baffled by young and handsome lovers, lenders by borrowers. Stoll is certainly right, but the question is whether Shakespeare has done something more than merely appeal to the feelings any crowd has in a theater in favor of prodigal young lovers and against old misers. As I see it, he has expressed important things about the relations of love and hate to wealth. When he kept to old tales, he not only made plausible protagonists for them, but also, at any rate when his luck held, he brought up into a social focus deep symbolic meanings. Shylock is an ogre, as Middleton Murry said, but he is the ogre of money power. The old tale of the pound of flesh involved taking literally the proverbial metaphors about money-lenders "taking it out of the hide" of their victims, eating them up. Shakespeare keeps the unrealistic literal business, knife-sharpening and all; we accept it, because he makes it express real human attitudes:

> If I can catch him once upon the hip,
> I will feed fat the ancient grudge I bear him.
> (I.iii.47–48)

So too with the fairy-story caskets at Belmont: Shakespeare makes Bassanio's prodigal fortune meaningful as an expression of the triumph of human, social relations over the relations kept track of by accounting. The whole play dramatizes the conflict between the mechanisms of wealth and the masterful, social use of it. The happy ending, which abstractly considered as an event is hard to credit, and the treatment of Shylock, which abstractly considered as justice is hard to justify, *work* as we actually watch or read the play because these events express relief and triumph in the achievement of a distinction.

★ ★ ★

The troth-plight rings which Bassanio and Gratiano have given away are all that remain of plot to keep the play moving after the trial. It is a slight business, but it gives the women a teasing way to relish the fact that they have played the parts of men as they give up the liberty of that disguise to become wives. And the play's general subject is continued, for in getting over the difficulty, the group provides one final demonstration that human relationships are stronger than their outward signs. Once more, Bassanio expresses a harassed perplexity about obligations in conflict; and Portia gayly pretends to be almost a Shylock about this lover's bond, carrying the logic of the machinery to absurd lengths before showing, by the new gift of the ring, love's power to set debts aside and begin over again.

★ ★ ★

The figure of Shylock is like some secondary figure in a Rembrandt painting, so charged with implied life that one can forget his surroundings. To look sometimes with absorption at the suffering, raging Jew alone is irresistible. But the more one is aware of what the play's whole design is expressing through Shylock, of the comedy's high seriousness in its concern for the grace of community, the less one wants to lose the play Shakespeare wrote for the sake of one he merely suggested.

Shakespeare's Festive Comedy A Study of Dramatic Form and Its Relation to Social Custom. 1959. Chap. 7.

[268] *W. H. Auden*

The action of *The Merchant of Venice* takes place in two locations, Venice and Belmont, which are so different in character that to produce the play in a manner which will not blur this contrast and yet preserve a unity is very difficult. If the spirit of Belmont is made too predominant, then Antonio and Shylock will seem irrelevant, and vice versa. In *Henry IV,* Shakespeare intrudes Falstaff, who by nature belongs to the world of *opera buffa,* into the historical world of political chronicle with which his existence is incompatible, and thereby, consciously or unconsciously, achieves the effect of calling in question the values of military glory and temporal justice as embodied in Henry of Monmouth. In *The Merchant of Venice* he gives us a similar contrast—the romantic fairy story world of Belmont is incompatible with the historical reality of money-making Venice—but this time what is called in question is the claim of Belmont to be the Great Good Place, the Earthly Paradise. Watching *Henry IV,* we become convinced that our aesthetic sympathy with Falstaff is a profounder vision than our ethical judgment which must side with Hal. Watching *The Merchant of Venice,* on the other hand, we are compelled to acknowledge that the attraction which we naturally feel towards Belmont is highly questionable. On that account, I think *The Merchant of Venice* must be classed among Shakespeare's "Unpleasant Plays."

★ ★ ★

Without the Venice scenes, Belmont would be an Arcadia without any relation to actual times and places, and where, therefore, money and sexual love have no reality of their own, but are symbolic signs for a community in a state of grace. But Belmont is related to Venice though their existences are not really compatible with each other. This incompatibility is brought out in a fascinating way by the difference between Belmont time and Venice time. Though we are not told exactly how long the period is before Shylock's loan must be repaid, we know that it is more than a month. Yet Bassanio goes off to Belmont immediately, submits immediately on arrival to the test of the caskets, and has just triumphantly passed it when Antonio's letter arrives to inform him that Shylock is about to take him to court and claim his pound of flesh. Belmont, in fact, is like one of those enchanted palaces where time stands still. But because we are made aware of Venice, the real city, where time is real, Belmont becomes a real society to be judged by the same standards we apply to any other kind of society. Because of Shylock and Antonio, Portia's inherited fortune becomes real money which must have been made in this world, as all fortunes are made, by toil, anxiety, the enduring and inflicting of suffering. Portia we can admire because, having seen her leave her Earthly Paradise to do a good deed in this world (one notices, incidentally, that in this world she appears in disguise), we know that she is aware of her wealth as a moral responsibility, but the other inhabitants of Belmont, Bassanio, Gratiano, Lorenzo and Jessica, for all their beauty and charm, appear as frivolous members of a leisure class, whose carefree life is parasitic upon the labors of others, including usurers. When we learn that Jessica has spent fourscore ducats of her father's money in an evening and bought a monkey with her mother's ring, we cannot take this as a comic punishment for Shylock's sin of avarice; her behavior seems rather an example of the opposite sin of conspicuous waste. Then, with the example in our minds of self-sacrificing love as displayed by Antonio, while we can enjoy the verbal felicity of the love duet between Lorenzo and Jessica, we cannot help noticing that the pairs of lovers they recall, Troilus and Cressida, Aeneas and Dido, Jason and Medea, are none of them examples of self-sacrifice or fidelity. Recalling that the inscription on the leaden casket ran, "Who chooseth me, must give and hazard all he hath," it occurs to us that we have seen two characters do this. Shylock, however unintentionally, did, in fact, hazard all for the sake of destroying the enemy he hated, and Antonio, however unthinkingly he signed the bond, hazarded all to secure the happiness of the friend he loved. Yet it is precisely these two who cannot enter Belmont. Belmont would like to believe that men and women are either good or bad by nature, but Shylock and Antonio remind us that this is an illusion: in the real world, no hatred is totally without justification, no love totally innocent.

"Brothers & Others." *The Dyer's Hand and Other Essays.* 1962.

A Midsummer Night's Dream

[269] *E. K. Chambers*

Love, as interpreted by the comic spirit, is a certain fine lunacy in the brain of youth; not an integral part of life, but a disturbing element in it. The lover is a being of strange caprices and strange infidelities, beyond the control of reason, and swayed with every gust of passion. He is at odds for the time with all the established order of things, a rebel against the authority of parents, a rebel against friendship, a rebel against his own vows. This is love as it figures in comedy, and in the presentation and analysis of this lies the point of the play.

Introduction. *Midsummer Night's Dream.* Red Letter Shakespeare. 1905. *Shakespeare: A Survey.* 1925.

[270] *Enid Welsford*

The plot is a pattern, a figure, rather than a series of events occasioned by human character and passion, and this pattern, especially in the moonlight parts of the play, is the pattern of a dance.

> 'Enter a Fairie at one doore, and Robin Goodfellow at another . . . Enter the King of Fairies, at one doore, with his traine; and the Queene, at another with hers.'

The appearance and disappearance and reappearance of the various lovers, the will-o'-the-wisp movement of the elusive Puck, form a kind of figured ballet. The lovers quarrel in a dance pattern: first, there are two men to one woman and the other woman alone, then for a brief space a circular movement, each one pursuing and pursued, then a return to the first figure with the position of the women reversed, then a cross-movement, man quarrelling with man and woman with woman, and then, as finale, a general setting to partners, including not only lovers but fairies and royal personages as well.

The Court Masque. 1927. Chap. XII.

[271] *S. C. Sen Gupta*

Shakespeare does not enter into the subtle distinctions between the characters of Lysander and Demetrius or between those of Helena and Hermia. These distinctions are irrelevant, because the lovers themselves were guided by impulse rather than by reason for which delicate nuances of emotion are illusory. It is the tenacity with which the lovers stick to their first choice that makes them apt symbols of Theseus' philosophy of life: it is their perverse intensity that places them in the category of madmen who cannot distinguish between a bush and a bear. If the rivals were carefully distinguished from each other, there might be some rational justification for selecting one of them in preference to the other and, if that were so, Theseus' philosophy of 'cool reason' would be inapplicable to the lovers. Thus it may be said that Shakespeare succeeds in embodying a particular philosophy of life in adequate dramatic shape by neglecting nuances of character. In *A Midsummer Night's Dream,* romance merges into symbolist drama. The potent juice which, working erratically, gives rise to strange complications is in its proper place here, because even in its wildest misapplication it is not more perverse than the capricious emotion we call love. It is a fitting symbol for the 'shaping fantasies' which the lover or the lunatic 'apprehends' and which cool reason can neither 'comprehend' nor approve of.

★ ★ ★

Bottom is prosaic to the backbone, being but a rude mechanic whose occupation keeps him in constant touch with the earth. Philosophically, he is a realist, but the central paradox of his character is that he does not understand reality. That is why he seems to be a puzzle, a mixture of contradictory traits. When he is left to himself, he is as clear-headed as he is hard-handed, but when we find him grappling with reality he acts like a dreamer. 'Bottom,' says Hazlitt, 'seems to have understood the subject of dramatic illusion at least as well as any modern essayist.' His ideas on the subject are logical and unambiguous and his arrangements precise and detailed. Being a realist, he does not leave anything to the imagination; every little detail must be represented with as much accuracy as possible . . . Being devoid of romantic imagination, he cannot enter into the minds of the spectators and gauge their capacities. His solicitude for the poor audience betrays lack of that inner sympathy which is the product of imagination. His instructions about the representation of the lion and the wall are but an indication of the absurdity to which realism unenlivened by imaginative understanding may lead a dramatic producer.

Shakespearian Comedy. 1950. Chaps. III–IV.

[272] *J. B. Priestley*

Lastly there is Bottom (and with him, of course, his companions), who is neither a flickering elf nor a bewildered passionate lover, but a man of this world, comfortably housed in flesh, a personage of some note among the artisans of Athens and, we have no doubt, in spite of certain unmistakable signs of temperament in him, a worthy dependable householder. We suspect that he has, somewhere in the background, a shrewish wife who spends her time alternately seeing through her husband and being taken in by him, for he is essentially one of those large, heavy-faced, somewhat vain and patronising men, not without either humour or imagination, who always induce in women alternating moods of irritation and adoration. Among his fellow artisans, Bottom is clearly the ladies' man, the gallant. He it is who shows himself sensitive to the delicacy of the sex in the matter of the killing and the lion, and we feel that his insistence upon a prologue, "a device to make all well," is only the result of his delicacy and chivalry. Snout and Starveling, who hasten to agree with him, are simply a pair of whimpering poltroons, who have really no stomach for swords and killing and raging melodrama and are afraid of the consequences if they should startle the audience. But Bottom, we feel, has true sensibility and in his own company is the champion of the sex; he knows that it is a most dreadful thing to bring in the lion, that most fearful wild-fowl, among ladies, and his sketch of the prologue has in it the true note of artful entreaty . . .

★ ★ ★

Against the background of the whole play, which is only so much gossamer and moonlight, the honest weaver appears anything but romantic, a piece of humorous, bewildered flesh, gross, earthy. He is a trades-unionist among butterflies, a ratepayer in Elfland. Seen thus, he is droll precisely because he is a most prosaic soul called to a most romantic destiny. But if we view him first among his own associates, we shall see that he is the only one of them who was fit to be "translated."

★ ★ ★

When the players are first met together and the parts are being given out, it is not just Bottom's conceit that makes him want to play every part himself. Of all those present, he is the only one who shows any passion for the drama itself, the art of acting, the enthralling business of moving and thrilling an audience. The others are only concerned with getting through their several tasks in the easiest and safest manner, with one eye on the hangman and the other on the exchequer. But the creative artist is stirring in the soul of Bottom; his imagination is catching fire; so that no sooner is a part mentioned than he can see himself playing it, and playing it in such a manner as to lift the audience out of their seats . . . All this shows the eagerness and the soaring imagination of the artist, and if it shows too an unusual vanity, a confidence in one's ability to play any number of parts better than any one else could play them, a confidence so gigantic that it becomes ridiculous, it must be remembered that vanity and a soaring imagination are generally inseparable. It is clear that a man cannot play every part, cannot be lover, tyrant, lady, and lion at once; but it is equally clear that every man of imagination and spirit ought to want to play every part. It is better to be vain, like Bottom, than to be dead in the spirit, like Snug or Starveling. If it is a weakness to desire to play lover, lady, and lion, it is a weakness of great men, of choice, fiery, and fantastic souls who cannot easily realise or submit to the limitations pressing about our puny mortality. The whole scene, with our friend, flushed and triumphant, the centre of it, is droll, of course, but we really find it droll because we are being allowed to survey it from a height and know that the whole matter is ridiculous and contemptible. These fellows, we can see, should never have left their benches to follow the Muses. But to the gods, the spectacle of Bottom, soaring and magnificent, trying to grasp every part, would be no more ridiculous than the spectacle of Wagner perspiring and gesticulating at Bayreuth: they are both artists, children of vanity and vision, and are both ridiculous and sublime. We can see how droll Bottom is throughout this scene because Shakespeare, having seated us among the gods, has invited us to remark the droll aspects of the situation; but to Flute and Starveling Bottom is a man to be admired and wondered at, and probably to Flute's eldest son (that promising young bellows-mender), to whom he has condescended on one or two occasions, our droll weaver is the greatest man in the world, a hero and an artist, in short, a Wagner. We have but to seat ourselves again among the gods to see that "the best in this kind are but shadows," at once droll, heroic, and pitiful, capering for a little space between darkness and darkness.

"Bully Bottom." *The English Comic Characters.* 1925.

[273] *C. L. Barber*

Shakespeare was not *simply* writing out folklore which he heard in his youth, as Romantic critics liked to assume. On the contrary, his fairies are produced by a complex fusion of pageantry and popular game, as well as popular fancy. Moreover, . . . they are not serious in the menacing way in which the people's fairies were serious. Instead they are serious in a very different way, as embodiments of the May-game experience of eros in men and women and trees and flowers, while any superstitious tendency to believe in their literal reality is mocked. The whole night's action is presented as a release of shaping fantasy which brings clarification about the tricks of strong imagination. We watch a dream; but we are awake, thanks to pervasive humor about the tendency to take fantasy literally, whether in love, in superstition, or in Bottom's mechanical dramatics. As in

Love's Labour's Lost the folly of wit becomes the generalized comic subject in the course of an astonishing release of witty invention, so here in the course of a more inclusive release of imagination, the folly of fantasy becomes the general subject, echoed back and forth between the strains of the play's imitative counterpoint.

★ ★ ★

The comedy's irony about love's motives and choices expresses love's power not as an attribute of special personality but as an impersonal force beyond the persons concerned. The tragedies of love, by isolating Romeo and Juliet, Antony and Cleopatra, enlist our concern for love as it enters into unique destinies, and convey its subjective immensity in individual experience. The festive comedies, in presenting love's effect on a group, convey a different sense of its power, less intense but also less precarious.

★ ★ ★

The woods are a region of passionate excitement where, as Berowne said, love "adds a precious seeing to the eye." This precious seeing was talked about but never realized in *Love's Labour's Lost;* instead we got wit. But now it is realized; we get poetry. Poetry conveys the experience of amorous tendency diffused in nature; and poetry, dance, gesture, dramatic fiction, combine to create, in the fairies, creatures who embody the passionate mind's elated sense of its own omnipotence. The woods are established as a region of metamorphosis, where in liquid moonlight or glimmering starlight, things can change, merge and melt into each other. Metamorphosis expresses both what love sees and what it seeks to do.

★ ★ ★

The confident assumption dominant in *A Midsummer Night's Dream,* that substance and shadow can be kept separate, determines the peculiarly unshadowed gaiety of the fun it makes with fancy. Its organization by polarities—everyday-holiday, town-grove, day-night, waking-dreaming—provides a remarkable resource for mastering passionate experience. By a curious paradox, the full dramatization of holiday affirmations permitted "that side" of experience to be boxed off by Theseus. If we take our stand shoulder to shoulder with Theseus, the play can be an agency for distinguishing what is merely "apprehended" from what is "comprehended." Shakespeare's method of structuring is as powerful, in its way, as Descartes' distinction between mind and body, the formidable engine by which the philosopher swept away "secondary qualities" so that mathematical mind might manipulate geometrical extension. If we do not in our age want to rest in Theseus' rationalistic position (any more than in Descartes'), it remains a great achievement to have got there, and wherever we are going in our sense of reality, we have come via that standing place.

Theseus, moreover, does not quite have the last word, even in this play: his position is only one stage in a dialectic. Hippolyta will not be reasoned out of her wonder, and answers her new Lord with

> But all the story of the night told over,
> And all their minds transfigur'd so together,
> More witnesseth than fancy's images
> And grows to something of great constancy;
> But howsoever, strange and admirable.
>
> (V.i.23–27)

Did it happen, or didn't it happen? The doubt is justified by what Shakespeare has shown us. We are not asked to think that fairies exist. But imagination, by presenting these figments, has reached to something, a creative tendency and process. What is this process? Where is it? What shall we call it? It is what happens in the play. It is what happens in marriage. To name it requires many words, words in motion—the words of *A Midsummer Night's Dream.*

Shakespeare's Festive Comedy A Study of Dramatic Form and Its Relation to Social Custom. 1959. Chap. 6.

Much Ado About Nothing

[274] *G. B. Shaw*

Much Adoodle-do . . . It is a shocking bad play, and can only be saved by Dogberry picking it up at the end, when Beatrice and Benedick are worn out after the church scene.

Ellen Terry and Bernard Shaw A Correspondence, ed. Christopher St. John. 1932. Letter of 3 June 1903.

[275] *Algernon Charles Swinburne*

If it is proverbially impossible to determine by selection the greatest work of Shakespeare, it is easy enough to decide on the date and the name of his most perfect comic masterpiece. For absolute power of composition, for faultless balance and blameless rectitude of design, there is unquestionably no creation of his hand that will bear comparison with *Much Ado about Nothing.*

A Study of Shakespeare. 1880. "Second Period: Comic and Historic."

[276] *William Hazlitt*

Perhaps that middle point of comedy was never more nicely hit in which the ludicrous blends with the tender, and our follies, turning round against themselves in support of our affections, retain nothing but their humanity.

Dogberry and Verges in this play are inimitable specimens of quaint blundering and misprisions of meaning; and are a standing record of that formal gravity of pretension and total want of common understanding, which Shakespear no doubt copied from real life, and which in the course of two hundred years appear to have ascended from the lowest to the highest offices in the state.

Characters of Shakespear's Plays. 1817.

[277] *S. C. Sen Gupta*

A person who falls in love with a particular woman, then woos her by proxy, gets suspicious about the intentions of the friend who has done the wooing for him, is engaged to the lady, then shortly after is easily led to suspect her virtue, condemns her on the slightest evidence, laments at what he thinks is her grave, and, finally, before the tears are dry, passes on to marry another woman, is not a man with an individual personality but is only a conglomeration of romantic postures.

Shakespearian Comedy. 1950. Chap. 5.

[278] *Lewis Carroll (Charles L. Dodgson)*

My difficulty is this:—Why in the world did not Hero (or at any rate Beatrice on her behalf) prove an 'alibi' in answer to the charge? It seems certain that she did *not* sleep in her room that night; for how could Margaret venture to open the window and talk from it, with her mistress asleep in the room? It would be sure to wake her. Besides Borachio says, after promising that Margaret shall speak with him out of Hero's chamber window, 'I will so fashion the matter that Hero shall be absent.' (*How* he could possibly manage any such thing is another difficulty, but I pass over that.) Well then, granting that Hero slept in some other room that night, why didn't she say so? When Claudio asks her: 'What man was he [you] talked with yesternight out at your window betwixt twelve and one?' why doesn't she reply: 'I talked with no man at that hour, my lord. Nor was I in my chamber yesternight, but in another, far from it, remote.' And this she could, of course, prove by the evidence of the housemaids, who must have known that she had occupied another room that night.

But even if Hero might be supposed to be so distracted as not to remember where she had slept the night before, or even whether she had slept *anywhere,* surely *Beatrice* has her wits about her! And when an arrangement was made, by which she was to lose, for one night, her twelve-months' bedfellow, is it conceivable that she didn't know *where* Hero passed the night? Why didn't *she* reply:

'But good my lord sweet Hero slept not there:
She had another chamber for the nonce.
'Twas sure some counterfeit that did present
Her person at the window, aped her voice,
Her mien, her manners, and hath thus deceived
My good Lord Pedro and this company?'

With all these excellent materials for proving an 'alibi' it is incomprehensible that no one should think of it. If only there had been a barrister present, to cross-examine Beatrice!

'Now, ma'am, attend to me, please, and speak up so that the jury can hear you. Where did you sleep last night? Where did Hero sleep? Will you swear that she slept in her own room? Will you swear that you do not know where she slept?' I feel inclined to quote old Mr. Weller and to say to Beatrice at the end of the play (only I'm afraid it isn't etiquette to speak across the footlights):

'Oh, Samivel, Samivel, vy vornt there a halibi?'

Letter quoted by Ellen Terry, *The Story of My Life.* 1908. Chap. XIV.

[279] *John Masefield*

The subject of the play is the power of hearsay, of report, of the thing overheard and repeated, to alter human destiny. Since the great wars began among us we have all known the withering power of calculated falsity and can trace its path in human disaster. Shakespeare had seen something of this of course on the tiny scale possible in Tudor politics. In *Much Ado* he was concerned with the lesser daily worry of discovering that what the soldier said is not evidence, nor fact.

The play all hangs upon mis-report. Antonio's man, listening behind a hedge, overhears Don Pedro telling Claudio that he will woo Hero. His report of the eavesdropping conveys no notion of the truth, but leads, no doubt, to a bitter moment for Hero. Borachio, hiding behind the arras, overhears the real truth of the matter. His report of the eavesdropping leads to the brink of the grave. Don John and Borachio vow to Claudio that they overheard Don Pedro making love to Hero. The report gives Claudio a bitter moment. Benedick, reporting to the same tune, intensifies his misery.

Benedick, overhearing the report of Beatrice's love for him, changes his mind about marriage. Beatrice, hearing of Benedick's love for her, changes her mind about men. Claudio, hearing Don John's report of Hero, behaves like one who is neither a lover nor a gentleman. Leonato, hearing Claudio's report of Hero, behaves like one who has neither affection nor sense. The marriage is broken-off; Hero lies, supposedly dead; while Don John goes off unquestioned: all this has happened through mis-report.

However, the watch men on duty have overheard Borachio's report of his villainy; they are able to change the tragedy to comedy; but not until report has been shown to be stronger than any human affection or acquired quality save the love of one unmarried woman for another; and that strongest of all things, a fool in authority.

William Shakespeare. 1954.

[280] *Francis Fergusson*

The opening scene, in which Leonato's household prepares to celebrate the return of the Duke, Benedick and Claudio from their comic-opera war, tells us what the play is really about: it is a festive occasion, a celebration of a certain evanescent but recurrent human experience. The experience is real in its way, all may recognize it, but under its spell everything the characters do is much ado about nothing. The progress of the underlying action of the play as a whole is therefore marked by a series of somewhat dreamy and deluded festive occasions. The first of these is Leonato's masked ball, in Act II, a visible and musical image of the action. Then comes Dogberry's nocturnal and incomprehensible charge to the Watch: a farcical version of the theme. The fourth act consists chiefly of the marriage which turns out to be no marriage at all, but a bad dream. In the fifth act there is Claudio's funeral tribute to Hero, by night, at her supposed tomb; but this is a funeral which is no funeral, corresponding to the marriage which was no marriage. After that pathetic and comic expiatory rite, daylight returns, the torches are put out, and we are ready for the real and double marriage, in daylight, with the ladies unmasked at last, which ends the play in dance and song.

We are just beginning to understand the technical value of the "ceremonious occasion" as an element of plot, though it has been used in countless ways from Aristophanes to Henry James. When people assemble for a ceremonious occasion (whether it be the festival of Dionysos or one of James's thorny tea parties) they must abate, or conceal, their purely individual purposes, and recognize the common concern which brings them together. A dramatist may use the festive occasion, therefore, to shift his audience's attention from the detail of the literal intrigue to some general plight which all more or less unwittingly share. All are social and political animals; all must suffer spring, mating, and death. Ceremonious occasions are especially useful to dramatists who are seeking poetry, which, as Aristotle remarked, is concerned with something more general than the particular facts, the unique events, of human life. The point—the comic point—of *Much Ado*—is poetic in that sense, and hence it is the festive ensemble scenes which most clearly adumbrate the basic vision of the play.

★ ★ ★

In this [the final] scene the main contrasting themes of the play are brought together, and very lightly and quickly resolved: marriage true and false, masking and unmasking, the delusion and truth of youthful love. The harmonies may all be heard in Beatrice's and Benedick's words. The exchange is in prose, but (like the prose of Leonato's masked ball) it has a rhythm and a varied symmetry suggesting the formality of a dance figure. The key words—love, reason, day, light, pity, peace—make music both for the ear and for the understanding as they echo back and forth, deepening in meaning with each new context. The effect of the scene as a whole is epitomized in Beatrice's and Benedick's heavenly double-take: their foolish idiosyncrasy is clear, but some joyful flood of acceptance and understanding frees them, for the moment, and lifts them beyond it. Is this effect "comic"? I do not know; I think it is intended to bring a smile, not for the windup of this little plot, but for the precarious human condition.

"*The Comedy of Errors* and *Much Ado About Nothing.*" *Sewanee Review.* Winter, 1954. Retitled "Two Comedies" in *The Human Image in Dramatic Literature.* 1957.

Othello

[281] *Samuel Johnson*

The beauties of this play impress themselves so strongly upon the attention of the reader, that they can draw no aid from critical illustration. The fiery openness of *Othello,* magnanimous, artless, and credulous, boundless in his confidence, ardent in his affection, inflexible in his resolution, and obdurate in his revenge; the cool malignity of *Iago,* silent in his resentment, subtle in his designs, and studious at once of his interest and his vengeance; the soft simplicity of *Desdemona,* confident of merit, and conscious of innocence, her artless perseverance in her suit, and her slowness to suspect that she can be suspected, are such proofs of *Shakespeare's* skill in human nature, as, I suppose, it is vain to seek in any modern writer. The gradual progress which *Iago* makes in the Moor's conviction, and the circumstances which he employs to inflame him, are so artfully natural, that, though it will perhaps not be said of him as he says of himself, that he is *a man not easily jealous,* yet we cannot but pity him when at last we find him *perplexed in the extreme.*

There is always danger lest wickedness conjoined with abilities should steal upon esteem, though it misses of approbation; but the character of *Iago* is so conducted, that he is from the first scene to the last hated and despised.

Even the inferiour characters of this play would be very conspicuous in any other piece, not only for their justness but their strength. *Cassio* is brave, benevolent, and honest, ruined only by his want of stubbornness to resist an insidious invitation. *Roderigo's* suspicious credulity, and impatient submission to the cheats which he sees practised upon him, and which by persuasion he suffers to be repeated, exhibit a strong picture of a weak mind betrayed by unlawful desires, to a false friend; and the virtue of *Æmilia* is such as we often find, worn loosely, but not cast off, easy to commit small crimes, but quickened and alarmed at atrocious villanies.

The Plays of William Shakespeare. 1765. Vol. VIII.

[282] *Charlotte Lennox*

The Character of *Iago,* says this Critic [Rymer], is against common Sense and Nature. "*Shakespear* would pass upon us a close, dissembling, false, insinuating Rascal, instead of an open-hearted, frank plain dealing Soldier; a Character constantly worn by them for some Thousands of Years in the World."

The Soldiers are indeed greatly obliged to Mr. *Rymer* for this Assertion, but though it may in general be true, yet surely it is not absurd to suppose that some few Individuals amongst them may be close dissembling Villains.

Iago was a Soldier, it is true, but he was also an *Italian;* he was born in a Country remarkable for the deep Art, Cruelty, and revengeful Temper of its Inhabitants. To have painted an *Italian* injured, or under a Suspicion of being injured, and not to have shewn him revengeful, would have been mistaking his Character.

It is with Justice indeed that Mr. *Rymer* condemns *Shakespear* for that unnecessary and diabolical Cruelty he makes *Iago* guilty of in urging *Othello* to the Murder of the innocent Lady who had never offended him; his Point was gained by making *Othello* jealous, and procuring his Consent to the Death of *Cassio,* who stood in his Way to Preferment: But the Murder of *Desdemona* was such an Excess of wanton Cruelty, that one can hardly conceive it possible a Man could be so transcendently wicked.

Cinthio indeed makes *Iago* not only urge *Othello* to the Murder of his Wife, but is himself the Perpetrator of it; this seems still more absurd; but he tells us, that he had been violently in love with *Desdemona,* and the Indifference she had discovered towards him converted his Love into a settled Hatred.

Shakespear injudiciously copies *Cinthio* in making *Iago* confess a Passion for *Desdemona,* as it rendered his urging on her Murder less probable; since in the Play *Iago* had no Opportunity of declaring that Love to her, and consequently could not be stimulated by her Contempt of him to act so cruel a Part against her.

But he has greatly improved on the Novelist by making him jealous of the Moor with his own Wife; this Circumstance being sufficient, in an *Italian* especially, to account for the Revenge he takes on *Othello,* though his Barbarity to *Desdemona* is still unnatural.

"Observations on the Use *Shakespear* has made of the foregoing Novel in his Tragedy of *Othello,* or the *Moor* of *Venice.*" *Shakespear Illustrated.* Vol. 1. 1753.

[283] *Samuel Taylor Coleridge*

. . . Iago's coolness, the coolness of a preconceiving *experimenter.*

★ ★ ★

. . . a true feeling of Iago's—the dread of contempt habit[ual] to those who encourage in themselves and have their keenest pleasure in the feeling and expression of contempt for others. His high self-opinion—and how a wicked man employs his real feelings as well as assumes those most alien from his own, as instruments of his purpose.

★ ★ ★

Iago's passionless character, all *will* in intellect . . .

★ ★ ★

. . . the motive-hunting of motiveless malignity—how awful! In itself fiendish; while yet he was allowed to bear the divine image, too fiendish for his own steady view. A being next to devil, only *not* quite devil—and this Shakespeare has attempted—executed—without disgust, without scandal!

Notes on the Tragedies. Raysor I, 45, 49.

[284] *William Hazlitt*

The character of Iago is one of the supererogations of Shakespear's genius. Some persons, more nice than wise, have thought this whole character unnatural, because his villainy is *without a sufficient motive.* Shakespear, who was as good a philosopher as he was a poet, thought otherwise. He knew that the love of power, which is another name for the love of mischief, is natural to man. He would know this as well or better than if it had been demonstrated to him by a logical diagram, merely from seeing children paddle in the dirt or kill flies for sport. Iago in fact belongs to a class of character, common to

Shakespear and at the same time peculiar to him; whose heads are as acute and active as their hearts are hard and callous. Iago is to be sure an extreme instance of the kind; that is to say, of diseased intellectual activity, with the most perfect indifference to moral good or evil, or rather with a decided preference of the latter, because it falls more readily in with his favourite propensity, gives greater zest to his thoughts and scope to his actions. He is quite or nearly as indifferent to his own fate as to that of others; he runs all risks for a trifling and doubtful advantage, and is himself the dupe and victim of his ruling passion—an insatiable craving after action of the most difficult and dangerous kind. 'Our ancient' is a philosopher, who fancies that a lie that kills has more point in it than an alliteration or an antithesis; who thinks a fatal experiment on the peace of a family a better thing than watching the palpitations in the heart of a flea in a microscope; who plots the ruin of his friends as an exercise for his ingenuity, and stabs men in the dark to prevent *ennui.* His gaiety, such as it is, arises from the success of his treachery; his ease from the torture he has inflicted on others. He is an amateur of tragedy in real life; and instead of employing his invention on imaginary characters, or long-forgotten incidents, he takes the bolder and more desperate course of getting up his plot at home, casts the principal parts among his nearest friends and connections, and rehearses it in downright earnest, with steady nerves and unabated resolution.

Characters of Shakespear's Plays. 1817.

[285] *Algernon Charles Swinburne*

Malignant as he [Iago] is, the very subtlest and strongest component of his complex nature is not even malignity. It is the instinct of what Mr. Carlyle would call an inarticulate poet. . . . if it be better to make a tragedy than to write one, to act a poem than to sing it, we must allow to Iago a station in the hierarchy of poets very far in advance of his creator's. None of the great inarticulate may more justly claim place and precedence. With all his poetic gift, he has no poetic weakness. . . . He has within him a sense or conscience of power incomparable: and this power shall not be left, in Hamlet's phrase, 'to fust in him unused.' A genuine and thorough capacity for human lust or hate would diminish and degrade the supremacy of his evil. He is almost as far above or beyond vice as he is beneath or beyond virtue. And this it is that makes him impregnable and invulnerable.

A Study of Shakespeare. 1880. "Third Period: Tragic and Romantic."

[286] *Theodore Spencer*

If we look at him [Iago] from the formalistic point of view, keeping the moralities and the interludes in mind, we can see him as the equivalent of the Vice, who manipulates all the action, until he is exposed at the end. From another point of view we can think of him as the typical Machiavellian, all intrigue, egoism and *virtú,* who enjoys evil, like Marlowe's Barabas, for its own sake. Or we can think of him as a neo-Senecan villain-hero, out to justify himself against a set of circumstances that have combined to oppress him. Literary historians have seen him in all three aspects, separately or combined, and if we enjoy being literary historians it may help us to understand him to think of him in these terms. But I doubt if Shakespeare thought of him in such a fashion, and it is perhaps wiser to discuss Iago in more direct relation to human nature.

★ ★ ★

The terrible thing about Iago, if we think of him (as Shakespeare thought of him) in terms of Elizabethan psychology, is that he is a thoroughly rational human being. As Bradley says, "not Socrates himself, not the ideal sage of the Stoics, was more lord of himself than Iago appears to be." Othello's nobility, his apparent control of his passions, was directed, until Iago got hold of him, to good purposes; to the service of the state, to the right kind of love. But Iago is a man without passions; he is an embodiment of one layer of human activity which has no relation to any other layers; he is separated from ordinary human beings on both sides of his nature, the lower and the higher. He has no lust to link him with the animals, and he has no capacity for seeing himself in relation to the state or the universal order of things. He is an unscrupulous individualist.

> "Virtue! a fig! 'tis in ourselves that we are thus, or thus. Our bodies are our gardens, to the which our wills are gardeners; so that if we will plant nettles or sow lettuce, . . . either to have it sterile with idleness or manured with industry, why, the power and corrigible authority of this lies in our wills." (i, 3, 322)

He knows all the right things, but he perverts the familiar doctrine to his own cynical ends:

> "If the balance of our lives had not one scale of reason to poise another of sensuality, the blood and baseness of our natures would conduct us to most preposterous conclusions; but we have reason to cool our raging motions, our carnal stings, our unbitted lusts, whereof I take this that you call love to be a sect or scion."

The last phrase gives him away—"I take this that you call love"; it is obvious that he knows nothing about it. He is an emotional eunuch. That is why he talks so much about lust. Lust is something that as a man of the world he has always heard about, and so he attributes it to everybody, even himself, since he wants to be like other people. For example, he urges himself forward to his attack on Othello by forcing an artificial set of emotions, based on a sexual jealousy about which he really knows nothing:

> Now, I do love her too;
> Not out of absolute lust, —though peradventure
> I stand accountant for as great a sin,—
> But partly led to diet my revenge,
> For that I do suspect the lusty Moor
> Hath leap'd into my seat; the thought whereof
> Doth like a poisonous mineral gnaw my inwards.
> (ii, 1, 303)

Coleridge's notorious phrase about Iago's soliloquies, that they represent the "motive-hunting of a motiveless malignity," is true in one sense, for although we do not have to think of Iago as an abstract personification of evil, he does, in the very reasons (none of them followed up) that he gives for his villainous actions, try to see himself in relation to ordinary human motives and behavior. He gives one explanation after another for his hatred of Othello, partly to make his behavior superficially plausible, and partly to assure himself that it is justified. But none of these reasons is convincing; they do not even sound convincing to Iago himself—"the thought whereof doth like a poisonous mineral gnaw my inwards": this is fairly stagey language; it has no real feeling in it, and we are not surprised never to hear of Iago's jealousy again. That venomous opportunist has merely conjured it up as one of his several attempts to make himself seem natural, and to make his villainy seem natural to the audience.

★ ★ ★

In fact we may think of Iago as being compounded of three concepts of human nature—not merely literary concepts—that were at this time familiar to both Shakespeare and his age: the concept of the difference between outer show and inner fact, the concept of the evil man as an individualist, and, connected with this, the concept of the evil man as the *incomplete* man, the man who does not contain all the psychological levels that should make up a human being. Shakespeare's vision of evil probed very deep when he conceived Iago, for the frightening thing about Iago, as I have said, is that from one point of view he represents the Renaissance ideal of the man whose reason controls his passions, and yet he is wholly bad.

Shakespeare and the Nature of Man. 1942. Chap. V.

[287] *Bernard Spivack*

. . . by every indication, he [Iago] is intended as a coward, just as he was featured by Cinthio: "a very great coward, yet his carriage and conversation were so haughty and full of pretension, that you would have taken him for a Hector or an Achilles." There is no reason to believe that the play changes this estimate. He is fluent with his dagger, but only in special circumstances: Cassio receives it anonymously in the dark, Roderigo already wounded and on his back, his wife when he is cornered ("Fie! your sword upon a woman?"); and he likes to stab and run. Finally, we can draw conviction on this point from the fact that to Cassio he is "the bold Iago" and to Lodovico "a very valiant fellow"; for, without exception, every moral attribute applied to him by anyone in the play is an ironic finger pointing to the truth of its opposite.

Shakespeare and the Allegory of Evil The History of a Metaphor in Relation to His Major Villains. 1958. Chap. XII.

[288] *W. H. Auden*

In trying to understand Iago's character one should begin, I believe, by asking why Shakespeare should have gone to the trouble of inventing Roderigo, a character who has no prototype in Cinthio. From a stage director's point of view, Roderigo is a headache. In the first act we learn that Brabantio had forbidden him the house, from which we must conclude that Desdemona had met him and disliked him as much as her father. In the second act, in order that the audience shall know that he has come to Cyprus, Roderigo has to arrive on the same ship as Desdemona, yet she shows no embarrassment in his presence. Indeed, she and everybody else, except Iago, seem unaware of his existence, for Iago is the only person who ever speaks a word to him. Presumably, he has some official position in the army, but we are never told what it is. His entrances and exits are those of a puppet: whenever Iago has company, he obligingly disappears, and whenever Iago is alone and wishes to speak to him, he comes in again immediately.

Moreover, so far as Iago's plot is concerned, there is nothing Roderigo does which Iago could not do better without him. He could easily have found another means, like an anonymous letter, of informing Brabantio of Desdemona's elopement and, for picking a quarrel with a drunken Cassio, he has, on his own admission, other means handy.

> Three lads of Cyprus, noble swelling spirits
> That hold their honour in a wary distance,
> The very elements of this warlike isle
> Have I to-night flustered with flowing cups.

Since Othello has expressly ordered him to kill Cassio, Iago could have murdered him without fear of legal investigation. Instead, he not only chooses as an accomplice a man whom he is cheating and whose suspicions he has constantly to allay, but also a man who is plainly inefficient as a murderer and also holds incriminating evidence against him.

A man who is seriously bent on revenge does not take unnecessary risks nor confide in anyone whom he cannot trust or do without. Emilia is not, as in Cinthio, Iago's willing accomplice, so that, in asking her to steal the handkerchief, Iago is running a risk, but it is a risk he has to take. By involving Roderigo in his plot, he makes discovery and his own ruin almost certain. It is a law of drama that, by the final curtain, all secrets, guilty or innocent, shall have been revealed so that all, on both sides of the footlights, know who did or did not do what, but usually the guilty are exposed either because, like Edmund, they repent and confess or because of events which they could not reasonably have foreseen. Don John could not have foreseen that Dogberry and Verges would overhear Borachio's conversation, nor Iachimo that Pisanio would disobey Posthumus' order to kill Imogen, nor King Claudius the intervention of a ghost.

Had he wished, Shakespeare could easily have contrived a similar kind of exposure for Iago. Instead, by giving Roderigo the role he does, he makes Iago as a plotter someone devoid of ordinary worldly common sense.

One of Shakespeare's intentions was, I believe, to indicate that Iago desires self-destruction as much as he desires the destruction of others but, before elaborating on this, let us consider Iago's treatment of Roderigo, against whom he has no grievance—it is he who is injuring Roderigo—as a clue to his treatment of Othello and Cassio.

When we first see Iago and Roderigo together, the situation is like that in a Ben Jonson comedy—a clever rascal is gulling a rich fool who deserves to be gulled because his desire is no more moral than that of the more intelligent avowed rogue who cheats him out of his money. Were the play a comedy, Roderigo would finally realize that he had been cheated but would not dare appeal to the law because, if the whole truth were made public, he would cut a ridiculous or shameful figure. But, as the play proceeds, it becomes clear that Iago is not simply after Roderigo's money, a rational motive, but that his main game is Roderigo's moral corruption, which is irrational because Roderigo has given him no cause to desire his moral ruin. When the play opens, Roderigo is shown as a spoiled weakling, but no worse. It may be foolish of him to hope to win Desdemona's affection by gifts and to employ a go-between, but his conduct is not in itself immoral. Nor is he, like Cloten in *Cymbeline,* a brute who regards women as mere objects of lust. He is genuinely shocked as well as disappointed when he learns of Desdemona's marriage, but continues to admire her as a woman full of most blessed condition. Left to himself, he would have had a good bawl, and given her up. But Iago will not let him alone. By insisting that Desdemona is seducible and that his real rival is not Othello but Cassio, he brings Roderigo to entertain the idea, originally foreign to him, of becoming a seducer and of helping Iago to ruin Cassio. Iago had had the pleasure of making a timid conventional man become aggressive and criminal. Cassio beats up Roderigo. Again, at this point, had he been left to himself, he would have gone no further, but Iago will not let him alone until he consents to murder Cassio, a deed which is contrary to his nature, for he is not only timid but also incapable of passionate hatred.

> I have no great devotion to the deed:
> And yet he has given me satisfying reasons.
> 'Tis but a man gone.

Why should Iago want to do this to Roderigo? To me, the clue to this and to all Iago's conduct is to be found in Emilia's comment when she picks up the handkerchief.

> My wayward husband hath a hundred times
> Wooed me to steal it . . .
> what he'll do with it
> Heaven knows, not I,
> I nothing but to please his fantasy.

As his wife, Emilia must know Iago better than anybody else does. She does not know, any more than the others, that he is malevolent, but she does know that her husband is addicted to practical jokes. What Shakespeare gives us in Iago is a portrait of a practical joker of a peculiarly appalling kind . . .

★ ★ ★

Cassio is a ladies' man, that is to say, a man who feels most at home in feminine company where his looks and good manners make him popular, but is ill at ease in the company of his own sex because he is unsure of his masculinity. In civilian life he would be perfectly happy, but circumstances have made him a soldier and he has been forced by his profession into a society which is predominantly male. Had he been born a generation earlier, he would never have found himself in the army at all, but changes in the technique of warfare demand of soldiers, not only the physical courage and aggressiveness which the warrior has always needed, but also intellectual gifts. The Venetian army now needs mathematicians, experts in the science of gunnery. But in all ages, the typical military mentality is conservative and resents the intellectual expert.

> A fellow
> That never set a squadron in the field
> Nor the division of a battle knows
> More than a spinster . . . mere prattle without practise
> Is all his soldiership

is a criticism which has been heard in every army mess in every war. Like so many people who cannot bear to feel unpopular and therefore repress their knowledge that they are, Cassio becomes quarrelsome when drunk, for alcohol releases his suppressed resentment at not being admired by his comrades in arms and his wish to prove that he is what he is not, as "manly" as they are. It is significant that, when he sobers up, his regret is not that he has behaved badly by his own standards but that he has lost his reputation. The advice which Iago then gives him, to get Desdemona to plead for him with Othello, is good advice in itself, for Desdemona obviously likes him, but it is also exactly the advice a character-type like Cassio will be most willing to listen to, for feminine society is where he feels most at home.

Emilia informs Cassio that, on her own initiative, Desdemona has already spoken on his behalf and that Othello has said he will take the safest occasion by the front to restore him to his post. Hearing this, many men would have been content to leave matters as they were, but Cassio persists: the pleasure of a heart-to-heart talk with a lady about his fascinating self is too tempting.

While he is talking to Desdemona, Othello is seen approaching and she says:

Stay and hear me speak.

Again, many men would have done so, but Cassio's uneasiness with his own sex, particularly when he is in disgrace, is too strong and he sneaks away, thus providing Iago with his first opportunity to make an insinuation.

Cassio is a ladies' man, not a seducer. With women of his own class, what he enjoys is socialized eroticism; he would be frightened of a serious personal passion. For physical sex he goes to prostitutes and when, unexpectedly, Bianca falls in love with him, like many of his kind, he behaves like a cad and brags of his conquest to others. Though he does not know who the owner of the handkerchief actually is, he certainly knows that Bianca will think that it belongs to another woman, and to ask her to copy it is gratuitous cruelty. His smiles, gestures and remarks about Bianca to Iago are insufferable in themselves; to Othello, who knows that he is talking about a woman, though he is mistaken as to her identity, they are an insult which only Cassio's death can avenge.

★ ★ ★

If one compares *Othello* with the other plays in which Shakespeare treats the subject of male jealousy, *The Winter's Tale* and *Cymbeline,* one notices that Othello's jealousy is of a peculiar kind.

Leontes is a classical case of paranoid sexual jealousy due to repressed homosexual feelings. He has absolutely no evidence that Hermione and Polixenes have committed adultery and his entire court are convinced of their innocence, but he is utterly possessed by his fantasy. As he says to Hermione: "Your actions are my dreams." But, mad as he is, "the twice-nine changes of the Watery Starre" which Polixenes has spent at the Bohemian court, make the act of adultery physically possible so that, once the notion has entered his head, neither Hermione nor Polixenes nor the court can prove that it is false. Hence the appeal to the Oracle.

Posthumus is perfectly sane and is convinced against his will that Imogen has been unfaithful because Iachimo offers him apparently irrefutable evidence that adultery has taken place.

But both the mad Leontes and the sane Posthumus react in the same way: "My wife has been unfaithful; therefore she must be killed and forgotten." That is to say, it is only as husbands that their lives are affected. As king of Bohemia, as a warrior, they function as if nothing has happened.

In *Othello,* thanks to Iago's manipulations, Cassio and Desdemona behave in a way which would make it not altogether unreasonable for Othello to suspect that they were in love with each other, but the time factor rules out the possibility of adultery having been actually committed. Some critics have taken the double time in the play to be merely a dramaturgical device for speeding the action which the audience in the theatre will never notice. I believe, however, that Shakespeare meant the audience to notice it as, in *The Merchant of Venice,* he meant them to notice the discrepancy between Belmont time and Venice time.

If Othello had simply been jealous of the feelings for Cassio he imagined Desdemona to have, he would have been sane enough, guilty at worst of a lack of trust in his wife. But Othello is not merely jealous of feelings which might exist; he demands proof of an act which could not have taken place, and the effect on him of believing in this physical impossibility goes far beyond wishing to kill her: it is not only his wife who has betrayed him but the whole universe; life has become meaningless, his occupation is gone.

This reaction might be expected if Othello and Desdemona were a pair like Romeo and Juliet or Antony and Cleopatra whose love was an all-absorbing Tristan-Isolde kind of passion, but Shakespeare takes care to inform us that it was not.

When Othello asks leave to take Desdemona with him to Cyprus, he stresses the spiritual element in his love.

> I therefore beg it not
> To please the palate of my appetite
> Nor to comply with heat, the young affects
> In me defunct, and proper satisfaction,
> But to be free and bounteous of her mind.

Though the imagery in which he expresses his jealousy is sexual—what other kind of images could he use?—Othello's marriage is important to him less as a sexual relationship than as a symbol of being loved and accepted as a person, a brother in the Venetian community. The monster in his own mind too hideous to be shown is the fear he has so far repressed that he is only valued for his social usefulness to the City. But for his occupation, he would be treated as a black barbarian.

The overcredulous, overgood-natured character which, as Iago tells us, Othello had always displayed is a telltale symptom. He had *had* to be overcredulous in order to compensate for his repressed suspicions. Both in his happiness at the beginning of the play and in his cosmic despair later, Othello reminds one more of Timon of Athens than of Leontes.

Since what really matters to Othello is that Desdemona should love him as the person he really is, Iago has only to get him to suspect that she does not, to release the repressed fears and resentments of a lifetime, and the question of what she has done or not done is irrelevant.

★ ★ ★

Everybody must pity Desdemona, but I cannot bring myself to like her. Her determination to marry Othello—it was she who virtually did the proposing—seems the romantic crush of a silly schoolgirl rather than a mature affection; it is Othello's adventures, so unlike the civilian life she knows, which captivate her rather than Othello as a person. He may not have practiced witchcraft, but, in fact, she is spellbound. And despite all Brabantio's prejudices, her deception of her own father makes an unpleasant impression: Shakespeare does not allow us to forget that the shock of the marriage kills him.

Then, she seems more aware than is agreeable of the honor she has done Othello by becoming his wife. When Iago tells Cassio that "our General's wife is now the General" and, soon afterwards soliloquizes

> His soul is so infettered to her love
> That she may make, unmake, do what she list
> Even as her appetite shall play the god
> With his weak function

he is, no doubt, exaggerating, but there is much truth in what he says. Before Cassio speaks to her, she has already discussed him with her husband and learned that he is to be reinstated as soon as is opportune. A sensible wife would have told Cassio this and left matters alone. In continuing to badger Othello, she betrays a desire to prove to herself and to Cassio that she can make her husband do as she pleases.

Her lie about the handkerchief is, in itself, a trivial fib but, had she really regarded her husband as her equal, she might have admitted the loss. As it is, she is frightened because she is suddenly confronted with a man whose sensibility and superstitions are alien to her.

Though her relation with Cassio is perfectly innocent, one cannot but share Iago's doubts as to the durability of the marriage. It is worth noting that, in the willow-song scene with Emilia, she speaks with admiration of Ludovico and then turns to the topic of adultery. Of course, she discusses this in general terms and is shocked by Emilia's attitude, but she does discuss the subject and she does listen to what Emilia has to say about husbands and wives. It is as if she had suddenly realized that she had made a *mésalliance* and that the sort of man she ought to have married was someone of her own class and color like Ludovico. Given a few more years of Othello and of Emilia's influence and she might well, one feels, have taken a lover.

"The Joker in the Pack." *The Dyer's Hand and Other Essays.* 1962.

[289] *Ellen Terry*

The fact is that . . . the foreign temperament is better fitted to deal with Othello than the English. Shakespeare's French and Italians, Greeks and Latins, medievals and barbarians, fancifuls and reals, all have a dash of Elizabethan English men in them, but not Othello.

The Story of My Life. 1908. Chap. IX.

[290] *G. G. Sedgewick*

Note, first [in Act II], how Cassio is picked out and shaped as a means toward the end. A text for the lesson is in the words . . . "Cassio's a proper man." We watch him gaining body, from our vantage point of knowledge, and Iago is watching him also and giving significance to what we see. We heard of him in the first lines of the play, and we have seen him once or twice on the stage. The style of his first notable speeches in the second act is significant: along with everything else we learn about him, it suggests "the wealthy curled darlings of our nation" whom Desdemona rejected for the Moor.

★ ★ ★

There is something indefinable—but it is certainly ironic—in what immediately follows: "(*Trumpet within.*) The Moor! I know his trumpet." Othello appears and in the ecstasy of reunion utters—one almost says chants—lines that to the audience have an Aeschylean foreboding:

> . . . not another comfort like to this
> Succeeds in unknown fate . . .
> It stops me here: it is too much of joy.

Note how extraordinarily brief this episode is! Then, with the visible contrast between Cassio and the Moor fresh to the memory, we are quickly led back with Iago to the old theme now given exact and specific point: ". . . there should be . . . to give satiety a fresh appetite, loveliness in favour, sympathy in years, manners, and beauties: all which the Moor is defective in"; while as for Cassio—". . . the knave is handsome, young, and hath all those requisites in him that folly and green minds look after; a pestilent complete knave; and the woman hath found him already." The case that Iago makes is abominable; but, in spite of that, he makes it sound nearly as "probable and palpable to thinking" as it had been to Brabantio. Besides—and this is the really important thing—we are in the theatre, and we can already see Iago's bad case being made good: "Villainous thoughts, Roderigo, . . . marshal the way." The ironic sense watches Cassio with a sort of pity; we *see* him being deliberately shaped as a tool proper to Iago's hand; and there is a beginning of terror as it watches, and thinks of, the Moor and his wife.

Turn back, now, for a moment to where Desdemona is anxiously awaiting the arrival of her husband. The episode is, or used to be, difficult for the "unco guid," as being too coarse for what ought to be Desdemona's taste. One is reminded of the New England editor who thought Shakespeare killed off Mercutio so that Romeo would not have to introduce him to Juliet. Luckily tastes differ and change. It is not very disturbing morally that Desdemona should egg Iago on to his doggerel about the ways of women; but it *is* dramatically disturbing that she should turn to him for diversion. The elegant Cassio is a bit uncomfortable, but only about Iago's etiquette: "You may relish him more in the soldier than in the scholar." The notable and ominous thing about the business is its naturalness, its good nature even. For it amuses Iago to amuse people, especially pretty women. With great and willing tact he relieves the tensity of the moment; he is a nice judge of person and occasion. The irony is that we know the mild ribaldry of his jokes to be but a pale reflection of his opinions; and, much more important, that the bodyguard whom Othello trusted in Venice has won the complete confidence of Desdemona. He has fooled her, as he has fooled Roderigo, Brabantio, the Moor, and as he will fool Cassio presently. Everybody on the stage, so we see, has every reason to trust him implicitly—every reason, that is, *except the knowledge which only the spectator has.*

Of Irony Especially in Drama. (Alexander Lectures, 1934.) University of Toronto Press, 1948. Lect. IV.

[291] *G. B. Shaw*

The element of accident in Tragedy has always been its weak spot; for though an accident may be sensational, nothing can make it interesting or save it from being irritating. Othello is spoilt by a handkerchief, as Shakespear found out afterwards when he wrote A Winter's Tale.

"Tolstoy: Tragedian or Comedian?" (Substance of an extemporized speech made at the Tolstoy Commemoration at Kingsway Hall in London on November 30, 1921.) XXIX, 277.

Richard II

[292] *Algernon Charles Swinburne*

Even after a lifelong study of this as of all other plays of Shakespeare, it is for me at least impossible to determine what I doubt if the poet could himself have clearly defined—the main principle, the motive and the meaning, of such characters as York, Norfolk, and

Aumerle. The Gaveston and the Mortimer of Marlowe are far more solid and definite figures than these; yet none after that of Richard is more important to the scheme of Shakespeare. They are fitful, shifting, vaporous: their outlines change, withdraw, dissolve, and 'leave not a rack behind.' They, not Antony, are like the clouds of evening . . . 'They cannot hold this visible shape' in which the poet at first presents them even long enough to leave a distinct image, a decisive impression for better or for worse, upon the mind's eye of the most simple and open-hearted reader. . . . You cannot descry so much as the original intention of the artist's hand which began to draw and relaxed its hold of the brush before the first lines were firmly traced. And in the last, the worst and weakest scene of all, in which York pleads with Bolingbroke for the death of the son whose mother pleads against her husband for his life, there is a final relapse into rhyme and rhyming epigram, into the 'jigging vein' dried up (we might have hoped) long since by the very glance of Marlowe's Apollonian scorn. It would be easy, agreeable, and irrational to ascribe without further evidence than its badness this misconceived and misshapen scene to some other hand than Shakespeare's. It is below the weakest, the rudest, the hastiest scene attributable to Marlowe, it is false, wrong, artificial beyond the worst of his bad and boyish work; but it has a certain likeness for the worse to the crudest work of Shakespeare. It is difficult to say to what depths of bad taste the writer of certain passages in *Venus and Adonis* could not fall before his genius or his judgment was full grown. To invent an earlier play on the subject and imagine this scene a surviving fragment, a floating waif of that imaginary wreck, would in my opinion be an uncritical mode of evading the question at issue. It must be regarded as the last hysterical struggle of rhyme to maintain its place in tragedy; and the explanation, I would fain say the excuse, of its reappearance may perhaps be simply this: that the poet was not yet dramatist enough to feel for each of his characters an equal or proportionate regard; to divide and disperse his interest among the various crowd of figures which claim each in its place, and each after its kind, a fair and adequate share of their creator's attention and sympathy. His present interest was here wholly concentrated on the single figure of Richard; and when that for the time was absent, the subordinate figures became to him but heavy and vexatious encumbrances, to be shifted on and off the stage with as much of haste and as little of labour as might be possible to an impatient and uncertain hand.

A Study of Shakespeare. 1880. "First Period: Lyric and Fantastic."

[293] *Samuel Taylor Coleridge*

In this scene [I.iv] a new light is thrown on Richard's character. Until now he has appeared in all the beauty of royalty; but here, as soon as he is left to himself, the inherent weakness of his character is immediately shown. It is a weakness, however, of a peculiar kind, not arising from want of personal courage, or any specific defect of faculty, but rather an intellectual feminineness which feels a necessity of ever leaning on the breast of others, and of reclining on those who are all the while known to be inferiors. To this must be attributed as its consequences all Richard's vices, his tendency to concealment, and his cunning, the whole operation of which is directed to the getting rid of present difficulties. Richard is not meant to be a debauchee; but we see in him that sophistry which is common to man, by which we can deceive our own hearts, and at one and the same time apologize for, and yet commit, the error. Shakespeare has represented this character in a very peculiar manner. He has not made him amiable with counterbalancing faults; but has openly and broadly drawn those faults without reserve, relying on Richard's disproportionate sufferings and gradually emergent good qualities for our sympathy; and this was possible, because his faults are not positive vices, but spring entirely from defect of character.

Notes on the History Plays. Raysor I, 148–49.

[294] *Edward Dowden*

Richard, to whom all things are unreal, has a fine feeling for "situations." Without true kingly strength or dignity, he has a fine feeling for the royal situation. Without any making real to himself what God or what death is, he can put himself, if need be, in the appropriate attitude towards God and towards death. Instead of comprehending things as they are, and achieving heroic deeds, he satiates his heart with the grace, the tenderness, the beauty, or the pathos of situations. Life is to Richard a show, a succession of images; and to put himself into accord with the aesthetic requirements of his position is Richard's first necessity. He is equal to playing any part gracefully which he is called upon by circumstances to enact. But when he has exhausted the aesthetic satisfaction to be derived from the situations of his life, he is left with nothing further to do. He is an amateur in living; not an artist.

Shakspere, His Mind and Art. 1874. Chap. IV.

[295] *Harold C. Goddard*

Though Bolingbroke was bent on getting the crown in the end, if Richard had not practically placed it on his head he might very well have asked no more at the moment than the restitution of his inheritance. There is nothing more provocative of violence than the dread of violence. The shrinking victim evokes a devil in the victor. The more Richard cowers, the more Henry tightens the screws. It is a vivid demonstration of the truth that fear and force are poles of a single entity. If a whirlwind meets a vacuum it naturally rushes into it. So force, into fear. Fear is as creative as faith. It brings into being what it imagines. The evil that stained the life of Henry IV from this day on was in no small measure of Richard's making.

The Meaning of Shakespeare. 1951. Chap. XV.

[296] *W. B. Yeats*

I cannot believe that Shakespeare looked on his Richard II. with any but sympathetic eyes, understanding indeed how ill-fitted he was to be King, at a certain moment of history, but understanding that he was lovable and full of capricious fancy, 'a wild creature' as Pater has called him. The man on whom Shakespeare modelled him had been full of French elegancies, as he knew from Hollingshead, and had given life a new luxury, a new splendour, and been 'too friendly' to his friends, 'too favourable' to his enemies. And certainly Shakespeare had these things in his head when he made his King fail, a little because he lacked some qualities that were doubtless common among his scullions, but more because he had certain qualities that are uncommon in all ages. To suppose that Shakespeare preferred the men who deposed his King is to suppose that Shakespeare judged men with the eyes of a Municipal Councillor weighing the merits of a Town Clerk . . . He saw indeed, as I think, in Richard II. the defeat that awaits all, whether they be Artist or Saint, who find themselves where men ask of them a rough energy and have nothing to give but some contemplative virtue, whether lyrical phantasy, or sweetness of temper, or dreamy dignity, or love of God, or love of His creatures. He saw that such a man through sheer bewilderment and impatience can become as unjust or as violent as any common man, any Bolingbroke or Prince John, and yet remain 'that sweet lovely rose.' The courtly and saintly ideals of the Middle Ages were fading, and the practical ideals of the modern age had begun to threaten the unuseful dome of the sky; Merry England was fading, and yet it was not so faded that the Poets could not watch the procession of the world with that untroubled sympathy for men as they are, as apart from all they do and seem, which is the substance of tragic irony. . . .

★ ★ ★

I have often had the fancy that there is some one Myth for every man, which, if we but knew it, would make us understand all he did and thought. Shakespeare's Myth, it may be, describes a wise man who was blind from very wisdom, and an empty man who thrust him from his place, and saw all that could be seen from very emptiness. It is in the story of Hamlet, who saw too great issues everywhere to play the trivial game of life, and of Fortinbras, who came from fighting battles about 'a little patch of ground' so poor that one of his Captains would not give 'six ducats' to 'farm it,' and who was yet acclaimed by Hamlet and by all as the only befitting King. And it is in the story of Richard II., that unripened Hamlet, and of Henry V., that ripened Fortinbras.

"At Stratford-on-Avon." *The Speaker.* May 11, 18, 1901. *Ideas of Good and Evil.* 1903.

[297] *Walter Pater*

One gracious prerogative, certainly, Shakespeare's English kings possess: they are a very eloquent company, and Richard is the most sweet-tongued of them all. In no other play perhaps is there such a flush of those gay, fresh, variegated flowers of speech—colour and figure, not lightly attached to, but fused into, the very phrase itself—which Shakespeare cannot help dispensing to his characters, as in this "play of the Deposing of King Richard the Second," an exquisite poet if he is nothing else, from first to last, in light and gloom alike, able to see all things poetically, to give a poetic turn to his conduct of them, and refreshing with his golden language the tritest aspects of that ironic contrast between the pretensions of a king and the actual necessities of his destiny. What a garden of words! With him, blank verse, infinitely graceful, deliberate, musical in inflexion, becomes indeed a true "verse royal," that rhyming lapse, which to the Shakespearian ear, at least in youth, came as the last touch of refinement on it, being here doubly appropriate. His eloquence blends with that fatal beauty, of which he was so frankly aware, so amiable to his friends, to his wife, of the effects of which on the people his enemies were so much afraid, on which Shakespeare himself dwells so attentively as the "royal blood" comes and goes in the face with his rapid changes of temper. As happens with sensitive natures, it attunes him to a congruous suavity of manners, by which anger itself became flattering: it blends with his merely youthful hopefulness and high spirits, his sympathetic love for gay people, things, apparel —"his cote of gold and stone, valued at thirty thousand marks," the novel Italian fashions he preferred, as also with those real amiabilities that made people forget the darker touches of his character, but never tire of the pathetic rehearsal of his fall, the meekness of which would have seemed merely abject in a less graceful performer.

★ ★ ★

Shakespeare supposes him an over-confident believer in that divine right of kings, of which people in Shakespeare's time were coming to hear so much; a general right, sealed to him (so Richard is made to think) as an ineradicable personal gift by the touch—stream rather, over head and breast and shoulders—of the "holy oil" of his consecration at Westminster . . . And nowhere is there so emphatic a reiteration as in *Richard the Second* of the sentiment which those singular rites were calculated to produce.

Not all the water in the rough rude sea
Can wash the balm from an anointed king,—

as supplementing another, almost supernatural, right.—"Edward's seven sons," of whom Richard's father was one,

Were as seven phials of his sacred blood.

But this, too, in the hands of Shakespeare, becomes for him, like any other of those fantastic, ineffectual, easily discredited, personal graces, as capricious in its operation on men's wills as merely physical beauty, kindling himself to eloquence indeed, but only giving double pathos to insults which "barbarism itself" might have pitied—the dust in his face, as he returns, through the streets of London, a prisoner in the train of his victorious enemy.

How soon my sorrow hath destroyed my face!

he cries, in that most poetic invention of the mirror scene, which does but reinforce again that physical charm which all confessed. The sense of "divine right" in kings is found to act not so much as a secret of power over others, as of infatuation to themselves. And of all those personal gifts the one which alone never altogether fails him is just that royal utterance, his appreciation of the poetry of his own hapless lot, an eloquent self-pity, infecting others in spite of themselves, till they too become irresistibly eloquent about him.

In the Roman Pontifical, of which the order of Coronation is really a part, there is no form for the inverse process, no rite of "degradation," such as that by which an offending priest or bishop may be deprived, if not of the essential quality of "orders," yet, one by one, of its outward dignities. It is as if Shakespeare had had in mind some such inverted rite, like those old ecclesiastical or military ones, by which human hardness, or human justice, adds the last touch of unkindness to the execution of its sentences, in the scene where Richard "deposes" himself, as in some long, agonising ceremony, reflectively drawn out, with an extraordinary refinement of intelligence and variety of piteous appeal, but also with a felicity of poetic invention, which puts these pages into a very select class, with the finest "vermeil and ivory" work of Chatterton or Keats.

★ ★ ★

. . . the play of *Richard the Second* does, like a musical composition, possess a certain concentration of all its parts, a simple continuity, an evenness in execution, which are rare in the great dramatist. With *Romeo and Juliet,* that perfect symphony (symphony of three independent poetic forms set in a grander one[1] which it is the merit of German criticism to have detected) it belongs to a small group of plays, where, by happy birth and consistent evolution, dramatic form approaches to something like the unity of a lyrical ballad, a lyric, a song, a single strain of music.

[1] The Sonnet: the Aubade: the Epithalamium.

"Shakespeare's English Kings." *Scribner's Magazine.* April, 1889. *Appreciations.* 1889.

Richard III

[298] *G. B. Shaw*

The world being yet little better than a mischievous schoolboy, I am afraid it cannot be denied that Punch and Judy holds the field still as the most popular of dramatic entertainments. And of all its versions, except those which are quite above the head of the man in the street, Shakespear's Richard III is the best. It has abundant devilry, humor, and character, presented with luxuriant energy of diction in the simplest form of blank verse. Shakespear revels in it with just the sort of artistic unconscionableness that fits the theme. Richard is the prince of Punches: he delights Man by provoking God, and dies unrepentant and game to the last. His incongruous conventional appendages, such as the Punch hump, the conscience, the fear of ghosts, all impart a spice of outrageousness which leaves nothing lacking to the fun of the entertainment, except the solemnity of those spectators who feel bound to take the affair as a profound and subtle historic study.

"Richard Himself Again." *The Saturday Review.* 26 December 1896. XXIV, 299.

[299] *John Palmer*

The eternal bully speaks to the everlasting trollop—and knows that he will prevail. When he throws himself at Anne's feet and protests that he has never sued thus to a living soul, his flattery is meant to impress, but not to deceive, a woman already impotent to resist him. Richard's humility and the lady's scorn are at this stage equally fictitious. She is already won.

★ ★ ★

Richard, who knew in advance that he would prevail, nevertheless expresses amazement at his success. Note, however, the quality of his exultation. He says nothing of the advantages to be derived from his marriage. Nor does he directly dwell upon it as a triumph of his will and person. His delight is more keen and sinister than that of a merely able man who comes off with flying colours from a difficult enterprise. The mainspring of his pleasure is to have proved that his measureless contempt of human nature, with its weak affections and silly scruples, is justified. His success with Lady Anne vindicates his whole philosophy of life.

★ ★ ★

Everything in Richard's world—even his deformity—nourishes his sense of power. There is nothing negative in his character. He never sins, for sin implies a breach of the moral law accepted by the sinner. Richard has his own code. To that he is always faithful and so lives happy as the day is long.

Political Characters of Shakespeare. 1945. Chap. II.

[300] *Hazelton Spencer*

In substance, then, *Richard the Third* is chronicle history; in form it is tragedy; but in tone it is hardly more than melodrama. The hero is not merely not a good man, he is not a good hero. Macbeth is carefully built up at the outset as a noble leader of men; and though he falls into wicked courses and deserves his fate, nobility hangs round him still. His tragedy inspires awe and pity—for him and for the human race. Richard is all villain and always villain, and at the end the real hero is Richmond. The fall of Crookback can not move us deeply; he is too isolated from humanity—there is no drop of the milk of human kindness in him. Even when he wakes from his dream it is fear he feels, not remorse.

The Art and Life of William Shakespeare. 1940. Chap. 4.

Romeo and Juliet

[301] *Samuel Johnson*

The Nurse is one of the characters in which the Authour delighted: he has, with great subtility of distinction, drawn her at once loquacious and secret, obsequious and insolent, trusty and dishonest.

The Plays of William Shakespeare. 1765. Vol. VIII.

[302] *Samuel Taylor Coleridge*

. . . in the Nurse you have all the garrulity of old age, and all its fondness; for the affection of old-age is one of the greatest consolations of humanity. . . .

You have also in the Nurse the arrogance of ignorance, with the pride of meanness at being connected with a great family. You have the grossness, too, which that situation never removes, though it sometimes suspends it; and, arising from that grossness, the little low vices attendant upon it, which, indeed, in such minds are scarcely vices . . .

Another point ought to be mentioned as characteristic of the ignorance of the Nurse:—it is, that in all her recollections, she assists herself by the remembrance of visual circumstances.

The Lectures of 1811–12. VII. Raysor II, 133–34.

[303] *Harold C. Goddard*

The world has long since decided what to think of a man who lets himself be called a villain without retaliating. Romeo, to put it in one word, proves himself, according to the world's code, a mollycoddle. And indeed a mollycoddle might act exactly as Romeo appears to. But if Romeo is a mollycoddle, then Jesus was a fool to talk about loving one's enemies, for Romeo, if anyone ever did, is doing just that at this moment. And Juliet was demented to talk about love being boundless and infinite, for here Romeo is about to prove that faith precisely true. Those who think that Jesus, and Juliet, and Romeo were fools will have plenty of backing. The "fathers" will be on their side. They will have the authority of the ages and the crowd. Only a philosopher or two, a few lovers, saints, and poets will be against them. The others will echo the

O calm, dishonourable, vile submission!

with which Mercutio draws his rapier and begins hurling insults at Tybalt that make Tybalt's own seem tame . . .

★ ★ ★

. . . the scene is like the court scene in *The Merchant of Venice* when we gloat over Shylock's discomfiture. Here, as there, not only our cooler judgment when we are alone but all the higher implications of the tragedy call for a reversal of our reactions when with the crowd. In this calmer retrospect, we perceive that between his hero's entrance and exit in this scene Shakespeare has given us three Romeos, or, if you will, one Romeo in three universes. First we see him possessed by love and a spirit of universal forgiveness. From this he falls, first to reason and an appeal to law, then to violence—but violence in a negative or "preventive" sense. Finally, following Mercutio's death, he passes under the control of passion and fury, abetted by "honour," and thence to vengeance and offensive violence. In astrological terms, he moves from Venus, through the Earth, to Mars. It is as if Dante's *Divine Comedy* were compressed into eighty lines and presented in reverse—Romeo in an inverted "pilgrimage" passing from Paradise, through Purgatory, to the Inferno.

The Meaning of Shakespeare. 1951. Chap. XIII.

[304] *Samuel Taylor Coleridge*

As the audience knew that Juliet is not dead, this scene [IV. v] is, perhaps, excusable. At all events, it is a strong warning to *minor* dramatists not to introduce at one time many different characters agitated by one and the same circumstance. It is difficult to understand what *effect,* whether that of pity or laughter, Shakespeare meant to produce—the occasion and the characteristic speeches are so little in harmony: *ex. gratia,* what the Nurse says is excellently suited to the Nurse's character, but grotesquely unsuited to the occasion.

Notes on the Tragedies. Raysor I, 11.

[305] *Harley Granville-Barker*

The first thing to mark about Juliet, for everything else depends on it, is that she is, to our thinking, a child. Whether she is Shakespeare's fourteen or Brooke's sixteen makes little difference; she is meant to be just about as young as she can be; and her actual age is trebly stressed. Her tragedy is a child's tragedy; half its poignancy would be gone otherwise. Her bold innocence is a child's, her simple trust in her Nurse; her passionate rage at the news of Tybalt's death is easily pardonable in a child, her terrors when she takes the potion are doubly dreadful as childish terrors. The cant saying that no actress can play Juliet till she is too old to look her should therefore go the way of all parroted nonsense. A Juliet must have both the look and the spirit of a girl of from fourteen to sixteen, and any further sophistication—or, worse, a mature assumption of innocence—will be the part's ruin. One must not compare her, either, to the modern girl approaching independence, knowing enough to think she knows more, ready to disbelieve half she is told. Life to Juliet, as she glimpsed it around her, was half jungle in its savagery, half fairy tale; and its rarer gifts were fever to the blood. A most precocious young woman from our point of view, no doubt; but the narrower and intenser life of her time ripened emotion early.

Not that there is anything of the budding sensualist in her; for to be sensual is to be sluggish, not fevered. Her passion for Romeo is ruled by imagination. And were this not the true reading of it, Shakespeare would have been all but compelled, one may say, to make it so; doubly compelled. Of what avail else would be his poetry, and through what other medium could a boy-actress realise the part? The beauty of the girl's story, and its agonies too, have imagination for their fount. The height of her joy (anticipated, never realised) is reached in the imaginative ecstasy of

> Gallop apace, you fiery-footed steeds. . . .

And she suffers to the full, even in thinking of them, all the shame of the marriage to Paris and the terrors of the vault.

★ ★ ★

The simplest reason for Juliet's leave-taking of life being short is that Romeo's has been long. But, theatrical effect apart, the sudden brutal blow by which her childish faith in the 'comfortable Friar' is shattered, and her unquestioning choice of death, make a fitting end to the desperate confidence of her rush to escape from what is worse than death to her. In the unreflecting haste of it all lies her peculiar tragedy. One day a child, and the next a woman! But she has not grown older as Romeo has, nor risen to an impersonal dignity of sorrow. Shakespeare's women do not, for obvious reasons, so develop. They are vehicles of life, not of philosophy. Here is a life cut short in its brightness; and it is a cruel business, this slaughter of a child betrayed.

Prefaces to Shakespeare. Second Series. 1930.

[306] *H. B. Charlton*

Shakespeare was casting in fresh directions to find the universality, the momentousness, and above all the inevitability of all-compelling tragedy. In particular, he was experimenting with a new propelling force, a new final sanction as the determinant energy, the *ultima ratio* of tragedy's inner world; and though *Romeo and Juliet* is set in a modern Christian country, with church and priest and full ecclesiastical institution, the whole universe of God's justice, vengeance and providence is discarded and rejected from the directing forces of the play's dramatic movement. In its place, there is a theatrical resuscitation of the half-barbarian, half-Roman deities of Fate and Fortune.

★ ★ ★

But how far can a Roman sense of Fate be made real for a modern audience? It is no mere matter of exciting thought to 'wander through eternity' in the wake of the mystery which surrounds the human lot. Mystery must take on positive shape, and half-lose itself in dread figures controlling human life in their malice. The forms and the phrases by which these powers had been invoked were a traditional part in the inheritance of the Senecan drama which came to sixteenth-century Europe. Fortuna, Fatum, Fata, Parcae: all were firmly established in its *dramatis personae.* Moreover their rôle in

Virgilian theocracy was familiar to all with but a little Latin . . .

But with what conviction could a sixteenth-century spectator take over these ancient figures? Even the human beings of an old mythology may lose their compelling power; 'what's Hecuba to him, or he to Hecuba?' But the gods are in a much worse case; pagan, they had faded before the God of the Christians: *Vicisti, Galilæe!* Fate was no longer a deity strong enough to carry the responsibility of a tragic universe; at most, it could intervene casually as pure luck, and bad luck as a motive turns tragedy to mere chance. It lacks entirely the ultimate tragic ἀνάγκη [necessity]. It fails to provide the indispensable inevitability.

Is then Shakespeare's *Romeo and Juliet* an unsuccessful experiment? To say so may seem not only profane but foolish. In its own day, as the dog's-eared Bodley Folio shows, and ever since, it has been one of Shakespeare's most preferred plays. It is indeed rich in spells of its own. But as a pattern of the idea of tragedy, it is a failure. Even Shakespeare appears to have felt that, as an experiment, it had disappointed him. At all events, he abandoned tragedy for the next few years and gave himself to history and to comedy; and even afterwards, he fought shy of the simple theme of love, and of the love of anybody less than a great political figure as the main matter for his tragedies.

Nevertheless it is obvious that neither sadism nor masochism is remotely conscious in our appreciation of *Romeo and Juliet,* nor is our 'philanthropy' offended by it. But the achievement is due to the magic of Shakespeare's poetic genius and to the intermittent force of his dramatic power rather than to his grasp of the foundations of tragedy.

Shakespearian Tragedy. 1948. Chap. III.

[307] *Harold C. Goddard*

In retrospect, Shakespeare's plays, which in one sense culminate in *King Lear* and in another in *The Tempest,* are seen to deal over and over with the same underlying subject that dominates the Greek drama: the relation of the generations. *Romeo and Juliet,* as the first play of its author in which this subject is central, assumes a profound seminal as well as intrinsic interest on that account. It points immediately in this respect to *Henry IV* and *Hamlet,* and ultimately to *King Lear* and *The Tempest.*

This theme of "the fathers" is merely another way of expressing the theme of "the stars." For the fathers are the stars and the stars are the fathers in the sense that the fathers stand for the accumulated experience of the past, for tradition, for authority, and hence for the two most potent forces that mold and so impart "destiny" to the child's life. Those forces, of course, are heredity and training, which between them create that impalpable mental environment, inner and outer, that is even more potent than either of them alone. The hatred of the hostile houses in *Romeo and Juliet* is an inheritance that every member of these families is born into as truly as he is born with the name Capulet or Montague. Their younger generations have no more choice in the matter than they have choice of the language they will grow up to speak. They suck in the venom with their milk. "So is the will of a living daughter curbed by the will of a dead father," as Portia puts it in *The Merchant of Venice.* The daughter may be a son and the father may be living, but the principle is the same. Thus the fathers cast the horoscopes of the children in advance —and are in that sense their stars. If astrology is itself, as it is, a kind of primitive and unconscious psychology, then the identity of the stars and the fathers becomes even more pronounced.

The Meaning of Shakespeare. 1951. Chap. XIII.

[308] *Donald A. Stauffer*

Even more obvious, in this play love becomes the teacher of society. Shakespeare was never more patently the schoolmaster than in his repeated moralizing that love must destroy hate: The prologue tells us that the misadventured piteous overthrows of the two lovers bury their parents' strife. Nothing could remove the continuance of their parents' rage except their children's end. The moral lesson is so shaped formally that it becomes the main theme of the drama: the opening scene stops the bitter feud temporarily; the middle act results in two deaths and the separation of the lovers when murderous quarreling breaks out again; the closing scene offers the sacrifice of innocents to wipe out in blood the cursed strife of the old partisans. Church and state combine at the end to arraign the hate-filled families. The Friar presents himself "both to impeach and purge." And the Prince of Verona speaks the ironic moral:

Capulet, Montague,
See what a scourge is laid upon your hate,
That heaven finds means to kill your joys with love!

"All are punish'd." Yet the houses are reconciled in clasped hands, and golden statues shall rise as memorials to these "Poor sacrifices of our enmity!" The universe is guided by "the rigour of severest law"; and Time works inevitably "to wrong the wronger till he render right." Insofar as this play is a tragedy of fate—and Shakespeare sets up dozens of signposts pointing toward the foregone moral conclusion—all accidents and events work toward the final sacrifice. Romeo and Juliet are puppets, since the moral punishment of the raging clans becomes more powerful in proportion to the innocence and helplessness of the sacrifices. In no other play does Shakespeare envisage a general moral order operating with such inhuman, mechanical severity.

⋆ ⋆ ⋆

Shakespeare has found skill adequate to his ambition. Nothing but the finest part of pure love inhabits his scenes of romantic enchantment—the courtship at the ball, the moonlit wooing, the bridal night. He has intensified its purity by contrasting it with Romeo's first posings, with Capulet's bargainings and tantrums, with Mercutio's bawdry, with the Friar's benign philosophizing, and with the nurse's loose opportunism. He has shown that love makes lovers fearless. He sings its hymn in Juliet's epithalamium; and consecrates it as rising above life, in the successive draughts, of sleep and of death, which each lover drinks to the other. His favorite theme of Death the Bridegroom he has introduced when the lean abhorred monster, in Romeo's imaginings, keeps Juliet "in dark to be his paramour."

Above all, he has brought out the pathos of love by violent contrasts. Time hurries all things away, and in the lightning imagery the kiss and the consummation are as fire and powder. Frail love, surrounded by disasters, becomes a thing of light in blackness, itself "like a rich jewel in an Ethiop's ear." All is loneliness: Juliet is deserted by her father, then by her mother, then by her nurse, until she is left only with the power to die, or to consign herself to the horrible vault. Romeo is exiled—and indeed through the middle scenes "banished! banished!" beats like a pulse. Desperate and exiled, love knows only enemies, ranging from the vulgar nurse to "love-devouring death" itself.

The secret of the play is that the deaths of the lovers are *not* the result of the hatred between the houses, nor of any other cause except love itself, which seeks in death its own restoring cordial. Love conquers death even more surely than it conquers hate. It sweeps aside all accidents, so that fate itself seems powerless. Time is conquered, in that first stirring of a belief that Shakespeare came later to trust completely: that the intensity of an emotion towers above its temporal duration or success.

Shakespeare's World of Images. 1949. Chap. II.

[309] *Harold S. Wilson*

Here, then, in the play as we have it, is the design—an arbitrary one, to be sure—of "a greater power than we can contradict," that finds means to humble the rival houses "with love." It is a stern conception of Providence, to the working of whose purposes human beings are blind, which fulfils the moral law that the hatred of the elders shall be visited upon the children—"poor sacrifices of our enmity," as Capulet describes them—yet whose power turns hatred in the end to love. The design of the tragedy has been a Christian moral, implicit but still sufficiently manifest to the thoughtful. Herein lies the rationale of the play's structure. The three entrances of the Prince mark the three stages of the action intended to show a chain of seeming accidents issuing in a moral design adumbrated in the sonnet-prologue, implicit from the beginning. The final entrance of the Prince marks the logical climax of a tightly built narrative scheme. This concluding stage of the action reveals, in recapitulation, the significance of the whole design, a design in which the catastrophic deaths of the lovers contribute but a part; the punishment of the elders, and still more their reconciliation, complete the pattern.

On the Design of Shakespearian Tragedy. University of Toronto Press, 1957. Chap. II.

The Taming of the Shrew

[310] *Nevill Coghill*

The Taming of the Shrew has often been read and acted as a wife-humiliating farce in which a brute fortune-hunter carries all, including his wife's spirit, before him, to the general but vicarious joy of hen-pecked husbands. Yet it is not so at all. True, it is based on the medieval conception of the obedience owed by a wife to her wedded lord, a conception generously and charmingly asserted by Katerina at the end. But it is a total misconception to suppose she has been bludgeoned into it. Indeed if either of them has triumphed in the art and practice of matrimony it is she.

Let us in the first place consider *why* she is a shrew; Shakespeare has made perfect preparation for this aspect of her character. She is a girl of spirit, yet has to endure a father who has openly made a favourite of her sly younger sister, and who is willing, even more openly, to sell his daughters to the highest bidder. We can see the sort of man he is from the marriage-market scene (II.i). We see, too, what sort of girl her petted sister is, with her pretended submissions and *minauderies* which culminate first in a clandestine and double-faced elopement, then in a contempt of her husband's authority and prestige. Thus environed, what choice has Katerina but to show her disdainful temper if she is to keep her self-respect?

Petruchio is a self-admitted fortune-hunter, but he is also a good-natured, vigorous, candid and likeable chap. No doubt whatever is left that he admires Katerina for herself on sight. Though he is loud-mouthed and given to swaggering, he is not contemptible; the companions of Beowulf would have approved of him. *Beot he gelæste.* To Katerina he must moreover seem her one hope of escaping from that horrible family. The defensive technique of shrewishness was no final solution to her troubles. It was too negative. Yet she had adopted it so long that it seemed to have become second nature to her.

It is this which Petruchio is determined to break in her, not her spirit. And he chooses a technique of practical jokes to do so.

At first she does not see the point, for his Hotspur manners are too violent. Still she senses, while resenting, his claim to love her, oddly though it conflicts with his boisterous and not very kindly behaviour:

> And that which spights me more than all these wants,
> He does it under name of perfect loue.

It is not until he positively declares that the sun is the moon that the joke breaks upon her in its full fantasy, and it is then that she wins her first and final victory by showing she has a sense of fun as extravagant as his own, and is able to go beyond him; so, entering the joke, she addresses the ancient Vincentio as if he were a

> Yong budding Virgin, faire, and fresh, & sweet

and when Petruchio whirls about once more with a

> Why how now Kate, I hope thou art not mad,
> This is a man old, wrinckled, faded, withered,
> And not a Maiden as thou saist he is

she reaches her top triumph of wit, proving herself more than his match in spirit with this disclaimer, and blaming the sun (or should it have been the moon?):

> Pardon old father my mistaking eies,
> That haue bin so bedazzled with the sunne. . . .

After that, victory is all hers, and like most human wives that are the superiors of their husbands she can afford to allow him mastery in public. She has secured what her sister Bianca can never have, a happy marriage; and her solution is not far from that imagined by Chaucer for Dorigen and Arveragus in the *Franklin's Tale.* She will certainly run him in private, though her honour in public must of course depend on his:

> Save that the name of soverayntee,
> That wolde he have for shame of his degree.

"The Basis of Shakespearian Comedy." (The substance of a lecture delivered in 1949 at Stratford-upon-Avon.) *Essays and Studies 1950.*

The Tempest

[311] *James Russell Lowell*

If I read it rightly, it is an example of how a great poet should write allegory,—not embodying metaphysical abstractions, but giving us ideals abstracted from life itself, suggesting an under-meaning everywhere, forcing it upon us nowhere, tantalizing the mind with hints that imply so much and tell so little, and yet keep the attention all eye and ear with eager, if fruitless, expectation. Here the leading characters are not merely typical, but symbolical,—that is, they do not illustrate a class of persons, they belong to universal Nature. Consider the scene of the play. Shakespeare is wont to take some familiar story, to lay his scene in some place the name of which, at least, is familiar,—well knowing the reserve of power that lies in the familiar as a background, when things are set in front of it under a new and unexpected light. But in the *Tempest* the scene is laid nowhere, or certainly in no country laid down on any map. Nowhere, then? At once nowhere and anywhere,—for it is in the soul of man, that still vexed island hung between the upper and the nether world, and liable to incursions from both. There is scarce a play of Shakespeare's in which there is such variety of character, none in which character has so little to do in the carrying on and development of the story. But consider for a moment if ever the Imagination has been so embodied as in Prospero, the Fancy as in Ariel, the brute Understanding as in Caliban, who, the moment his poor wits are warmed with the glorious liquor of Stephano, plots rebellion against his natural lord, the higher Reason. Miranda is mere abstract Womanhood, as truly so before she sees Ferdinand as Eve before she was wakened to consciousness by the echo of her own nature coming back to her, the same, and yet not the same, from that of Adam. Ferdinand, again, is nothing more than Youth, compelled to drudge at something he despises, till the sacrifice of will and abnegation of self win him his ideal in Miranda. The subordinate personages are simply types; Sebastian and Antonio, of weak character and evil ambition; Gonzalo, of average sense and honesty; Adrian and Francisco, of the walking gentlemen who serve to fill up a world. They are not characters in the same sense with Iago, Falstaff, Shallow, or Leontius; and it is curious how every one of them loses his way in this enchanted island of life, all the victims of one illusion after another, except Prospero, whose ministers are purely ideal. The whole play, indeed, is a succession of illusions, winding up with those solemn words of the great enchanter who had summoned to his service every shape of merriment or passion, every figure in the great tragi-comedy of life, and who was now bidding farewell to the scene of his triumphs.

"Shakespeare Once More." *North American Review*. 1868. *Among My Books*. 1870.

[312] *Mark Van Doren*

If Shakespeare thought of "The Tempest" as the last play he would write he may have said to himself—silently, we must assume—that he could afford to let action come in it to a kind of rest; that its task was not so much to tell a story as to fix a vision; that the symbols he hitherto had defined his art by concealing might now confess themselves, even obtrude themselves, in measured dance and significant song; and that while he was at it he would recapitulate his poetic career. It is interesting to conjecture thus, but it is perilous. "The Tempest" does bind up in final form a host of themes with which its author has been concerned. It is a mirror in which, if we hold it very still, we can gaze backward at all of the recent plays; and behind them will be glimpses of a past as old as the tragedies, the middle comedies, and even "A Midsummer Night's Dream." Or it is a thicket of resonant trees, in an odd angle of the Shakespearean wood, which hums with echoes of every distant aisle. And certainly its symbols expose themselves as their ancestors in Shakespeare seldom or never did. The play seems to order itself in terms of its meanings; things in it stand for other things, so that we are tempted to search its dark backward for a single meaning, quite final for Shakespeare and quite abstract. The trouble is that the meanings are not self-evident. One interpretation of "The Tempest" does not agree with another. And there is deeper trouble in the truth that any interpretation, even the wildest, is more or less plausible. This deep trouble, and this deep truth, should warn us that "The Tempest" is a composition about which we had better not be too knowing. If it is one of Shakespeare's successes, and obviously it is, it will not yield its secret easily; or it has no secret to yield. Notwithstanding its visionary grace, its tendency toward lyric abstraction, it keeps that lifelike surface and that humor with which Shakespeare has always protected his meaning if he had one: that impenetrable shield off which the spears of interpretation invariably glance—or return, bent in the shaft and dulled at the point, to the hand of the thrower. It may well be that Shakespeare in "The Tempest" is telling us for the last time, and consciously for the last time, about the world. But what he is telling us cannot be simple, or we could agree that it is this or that. Perhaps it is this: that the world is not simple. Or, mysteriously enough, that it is what we all take it to be, just as "The Tempest" is whatever we would take it to be. Any set of symbols, moved close to this play, lights up as in an electric field. Its meaning, in other words, is precisely as rich as the human mind, and it says that the world is what it is. But what the world is cannot be said in a sentence. Or even in a poem as complete and beautiful as "The Tempest."

Shakespeare. 1939.

[313] *John Dryden*

To return once more to Shakespeare; no man ever drew so many characters, or generally distinguished 'em better from one another, excepting only Johnson. I will instance but in one, to show the copiousness of his intention; it is that of Caliban, or the monster, in the *Tempest.* He seems there to have created a person which was not in Nature, a boldness which, at first sight, would appear intolerable; for he makes him a species of himself, begotten by an incubus on a witch . . . Whether or no his generation can be defended, I leave to philosophy; but of this I am certain, that the poet has most judiciously furnished him with a person, a language, and a character, which will suit him, both by father's and mother's side: he has all the discontents and malice of a witch, and of a devil, besides a convenient proportion of the deadly sins; gluttony, sloth, and lust, are manifest; the dejectedness of a slave is likewise given him, and the ignorance of one bred up in a desert island. His person is monstrous, and he is the product of unnatural lust; and his language is as hobgoblin as his person; in all things he is distinguished from other mortals.

Troilus and Cressida, or Truth found too late; a Tragedy: with a Preface containing the Grounds of Criticism in Tragedy. 1679. Ker I, 219–20.

[314] *Samuel Taylor Coleridge*

The character of Caliban is wonderfully conceived: he is a sort of creature of the earth, as Ariel is a sort of creature of the air. He partakes of the qualities of the brute, but is distinguished from brutes in two ways:—by having mere understanding without moral reason; and by not possessing the instincts which pertain to absolute animals. Still, Caliban is in some respects a noble being: the poet has raised him far above contempt: he is a man in the sense of the imagination: all the images he uses are drawn from nature, and are highly poetical; they fit in with the images of Ariel. Caliban gives us images from the earth, Ariel images from the air. Caliban talks of the difficulty of finding fresh water, of the situation of morasses, and of other circumstances which even brute instinct, without reason, could comprehend. No mean figure is employed, no mean passion displayed, beyond animal passion, and repugnance to command.

The Lectures of 1811–12. IX. Raysor II, 177–78.

[315] *Richard G. Moulton*

If ever a 'child of nature' has been painted it is Miranda. Brought up from infancy on the island without ever seeing one of her sex, she has been formed by nature alone; analysis can discover in her only the elementary features of female character, unconditioned by social forms or by individuality; she might almost be called a desert island of humanity. The most distinctive note of Miranda is a simplicity that acts like a charm, and, in the wooing scenes, needs the best acting to distinguish it from forwardness; it becomes a childlike *naïveté* of admiration when she first has the chance of seeing 'how beauteous mankind is.' Yet there is in her plenty of womanly strength: capacity for the most vivid appreciation of nature in the storm, and the 'very virtue of compassion' for those suffering in it; she exhibits an equally quick and intelligent play of emotion as she follows her father's story, and still more at the end of the scene, where she is distracted between two tendernesses. For beauty, Miranda is almost a definition of ideal—'created of every creature's best.' And her creed seems to be a simple faith in beauty: even the 'brave vessel' she doubts not contains 'noble creatures in her,' and this instinctive confidence that a fair outside must mean fairness within leaps forth to defend Ferdinand when, in the glory of his youthful beauty, he stands accused of treachery.

> There's nothing ill can dwell in such a temple:
> If the ill spirit have so fair a house,
> Good things will strive to dwell with't.

At the opposite pole from Miranda, yet equally with her linked to the idea of nature, stands Caliban, the natural savage, or wild man of the woods: we shall see later on that this does not exhaust the description of Caliban, but this is undoubtedly one aspect of him. And in connection with this Shakespeare has thrown in an effect of a very special kind, one which, when we consider the date of the play, seems almost a flash of prophecy. The name 'Caliban' is an anagram for 'cannibal'; and in a single dialogue between Caliban and Prospero we have painted, in successive clauses, the whole history of the relations between savage races and civilisation, wherever at least that civilisation has not been reinforced by the elevating power of religion. First, we have the wrongs of the savage, and his dispossession by the white man:

> This island's mine, by Sycorax my mother,
> Which thou takest from me.

Next, we see the early and pleasant relations between the two; the white man pets the savage almost like an animal,—

When thou camest first,
Thou strokedst me and madest much of me, wouldst
give me
Water with berries in't—

There is an interchange of good offices, education on the one side, on the other reverence and gifts of natural riches:

[Thou wouldest] teach me how
To name the bigger light, and how the less,
That burn by day and night: and then I lov'd thee
And show'd thee all the qualities o' the isle,
The fresh springs, brine-pits, barren place and
fertile.

But soon there appears a moral gulf between the two that forbids equal intercourse:

Thy vile race,
Though thou didst learn, had that in't which
good natures
Could not abide to be with.

There is nothing for it but the forced domination of the white man:

Therefore wast thou
Deservedly confined into this rock,
Who hadst deserved more than a prison.

So that the gift of civilisation is turned into a curse:

You taught me language; and my profit on't
Is, I know how to curse!

And a later scene completes the analogy, and exhibits civilisation introducing one undeniably new gift into savage life—the gift of intoxicating drink! In this way Caliban presents the aborigines of nature crushed beneath the advance of artificial life. Yet the impartial dramatist finds an attractiveness even for him. Beside Caliban, the dregs of natural life, he places the drunken sailors, the dregs of civilisation: and as Caliban kneels to Stephano we feel that the savage is the nobler of the two, for he has not exhausted his faculty of reverence.

Shakespeare as a Dramatic Artist. 2d ed. 1888. Chap. XII.

[316] *Derek Traversi*

The keynote of the whole play, which Ariel comes to emphasize, is indeed *judgement.* Only when the good and evil in human nature have been understood and separated (for just separation can only follow upon understanding) will the final reconciliation and restoration of harmony take place. This moral judgement is based in *The Tempest* upon an objective sanction which . . . needs to be proved in operation. For this purpose—and really for this purpose alone—the various actors in the forgotten story of Naples and Milan have been brought together through the providential action of the storm upon 'this most desolate isle', 'where man doth not inhabit'. Desolate surely because the work of purgation which is about to be accomplished needs to be accompanied by abstinence and a certain asceticism; and desolate too, because it is not a place upon which men are to live their full civilized lives—after the final reconciliation it is left by all, except those whose nature debars them from playing a part in the 'brave new world' of beings at once spiritualized and social to which they are now being offered entry—but on which they are to achieve moral understanding and learn to accept the judgement passed upon them. It is upon their acceptance of the tremendous accusation now worded by Ariel, which touches the deepest nature of each of them, that their possibility of salvation will depend. They have been brought to the island to *learn*, and, through learning, to leave a world of shadow and fancy for re-assimilation into a truly civilized order.

Shakespeare: The Last Phase. 1955. Chap. V.

[317] *Bernard Knox*

Below the strange and brilliant surface composed of medieval magic and Renaissance travel tales, the initial situation, the nature and relationships of most of the characters, the development of the action and its final solution are all conjugations of the basic paradigms of classical comedy.

One of the most influential of these paradigms relates to the existence in ancient society of a dividing line stricter and more difficult to cross than any social barrier has been since: the distinction between slave and free. The free man could not imagine a misfortune worse than slavery, nor the slave a greater blessing than freedom. Slave and free were not so much separate classes as separate worlds: Aristotle could go so far as to claim that they were separate natures. This division was the most important sociological datum of ancient society, affecting men's attitude toward each other with a power almost as great as that of natural differences of sex or color. Among other things it provided a fixed contrast of condition and standards on which comedy could be based.

★ ★ ★

In the comedy of the fourth century the magnificent fantasy and political wit of Aristophanes are sadly lacking, but the theme of contrast between slave and free remains. In the domestic comedy of Menander and his contemporaries (the models of the Roman comic poets) the theme crystallizes into a variety of stock patterns, which have exerted enormous influence on comedy ever since.

In this comedy the master design is always more or less the same. A domestic problem involving the free members of the household (usually, in Menander, a marriage or a seduction—sometimes both) is eventually solved through complicated intrigues which involve the slave members of the household. The comedy proceeds on two social levels which interpenetrate, often on two plot levels as well, which also interpenetrate. The slave characters (and a host of technically free but hardly distinguishable lower-class types such as parasites, butlers, cooks, and pimps) have their own problems (the attainment of freedom, a free meal or a free drink), the solution of which is artfully made to depend on the solution of the problem of the free characters. A typical paradigm is the plot in which a clever slave, by intelligent initiative and intrigue (often directed against his less intelligent fellow-slaves) solves his master's problem (which may range from finding a wife to marrying off a child) and, as a reward for his services, gains his private objective, his liberty.

This is a slave who has the intelligence of, and eventually attains the status of, a free man; but there is another type of slave who is a convenient vehicle for the traditional servile humor. This one provides the sullen bad temper, the cursing, the drunkenness, the indecency, the thievishness, and cowardice which are the traditional characteristics of the comic slave. He may have the same ambition as his cleverer fellow, but not the same capacity; he forms grand designs, but through stupidity (often through the direct intervention of the clever slave) he fails miserably, and is humiliated and punished with blows or a stint at the mill.

While the slaves, in aspiration and action, trespass on the confines of the free world, the free-born may find themselves, as foundlings, kidnapped children, or prisoners of war, temporary denizens of the slave world; their identification and restoration to freedom (and usually marriage) is the play's denouement, and usually coincides with, and balances, the liberation of the clever slave or the restoration of the stupid slave to his proper station, or both. Together with these contrasts of condition there are deeper contrasts of nature; free men can think and act like slaves and slaves rise superior in intelligence or emotion to their masters.

★ ★ ★

But in *The Tempest,* a Utopia which Shakespeare invented for himself (as Gonzalo invents his in the play), there is no need to translate the classic form: it can be used literally. Prospero is master (and incidentally an irritable old man with a marriageable daughter) and Ariel and Caliban are slaves. Prospero as sorcerer has the power to enslave and release the free men too: this contrast is relevant for all the characters of the play—one of its main components is what Brower has called "the slavery-freedom continuity." "The 'slaves' and 'servants' of the play," he points out, "suffer various kinds of imprisonment, from Ariel in his 'cloven pine' to Ferdinand's mild confinement, and before the end of Act IV everyone except Prospero and Miranda has been imprisoned in one way or another. During the course of Act V all the prisoners except Ferdinand (who has already been released) are set free. . . ."[1]

★ ★ ★

Prospero has already been recognized as "sometime *Millaine*" and restored to *his* proper station—"thy dukedom I resigne"—the marriage of Ferdinand and Miranda is arranged; all that remains is to free the clever slave—"to the elements Be free, and fare thou well"—and the play, except for a version of the conventional Plautine request for applause, is over, the traditional paradigm complete. Gonzalo is given the speech in which the loose ends are tied together and the pattern of restoration spelled out:

In one voyage
Did *Claribell* her husband finde at *Tunis,*
And *Ferdinand* her brother, found a wife,
Where he himselfe was lost: *Prospero* his Dukedome
In a poore Isle:

[1] R. A. Brower, *The Fields of Light* (Oxford, 1951), p. 110.

So far we are still within the recognizable limits of the ancient plan, but Gonzalo's closing words (though they continue the metaphor of liberation) can serve to remind us that this plan is only the bare outline of a poetic structure which in feeling and imagination as far surpasses Plautine comedy as "great'st do's least":

> —*Prospero* his Dukedome
> In a poore Isle: and all of us, our selves,
> When no man was his owne.

"*The Tempest* and the Ancient Comic Tradition." *English Stage Comedy*, English Institute Essays, 1954. 1955.

[318] *Nevill Coghill*

What story then, familiar to Shakespeare and to his audience, does this *Tempest* story of a man and woman exiled from their natural inheritance for the acquisition of a forbidden knowledge resemble? An answer leaps readily to mind; it resembles the story of Adam and Eve, type-story of our troubles. *The Tempest* also contains the story of Prospero and his brother Anthonio, that has something of the primal, eldest curse upon it, something near a brother's murder. There is in *Genesis,* as well as the story of Adam and Eve, the story of Cain and Abel. But in *The Tempest* there is also a turn in both stories by which there is a repentance and a forgiveness, and a homecoming in harmony. This is the shape of the promise of the New Testament and of the Second Adam. There is the hope of a return to Paradise when we come to die. Trouble will turn to joy.

"The Basis of Shakespearian Comedy." (The substance of a lecture delivered in 1949 at Stratford-upon-Avon.) *Essays and Studies 1950.*

[319] *Arthur Quiller-Couch*

And I conclude by asseverating that were a greater than Ariel to wing down from Heaven and stand and offer me to choose which, of all the books written in the world, should be mine, I should choose—not the *Odyssey,* not the *Aeneid,* not the *Divine Comedy,* not *Paradise Lost;* not *Othello* nor *Hamlet* nor *Lear;* but this little matter of 2000 odd lines—*The Tempest.* 'What?—rather than *Othello* or than *Lear?*' 'Yes: for I can just imagine a future age of men, in which *their* characterisation has passed into a curiosity, a pale thing of antiquity; as I can barely imagine, yet can just imagine, a world in which the murder of Desdemona, the fate of Cordelia, will be considered curiously, as brute happenings proper to a time out-lived; and again, while I reverence the artist who in *Othello* or in *Lear* purges our passion, forcing us to weep for present human woe, *The Tempest*, as I see it, forces diviner tears, tears for sheer beauty; with a royal sense of this world and how it passes away, with a catch at the heart of what is to come. And still the sense is royal: it is the majesty of art: we *feel* that we are greater than we know. So on the surge of our emotion, as on the surges ringing Prospero's island, is blown a spray, a mist. Actually it dwells in our eyes, bedimming them: and as involuntarily we would brush it away, there rides in it a rainbow; and its colours are wisdom and charity, with forgiveness, tender ruth for all men and women growing older, and perennial trust in young love.

Shakespeare's Workmanship. 1918. Chap. XVII.

Timon of Athens

[320] *Samuel Taylor Coleridge*

. . . where shall we class the *Timon of Athens*? Immediately below *Lear*. It is a *Lear* of the satirical drama, a *Lear* of domestic or ordinary life—a local eddy of passion on the high road of society, while all around are the week-day goings on of wind and weather—a *Lear*, therefore, without its soul-scorching flashes, its ear-cleaving thunder-claps, its meteoric splendors, without the contagion and fearful sympathies of nature, the Fates, the Furies, the frenzied elements dancing in and out, now breaking thro' and scattering, now hand in hand with, the fierce or fantastic group of human passions, crimes, and anguishes, reeling on the unsteady ground in a wild harmony to the swell and sink of the earthquake.

Notes on the Comedies. Raysor I, 108–9.

[321] *Edward Dowden*

It would seem that about this period [when he wrote *Timon*] Shakspere's mind was much occupied with the questions, In what temper are we to receive the injuries inflicted upon us by our fellow men? How are we to bear ourselves towards those that wrong us? How shall we secure our inward being from chaos amid the evils of the world? How shall we attain to the most just and noble attitude of soul in which life and the injuries of life may be confronted? Now, here, in Timon we see one way in which a man may make his response to the injuries of life; he may turn upon the world with a fruitless and suicidal rage. Shakspere was interested in the history of Timon, not merely as a dramatic study, and not merely for the sake of moral edification, but because he recognised in the Athenian misanthrope one whom he had known, an intimate acquaintance, the Timon of Shakspere's own breast. Shall we hesitate to admit that there was such a Timon in the breast of Shakspere? We are accustomed to speak of Shakspere's gentleness and Shakspere's tolerance so foolishly, that we find it easier to conceive of Shakspere as indulgent towards baseness and wickedness, than as feeling measureless rage and indignation against them—rage and indignation which would sometimes flash beyond their bounds, and strike at the whole wicked race of man. And it is certain that Shakspere's delight in human character, his quick and penetrating sympathy with almost every variety of man, saved him from any persistent injustice towards the world. But it can hardly be doubted, that the creator of Hamlet, of Lear, of Timon, saw clearly, and felt deeply, that there is a darker side to the world and to the soul of man.

The Shakspere invariably bright, gentle, and genial is the Shakspere of a myth. The man actually discoverable behind the plays was a man tempted to passionate extremes, but of strenuous will, and whose highest self pronounced in favour of sanity. Therefore he resolved that he would set to rights his material life, and he did so. And again he resolved that he would bring into harmony with the highest facts and laws of the world his spiritual being; and that in his own high fashion he accomplished also. The plays impress us as a long study of self-control,—of self-control at one with self-surrender to the highest facts and laws of human life. Shakspere set about attaining self-mastery, not of the petty, pedantic kind, which can be dictated by a director, or described in a manual, but large, powerful, luminous, and calm; and by sustained effort he succeeded in attaining this in the end. It is impossible to conceive that Shakspere should have traversed life, and felt its insufficiencies, and injuries, and griefs, without incurring Timon's temptation,—the temptation to fierce and barren resentment. What man or woman, who has sought good things, and with whom life has not gone altogether smoothly and pleasantly, has not known, if not for days and weeks then for hours, if not for hours then for intense moments, a Timon within him, incapable for the while of making any compromise with the world, and fiercely abandoning it with cries of weak and passionate revolt? And when again such a man accepts life, and human society, it is not what it had been before. The music of his life is a little lowered throughout; the pegs are set down. Or what had been a nerve is changed to a sinew. Or he finds himself a little more indifferent to pain. Or now and then a pungent sentence escapes his lips, which is unintelligible to those who had only known his former self.

In the character of Timon, Shakspere gained dramatic remoteness from his own personality. It would have been contrary to the whole habit of the dramatist's genius to have used one of his characters merely as a mask to conceal his visage, while he relieved himself with lyrical vehemence of the feelings that oppressed him. No: Shakspere, when Timon was written, had attained self-possession, and could transfer himself with real disinterestedness into the person of the young Athenian favourite of fortune. This, in more than one instance, was Shakspere's method,—having discovered some single central point of sympathy between his chief character and his past or present self, to secure freedom from all mere lyrical intensity by studying that one common element under conditions remote from those which had ever been proper or peculiar to himself.

Shakspere, His Mind and Art. 1874. Chap. VIII.

Troilus and Cressida

[322] *John Dryden*

For the play itself, the author seems to have begun it with some fire; the characters of Pandarus and Thersites are promising enough; but as if he grew weary of his task, after an entrance or two, he lets them fall: and the latter part of the tragedy is nothing but a confusion of drums and trumpets, excursions and alarms. The chief persons, who give name to the tragedy, are left alive; Cressida is false, and is not punished. Yet, after all, because the play was Shakespeare's, and that there appeared in some places of it the admirable genius of the author, I undertook to remove that heap of rubbish under which many excellent thoughts lay wholly buried.

Troilus and Cressida, or Truth found too late; a Tragedy: with a Preface containing the Grounds of Criticism in Tragedy. 1679. Ker I, 203–4.

[323] *Algernon Charles Swinburne*

The hysterics of the eponymous hero and the harlotries of the eponymous heroine remove both alike beyond the outer pale of all rational and manly sympathy; though Shakespeare's self may never have exceeded or equalled for subtle and accurate and bitter fidelity the study here given of an utterly light woman, shallow and loose and dissolute in the most literal sense, rather than perverse or unkindly or unclean; and though Keats alone in his most perfect mood of lyric passion and burning vision as full of fragrance as of flame could have matched and all but overmatched those passages in which the rapture of Troilus makes pale and humble by comparison the keenest raptures of Romeo.

A Study of Shakespeare. 1880. "Third Period: Tragic and Romantic."

[324] *Tucker Brooke*

I cannot believe that Shakespeare shared the contempt which the Elizabethan public generally and the race of modern critics have felt for Cressida. She is a more helpless being than Chaucer's Criseyde, a flower growing in Trojan slime, a little soiled from the first and shrinkingly conscious of her predestined pollution; yet Shakespeare's attitude to her is much more that of Chaucer than that of Ulysses, or of Sir Sidney Lee. In her relations with both her lovers he shows us the pathos of a daintiness reaching vainly after nobility, a wistful sincerity which knows it lacks strength to be the thing it should be. "Sweet, bid me hold my tongue," says she to Troilus in her most candid and assured moment—

> For in this rapture I shall surely speak
> The thing I shall repent;

and to Diomed in her last scene, with hardly less candor and simplicity,

Sweet honey Greek, tempt me no more to folly.

Ancient Pistol may gibe at "the lazar kite of Cressid's kind," and the cold Ulysses cry, "Fie, fie upon her!" But Shakespeare does not cry "Fie!" Rather, I think, we hear him whisper, "But yet the pity of it, Ulysses! O Ulysses, the pity of it!"

"Shakespeare's Study in Culture and Anarchy." *The Yale Review.* 1928. *Essays on Shakespeare and Other Elizabethans.* 1948.

[325] *Samuel Taylor Coleridge*

The character of Thersites well deserves a more particular attention, as the Caliban of demagogues' life—the admirable portrait of intellectual power deserted by all grace, all moral principle, all not momentary purpose; just wise enough to detect the weak head, and fool enough to provoke the armed fist of his betters; whom malcontent Achilles can inveigle from malcontent Ajax, under the condition that he shall be called on to do nothing but to abuse and slander and that he shall be allowed to abuse as much and as purulently as he likes—that is, as [he] can; in short, a mule, quarrelsome by the original discord of its nature, a slave by tenure of his own baseness, made to bray and be brayed, to despise and be despicable.

Notes on the Comedies. Raysor I, 111.

[326] *Harold S. Wilson*

The reversal of human values has been complete. The Trojan War which might have ended with the restoration of Helen, goes on. Paris keeps Meneleus's queen, and the wrong is perpetuated. The faith of Troilus lies bleeding, betrayed by the wantonness of Cressida; she is won and held by a man of her own kind, and Troilus is not even able to avenge himself upon Diomede. The honour of Hector succumbs to the brutal treachery of Achilles, and the doom of Troy is clearly foreshadowed. Brutality, treachery, lust are everywhere in the ascendant; the forces of disorder and dishonour have triumphed. We have seen the amiable weaknesses through which the Trojans succumb—Hector's imprudent sense of honour, the rash inexperience of Troilus in both love and war; but the successful forces are wholly odious—the shrewd licentiousness of Diomede, the heartlessness of

Cressida, the impudent and brutal pride of Achilles. These are all simply human motives. There is nowhere any implication of a power that transcends the human measure. This is the world of men, and it is a disordered world, as Ulysses' thematic speech pictures it . . .

On the Design of Shakespearian Tragedy. 1957. Chap. V.

[327] *Tucker Brooke*

Where another writer might have attempted to mediate between these two irreconcilable accounts [Caxton's *Destruction of Troy*, Chapman's *Iliad*], Shakespeare has seized the essential spirit of each, poetically intensified it, and hurled both, unmixed and forever unmixable, into the seething vortex of his play. Thus he produces a milieu for Troilus and Cressida, the forlorn and fated lovers, wandering between two worlds: the effete, immoral, over-refined world of Troy, and the brutal, quarrelsome, cynical world of the Greeks. Paris is on the one side, Diomed on the other. Shakespeare makes each of these environments develop its special type figure, emblematic of the worst in itself. . . .

Thersites chants an interpretative, accusing chorus to all the Greek scenes. Opposite him, at the other pole of foulness, stands the evil genius of Troy, the Lord Pandarus—Chaucer's Pandarus grown old, impotent, and rotten, but still every inch a lord, sure of welcome in any Merry Monarch's court: urbane, genuinely good-tempered, and still, I insist, likable, with a candy deal of courtesy and a Falstaffian love of young rogues; in fact a Belial than whom "a fairer person lost not heaven." Pandarus and Thersites are the Scylla and Charybdis of the lovers' voyage, and their extremes meet in one only point—in lechery, which they keep shrieking, lisping, and insinuating till the echoes meet and merge like a miasma over the whole play, and all the nobility of life is choked.

Greater scenes and more magnificent lines than some that are found in *Troilus and Cressida* it is agreed that Shakespeare seldom wrote. The question is, what was his purpose? I cannot help imagining that he is, however subconsciously, anatomizing the England of the dying Elizabeth: within the wall, the febrile Essex type of decadent chivalry; without, the strident go-getters of the newer dispensation: Cecil-Ulysses and Ralegh-Diomed. I take it that Shakespeare glimpsed somehow the seriousness of the cleavage between Cavalier and Puritan, sensed in Thersites the lowering shadow of Prynne and the iconoclasts, foresaw in Pandarus the portent of the scandalous Carr, Earl of Somerset. Indeed, when reading the great culminating scene (the second of Act V), in which Troilus, the heart-broken young cavalier, and the shrewd old puritan, Ulysses, are drawn together against a giddy and immoral universe, one may almost feel that the writing is prophetic—that the thing must have happened, not at ancient Troy but forty years after the play was created, on some night when Royalist and Cromwellian met beneath the walls of Oxford.

"Shakespeare's Study in Culture and Anarchy." *The Yale Review.* 1928. *Essays on Shakespeare and Other Elizabethans.* 1948.

Twelfth Night

[328] *J. B. Priestley*

Sir Toby . . . is by no means a simpleton. Nor is he, on the other hand, a comic genius like Falstaff, whose world has been transformed into an ideally comic world, whose whole life, whose every speech and action, are devised to further ease, enjoyment, and laughter. Sir Toby, in his own coarse, swashbuckling manner, is witty, but he is not the cause of wit in other men. He does not transform himself into an object of mirth, content so long as men are laughing and the comic spirit is abroad, but, like any bullying wag of the tap-room, looks for a butt in the company. He is really nothing more than an elderly schoolboy with a prodigious thirst and far too much spare time on his hands: the type is not uncommon.

★ ★ ★

But it is Sir Andrew's amazing simplicity, his almost pathetic naïvety, his absolute lack of guile, that make him so richly absurd. And with these there goes a certain very characteristic quality, the unanalysable factor, that is present in every remark he makes; every speech has a certain Aguecheek flavour or smack that is unmistakable; even as we read we can hear the bleating of his plaintive little voice. His best trait is one that he shares with every simpleton, and that is a childlike capacity for enjoyment, which is really born of a sense of wonder, the ability to marvel at and relish the commonest things, to see the world innocently and freshly, a sense that withers among brighter wits and natures richer in experience but blooms for ever with the extremes of humankind, the utter simpletons and the great geniuses. Sir Andrew has this capacity, and it entitles him to a place at the revels. In spite of his starts and frights, his loss of two thousand ducats and his broken head, it is clear that he has enjoyed himself hugely in the company of his admired Sir Toby, and that he will return to his distant estate bubbling with a confused tale of strange happenings and great personages that will be meat and drink to him for years. It is true that he has been everybody's butt, but then he does not know it; he is happily protected from all such discoveries and will be all his life; so that he might almost be said to have the best of the laugh, for whereas the others are living in this world, he is still dwelling in Eden.

"The Illyrians." *The English Comic Characters.* 1925.

[329] *Bertrand Evans*

In the world of *Twelfth Night,* as in the worlds of the comedies just preceding, the spirit of the practiser prevails. Seven of the principal persons are active practisers, and they operate six devices. All action turns on these, and the effects of the play arise from exploitation of the gaps they open. During all but the first two of eighteen scenes we have the advantage of some participant; in seven—an unusually high proportion—we hold advantage over all who take part. In the course of the action, every named person takes a turn below our vantage-point, and below the vantage-point of some other person or persons: in this play neither heroine nor clown is wholly spared. Although Viola shares the great secret with us alone, Shakespeare early establishes our vantage-point above hers, and once even makes her the unwitting victim of another's practice. Although Feste is either 'in' on most practices or unaffected by them, he, with all Illyria, is ignorant of the main secret of the play, the identity of 'Cesario'. Here, then, even heroine and clown stand below us, and below them the others range down to the bottom, where sit Aguecheek and Malvolio in chronic oblivion. Though also victims of others' practices, neither needs deceiving to be deceived—Nature having practised on them once for all.

But if all are exposed at some time in ignorance of their situations, yet all but Orsino and Malvolio have compensatory moments when they overpeer others: even Aguecheek, though a fool the while, briefly enjoys advantage over Malvolio. The awarenesses in *Twelfth*

Night are so structured that an overpeerer gloating in his advantage is usually himself overpeered by another participant or by us: thus Sir Toby exults in his advantage over 'Cesario', knowing that Sir Andrew is not the 'devil in a private brawl' he would have 'Cesario' believe—but at the same time 'Cesario' holds advantage over him in knowing that 'Cesario' is a fiction; and the last laugh is ours, on Sir Toby, for even he would hardly have made his jest of a duel had he known 'Cesario' truly. From much use of such arrangements, in which a participant's understanding is inferior with respect to some elements of a situation and superior with respect to others, emerge the richest effects of *Twelfth Night* and some of the finest in Shakespeare.

Shakespeare's Comedies. 1960. Chap. IV.

[330] *Mark Van Doren*

"He hath been most notoriously abus'd" (v, i, 387). Olivia's line rights Malvolio's wrong, but her household will never grant him the last justice of love. Where there is such difference there cannot be love. That is what "Twelfth Night" is most interested in saying, and saying with an impartiality which precludes sentiment. The balance between Malvolio and his enemies is delicate; they are attractive, as all loose livers are, yet there is an integrity in his tightness, a loftiness other than the misguided one, which we cannot but respect. Modern audiences have bestowed more sympathy upon Malvolio than Shakespeare perhaps intended, so that the balance is now not what it was. It can scarcely be overthrown, however, whatever changes the whirligig of time brings in. The foundation for comedy here is too firm for that, the counterpoint of effects is too sanely arranged. This world of music and mannerly sadness is not sentimentally conceived. Even within its gates the violin voice of Orsino is corrected by the bawling bass of Sir Toby, and the elegant neuroses of the nobility are parodied on servants' tongues. "Now, the melancholy god protect thee," calls Feste after Orsino, mocking him. And Fabian, told of the plot against Malvolio, can rub his hands and say: "If I lose a scruple of this sport, let me be boil'd to death with melancholy" (II, v, 2–4). A balance of tones is maintained, indeed, everywhere in "Twelfth Night." Nature and artifice, sanity and sentiment, are so equally at home here that they can with the greatest difficulty be distinguished from one another; nor in our delight are we disposed to try.

All the while, of course, a story of twins is being told, and three cases of love at first sight (Viola and Orsino, Olivia and Viola, Sebastian and Olivia) are being dove-tailed into a pattern of romance. Shakespeare's interest in Viola cannot be doubted.

> My father had a daughter lov'd a man,
> As it might be, perhaps, were I a woman,
> I should your lordship.
>
> (II, iv, 110–2)

Nor can that of the audience, for she is Julia grown to greatness. But other portions of the pattern deserve and are given only such attention as is necessary. The confusion of the twins and the farce of the fencing-match are not what the comedy is essentially about, any more than the marriage of Olivia and Sebastian is—and the perfunctoriness of Shakespeare's feeling with respect to that marriage is clearly confessed in the kind of verse he gives the priest to speak (V, i, 159–66). Even Viola, much as we like her, stands a little to one side of the center. The center is Malvolio. The drama is between his mind and the music of old manners.

Shakespeare. 1939.

[331] *Donald A. Stauffer*

If it is possible, *Twelfth Night* goes even further than *As You Like It* in the idealization of love. Shakespeare never surpassed the scenes between Viola and Orsino, or between Viola and Olivia, in the lively and sensitive conversation of pleasant and gently nurtured young men and women. If Rosalind's humor keeps her love from extremes, Viola's unassuming fidelity sets the seal upon hers. It is so perfectly proportioned, so much of the purest essence of what love ought to be, that in comparison even the fine natures of the Duke and Olivia seem unformed, as though they were yet young and new in that emotion which in Viola was a natural instinct. Orlando in *As You Like It* is much preoccupied with gentility and good manners, and their relation to birth, education, position, and riches. But Viola is gentleness in action. There is no more to be argued or learned or said. The melancholy which is so mysteriously associated with love, which Shakespeare smiles at in his lovers sighing like furnaces, which seems almost an affectation in the early Romeo and Duke Orsino and even in Antonio in *The Merchant of Venice*, is transmuted in Viola into pathos and tenderness. The quintessence of love, in which the personal fever or madness has been refined into noble sympathy, is close to that charity which Paul exalts in his letter to the Corinthians. In Viola, this conception is realized with all the complexity possible to developed dramatic art. It is not fossilized in a few wise sayings, in formal soliloquies, or in the neat opinions of others. The finest ideals live in persons, not in copybooks. Shakespeare's power to present moral ideas—and if charity is not a moral idea, where is one to be found?—is now so subtle and comprehensively *dramatic* that to summarize adequately Viola's spirit would be to reproduce all the scenes in which she appears—or better, to produce the play. Her "soft and tender breeding" shows in her every action, but most, of course, in her wooing Olivia for Orsino as, she tells her, "your servant's servant," loyal to her master against her own true love. She must therefore seem scornful to Olivia while she pities her—"Poor lady, she were better love a dream!"—and loyal to Orsino's passion in her own silence and obedience, so that true love is seen not in tears, but "smiling at grief. Was not this love indeed?" With something of the unmixed innocence of Desdemona, who believes that unchaste women must be mere fictions, Viola holds that pity is common and natural enough to all men: "for 'tis a vulgar proof That very oft we pity enemies."

The melancholy that touches the gentle scenes of this play is rarely directly expressed, yet it manages to make the lovers in *Much Ado* seem almost boisterous in comparison, and those in *As You Like It* appear pert. It is the Keatsian melancholy, that "dwells with beauty, beauty that must die." "Women are as roses," says the Duke, and Viola answers:

> And so they are; alas, that they are so!
> To die, even when they to perfection grow!
>
> (II, iv, 41–2)

With this play Shakespeare touches the pinnacles of romantic love, after a long and arduous ascent. Never again does he repeat the theme in the same key. There is about it the merest trace of that melancholy evanescence of an ideal achieved, like the sadness that is part of the beauty on the faintly smiling face of Giorgione's sleeping Venus.

Such effects must have their symbol and embodiment, which Shakespeare here secures through the music that fills the play from the first line—"If music be the food of love, play on"—to the song that ends the play "With hey, ho, the wind and the rain." The artifice and ambition of *Love's Labour's Lost,* written just a few years before, are far from the simplicity and sincerity to which this play returns as if it were going home. The wedding of love to simple nature is celebrated again in the praise accorded to one of the sad songs that is sung:

it is old and plain.
The spinsters and the knitters in the sun,
And the free maids that weave their thread with bones,
Do use to chant it. It is silly sooth,
And dallies with the innocence of love
Like the old age. (II, iv, 44–9)

Music is the perfect symbol for this exalted theme of love, as is seen in Viola's comment: "It gives a very echo to the seat Where Love is thron'd," and in the Duke's reply: "Thou dost speak masterly."

Shakespeare's World of Images. 1949. Chap. III.

The Two Gentlemen of Verona

[332] *Samuel Johnson*

In this play there is a strange mixture of knowledge and ignorance, of care and negligence. The versification is often excellent, the allusions are learned and just; but the author conveys his heroes by sea from one inland town to another in the same country; he places the Emperour at *Milan* and sends his young men to attend him, but never mentions him more; he makes *Protheus,* after an interview with *Silvia,* say he has only seen her picture, and, if we may credit the old copies, he has by mistaking places, left his scenery inextricable. The reason of all this confusion seems to be, that he took his story from a novel which he sometimes followed, and sometimes forsook, sometimes remembred, and sometimes forgot.

The Plays of William Shakespeare. 1765. Vol. I.

[333] *Hazelton Spencer*

Plot, as in *Errors* and *The Shrew,* is more important than character, ideas, or literary polish; but now the core of the plot is love. Shakespeare's first resort to the romantic bag of tricks, to which he went again and again throughout the rest of his career, provides lovers' crosses and double-crosses, a loving maid disguised as a lad, a rope ladder and flight from a tyrannical father, exile, outlaws in the greenwood, a serenade, a rendezvous at a friar's cell, a ring for a token, attempted rape and rescue, and at last forgiveness all round and a dash of heroics that do not quite come off.

The Art and Life of William Shakespeare. 1940. Chap. 3.

The Winter's Tale

[334] *G. B. Shaw*

Leontes is a magnificent part, worth fifty Othellos (Shakespear knew nothing about jealousy when he wrote Othello), as modern as Ibsen, and full of wonderful music—"I have tremor cordis on me" and so on.

Ellen Terry and Bernard Shaw A Correspondence. Ed. Christopher St. John. 1932. Letter of 1 November 1895.

[335] *E. M. W. Tillyard*

Perdita . . . is one of Shakespeare's richest characters; at once a symbol and a human being. She is the play's main symbol of the powers of creation. And rightly, because, as Leontes was the sole agent of destruction, so it is fitting, ironically fitting, that the one of his kin whom he had thrown out as bastard should embody the contrary process. Not that Leontes, as a character, is the contrary to Perdita. *His* obsession is not a part of his character but an accretion. Her true contrary is Iago. It is curious that Iago should ever have been thought motiveless. The desire to destroy is a very simple derivative from the power-instinct, the instinct which in its evil form goes by the name of the first of the deadly sins, Pride. It was by that sin that the angels fell, and at the end of *Othello* Iago is explicitly equated with the Devil. Shakespeare embodied all his horror of this type of original sin in Iago. He was equally aware of original virtue, and he pictured it, in Perdita, blossoming spontaneously in the simplest of country settings. There is little direct reference to her instincts to create; but they are implied by her sympathy with nature's lavishness in producing flowers, followed by her own simple and unashamed confession of wholesome sensuality . . . The great significance of Perdita's lines lies partly in the verse, which (especially at the close) is leisurely, full, assured, matured, suggestive of fruition, and acutely contrasted to the tortured, arid, and barren ravings of Leontes, and which reinforces that kinship with nature and healthy sensuality mentioned above. But it lies also in the references to the classical Pantheon. The gods of Greece and Rome occur very frequently in the last plays of Shakespeare and are certainly more than mere embroidery. Apollo is the dominant god in *The Winter's Tale,* and his appearance in Perdita's speech is meant to quicken the reader to apprehend some unusual significance. He appears as the bridegroom, whom the pale primroses never know, but who visits the other flowers. Not to take the fertility symbolism as intended would be a perverse act of caution. Perdita should be associated with them, as symbol both of the creative powers of nature, physical fertility, and of healing and re-creation of the mind. She is like Milton's youthful Ceres,

> Yet virgin of Proserpina from Jove,

or his Eve, mistress of the flowers of Paradise.

Shakespeare's Last Plays. 1938. Chap. II.

[336] *Derek Traversi*

[Autolycus'] comic function is that of one who is regarded as a little apart from the main structure, whose behaviour is in some sense irreducible to the social values of the play, calculated to throw upon the symbolic symmetry itself a touch of relativity, a sense of the incalculable individuality of the processes of life. Yet, although he is not identified, or indeed identifiable, with any neatly rounded scheme, there exists a relation between Autolycus and the complete conception; his vivacious spontaneity has something to contribute to the life-blood of the action, to the vitality without which it would be no more than an abstract play of empty symbols. This is indicated clearly in the song with which he makes his entry. If *The Winter's Tale* is built upon a pattern which reflects the movement of the seasons, from winter through the rebirth of spring to the full consummation of summer, it is clearly fitting at this point, as an introduction to the following Whitsun pastoral, that this song should indicate the restoration to life of the processes of nature after the prolonged recess of winter. Autolycus' song represents 'the sweet', the tender, reborn heart of the year; its concern is with the daffodil new-flowering and the impulse of the 'blood' that sets the 'pugging tooth' on edge, that finds its human counterpart, intensely alive and impatient of all social restraint, in the meeting with 'the doxy over the dale' and in 'tumbling in the hay'. In Autolycus the sense of freedom takes the form of an abandonment of all normal social forms and restraints, the positively valuable and the merely conventional alike. He tells us that he once served Prince Florizel but is now 'out of service'; his relation to the social world is in one sense that of an outcast, threatened with the terrors of 'beating and hanging', but in another that of a free man exercising a vitality which rests on the action of 'blood' and needs itself to be considered in relation to the complete experience offered by the play.

The key to Autolycus, and to his peculiar position in the action, can, indeed, be defined in the phrase from his own song that 'the red blood reigns in the winter's pale'. The reference to winter implies at once a contrast and a point of reference. It connects the episode now before us with the play's title, and establishes a relationship between the birth of spring in the heart of winter and the affirmation of the warm, living 'blood' of youth against the jealousy and care-laden envy of age, an affirmation shortly to be confirmed in the contrast between the young lovers and their elders. In Autolycus himself, of course, this outpouring of spontaneous life moves on the margin of social forms. It has indeed a predatory aspect comically expressed in his first action, the picking of the Clown's pocket; but this itself is, to some degree, a devaluation of his victim's new-found riches and the social pretensions which these have aroused in him. It represents, in any case, an element which will have in due course to be related, as far as may be, to the growing harmony. For the new and natural life expressed in the resurrection of spring is to be, once assumed into fully 'gracious' forms of living, a prelude to the final reconciliation; and the main significance of the pastoral which follows, thus stated in the form of an introductory theme, lies in its relation to the birth of spring out of winter, and life—even in the form of wayward, anarchic impulse—on the margin of social forms and conventions.

Shakespeare: The Last Phase. 1955. Chap. IV.

III. Some Poets on Shakespeare

[337] *Ben Jonson*

To the Memory of my beloued, the Avthor Mr. William Shakespeare: and what he hath left vs.

To drawn no enuy (*Shakespeare*) on thy name,
Am I thus ample to thy Booke, and Fame:
While I confesse thy writings to be such,
As neither *Man,* nor *Muse,* can praise too much.
'Tis true, and all mens suffrage. But these wayes
Were not the paths I meant vnto thy praise:
For seeliest Ignorance on these may light,
Which, when it sounds at best, but eccho's right;
Or blinde Affection, which doth ne're aduance
The truth, but gropes, and vrgeth all by chance;
Or crafty Malice, might pretend this praise,
And thinke to ruine, where it seem'd to raise.
These are, as some infamous Baud, or Whore,
Should praise a Matron. What could hurt her more?
But thou art proofe against them, and indeed
Aboue th'ill fortune of them, or the need.
I, therefore will begin. Soule of the Age!
The applause! delight! the wonder of our Stage!
My *Shakespeare,* rise; I will not lodge thee by
Chaucer, or *Spenser,* or bid *Beaumont* lye
A little further, to make thee a roome:
Thou art a Moniment, without a tombe,
And art aliue still, while thy Booke doth liue,
And we haue wits to read, and praise to giue.
That I not mixe thee so, my braine excuses;
I meane with great, but disproportion'd *Muses:*

For, if I thought my iudgement were of yeeres,
I should commit thee surely with thy peeres,
And tell, how farre thou didst our *Lily* out-shine,
Or sporting *Kid,* or *Marlowes* mighty line.
And though thou hadst small *Latine,* and lesse *Greeke,*
From thence to honour thee, I would not seeke
For names; but call forth thund'ring *Æschilus,*
Euripides, and *Sophocles* to vs,
Paccuuius, Accius, him of *Cordoua* dead,
To life againe, to heare thy Buskin tread,
And shake a Stage: Or, when thy Sockes were on,
Leaue thee alone, for the comparison
Of all, that insolent *Greece,* or haughtie *Rome*
Sent forth, or since did from their ashes come.
Triumph, my *Britaine,* thou hast one to showe,
To whom all Scenes of *Europe* homage owe.
He was not of an age, but for all time!
And all the *Muses* still were in their prime,
When like *Apollo* he came forth to warme
Our eares, or like a *Mercury* to charme!
Nature her selfe was proud of his designes,
And ioy'd to weare the dressing of his lines!
Which were so richly spun, and wouen so fit,
As, since, she will vouchsafe no other Wit.
The merry *Greeke,* tart *Aristophanes,*
Neat *Terence,* witty *Plautus,* now not please;
But antiquated, and deserted lye
As they were not of Natures family.
Yet must I not give Nature all: Thy Art,
My gentle *Shakespeare,* must enioy a part
For though the *Poets* matter, Nature be,
His Art doth giue the fashion. And, that he,
Who casts to write a living line, must sweat,
(Such as thine are) and strike the second heat
Vpon the *Muses* anuile: turne the same,
(And himselfe with it) that he thinkes to frame;
Or for the lawrell, he may gaine a scorne,
For a good *Poet's* made, as well as borne.
And such wert thou. Looke how the fathers face
Lives in his issue, euen so, the race

Of *Shakespeares* minde, and manners brightly shines
In his well torned, and true-filed lines:
In each of which, he seemes to shake a Lance,
As brandish't at the eyes of Ignorance.
Sweet Swan of *Auon!* what a sight it were
To see thee in our waters yet appeare,
And make those flights vpon the bankes of *Thames,*
That so did take *Eliza,* and our *Iames!*
But stay, I see thee in the *Hemisphere*
Aduanc'd, and made a Constellation there!
Shine forth, thou Starre of *Poets,* and with rage,
Or influence, chide, or cheere the drooping Stage;
Which, since thy flight from hence, hath mourn'd like night,
And despaires day, but for thy Volumes light.

Mr. William Shakespeares Comedies, Histories, & Tragedies. 1623.

[338] *John Milton*

An Epitaph on the admirable Dramaticke Poet,
W. Shakespeare

What neede my *Shakespeare* for his honour'd bones,
The labour of an Age in piled stones
Or that his hallow'd Reliques should be hid
Under a starre-ypointing Pyramid?
Deare sonne of Memory, great Heir of *Fame,*
What needst thou such dull witnesse of thy Name?
Thou in our wonder and astonishment
Hast built thy selfe a lasting Monument:
For whil'st to th' shame of slow-endevouring Art
Thy easie numbers flow, and that each part
Hath from the leaves of thy unvalud Booke,
Those Delphick Lines with deepe Impression tooke,
Then thou our fancy of herselfe bereaving,
Dost make us Marble with too much conceving,
And so Sepulcher'd in such pompe dost lie
That Kings for such a Tombe would wish to die.

Mr. William Shakespeares Comedies, Histories, and Tragedies. 1632.

[339] *John Milton*

Then to the well-trod stage anon,
If *Jonsons* learned Sock be on,
Or sweetest *Shakespear* fancies childe,
Warble his native Wood-notes wilde

"L'Allegro." (1632?) *Poems of Mr.* John Milton. 1645. Lines 131–34.

[340] *John Dryden*

As when a Tree's cut down the secret root
Lives under ground, and thence new Branches shoot;
So, from old *Shakespear*'s honour'd dust, this day
Springs up and buds a new reviving Play.
Shakespear, who (taught by none) did first impart
To *Fletcher* Wit, to labouring *Johnson* Art.
He Monarch-like gave those his subjects law,
And is that Nature which they paint and draw.
Fletcher reach'd that which on his heights did grow,
Whilst *Johnson* crept and gather'd all below.
This did his Love, and this his Mirth digest:
One imitates him most, the other best.
If they have since out-writ all other men,
'Tis with the drops which fell from *Shakespear*'s Pen.
The Storm which vanish'd on the Neighb'ring shore,
Was taught by *Shakespear*'s Tempest first to roar.
That innocence and beauty which did smile
In *Fletcher*, grew on this *Enchanted Isle*.
But *Shakespear*'s Magick could not copy'd be,
Within that Circle none durst walk but he.
I must confess 'twas bold, nor would you now,
That liberty to vulgar Wits allow,
Which works by Magick supernatural things:
But *Shakespear*'s pow'r is sacred as a King's.
Those Legends from old Priest-hood were receiv'd,
And he then writ, as people then believ'd.

The Tempest, or the Enchanted Island; a Comedy. (1667) 1670. Prologue. Lines 1–26.

[341] *John Dryden*

To begin, then, with Shakespeare. He was the man who of all modern, and perhaps ancient poets, had the largest and most comprehensive soul. All the images of Nature were still present to him, and he drew them, not laboriously, but luckily; when he describes any thing, you more than see it, you feel it too. Those who accuse him to have wanted learning, give him the greater commendation: he was naturally learn'd; he needed not the spectacles of books to read Nature; he looked inwards, and found her there. I cannot say he is every where alike; were he so, I should do him injury to compare him with the greatest of mankind. He is many times flat, insipid; his comic wit degenerating into clenches, his serious swelling into bombast. But he is always great, when some great occasion is presented to him; no man can say he ever had a fit subject for his wit, and did not then raise himself as high above the rest of poets,

Quantum lenta solent inter viburna cupressi.

[As cypresses do among the drooping undergrowth.
Virgil. Eclogue I. 25.]

★ ★ ★

If I would compare him [Jonson] with Shakespeare, I must acknowledge him the more correct poet, but Shakespeare the greater wit. Shakespeare was the Homer, or father of our dramatic poets; Johnson was the Virgil, the pattern of elaborate writing; I admire him, but I love Shakespeare.

An Essay of Dramatick Poesie. 1668. Ker I, 79–80, 82–83.

[342] *John Dryden*

. . . the excellency of that poet [Shakespeare] was, as I have said, in the more manly passions; Fletcher's in the softer: Shakespeare writ better betwixt man and man; Fletcher, betwixt man and woman: consequently, the one described friendship better, the other love: yet Shakespeare taught Fletcher to write love: and Juliet and Desdemona are originals. 'Tis true, the scholar had the softer soul; but the master had the kinder. Friendship is both a virtue and a passion essentially; love is a passion only in its nature, and is not a virtue but by accident: good nature makes friendship; but effeminacy love.

Shakespeare had an universal mind, which comprehended all characters and passions; Fletcher a more confined and limited: for though he treated love in perfection, yet honour, ambition, revenge, and generally all the stronger passions, he either touched not, or not masterly. To conclude all, he was a limb of Shakespeare.

Troilus and Cressida, or Truth found too late; a Tragedy: with a Preface containing the Grounds of Criticism in Tragedy. 1679. Ker I, 227–28.

[343] *Joseph Addison*

Among the *English*, *Shakespear* has incomparably excelled all others. That noble Extravagance of Fancy, which he had in so great Perfection, thoroughly qualified him to touch this weak superstitious Part of his Reader's Imagination; and made him capable of succeeding, where he had nothing to support him besides the Strength of his own Genius. There is something so wild and yet so solemn in the Speeches of his Ghosts, Fairies, Witches and the like Imaginary Persons, that we cannot forbear thinking them natural, tho' we have no Rule by which to judge of them, and must confess, if there are such Beings in the World, it looks highly probable they should talk and act as he has represented them.

Spectator. No. 419. Tuesday, July 1, 1712.

[344] *Joseph Addison*

. . . our Criticks do not seem sensible that there is more Beauty in the Works of a great Genius who is ignorant of the Rules of Art, than in those of a little Genius who knows and observes them . . . Our inimitable *Shakespear* is a Stumbling-block to the whole Tribe of these rigid Criticks. Who would not rather read one of his Plays, where there is not a single Rule of the Stage observed, than any Production of a modern Critick, where there is not one of them violated? *Shakespear* was indeed born with all the Seeds of Poetry, and may be compared to the Stone in *Pyrrhus*'s Ring, which, as *Pliny* tells us, had the Figure of *Apollo* and the Nine Muses in the Veins of it, produced by the spontaneous Hand of Nature, without any Help from Art.

Spectator. No. 592. Friday, Sept. 10, 1714.

[345] *Alexander Pope*

If ever any Author deserved the name of an *Original,* it was *Shakespear. Homer* himself drew not his art so immediately from the fountains of Nature . . . The Poetry of *Shakespear* was Inspiration indeed: he is not so much an Imitator, as an Instrument, of Nature; and 'tis not so just to say that he speaks from her, as that she speaks thro' him.

★ ★ ★

The *Power* over our *Passions* was never possess'd in a more eminent degree, or display'd in so different instances. Yet all along, there is seen no labour, no pains to raise them; no preparation to guide our guess to the effect, or be perceiv'd to lead toward it: But the heart swells, and the tears burst out, just at the proper places: We are surpriz'd, the moment we weep; and yet upon reflection find the passion so just, that we shou'd be surpriz'd if we had not wept, and wept at that very moment.

How astonishing is it again, that the passions directly opposite to these, Laughter and Spleen, are no less at his command! that he is not more a master of the *Great,* than of the *Ridiculous* in human nature; of our noblest tendernesses, than of our vainest foibles; of our strongest emotions, than of our idlest sensations!

Nor does he only excell in the Passions: In the coolness of Reflection and Reasoning he is full as admirable. His *Sentiments* are not only in general the most pertinent and judicious upon every subject; but by a talent very peculiar, something between Penetration and Felicity, he hits upon that particular point on which the bent of each argument turns, or the force of each motive depends. This is perfectly amazing, from a man of no education or experience in those great and publick scenes of life which are usually the subject of his thoughts: So that he seems to have known the world by Intuition, to have look'd thro' humane nature at one glance, and to be the only Author that gives ground for a very new opinion, That the Philosopher and even the Man of the world, may be *Born,* as well as the Poet.

Preface. *The Works of Shakespear.* 1725.

[346] *Samuel Johnson*

When Learning's Triumph o'er her barb'rous Foes
First rear'd the Stage, immortal *Shakespear* rose;
Each Change of many-colour'd Life he drew,

Exhausted Worlds, and then imagin'd new:
Existence saw him spurn her bounded Reign,
And panting Time toil'd after him in vain:
His pow'rful Strokes presiding Truth impress'd,
And unresisted Passion storm'd the Breast.

Prologue Spoken by Mr. Garrick at the Opening of the Theatre in Drury-Lane. 1747. Lines 1–8.

[347] *Samuel Taylor Coleridge*

If Shakspeare be the wonder of the ignorant, he is, and ought to be, much more the wonder of the learned: not only from profundity of thought, but from his astonishing and intuitive knowledge of what man must be at all times, and under all circumstances, he is rather to be looked upon as a prophet than as a poet. Yet, with all these unbounded powers, with all this might and majesty of genius, he makes us feel as if he were unconscious of himself, and of his high destiny, disguising the half god in the simplicity of a child.

The Lectures of 1811–12. IX. Raysor II, 181.

[348] *Samuel Taylor Coleridge*

Shakspeare is of no age. It is idle to endeavour to support his phrases by quotations from Ben Jonson, Beaumont and Fletcher, &c. His language is entirely his own, and the younger dramatists imitated him. The construction of Shakspeare's sentences, whether in verse or prose, is the necessary and homogeneous vehicle of his peculiar manner of thinking. His is not the style of the age. More particularly, Shakspeare's blank verse is an absolutely new creation . . .

I believe Shakspeare was not a whit more intelligible in his own day than he is now to an educated man, except for a few local allusions of no consequence. As I said, he is of no age—nor, I may add, of any religion, or party, or profession. The body and substance of his works came out of the unfathomable depths of his own oceanic mind: his observation and reading, which was considerable, supplied him with the drapery of his figures.

Table-Talk. 1835. Raysor II, 358.

[349] *John Keats*

. . . it struck me, what quality went to form a Man of Achievement especially in Literature, & which Shakespeare posessed so enormously—I mean *Negative Capability,* that is when man is capable of being in uncertainties, Mysteries, doubts, without any irritable reaching after fact & reason—Coleridge, for instance, would let go by a fine isolated verisimilitude caught from the Penetralium of mystery, from being incapable of remaining content with half knowledge. This pursued through Volumes would perhaps take us no further than this, that with a great poet the sense of Beauty overcomes every other consideration, or rather obliterates all consideration.

Letter to George and Tom Keats. 21, 27 (?) December 1817. *The Letters of John Keats 1814–1821.* Ed. Hyder Edward Rollins. 1958.

[350] *Matthew Arnold*

Shakespeare

Others abide our question. Thou art free.
We ask and ask: Thou smilest and art still,
Out-topping knowledge. For the loftiest hill
That to the stars uncrowns his majesty,
Planting his steadfast footsteps in the sea,
Making the Heaven of Heavens his dwelling-place,
Spares but the cloudy border of his base
To the foil'd searching of mortality:
And thou, who didst the stars and sunbeams know,
Self-school'd, self-scann'd, self-honour'd, self-secure,
Didst walk on Earth unguess'd at. Better so!
All pains the immortal spirit must endure,
All weakness that impairs, all griefs that bow,
Find their sole voice in that victorious brow.

The Strayed Reveller and Other Poems. 1849.

[351] *Herman Melville*

No utter surprise can come to him
Who reaches Shakspeare's core;

That which we seek and shun is there—
Man's final lore.

"The Coming Storm." *Battle-Pieces and Aspects of the War.* 1866. Lines 13–16.

[352] *Henry Wadsworth Longfellow*

Shakespeare

A vision as of crowded city streets,
With human life in endless overflow;
Thunder of thoroughfares; trumpets that blow
To battle; clamor, in obscure retreats,
Of sailors landed from their anchored fleets;
Tolling of bells in turrets, and below
Voices of children, and bright flowers that throw
O'er garden-walls their intermingled sweets!
This vision comes to me when I unfold
The volume of the Poet paramount,
Whom all the Muses loved, not one alone;—
Into his hands they put the lyre of gold,
And, crowned with sacred laurel at their fount,
Placed him as Musagetes on their throne.

A Book of Sonnets. 187–.

[353] *Robert Browning*

The Names

Shakespeare!—to such name's sounding, what succeeds
Fitly as silence? Falter forth the spell,—
Act follows word, the speaker knows full well,
Nor tampers with its magic more than needs.
Two names there are: That which the Hebrew reads
With his soul only: if from lips it fell,
Echo, back thundered by earth, heaven and hell,
Would own "Thou didst create us!" Naught impedes
We voice the other name, man's most of might,

Awesomely, lovingly: let awe and love
Mutely await their working, leave to sight
All of the issue as—below—above—
Shakespeare's creation rises: one remove,
Though dread—this finite from that infinite.

The Shakespearean Show-Book. 1884.

[354] *Edwin Arlington Robinson*

. . . he may scarcely give a Fool an exit
But we mark how he sees in everything
A law that, given we flout it once too often,
Brings fire and iron down on our naked heads.

"Ben Jonson Entertains a Man from Stratford." *Drama.* Nov., 1915. *The Man Against the Sky.* 1916. Lines 211–14.

[355] *D. H. Lawrence*

When I read Shakespeare I am struck with wonder
that such trivial people should muse and thunder
in such lovely language.

Lear, the old buffer, you wonder his daughters
didn't treat him rougher,
the old chough, the old chuffer.

And Hamlet, how boring, how boring to live with,
so mean and self-conscious, blowing and snoring
his wonderful speeches, full of other folk's whoring!

And Macbeth and his Lady, who should have been choring,
such suburban ambition, so messily goring
old Duncan with daggers!

How boring, how small Shakespeare's people are!
Yet the language so lovely! like the dyes from gas-tar.

Pansies. 1929.

[356] *George Barker*

It is particularly in his religious—his openly religious—passages that Shakespeare most admirably exercises that faculty for which Keats so deeply respected him. I mean that faculty Keats called the negative faculty . . . "when a man is capable of being in uncertainties, mysteries, doubts, without any irritable reaching after fact and reason." This negative capability, I think, is really part of a greater, a larger characteristic of Shakespeare in the particular and the poet proper in general. There is, I believe, a state of a spiritual neutrality about existence which, seen in operation, gives the impression of an effortless laboring, like the moon on a night of storm. This effortless laboring in a supreme neutrality is by no means a withdrawal from human affairs—it is rather a wandering up and down the no-man's-land in between the machine guns and the opposition of all natural factions. It is this supreme neutrality that appears to deprive the poet of his personal character and make of him a creature half sub-human and half superhuman. It is this supreme neutrality that permits the poet to delight in the apparent creation of evil, ugliness and despair. . . . This is that "universality" of Shakespeare's, a love of all created things which, exercising its force in all directions, cancels itself out and thus leaves the poet laboring, as I say, in a supreme neutrality. It resembles the impartiality of those heavenly bodies that turn their faces in all directions at once.

. . . the poet is a mystic who operates downward. He operates downward upon the world through the agency of the word, perceiving that every object, enshrining a divine idea, is therefore equally to be loved.

"William Shakespeare and the Horse with Wings." (Text of a lecture delivered on Shakespeare's birthday at Stratford-on-Avon). *Partisan Review*, Series 4. July–August, 1953.

Index